D0908287

I,
and
/

America,
Its Jews,
and the
Rise of Nazism

Gulie Ne'eman Arad

America, Its Jews, and the Rise of Nazism

Indiana University Press
Bloomington • Indianapolis

This book is a publication of

Indiana University Press
601 North Morton Street
Bloomington, IN 47404-3797 USA

http://www.indiana.edu/~iupress

Telephone orders   800-842-6796
Fax orders   812-855-7931
Orders by e-mail   iuporder@indiana.edu

© 2000 by Gulie Ne'eman Arad

The paper used in this publication meets the minimum requirements
of American National Standard for Information Sciences—Permanence of Paper for Printed Library Materials, ANSI Z39.48-1984.

Manufactured in the United States of America

Library of Congress Cataloging-in-Publication Data

Arad, Gulie Ne'eman, date
    America, its Jews, and the rise of Nazism / Gulie Ne'eman Arad.
    p.   cm.
    Includes bibliographical references and index.
    ISBN 0-253-33809-3 (cl : alk. paper)
    1. Jews—United States—Politics and government—19th cen-
tury. 2. Jews—United States—Politics and government—20th century. 3. Holocaust, Jewish (1939–1945)—Public opinion. 4. Public
opinion—Jews. 5. Public opinion—United States.   I. Title.

E184.36.P64 A73 2000
973.04'924—dc21
                                                          00-038910
1 2 3 4 5   05 04 03 02 01 00

contents

To Shlomo Arad (Goldberg)

and in memory of

Berta and Elimelech Goldberg
Two among the millions who perished without trace

acknowledgments

Completing a book is a joy, not least because of the opportunity to express much and long-overdue gratitude to the many individuals and institutions who generously provided me with guidance and support.

The Eva and Marc Besen Institute for the Study of Historical Consciousness, and The Joran-Sznycer Foundation, both at Tel Aviv University, helped facilitate the implementation of this project. The Memorial Foundation for Jewish Culture in New York also provided generous financial support on a number of occasions. My year's stay as a fellow at the University of Pennsylvania, Center for Judaic Studies, provided me with the priceless privilege of free time, a superb library, and a stimulating intellectual community. I wish to thank especially David Ruderman, the director, and Etty Lassman, who was always ready to extend a hand well beyond the call of duty.

Putting up with the whims of researchers is not an easy task and through the years I have come to cherish the invaluable knowledge and help of the many librarians and archivists who assisted me. I would like to extend my appreciation to the staffs of the following institutions: Wiener Library at Tel Aviv University; American Jewish Archives, Cincinnati, Ohio, especially to Kevin Proffitt; American Jewish Committee Record Center and the Blaustein Library, New York; YIVO, Institute of Jewish Research, New York; Jewish Collection, New York Public Library; American Jewish Historical Society Archives, Waltham, Massachusetts; Central Zionist Archives, Jerusalem.

The odyssey of seeing ideas take shape as a manuscript and then become a book can never be undertaken completely alone. I was fortunate to have had teachers, colleagues, and friends who have accompanied me on this journey. I benefited greatly from the opportunity to present and discuss various aspects of my work in various academic forums. I wish to thank Omer Bartov and Phillis Mack, Rutgers University; David Engel, New York University; Andrei S. Markovits, Center for European Studies, Harvard University; Peter Novick, University of Chicago; Alvin H. Rosenfeld, Indiana University, Bloomington; Richard Wolin, Rice University; Wolfgang Benz, Zentrum für

Antisemitismusforschung, Technische Universität Berlin. Gisela Bock, Freie Universität Berlin, has not only invited me on a number of occasions to discuss my work with her students and colleagues; she also generously opened her home and heart on my many visits to Berlin. Dalia Ofer, Hebrew University, Jerusalem, invited me to present my future project in a conference she organized. Her solid support and friendship mean much to me. My friend Gertrud Koch of the Kulturwissenschaftliches Institut Essen and Freie Universität Berlin provided me with numerous opportunities to air my ideas. With her constant nagging she proved instrumental in pushing me over the finishing line. Hans Mommsen gave me much encouragement by expressing interest in my work. I also wish to thank my dear colleage and friend Bat-Ami Zucker for her consistent interest in the project and her generosity in sharing with me the manuscript of her book before its publication.

I am particularly indebted to my teacher, colleague, and friend Saul Friedländer, whose knowledge and wisdom guided me first through my dissertation and then very steadfastly through the preparation of this book. Peter Novick was always there to provide generous and valuable critique. I thank them both for taking time in the midst of their overcrowded academic schedules to read the entire manuscript. Yvette Bendek-Maor's intellectual insights and linguistic skills are present throughout the book, but not least important is the warmth and support of the entire Maor family—Elie, Daniella, Gabrielle, and Maya—in whose home in New York I recovered from the many crises that accompany a project of this magnitude. Raya Cohen was always encouraging and eager to read whatever I placed on her own crowded desk. Mira, her daughter, provided much joy and the necessary reminders of what true life is. Nili Keren and her family were kind enough to remain my friends through the many years when I could not reciprocate their kindness.

Other friends and colleagues have been kind enough to read and comment on parts of the manuscript: Robert Liberles, Amnon Raz-Krakotzkin, Shimon Redlich, and Ilan Troen of Ben-Gurion University of the Negev, as well as Anita Shapira of Tel-Aviv University—I thank them all. My very special gratitude to Philippa Shimrat, from whose excellent judgement and editorial skills I have benefited greatly over the years. From all of these people I have received much support and good advice, but needless to say the usual formula holds—the mistakes are all mine.

At Indiana University Press it gives me great pleasure to thank Assistant Director and Senior Sponsoring Editor Janet Rabinowitch, who took me aboard and followed closely and attentively every phase of this project. Journals Manager Kathryn Caras, a friend and associate at *History & Memory* (of which I am co-editor), was a source of invaluable support. Marvin Keenan treated my manuscript as if it were his own. I thank him.

And I wish to make yet another and somewhat unusual acknowledgment about my personal past which inevitably must echo in this narrative. As a native of the Yishuv in Palestine, my first home dovetailed with one of Israel's largest immigrant camps. It was there that I struck up my first friendships with children who came from Europe after the war, to whom we the "natives" referred collectively as being from "there." We communicated in a unique language—a polyglot of Polish, Czech, Hungarian, German, and Yiddish. My parents, who were from "here," were terribly concerned about my poor language skills in Hebrew and shortly after my fifth birthday decided that proper education was in order. They took me to see the school principal, Dr. Jager, and asked him to accept me at school a year earlier than was customary. For my entry examination I was presented with a magazine cover and was pointedly asked "What color is it?" I answered, "Rot" (red in German). He asked again and I quickly replied, "Czerwony" (red in Polish). Having failed to identify it as "adom" (red in Hebrew), I was immediately accepted. This early socialization experience—the insistence on the primacy of the "here" over the "there"—shaped me as a person who never completely belonged to either.

When the Six Day War broke out in June 1967, some six years after I came to the United States, I was well on my way to becoming a strange hybrid of an American-Israeli-Jew. A major clue to my own transformation came in the immediate aftermath of this war when I discovered that I was among the few who did not make a dash for a "home run" to celebrate the great victory. I became concerned about what impact the occupation would have on Israeli society. In the years that followed I came to feel less Israeli and more Jewish. My sense of Jewishness had nothing to do with religion and everything to do with history. It was through a newly discovered consciousness of being a member of a minority in the greater American kaleidoscope, a mindset which has been the common experience of most Jews throughout the ages, that I came to feel a sense of belonging to a people.

In the early 1970s, shortly before the Yom Kippur War, I decided to return to Israel. A few years later I met Shlomo Arad—né Manfred Goldberg—who came from "there" and found his first home in the same immigrant camp which I embrace as my "here." For the past twenty-five years he has been my partner and friend in a life which by a shared need came to include both the here and the there. It is to him and to the memory of his parents that this book is dedicated.

abbreviations

AH	*American Hebrew*
AJA	American Jewish Archives
AJAJ	*American Jewish Archives Journal*
AJC	American Jewish Committee
AJCA	American Jewish Committee Archives
AJ Congress	American Jewish Congress
AJH	*American Jewish History*
AJHQ	*American Jewish Historical Quarterly*
AJHS	American Jewish Historical Society Archives
AJYB	*American Jewish Year Book*
C.V.	Central Association of German Citizens of the Jewish Faith
CZA	Central Zionist Archive, Jerusalem
FDR	Franklin Delano Roosevelt
FRUS	*Foreign Relations of the United States*
JDC (Joint)	American Jewish Joint Distribution Committee
JPS	Jewish Publication Society of America
JSS	*Jewish Social Studies*
JTA	Jewish Telegraphic Agency
LBIY	*Leo Baeck Institute Year Book*
NCRAC	National Community Relations Advisory Council
NYT	*The New York Times*
PAJHS	*Publications of the American Jewish Historical Society*
SSW	Stephen S. Wise
WJCC	World Jewish Congress Collection
YAJSS	*YIVO Annual of Jewish Social Science*
YIVO	Institute for Jewish Research, New York

America,
Its Jews,
and the
Rise of Nazism

Introduction

It is so difficult to find the beginning.
Or better: it is difficult to begin at the beginning.
And not try to go further back.
—Wittgenstein, *On Certainty*

In the collective memory of the millions of Jews who succeeded in escaping religious, racial, and political persecution—and no less in the minds of the millions who failed to do so—America was and remained the *goldene medine* (golden country). The fact that most who lived to see their dream come true were soon to discover that they had reached the "gilded medine" did little to spoil their dream. However, it is not my intention to argue for or against American exceptionalism or to point to the existence of a causal-determinant relationship between the Jews' history in America and their reactions to the Nazi catastrophe. Rather, my aim is to understand the American Jewish leadership's response to the rise of Nazism in Germany within the context of a century-long American experience.

It was roughly since the 1840s that American Jews began to devise the basic survival strategies of a sub-group, to master the "dos and don'ts" of the American political culture; to balance between the world they had left behind and a world where they were not yet fully at home; to strive, not always consistently or successfully, to preserve their old-world cultural patrimony *and* to become American. It was with these mighty acquisitions and certain losses that they faced myriad crises which culminated in the Nazi menace. It was only after, and in no small part as a result of, the Shoah and the establishment of the Jewish state that their previous patterns of behavior were partially breached.

The challenge that America's response to the Nazi menace occasions for historians is evident from the growing number of books and articles it continues to generate.[1] Whether it is the response of the United States government or the president, lay or clerical organizations, Jews or Christians, the mainstream or the Jewish press—there is hardly an aspect of this tragic era that has not commanded serious scholarly attention. Indeed, to add yet another volume to this crowded list calls for an explanation.

After learning much from reading this wealth of research, I nonetheless became increasingly convinced that despite this expanding body of knowledge a conspicuous gap between "knowing" and "understanding" persists. Narrowing this gap, especially with regard to the American Jewish response, is the main purpose of this study. The need for such an undertaking has been observed over the past three decades by a number of prominent historians. In 1979, without dismissing the then available studies out of hand, Henry Feingold stressed the need to "recognize that they are as much cries of pain as they are serious history."[2] A decade later Michael Marrus remarked that the tremendous output that uncovered "particular variations" on the theme of the bystanders' response to the Holocaust had failed to produce "breaks in the pattern" of research.[3]

More recently and in a similar vein, Jonathan Sarna questioned whether the subject of America and the Holocaust, as it had been approached, "warrant[s] continued investment of scholarly resources at the current extravagant level."[4] Presenting his own research priorities, Sarna identified a need for "a broadly-conceived study of the Holocaust's impact on American life generally and on American Jewish life in particular."[5] But he went on to suggest that

> what we may need even more, at this point is background and historical context: studies of American Jews' political life and culture stretching back into the nineteenth century, as well as in Europe, analyzing the stock of received political wisdom and experience that American Jews brought with them to the crisis of the 1930s and 1940s and then drew upon in formulating their response to it. In short, rather than viewing American aspects of the Holocaust in an historical vacuum, as is so often done today, we need to see it as part of the continuum of American Jewish history, one chapter in a long story that has not yet been adequately recounted.[6]

I have reached a similar conclusion the hard way. After laboring for months in various archives I came to realize that the evidence didn't support the picture I had sketched and that I may have been missing what it did suggest. I located the reasons for my misreading in the nature of the event itself and in my core subjects, the Jewish bystanders.

The exceptional holds much more fascination for us than the ordinary, and historians are no exception. Because it is stronger than the sum total of its *un*-historical components, a symbol of the profane in human behavior, and a reference point of our moral discourse, "Auschwitz" casts a shadow over all that preceded it. Indeed, in the historiography on the Holocaust the life experiences of the perpetrators, victims, or bystanders in the six years prior to the war, not to mention before it, are generally treated as little more than a prelude to the "Final Solution."[7] While no historian can disown Auschwitz when writing about any facet of this period, to situate the analysis within a closed referential framework of its catastrophic ending, when the real became unreal by the reality of the unthinkable, is likely to engender a *supra*-historical interpretation.

But what draws us to the extraordinary is more than naive fascination. As Jonathan Frankel poignantly observed, times of crisis can be remarkably telling for historians. For during such vulnerable interludes, realities of everyday existence that are better hidden during normal times surface most clearly. At such crossroads it is harder for illusions to survive, time-honored assumptions are more likely to falter, and reality normally too painful to face cannot be dodged.[8]

But the exceptional can also turn out to be a precarious domain for historians. Especially among distant observers, extreme situations encourage extreme explanations; they resist a fusion of the conventional and the extraordinary. By their very nature evil deeds tend to desensitize us to human behavior within what can be called the normal curve—allowing lesser evil and lesser good to go unheeded. Indeed, for that very reason extreme situations may prove a dubious place to seek historical lessons. Yet venturing to explore the American Jews' more distant past—with the aim of dissipating the fog that clouds our understanding of their response to what began as a racial ideology, evolved into oppressive persecution, and ended in the unthinkable murder of millions of Jews—may prove both a risky and an unpopular choice.

Historian Marc Bloch has fittingly noted that "obsession with origins" may lead us into a number of traps.[9] In addition to the elusiveness of the very notion of a beginning, there is the risk of equating origins with causes, and even worse, of seeking in the beginning a complete explanation for what followed. The search for origins is further challenged by the particular nature of the event under investigation. One significant clue to this difficulty was communicated to me by an anonymous reader of the manuscript of this book. In this reader's opinion, going back to the nineteenth century was little more than a "filler" that "did not really add to the heart of the topic, the response to the Holocaust." Needless to say, the decision about where to begin and where to end this historical account was neither arbitrary nor impartial.

My overall guide was the realization that probing the particular responses of American Jewry had to be lifted out of the narrow, parochial context in which it has usually been placed. Instead, it must be integrated into wider modalities of the culture that shaped them. In my view of culture I follow the late George Mosse, who rendered it "a state or habit of mind which is apt to become a way of life intimately linked to the challenges and dilemmas of contemporary society."[10] By de-ghettoizing the existence of the Jews in America in relation to the surrounding society and exposing the mutual interplay between the two, we may discern an unfolding development, an emerging pattern of behavior intertwined into an ever-broadening tapestry, in which the response to the Nazi anti-Jewish agenda is conceived not as some kind of deviation from the norm but as a continuous manifestation of the process of Americanization.

Adopting such an approach may help us avoid another debatable assumption which anticipates that exceptional circumstances will elicit exceptional responses and the resulting inclination to emphasize the elements of change and attenuate the forces of the continuum.[11] The magnitude of the event, its brutality and rancor, its toll in human lives—what Hannah Arendt characterized as the total moral collapse of respectable society[12]—tend to make us morally and emotionally predisposed to believe, and even insist, that the reactions of the witnesses should and could have matched the escalating Nazi terror in intensity. Yet such expectations are not borne out by the historical facts, which reveal, rather, that the Jewish leaders' modes of response to the German crisis in the course of 1933 set a pattern from which they did not deviate much, in either form or content, in the decade that followed.

To deflect what one historian accurately observed as "a strong tendency in historical writing on bystanders . . . to condemn, rather than to explain,"[13] this study undertakes to trace the impact that historical memory and the American experience had on the Jews' group cohesion, their political and social standing, and their own aspirations and probe the extent to which these variables prevailed upon their response to crisis situations which affected them as Jews.

By exploring what figured into the responses of American Jews to previous crises over the century that preceded the 1930s and by recognizing their desire to Americanize, I have come to believe that, more than the events themselves, it was the American experience which was instrumental in dictating and shaping their response to Nazism. More than the developments in Europe or the immediate domestic adversities of anti-Semitism or the Depression, it was the Jews' desire to adapt, and the host culture's conditions for acceptance, which shaped the Jewish response to this most catastrophic chapter in history. Yet it is important to emphasize that however much they may have been limited by objective circumstances, American Jews had choices to make and, like any other people, they acted upon a reality which in no small part was shaped by their own perceptions.

Historical developments and my focus on Jews' behavior during times of crisis moved my starting point back to 1840, when the Jews in America came to number some 15,000 and to constitute, however loosely, a community. It was in the same year that they were implicated for the first time in a major transnational crisis which unfolded in Damascus. My decision to end this study in the fall of 1942, when the Nazis' systematic extermination of the European Jews was confirmed by the State Department, was informed by my understanding that subsequently not much could have been expected of my principal subjects, the American Jewish leaders, in terms of rescue or influencing the policy makers. This periodization was also influenced by my attempt to avoid certain ahistorical biases that are often included in representations of the bystanders in connection with this extreme event. This calls for some further elaboration.

The response of the bystanders to the unfolding Nazi calamity is particularly susceptible to a dichotomous portrayal. If the victims and perpetrators lend themselves to an essentially absolute depiction of innocent and guilty, respectively, the bystanders a priori occupy an intractable middle position. As the victims' potential saviors or betrayers, they are generally exalted or condemned accordingly. The extent of the tragedy and the failure to reduce it, let alone prevent it, inspires a tacit moral-psychological posture that renders the bystanders as guilty until proven innocent. As has been aptly observed, the "indictment against the witnesses is as predictable as it is irresistible."[14] Furthermore, with the end result known, rescue becomes the indisputable expectation and the six million victims the equally indisputable failure. Post factum the millions of victims reinforce an intuitive-ethical inclination to evaluate the results of the American Jewish leaders' actions as a function of the sufferers' needs and not of the bystanders' means. Such an analysis is based on the fanciful notion that American Jews should have totally identified with the plight of their European co-religionists in the belief that unequivocal altruism, itself based on an idealized vision of kinship solidarity, could have overcome any objective or subjective obstacles to a determined will to help.[15] This is a deeply felt moral-emotional argument. But it is also deeply flawed.

The perspective of Auschwitz, which came to epitomize "a world gone mad,"[16] supports a rather curious template of periodization which regards the period between 1938 and the end of 1941 as the "refugee" phase, and confines the "rescue" phase to the years of mass extermination—when the likelihood of rescue was greatly diminished.[17] In a recent essay Henry Feingold implies that the earlier periodization, which he himself helped establish, is erroneous. In his revised understanding he now correctly claims that "rescue possibilities were far more promising during the refugee phase," which he now predates to 1933.[18]

Framing the core discussion on rescue within the time span of the mass killings which followed Germany's invasion of the Soviet Union and, no less momentously for American Jews, after the United States entered the war, when it is generally agreed that both priorities and capabilities for effecting rescue became highly improbable, carries the discourse outside history—it places it in the speculative realm of what should have been.[19] Stemming from a similar source is the common post-Auschwitz contention that American Jews could not have known that the Jews they did not save were going to die in a Holocaust.[20] This assertion is of course true, but such a reading of history is neither simple nor innocent. It points to what, in my mind, are various disturbing perceptions. It intimates that Auschwitz is a quantitative signifier; a code that thrusts us toward a numerical orientation which renders overlooking the fate of the tens, hundreds, and thousands of human lives that might have been saved more tolerable. It also alludes to an irking hierarchy of death —to a difference between dying in the Holocaust and dying, for example, from hunger or disease in a ghetto, or in the course of a "normal" pogrom. Furthermore, it overlooks the contemporary sufferers' own mindset, their feelings that the escalating harassment, which severely restricted their civil, social, and economic status and subjected them to occasional random violence, may well have earned them the dubious status of victims who merited rescue. But most interesting, it treats as settled fact the moot assumption that had American Jews known that there was going to be a Holocaust they could have and would have acted differently and saved Europe's Jews.

However, if we heed the perceptions of American Jews at the time, we learn that for them what transpired in 1933 was already anything but normal, and required "a complete reorientation of one's sense of reality as well as one's historical sense."[21] The fact remains that it was prior to the war that the German quota was consistently under-issued (except after the November 1938 pogrom) and many of the Jews who perceived the danger, had the means, and wished to leave were turned away on account of "legal technicalities."[22] In focusing our inquiry on the years *before* the Nazis embarked on implementing the "Final Solution" we are pleading a case in the name of six million lives instead of in the name of six million deaths.

There can be no certain answer as to why the years of extermination dominate both our history and memory: why America's failure to bomb Auschwitz and the Jewish leadership's consent to withhold information about the extermination pending verification by the State Department have become the ultimate symbols of American and Jewish indifference. But as former historian of the United States Holocaust Memorial Museum David Luebke has suggested, these non-events are much more "emotion-laden" and therefore more alluring than the issue of the restrictive immigration policies of the 1930s and 1940s. It is also easier, as he noted "to cope with helplessness after the fact, if you can convince yourself that mendacity, not circumstances, had produced it."[23] Historians cannot afford such an emotional succor.

Whose Story Is It, Anyway?

The protagonists of this history were Jewish American citizens who spoke and acted in the name of kinsmen in distant lands as representatives of organizations with no constituencies to speak of, of a community which at the time was little more than "the product of a messianic imagination."[24] It is also the story of those I call "the president's Jews"—people who were not necessarily involved in Jewish organizational life, but whose prominent positions in and around the Roosevelt administration earned them an important role in this narrative. They were mostly self-appointed leaders who together did not constitute a unified "leadership" but rather an odd coalition drawn from the American Jewish elite. This account is limited to those Jews who presented the "Jewish case" before the American decision makers. It is about emissaries who had enough faith in the "American dream" to cross the bridge that stretches between dissent and cooperation within America. Although these people did not represent the whole gamut of American Jewry, they nonetheless argued the case of millions of mostly mute Jews, new citizens for whom America was still a foreign country.

This was a difficult tale to tell, not only because it has no happy ending. It narrates a history of a people in their home that was not yet a home, of believers in a better world who discovered its evil and apathy. It is always a taxing experience for a historian to interpret fragments of people's lives, their ideas and feelings. It is more so when these lives and deeds are probed in connection with a catastrophe that claimed millions of lives. It is even more so when, as in my own case the subject is the historian's "own," with all the emotional and metahistorical baggage that it carries. For all these reasons I tried to be as receptive as I could and include the protagonists' own voices, with their own linguistic peculiarities, their preferred partialities, and their psychological and ideological leanings. While attempting to grant this iota of "justice" to the subjects, I am nonetheless aware that what they wrote was not always what they thought, and what they said was not always what they felt. Their feelings and thoughts remained with them.

Part One

Incoming

1

"Amerika du hast es besser"
German Jewish Immigrants in America

A nation, like a tree, does not thrive well till it is
engraffed with a foreign stock.
— Ralph Waldo Emerson, *Journals*, 1823

It was only in America that a civilization was conceived with the pronounced
intent of accommodating all (white) peoples.[1] For Jews this unprecedented
social experiment presented a unique opportunity: nowhere else could they
secure legal and political rights by merely coming to settle. The constitutional guarantee that "[N]o religious test shall ever be required as a qualifi-
cation to any office or public trust," coupled with the separation of church
and state as confirmed by the First Amendment, assured the entry of Jews
into the sphere of citizenship as individuals.

With the American spirit embodied in the notion of a fresh start, the New
World appeared an ideal ground for creating a new Jew no longer haunted
by his turbulent past.[2] In the oft-quoted words of Hector St. John de Crèvecoeur, in America "every thing tended to regenerate" the poor of Europe:
"new laws, a new mode of living, a new social system: here they become men."
But to become an American, the new immigrant was expected to leave behind
"all the ancient prejudices and manners, receive new ones from the new mode
of life he has embraced, the new government he obeys, and the new rank he
holds."[3]

However, in the experiences of most newcomers, these conditions were
easier to define than to realize. Modernity's promise to emancipate "individual life from collective destiny," and "to strip everyone of their parochial
clothing, liberating them by reducing them to pure human essence," was not
entirely fulfilled even for individual Jews who made the choice to abandon
their particular ties and join the universal civil order.[4] Jews (and Catholics),
whose foreignness was perceived as a threat to the Protestant majority culture, had a particularly hard time overcoming suspicion. Even in the United

States, where liberal democracy was by far more firmly rooted than anywhere else, individual Jews were quick to learn that equal protection under the law was not sufficient to guarantee them free and equal access to the social sphere. Indeed, well into the twentieth century they could hardly escape the stigma of being identified as members of a spurned and clannish group.

This was all the more painful for the German Jews who arrived in America. Discouraged by the setbacks caused by the periods of reaction following Napoleon's defeat in 1815, and later by the 1848 debacle, they had made the momentous decision to emigrate, hoping that in America they would harvest the promises of emancipation. They were attracted by the belief that in the New World, where peoplehood was not a *Volk*, "civil betterment" could lead to full acceptance into the new national community.[5]

Upon arriving in America they were prepared, even eager, for a change in their collective condition. Indeed, as the world opened up for them and new options competed for their loyalty, traditional religious hierarchies lost their power to preserve the tight structure of Jewish solidarity. In return for the privileges that were intrinsic to citizenship, Jews readily accorded the liberal state their undivided loyalty. As a result, the old form of communalism that cemented Jewish group existence was undermined.[6] German Jewish immigrants arrived in America well prepared; their sense of community was already diluted.

Yet, as they were to discover, in every situation of discontinuity there was much continuity left; even the alluring new environment and their strong desire to integrate did not entirely erase traditional attitudes. Religious animus against Jews was not left behind in the Old World. The medieval European Christian discourse of the demonic Christ-killer survived in America well into the mid-nineteenth century.[7] Endlessly wandering among the nations of the world, Jews continued to be perceived as aliens; because they were everywhere, they were thought to belong nowhere.[8] Jews continued to be identified as outsiders, which made them both collectively and individually extremely vulnerable.

There is no doubt that most Jews who immigrated to the United States wished to integrate into, if not completely assimilate to, American society.[9] Yet group consciousness, in part due to contingencies and in part to preference, did not die easily. But it survived on American terms.[10] In Jewish life communal responsibility was not only ordered by the Covenant, it was a proven tool for collective survival and a primordial political interest.[11] However, as Jews were to learn in America, the very nature of power in a pluralistic democracy placed restrictions on efforts to further particular group interests, a lesson they learned anew whenever they attempted to exercise influence on behalf of their fellow Jews abroad.[12]

Indeed, for Jews it was no easy matter to adjust to America's liberal doctrine in which the individual was viewed as the fundamental unit of political life. In American political culture social justice meant treating each individual's demands with equal concern; hence, showing preference for a particular group of individuals was regarded as unfair. Group separateness was considered an anathema to the central concepts of the American social-political experiment. Making one out of the many was the main idea of the melting pot, and becoming a *Homo Americanus* called for abandoning particular group interests and commitments. Embracing a particular identity was viewed as implying a fundamentally chauvinistic and degrading attitude toward the majority.[13]

Settling the conflict between "Americanism" and "Jewishness" and arriving at a synthesis that would enable them to remain Jewish and become Americans has therefore been an ongoing challenge for American Jews. The strain of the trials and tribulations that they encountered played a decisive role in shaping their consciousness and actions as Americans, as Jews, and as American Jews; it influenced not only the way in which they came to interact with the host society, but no less, perhaps, the way they interacted among themselves. As Ira Katznelson has noted, they were frequently reminded that

> they could not enter American life unimpeded, whether they chose to downplay or emphasize their identity as Jews. Either move, as it were, was encumbered with risks whose dimensions were difficult to discern. What American Jews sought, therefore, was an orienting stance that could protect them while they probed actually existing possibilities.[14]

Until recently the preferred reading of the American Jewish experience was very much in tune with the notion of American exceptionalism—a belief in America's unique destiny and history that stresses its liberality and the unrestricted access of Jews to its greatness.[15] It is difficult to argue with the exceptional achievements of Jews in America, but one should not neglect the ugly underside of their experience. Notwithstanding the guarantees of the Constitution, Jews were to discover that even in America laws and reality did not always correspond.[16] They had to struggle for their rights as Americans by challenging laws and treaties and filing lawsuits. To succeed they had to join coalitions and form alliances, but finding the right partners was not always easy or possible.

The experience of Jews in America followed neither a linear path nor a single trajectory; there were many and varied American Jewish experiences. How Jews fared in America depended on when they came, where they came from, and where they settled. Yet the Jewish community has often been studied with little regard for the social, cultural, ethnic, and political contexts in which Jews found themselves. The result is a narrow parochial focus where Jews are divorced from the general society in which, to some degree or other, they have lived. Such an approach generally tends to assume the existence of universal Jewish norms and thereby reduces empirical problems to theoretical assertions. This impedes the explications of the reasons for changed behaviors and responses by Jews, both as individuals and as a community.[17]

Basic to the understanding of Jewish life in America, as Benjamin Ginsberg has pointed out, is the realization that the triumph of liberalism in the United

States was not preordained by the mere existence of an immutable ideology. Rather, liberalism has prevailed as a result of the victories won by liberal forces in political struggles against opponents whose values were decidedly illiberal. As we shall see, when American liberalism was challenged so was the position of Jews in society.[18]

Our story begins with the German period of American Jewish history. It follows the process of the Americanization of German Jewish immigrants and the ways in which it affected their collective Jewish identity and their behavior as a group. More specifically, I will focus on how German Jews reacted as a collective to particular issues, both domestically and abroad: how they functioned in the public sphere and interacted with the political centers of power.

The Emergence of a Community

The German Jews who dreamed of freedom and searched for economic security were eager to believe, as Goethe wrote, "Amerika du hast es besser" (America, you have it better). It was not only their confidence in America that drove German Jews to uproot themselves, but also their pessimism about their future in Germany. The Jewish immigrants were poor and usually uneducated in either Jewish or secular learning, but being squeezed out by interacting social and economic forces and harassed by marriage restrictions, they had no other alternative than to search for a "new world." One Bavarian Jew who was anxious to believe in the soundness of his choice, upon being asked on the eve of his departure if he planned to return to his homeland after striking it rich in the United States, answered: "[N]ot until America becomes Bavarian."[19]

Prior to 1830 there was only a trickle of Jewish newcomers from Germany. But the 200,000 or so who arrived between 1830 and 1880 were a fraction of the 2.7 million Irish, 3 million Germans, 950,000 English, and 400,000 Scandinavians who arrived during the same period. From the outset several factors distinguished German Jews from other Jewish immigrant groups that came to build their home in America.[20] Unlike the others, they arrived with a strong dual ethnicity: they were both Jews and Germans. It was a long while before these Jews began to let go of their ties with German culture. They spoke German at home, prayed in German, and educated their children with German methods. Indeed, throughout most of the nineteenth century German Jews proudly accepted the German identity that Americans attributed to them.[21]

The close collaboration with the German Gentile community provided Jews with broader options than were available to the Sephardim who had preceded them and the East Europeans who were to follow them. Unlike these two groups, who mostly clustered in the urban centers of the Atlantic seaboard, German Jews followed the general population movement of the Germans to Wisconsin, Michigan, Ohio, upstate New York, Pennsylvania,

South Carolina, and Maryland. As a result of their geographical dispersion they enjoyed greater opportunities for their commercial pursuits. New York City, for example, which was later to absorb the majority of Russian Jews, became home to only about one-fifth of all the Germans who came through its port.[22]

Following in the footsteps of the waves of German immigration, Jews were invited to participate in the social life of the larger Germany community, where they were free, if they wished, to maintain a distinctive religious life. Although social anti-Semitism made this mix neither entirely equal nor always cordial, most Jews preferred to ignore "minor" mistreatment in return for the chance of quicker integration through the mediation of the Gentile German community.[23] There is a double irony in the fact that the Jews' desired integration into German society was achieved in America, where they were still outsiders.

Unlike the Sephardim or the Jews of Eastern Europe who came to the New World hoping to maintain a corporate religious community life, German Jews were anxious to be liberated from the rigidities that obligatory membership in Jewish *Gemeinden* (congregational communities) entailed. For them emancipation—the transition from a merely tolerated element of the population, subjected to legal discriminations, into citizens with equal rights—signified freedom of choice within society at large as well as within Jewish society. As Max Kohler noted, the liberty and self-assertiveness of the immigrants motivated "each little body or clique to form a separate and distinct congregation for itself . . . instead of coalescing . . . into a few large congregations or organizations."[24]

Indeed, for the first Jewish immigrants who came from Germany in the early nineteenth century, America's social openness and economic expansion proved very beneficial. Zealous to conquer the West, the nation eagerly awaited newcomers who would help to realize this dream. The spirit of the age was expressed in President John Tyler's message to Congress in 1841, where he extended an invitation to people of other countries

> to come and settle among us as members of our rapidly growing family, and for the blessings which we offer them we require of them to look upon our country as their country and to unite with us in the great task of preserving our institutions and thereby perpetuating our liberties.[25]

Feeling welcomed, Jews thrived in the land where "the dark clouds of sectarian prejudice seem everywhere to be fast fading away before the widely spreading light of right, reason and philosophy."[26] All the more so since in American society there was a growing belief that a new generation born in America "would be free from those errors generally imputed to the Jews, and participating in the blessings of liberty, would have every inducement to become valuable members of society."[27] In such an optimistic climate the centripetal forces that made disunity of Jewish life endemic were further reinforced by the social and geographical openness of American society. With internal restraints already weakened and external restraints removed, there was not much to mobilize for unity. Instead, Jewish newcomers used their independence to form a loose congregational life in which they were free to determine their own practices with regard to ritual as well as fiscal and organizational matters.[28] Although this high degree of decentralization suited the American surroundings and eased the entry of German Jews into the larger German community, they were soon to realize that whenever a crisis threatened their own particular group a particular united action was called for. But America society, they learned, rarely viewed such behavior with favor.

One such crisis occurred when the news of the Damascus affair reached America. In February 1840 a Capuchin monk and his servant disappeared in Damascus. The Ottoman government, convinced that Jews had killed the two, moved into the Jewish quarter and tortured several Jews until a confession to the murder was obtained. According to reports, seventy-two Jews were sentenced to be hanged and the entire Jewish community was under suspicion. In England the Board of Deputies of British Jews met in April and decided to approach the secretary of state for foreign affairs. During June and July the matter was broached in the British and French Parliaments as well as in the Jewish communities of those countries. After many deliberations it was decided that Sir Moses Montefiore from England and Adolphe Crémieux from France would go to Alexandria to persuade the pasha of Egypt, Muhammed Ali, to re-examine the Damascus case.[29]

For the United States the events in Damascus were extremely remote. The few brief mentions in the press mostly treated the charges with extreme skepticism. Without a central organization and a recognized leadership, American Jewry was also slow to respond to the crisis. It was only after the Jewish leadership in London decided to publicize the Montefiore-Crémieux mission and appealed openly to Jews around the world to engage in public protest that American Jews launched a public response. In late August and early September 1840 protest meetings took place in some six American cities. Although these assemblies were held too late to be of any consequence in resolving the Damascus affair, for in fact on August 28th Muhammed Ali promised to set the Jewish prisoners free, they gain in significance when viewed in historical perspective.

The reaction of American Jews, their first participation in an international Jewish campaign on behalf of their counterparts abroad, demonstrated that Jewish group consciousness had not dissipated. It also revealed that in America neither its existence nor its public expression could be taken for granted. Americanism as a national ideology did not look with favor upon acting on behalf of a particular group's interests.

In a speech about the Damascus crisis, Mordechai Manuel Noah, one of the most prominent Jews of his era and the editor of the *Evening Star* (an Anglo-American newspaper) articulated the view that however protected Jews in America might feel, their destiny was inescapably tied to that of the Jewish people:

> [I]t may be said that we are remote from the scene of these cruelties . . . that the Almighty has cast our lot in a country of laws administered alike to Jew and Gentile, that . . . we are exempt from such outrages. . . . We thank God that it is so. . . . But . . . in every country on earth in which the Almighty has fixed the destiny of the Jew . . . scattered by a wise Providence among every nation, we are still one people, governed by the same sacred laws and bound together by the same destiny; the cause of one is the cause of all.[30]

Isaac Leeser, who emerged as a prominent spokesman for American Jewry in the course of the Damascus affair and who in 1843 established the prestigious journal *The Occident and American Jewish Advocate,* was aware of the tension that existed between the particular imperative "all Israel are responsible for one another," on the one hand, and the American doctrine of citizenship on the other hand. Speaking before a meeting in Philadelphia in late August he made clear which one he thought should gain preference:

> We have no country of our own . . . under the shadow of which we can live securely; but we have a tie yet holier than a fatherland, a patriotism stronger than the community of one government, our . . . patriotism is the affection which unites the Israelite of one land to that of another. As citizens, we belong to the country we live in, but as believers in one God . . . we hail the Israelite as a brother, no matter if his home be the torrid zone or where the poles encircle the earth.[31]

There is no reason to doubt the sincerity of these sentiments but, as the behavior of America's Jews in this affair demonstrated, they did not necessarily guide their actions. For in fact, they were hesitant to ask their government to intervene on behalf of the Damascus Jews and, as Jonathan Frankel convincingly shows, the single initiative taken by the U.S. government was in response to the Lord Mayor of London, and *not* to an appeal by American Jews. Indeed, it was only *after* Secretary of State John Forsyth had sent a dispatch to Alexandria and President Martin Van Buren had expressed his sympathy and asked for repression of the horrors that American Jews organized public meetings to protest the Damascus persecution. By then the case was almost six months old and nearing its resolution.[32]

The fact that the actions of the U.S. government had no effects on the events in the Middle East did not stop American Jews from rejoicing at their success. The very fact that they had managed for the first time to act as a collective and, moreover, to rouse Christian public opinion on behalf of a Jewish cause was viewed by Jews as evidence of their acceptance in America on equal terms. Indeed, this achievement lingered on in their collective consciousness as the first in a series of American humanitarian diplomatic initiatives on behalf of persecuted Jews abroad.[33]

It is therefore not surprising that they interpreted Van Buren's intervention as a precedent for the future. His "voluntary act," they reasoned, was an assurance of sympathy: "In whatever may hereafter be attempted or done toward extending to the ancient race of Israel, wherever dispersed, the civil and religious privileges secured to us by the Constitution of this favored land."[34] With almost religious fervor American Jews embraced the doctrine of the "American mission" which, as expressed by Benjamin Franklin, promised that "the liberties of America will not only make that people happy, but will have some effect in diminishing the misery of those, who in other parts of the world groan under despotism."[35] American Jews invoked this doctrine as an endorsement to act on behalf of their fellow Jews abroad; it enabled them to be Americans and Jews at the same time. If America's recent struggle for independence made it all the more protective of the principles of sovereignty, at the same time it was also eager to spread the gospels of political freedom and human rights which underpinned its practice of humanitarian diplomacy. Jews were quick to learn how to put this principle to use for their own particular agendas and, because they were probably the main client for it, they were also its chief guardians.

As novices in the world of American politics, Jews overinterpreted the intent of the President's gesture, overlooking the fact that Van Buren may have taken this cost-free opportunity to remunerate Jews for their predominant loyalty to the Democratic party on the eve of a national election in which he faced the popular Harrison as a rival candidate.[36] Unbeknown to them, the Damascus affair had given them their first experience in the American "politics of gestures."

During this time the first fissures were beginning to appear in the wall of confidence that surrounded Jews in America. Although apprehensions about the Jews' safety in America were usually whispered in private, when the Philadelphia Congregation assembled to protest the events in Damascus, its president, Abraham Hart, publicly articulated the anxiety when he warned: "If such a calumny is not nipped in the bud, its effect will not be limited to any particular place, but will be extended to every part of the globe."[37] Those fears were not entirely unfounded. A decade later the *New York Herald* returned the Damascus affair to its front page, claiming that Jews had committed the murder in accordance with Talmudic injunctions. Even worse, as far as American Jews were concerned, was the "finding" that charges had been dropped because of dubious manipulations by the Rothschilds, the archetypal symbol of Jewish international power.[38]

Between Inclusion and Exclusion

Jews who arrived in America from Germany after the Damascus affair— swelling their number from 15,000 in 1840 to 50,000 in 1850 and 150,000 in 1860—encountered a chillier welcome than their forebears.[39] This much poorer and less sophisticated wave of newcomers concentrated in the crowded urban centers and underwent a painful process of proletarianization. The option of assimilating into the general German community became less available as their Gentile compatriots increasingly wished to distance themselves from these Jews.[40] By the 1840s social anti-Jewish biases began to surface: "to jew" was a popular verb, meaning to strike a sly deal, to use "non-Kosher" ethics in business transactions; the conniving and cheating Jewish merchant ("Shylock") became the worshipper of the golden calf ("rich as a Jew"); and having no homeland of their own, the Jew was everywhere the eternal alien.[41]

This exclusion was echoed in the Jewish sphere as well. The more Americanized Jews were disinclined to accept the "alien" and "uncouth" newcomers into their congregations. It was not so much the different degrees of piety or doctrinal distinctions that kept the old and the new apart, but rather the desire of native American Jews to assert their Americanism by separating themselves from Jewish "foreign" elements. Although the new immigrants were eager to adapt, they still sought the support of familiar traditions and hence tended to congregate around their own communities. The pattern was to repeat itself with each succeeding generation; the newcomers of one generation became the excluding elite of the next generation. Thus, for example, the New York synagogue Bene Jeshurun was founded in 1825 in protest against the discriminatory membership policy of the Shearith Israel synagogue, but already by the 1850s membership in Bene Jeshurun had become selective as well.[42]

These ambiguous attitudes toward the newcomers from both the wider American society and established Jewish communities induced them, more by need than by choice, to establish autonomous agencies outside the Jewish congregational framework. Synagogues were unable to meet the diverse social, cultural, and philanthropic needs of the burgeoning and increasingly excluded community of new immigrants.[43] The recognition that to "make it" as individuals called for organized group support was at the root of what was to develop into a distinctive ethnic community. What was beginning to emerge was a similar (Americanized) but separate (exclusively Jewish) institutional framework that tried to meet the needs of the immigrants who were frequently excluded by the larger American society.[44]

During the decade of the 1850s, the growing influx of new immigrants to America—over three million newcomers arrived between 1845 and 1854, the largest number to enter in one decade before the 1880s—kindled anti-foreign sentiments. Nativism took two basic forms. The first was anti-radicalism, which played on the fear that the class-conscious European newcomers would undermine the status quo. The second was Anti-Catholicism, which reached its peak in the 1850s around the Know-Nothing movement. The Irish and German Catholic immigrants who flooded America in the nineteenth century were viewed as agents dispatched by a foreign power to subvert American institutions. The nationalist nexus provided a home for both these sentiments, resulting in the conviction that outsiders were a peril to the American way of life.[45] While radicals and Catholics were defined as enemies of the nation, Protestantism was fused ever more inextricably into the substance of Americanism.[46] The fundamental aim was "to make America the world's great example of a truly Protestant republic."[47]

As usual in periods of religious revivalism and xenophobia, Jews felt the sting. The fact that Jews were eager to acculturate seems to have had little impact on the way American society perceived them. Judaism was depicted in missionary and conversionist literature as "a dead religion, long superseded by a loving and benevolent Christianity, and no longer relevant to civilization." Those who practiced Judaism "proved their moral backwardness and proverbial stiff-neckedness."[48] More than being an insult, these attitudes were perceived by Jews as a hazard to their claim to equality. The conversionists implied that for the Jews emancipation was not granted as a right but rather was a gift Christians made in order to bring about their conversion.[49] Although the derision that Jews encountered throughout the country was an irritant, they were not yet daunted. With Old World anti-Semitism as their reference point, they felt much less threatened in America, where anti-Jewish sentiments were not officially sanctioned by the government.

But protection of Jews by the state could not be taken for granted. In 1850, in the wake of negotiations of a commercial treaty between the United States and Switzerland, their equal status as citizens was challenged. The proposed treaty contained the restrictive clause that only Christians were "entitled to the enjoyment of the privileges guaranteed by the present Article in the Swiss Cantons." According to American Minister to Switzerland A. Dudley Mann, the measure was intended to keep out "undesirable" Jewish peddlers from Alsace, and he opined that individual American Jews would probably not be subjected to such harassment.[50]

Despite this reassurance, Jews in America were outraged that their citizenship status was not protected abroad. They drew up a petition to the Senate which was presented before the vote on ratification took place. Indeed, in the new treaty that was finally ratified in 1855 the language was modified but the discriminatory provision remained. The new version decreed that citizens of both countries should be admitted and treated equally, provided "it shall not conflict with the constitutional or legal provisions."[51] Although reference to exclusive Christian rights was deleted, Jews were still left at the mercy of the individual cantons which remained sovereign to refuse entry and commercial privileges to foreign Jews, or for that matter to others they wished to exclude.

Most Jewish leaders were reluctant to treat the matter as a sectarian issue, preferring instead to argue that the treaty discredited America's image in the world. Following internal bickering, a delegation of Jews met with President Buchanan in October 1857. They left satisfied with an apology and a promise to resolve the situation. In fact, they appear to have been gratified by the honor of meeting with the President; the Reform leader Rabbi Isaac Mayer Wise advised that communal agitation cease.[52] Isaac Leeser charged that American Jews, at the time mostly Reform, were shocked by the implications of the Swiss treaty because they had deceived themselves into believing that Jewish redemption had been secured in America. "We are in *Galuth* [exile]," he reminded his readers:

> We have our theoretical rights; but practically they are dependent on the will of those who have numbers on their side; and if we make all the noise in the

world, and brag aloud after our heart's content, *we are yet strangers* in stranger lands.[53]

It was not the fate of foreign Jews, in this case of Alsace, that goaded American Jews to react to the Swiss treaty. The case of the former Alsatian Jews was handled, however marginally, by Theodore S. Fay, the American minister to Switzerland, who in a long note to the Swiss government in 1858 called particular attention to their plight when he defended the rights of all Jews in the modern world, thereby confirming that the acceptance of American Jews could not be dissociated from the acceptance of other Jews.[54] Rather, what provoked the intense reaction to the Swiss treaty was a series of discriminatory domestic incidents and decrees (such as the Sunday Laws) that violated the Jews' constitutional rights on religious and civil grounds.[55] In this wider context the ratification of the treaty was interpreted as tacit recognition of Protestantism as a dominant or superior religion, which set Jews apart from other American citizens and, as such, designated them as second-class or less-than-equal citizens.

Indeed, what concerned American Jews was not so much the universal principle of religious liberty, although this was what they emphasized in the public discussion; rather, they were mobilized to act by a particular Jewish agenda. Convinced that the continuation of Jewish collective life depended on more than a common faith, American Jews searched for a course that would assure the survival of their ethnic identity. But by invoking religious liberty to sanction their historic nationality, Jews were inadvertently helping to sow the seeds of an American Jewish problem. The conservation of Jewish group consciousness by misappropriating the concept of religious liberty not only ran counter to the ideology of the melting pot, it also imperiled the Christian-Protestant credo which held that "the privacy of religious conscience is a right of individuals and not of collective entities."[56] The Jews' rejoinder was to endow the doctrine of separation of church and state, of which they were avid champions, with a meaning that was neither intended nor accepted by Protestant America. Under the flag of liberty of conscience they hoped to establish a sanctuary for preserving their "collective privacy."[57]

In 1858, eighteen years after the Damascus affair, American Jews again tried to use the principle of religious liberty to further a collective concern. Edgar Mortara, a six-year-old Jewish boy of Bologna, Italy, was forcibly abducted from his home by church authorities after a Catholic maid who worked at the Mortara home confessed that she had secretly baptized him. Urged by their European co-religionists to act, American Jews appealed again for governmental intercession on the basis of humanitarian diplomacy, making clear that they were not asking their government to interfere in the internal affairs of another state.[58]

But unlike in the case of the Damascus Jews, President Buchanan informed the representatives of the Jewish community that in the Mortara case, which did not involve torture and loss of life, "humanitarian diplomacy" could not be applied and nonintervention was the policy of the United States.[59] When Jews reminded the president of Van Buren's action during the Damascus incident, they were told that the previous case set no precedent.[60]

Indeed, the year 1858 was considerably different from 1840. The Buchanan administration was threatened with a domestic political upheaval that was brewing over the slavery issue and was sensitive to foreign criticism. As Buchanan told Isaac Leeser at a White House meeting in 1859, if America could stay neutral on a moral issue such as the Mortara case, it might teach the rest of the world to stay out of America's affairs. Jews, who represented some 50,000 Democratic voters, were no match in the political marketplace to the almost one million Irish Catholic loyal supporters. Moreover, the commitment of Jews to the Democratic Party was on the decline. Some of them resented the party's strong backing of the Irish in urban politics, while others deserted because the party defended slavery.[61]

Aware of the politicization of the Mortara affair, Republicans used it to pry Jews from the Democrats. The Know-Nothing movement used it to boost their anti-Catholic campaign, and the abolitionists used the public sympathy for the kidnapping of one victim to underscore national apathy toward the fate of the slaves. American Jews, highly divided, found themselves, by association, in a strange coalition with liberal Protestants and the nativist Know-Nothing movement. But unlike the other factions who used the affair to further their own agendas, they refrained from any activity that could be interpreted as Jewish group politics. On the contrary, Jews often made the point in public that they "wholly disclaim any wish . . . to be represented as a peculiar community."[62] In 1858 the *Northern Monthly* noted with some surprise that "we hear of the Irish vote, the German vote, but who ever hears of a Jewish vote?" The *American Israelite* was quick to assert that this was "the way things should be."[63]

Indeed, until late 1859 there was no central body that could claim to represent American Jewry. The failure to influence the Buchanan administration on behalf of Edgar Mortara induced a group of prominent New York Jews to follow the example of the British Board of Deputies, which had been formed in 1840 in response to the Damascus "blood libel," and organize a Board of Delegates of American Israelites. Its aim was "to secure and maintain Jewish civil and religious rights at home and abroad."[64] But since the Board represented only a narrow section of American Jewry, these self-appointed leaders carried little authority and achieved even less in uniting the community. More significant, the new agency avoided the real issue that irked Jews in America— how to air their collective interests in political terms and not be accused of clannish particularism. Although the founders of the Board of Delegates disclaimed any intent of creating a political body, the Sephardic elite and most German Jews stayed aloof from this communal venture, fearing that the very idea of a Jewish defense agency could be interpreted as lack of faith in the American system. Some even suggested that such an organization would raise the charge of operating "a state within a state."[65]

Upward Mobility Reawakens Old Prejudices

Focusing on incidents that induced Jews to engage with American society in the public and political spheres may create a distorted picture of intense group participation. But in fact, in mid-nineteenth-century America Jews were still rather invisible as a group. For the most part they were optimistic enough to venture on their own and find their niche in American society as individuals. It was during, and particularly after, the Civil War that Americans began to notice with increasing apprehension and distaste the swelling number of Jews and their rapid mobility that was markedly unmatched by any other immigrant group.[66] In 1865, Isaac Leeser gave bitter expression to the emerging new mood:

> With the great increase of Hebrew residents in America, their general prosperity has also augmented in the same ratio. . . . Now, if nothing else would cause prejudice, this circumstance will. . . . While we were poor and unsightly, we may be tolerated; but let us only look up, and become the social equals of our neighbors, and their ire be at once roused.[67]

Although during the Civil War Jews proved their patriotism when some 10,000 of them, far above their proportion in the population, joined both armies, the period brought a definite upsurge of anti-Jewish sentiments.[68] The most notorious instance was General Ulysses S. Grant's Order Number 11, issued on December 17, 1862. "The Jews *as a class*," it stated, "violating every regulation of trade established by the Treasury Department and also department orders, are hereby expelled from the department within twenty-four hours from the receipt of this order."[69] The background for this Order was widespread activity by cotton speculators in the western area under Grant's command. While some of them were undoubtedly Jews, Grant decided on collective punishment for all Jews in the district. The community leaders protested to President Abraham Lincoln, who issued a directive on January 4, 1863, that rescinded the order.[70] There is no reason to belittle the significance of this incident, but there is also a danger of making too much of it. It is likely that Grant's extreme response manifested, at least in part, national sensitivities carried to extremes in time of a war that threatened the survival of the Union. Under such circumstances, perhaps, anti-Jewish tendencies were as easy to inflame as to extinguish.

Indeed, Jews were not eager to strike back at Grant when he campaigned for the presidency in 1868. According to the national press, which raised the issue of the Jewish vote, the Democrats hoped Jews would disavow Grant, while the Republicans made an effort to retain their Jewish voters. As a group Jews were divided. Many deserted the Republicans, but there was a Hebrew Grant Club and some public pro-Grant proclamations of prominent individual laymen.[71] The *Jewish Messenger,* which five years earlier had promised to exact revenge, was now defending its neutrality by claiming that at present there was "no religious issue." It maintained that in fact political independence would gain outside respect, while voting as a class would only confirm the group libel propagated by Grant's order of expelling Jews "as a class."[72] Even a Democrat like Rabbi Isaac Mayer Wise, editor of the *Israelite* who, shortly after Order 11 had become a controversy, had announced that if Grant ever ran for the presidency it would be his duty to oppose him, hid under his rabbi's hat during the campaign, claiming that he had been expressing his views in a religious journal. Henceforth, it devolved upon "offended citizens" to act.[73]

As for Grant, he never again revealed any prejudice toward Jews. On the contrary, he appointed many Jews to public office, the better known of whom were Edward S. Solomon as governor of the Washington Territory and Joseph Seligman, whom he invited to serve as secretary of the treasury—an offer Seligman declined. Grant even demonstrated considerable interest in the fate of Jews overseas. When in 1870 pogroms broke out in Romania, he appointed a Jew to serve as consul in Bucharest in an effort to bring pressure on the government to cease the attacks on Jews.[74]

Jews protected their rights in the political sphere by adopting, at least outwardly, a neutral posture: there were to be no separate Jewish formations on political issues and the community leaders were to have no influence on political matters. Political affiliations and expressions were to be kept within the individual domain. But their experience during the Civil War pointed to the futility of professing a non-partisan position, for while Jews themselves were not unified on the war issues, the outbursts of Judeophobia were common both in the North and in the South.[75] The frequently repeated warning by Jews themselves that the misbehavior of the individual reflected upon the entire collective was confirmed.

Professing such neutrality in the much less controlled social and economic spheres was entirely to no avail. For it was in these domains that existing prejudice and discrimination found their most extreme expressions. It was the unmatched success of Jews as a group in achieving middle-class status, often within one generation, that evoked strong anti-Jewish sentiments during the Civil War era and after. Following the war, department stores across the urban landscape bearing such names as Straus, Lazarus, Altman, Bloomingdale, Filene, Gimbel, Wertheim, Saks, Bamberger, and Hecht, along with the Loebs, Kuhns, Seligmans, Guggenheims, Lehmans, and others who became household names in the world of finance, were glaring evidence that Jews had "arrived" in America. Their achievements, however, were not attributed to honest hard work. Rather, as Jews began to play a more conspicuous role in the economy, they increasingly came to be stigmatized as a disreputable and dishonest people. Credit-rating firms responded to the image of the Jewish "swindler" by imposing penalties for being "an Hebrew," and insurance companies refused to take on "Jew risks."[76] The fact that Jews overcame these obstacles, in part by resorting to their own credit networks, made them all the more feared and disliked. As John Higham has noted, Jews "lost in reputation as they gained in social and economic status."[77]

The period of commercial and industrial expansion in the decades following the Civil War allowed a small but notable group of Jews to take the great leap from rags to riches. Somewhat ironically, the fact that Jews were barred from representation in Yankee banking houses to which their capital entitled them drove them to establish investment banks of their own just at the time when the American economy was vying for finance capital. Most significant for Jews, who did not have it easy in the private sector, the federal government sought their collaboration in the "high-risk" rebuilding of the American nation after the war.[78] The Seligmans, for instance, played a key role in repaying and refunding the national debt by serving as agents in selling government securities in Europe, where the buyers were also overwhelmingly Jews. Financing the reconstruction of the South was hardly attractive for American or English investors who had first-hand knowledge of the shaky southern economy. They left these risky ventures to others—Jews like Joseph Seligman, Jacob Schiff, and Franklin Moses, who through their European Jewish banking connections were able to market even the most questionable securities.

Another opportunity was the construction of railroads, the national government's single most important industrial development project during this period. The government subsidized this undertaking by giving land grants to firms in exchange for construction of rail lines, but there was high demand for private financing to provide the capital for equipment and laying the tracks. The Seligmans and the Schiffs were there again, and their clients included every major railroad company in America. Jews were also present as active partners in America's imperialist enterprise, a move that brought them into close relations with governmental institutions. The Seligmans, for instance, extended credit to U.S. naval pay officers throughout the world, helping them meet the navy payroll obligations. But the highlight of their close link with the national government was their active involvement in the Panama Canal project in 1880. How far the wheel of fortune had changed for Jews can be exemplified by the offer the Seligmans made to former President Grant to head the Panama Canal Committee for a salary of $24,000 per year—but now it was his chance to turn them down. It is perhaps not surprising that this period of tremendous expansion, when fortunes were made and lost, was accompanied by corruption and scandals.[79]

Jews, so heavily involved in finance, politics, and society, figured prominently in the American imagination as symbols for the evils of the Gilded Age. These sentiments were fermented in two groups that lost the most in the economic transformations of the post–Civil War era. The first were western and southern radical agrarians, who were deeply distressed by the economic and political changes that came in the wake of the new industrial order. The second were old-stock New England patricians, who lost their economic and political pre-eminence to the new class of industrialists and financiers.[80]

Even in good times traditional anti-Jewish biases did not disappear among these two groups; in bad times the old myths were revitalized in response to contemporary frustrations. An increasingly diversified society character-ized by frenzied social climbing stimulated by the spirit of the age engen-dered insecurity among traditionally favored groups. Those whose status was compromised yearned for a positive self-definition and sought it through re-newed national pride in the Anglo-Saxon creed. Underlying the resurgence of the Anglo-Saxon tradition in the 1870s was the desire to forge a unique link between this "race" and America's national greatness. The newly elevated Anglo-Saxon culture, which made the ethnocentric residue of Jews all the more objectionable, was now recruited in the name of setting up "areas of ex-clusiveness that would mark off the favored groups and protect them against excessive contacts with outsiders."[81] For the Brahmins, the "outsiders" were the new commercial and financial parvenus who threatened to replace them as the nation's elite. Jews embodied for them the parvenu spirit; greedy, mate-rialistic, and uncouth, these nouveau riche capitalists were easily identified as the object of exclusion by the traditional elite.[82]

Hannah Arendt's remarks on the equivocal nature of equality are germane to understanding the predicament that Jews faced in America well into the twentieth century. "The more equal conditions are," she poignantly noted, "the less explanation there is for the differences that actually exist between people; and thus all the more unequal do individuals and groups become." In a society like America, she wrote, "where equality of conditions had been taken for granted, discrimination becomes the only means of distinction, a kind of universal law according to which groups may find themselves outside the sphere of civic, political and economic equality."[83]

Indeed, in America discrimination against Jews was usually restricted to the social sphere, which was largely outside government jurisdiction and not punishable by law. Hotels, resort areas, residential housing, professional and social clubs, and private education were the principal venues of discrimina-tion against Jews. The famous episode of Joseph Seligman, who in 1877 was refused accommodation in a Saratoga hotel, was by no means the first or an isolated occurrence. But the fact that even Seligman—a prominent banker and a friend of Presidents Lincoln and Grant with links to the various admin-istrations since the Civil War—encountered social discrimination ominously foreshadowed the looming pattern of Jewish exclusion.[84]

For German Jews the transition from the warm welcome that was first extended to them by American society to their rather abrupt rejection just as they were becoming Americanized was a painful experience. It spoke to the fact, as Ira Katznelson observed, that in an age of mass migration, assimila-tion of individuals, short of conversion, is an unlikely option. Contrary to their dreams and desires, and like other American ethnic groups in this pe-riod, Jews were forced back into a tightly based ethnic and religious enclave. In an increasingly concentrated urban setting they formed their own social space. Although separate, the independent institutions that Jews established were a remarkably close replica of the American model. It may appear some-what ironic that the Jewish elite coped with its ousting from American society by creating an alternative civil society that was modeled after the one that had rejected them. Indeed, Jews of German descent had hoped that from their separate but American-like environment they would gain a more favorable position from which to transact with the greater American society.[85] They had yet to acknowledge that in America "citizenship opened far fewer doors than they had imagined."[86]

It was the massive influx of East European Jews in the 1880s, followed by the xenophobic and nationalist decade of the nineties, that constituted the great divide in American Jewish history. It brought German Jewish oldcomers face to face with the praxis of American liberalism and obliged them to take stock of their position in American society. While trying to protect their gains under increasingly strenuous domestic circumstances, they were faced with an exceptional challenge as millions of their East European kin began to contemplate leaving their homelands. How they responded to this challenge is the subject of the next chapter.

2

A Community Transformed
The Influx from the East

As the Jewish population increases, animosity grows with it.
Nations love only themselves, not strangers. If we get too
close to the Americans with our language and customs,
they will be annoyed.
　　　　　—Abraham Cahan, "Are We Safe in America?"

The millions of Jews who immigrated from Eastern Europe to America arrived with two cultures: "One culture they carried deep within themselves, within their spiritual and psychic being. The other they bore upon themselves, like an outer garment."[1] But as they were to discover, what they cherished most in the shabby luggage they brought along was less than welcomed in their new home. Marcus Ravage expressed it masterfully after he painfully conquered the new tongue:

> The alien who comes here from Europe brings with him a deep-rooted tradition, a system of culture and tastes and habits—a point of view which is as ancient as his national experience and which has been engendered in him by his race and his environment. And it is this thing—this entire Old World soul of his—that comes in conflict with America as soon as he has landed.[2]

However, few knew, or cared, about the reality that awaited them. They clung instead to the well-known image of America as a haven for the oppressed, and wished to believe the raving reports that appeared in the Hebrew and Yiddish press about the *goldene medine* that welcomed Jews. Although a small number of the East European Jews, some 30,000, chose to resettle in Palestine, for most of them America was the preferred destination by the 1880s. "Give us a chance in your great and glorious land of liberty," read one plea for help that arrived in 1880. "Come, brothers of Israel in America, come to our help . . . let us touch the sacred soil of Washington." As one Russian newcomer recalled, "America was in everybody's mouth."[3]

America became even more alluring when the Russian Empire started to undergo a process of rapid transition. As the peasant-based economy began to disintegrate, many of the Jews who made their living serving it as small merchants were subjected to severe dislocation. But what made Jews especially vulnerable, and their adjustment to the new conditions significantly more difficult, was the general upheaval that permeated Russian life after the assassination of Alexander II in March 1881. In the heated mood of the post-assassination period, when the impoverished masses were caught in a situation of rising prices, substantial unemployment, and intense competition, a lashing out against the Jews, whose economic behavior and very existence were held in contempt, was the result. The Russian government had been caught totally unaware by the pogroms that followed, and it greatly feared the widespread disorder. Yet within a few months the government's position tilted strongly against the Jews. A year later, in 1882, the May Laws legislated economic discriminations against Jews which prohibited them from settling in villages and allowed villagers to expel Jews already living in them. The main impact of these regulations was to cut off the Jews from the peasantry, which in effect meant their economic collapse.[4]

In 1886 a strict *numerus clausus* limited Jews' access to university education, which dealt a severe blow to those who were still hoping to gain access to the developing middle class. After 1891, even the Jews who lived in the large cities and thereby avoided many of the hardships of their less fortunate co-religionists ran out of luck. Declared as illegal residents, they were evicted, first from Moscow's Zaryadye quarter and later from other cities. In Romania and Austria-Hungary the Jews did not fare much better than those in Russia, and indeed in all of these territories Jews needed to look for other options.

Hence, between 1881 and 1924, when America established national quotas for new immigrants, a mass exodus took place when approximately two and a half million Jews chose to flee their European fate.[5] They came in waves. As in other migrations, those who came first, however impoverished, were nonetheless liberated enough from traditional constraints and sufficiently mobile to take the momentous step of starting a new life in a strange new world. The first to leave were mostly poor and uneducated young people, those who had the least to lose. Coming primarily from urban areas, where Jews were squeezed by rapid industrialization, many of them were artisans who could easily transfer their skills abroad. Merchants and property owners who lived mostly in the larger cities were not quick to uproot, and those who did waited until the early years of the twentieth century to take the step. The professional class and the religious elite mostly stayed behind.[6]

Conflicting Tides: Mass Immigration and Nativism

The hundreds of thousands of East European Jews who began landing on American soil after 1881 received a mixed and a somewhat unexpected welcome. The 1880s and 1890s were crisis-ridden decades in American history. As the social and economic costs of rapid industrialization became more manifest, the notion of an ideal society began to fade. The gap between the "haves" and the "have-nots" could no longer be ignored and the result was a larger circle of discontented citizenry that began doubting the success of the system. In American thought, as John Higham described it, "an ingenuous faith in the open road westward had long supported belief in an open road upward. The eighties cast a shadow over both ideas at the same time. A new sense of 'closed space' compounded the emerging fears of a closed society."[7] American Jewish oldcomers were not spared the impact of this unrest. Moreover, in the 1880s anti-Semitic discrimination began spreading like "wildfire."[8]

The newcomers were nonetheless eagerly awaited by their potential industrial and commercial exploiters who vied for working hands—the cheaper, the better. Somewhat ironically, it was these conservative elements who, for the time being at least, professed to be optimistic about the successful blending of this mixture of immigrants into a new American nationality. The entrepreneurial class, which was eager to turn America into an industrial and technological giant, chose to view the new immigrants as an economic blessing and ignore the social costs to American society.

It was left to a new body of middle-class reformers to focus attention on the increased polarization of American society. Most reformers located the heart of the problem in the crowded slums of the rapidly expanding cities. Indeed, since that is where most of the immigrants settled, it was not difficult to identify them as the source of America's social ills. Therefore, rather paradoxically, it was these liberal reform elements who, while cherishing a belief in equal opportunities and upward mobility, were also the first to lose faith in the success of assimilation. Although they viewed the immigration problem in social rather than nationalistic terms, by linking it to the central issues of the day, the reformers provided respectability to anti-immigration sentiments.[9]

Initially, Jewish charity organizations viewed the immigration problem in much the same light as the reformers. But, it can be safely argued, Jewish apprehensions were largely a result of the particular troubled position of Jews in American society. "Please bear constantly in mind," the Russian Emigrant Relief Fund in New York wrote in October 1881 to the Alliance Israélite Universelle, "that the position of the Jews in America is not such that they can well afford to run any risk of incurring the ill-feeling of their fellow citizens."[10] The Board of Delegates of American Israelites confessed, not without some justification, that American Jews were powerless to care for the mass of immigrants.[11] One of the officers of the United Hebrew Charities— established in 1874 for the purpose of providing relief to needy Jews in America—complained:

> The dispatch of poor emigrants to America has long constituted a burden and unjust tax upon our large cities. . . . Complaints continue that it is habitual with benevolent organizations in certain cities in Europe to dispatch utterly helpless Jewish families to America—only to become a burden upon our charities.[12]

Indeed, it was left to America's Jews, themselves experiencing social and economic hardships, to bear the brunt of absorbing the greatest Jewish population movement since the Jews' expulsion from Spain. Although the Jews of Western Europe were the first to establish a network of organizations to provide relief for the East European Jews, the aim of the German, French, and British Jewish communities was to help them emigrate to America. As historian Elias Tcherikower observed, European Jews were afraid that Jews from the East "might engulf their countries. They therefore seized upon America as an ideal solution and resolved to direct the stream of immigrants to that 'vast free and rich country.'"[13] As to the costs, German Jews undertook to finance their journey westward across Europe and British Jews undertook to get them to their final destination in America.

American Jews were willing to help, but only a selective emigration that would be provided with financial assistance by European Jewry. But when the approximately 300,000 Jews who lived in America in 1881 came to realize that a mass exodus of hundreds of thousands and later millions was on the agenda—first in the 1880s from Russia, then at the turn of the century from Romania, and after 1905 from Russia again—it was perceived by some as "a bane to the country and a curse to all Jews."[14] One prominent Jewish observer suggested that it would be better to "send American-Jewish missionaries to Russia to civilize them there than give them an opportunity to russianize us."[15] When riots broke out in the Ukraine, the New York *Jewish Messenger* editorialized on May 20, 1881:

> It is very philanthropic to desire the Jews of Russia to leave that Empire . . . but to suggest that three million of them settle in America evidences more enthusiasm than common sense. . . . [It] is too difficult for one to view the advent of three million more with anything but trepidation.[16]

American Jews responded to these fears by setting forth strict limiting conditions for accepting new immigrants. During a meeting of relief organizations in Vienna, a representative of the Hebrew Emigrant Aid Society (HEAS, later re-established and renamed as the Hebrew Immigration Aid Society, HIAS) made it clear that American Jews

> would receive no more emigrants except in a few exceptional cases, confined to those . . . who could not be repatriated and who could not be disposed of in some European or non-American community, and these should be sent, with such sums and upon such conditions only as should be exacted by the HEAS, and only after the express consent of that Society had been obtained.[17]

Even the Baron de Hirsch Fund—established in New York in 1891 for the purpose of assisting the new immigrants and relieving the American community of some of the financial burden—was not accepted without conditions.[18] Oscar Straus, who was later appointed secretary of commerce under Theodore Roosevelt, warned Hirsch that the Fund was in no way to foster or encourage further emigration from Europe. If such was intended, then he (Straus) wanted no part of it.[19]

Although there was not much love lost between "old" German Jewish immigrants and East European Jews, it was more than personal dislike that accounted for their reluctance to see an influx of debilitated and pauperized Jewish masses immigrate to America.[20] Judging by the American climate at the time, their anxieties were not groundless. The nativist sentiments that had been brewing again since the 1880s reached hysterical intensity in the 1890s. The socially framed warnings about continued immigration by social reformers in the 1880s were reformulated in anti-foreign and nationalist terms in the 1890s.

The 1893–1897 depression only exacerbated the economic and social unrest in America. During this era of profound disruptive pressures, nationalism and jingoism functioned as a most powerful unifying force. Discontent was expressed in nationalist terms, and Americanism became the nation's civil religion. Its dogma called for a more restricted sense of nationality and was articulated in terms of deep suspicion of divided loyalty and resistance to Americanization.[21] A rather unlikely coalition—of Brahmins, rednecks, bourgeois, proletarians, reactionaries, and populists—joined against the "hordes" of aliens, who were depicted as a threat to American society, culture, and the Anglo-Saxon race.

Forces in favor of restricting immigration were gathering momentum. The patricians of New England, whose elite status was already challenged by a new elite made of robber barons, captains of industry, and representatives of the South and rural West (whose way of life was threatened by the industrial regime of the North), were at the forefront of this movement which reflected as much an attack on the industrial order as on immigrants. Tom Watson, the most important southern leader of the People's Party, summed up the situation: "The scum of creation has been dumped upon us. Some of our principal cities are more foreign than American." But he placed the blame for it upon the industrial class, "the manufacturers and bankers," who "wanted cheap labor and did not care how much harm to our future might be a consequence of their heartless policy."[22] The attitude of the American gentry was expressed most starkly by Henry Adams, grandson of President John Quincy Adams. In his autobiographical work, *The Education of Henry Adams*, he echoed the laments of his class when he wrote that he had "no place" in a society where Jews were in control of business, politics, and finance, where "a Polish Jew fresh from Warsaw or Cracow" had a "freer hand than he—American of Americans"—did.[23]

In 1894 a trio of Harvard-educated New England patricians founded the Immigration Restriction League, which soon achieved national prominence. The League focused its campaign on the threat posed by the new immigrants to America's institutions and way of life.[24] Two years later, Senator Henry Cabot Lodge of Massachusetts sponsored a bill calling for a literacy test to be taken by all immigrants before being admitted to the United States. It was passed by Congress, but President Grover Cleveland vetoed it, calling it a "radical departure from our national policy relating to immigration." (Twice more the literacy bill passed the Congress and twice more it was vetoed, once by President Taft in 1913 and again by President Wilson in 1915).[25] But anti-immigration sentiments did not subside.

Even in this pernicious climate, the potential for a strong alliance between the Populists and the traditional aristocracy of New England did not endure for long. As Benjamin Ginsberg has perceptively observed, the leaders of the new industrial order responded to patrician anti-Semitism by ridding themselves of Jews and making a place for the much-preferred traditional elite. And once these "American of Americans" gained a stake in the new regime, they became more tolerant of its failings. As for the Populists, left on their own they were crushed by the northeastern industrial regime in the 1896 elections. Thereafter, the impact of their brand of anti-capitalism and anti-Semitism was limited to the South.[26]

For American Jews, the nationalist nineties added a new potency to the Shylock stereotype, which in its updated version tended to obscure the distinctions between the "old" and "new" Jewish immigrants.[27] The more conventional reactions in the 1880s were against the culture and appearance of the new Jewish immigrants, which were relatively easy to alter. But by the 1890s Jews were being charged with the more serious offense of being capable of dominating or destroying the American economy. Typecast traditionally as being connected with gold, Jews in America were suspected of exerting pressure on the government to maintain the gold standard. At the Democratic national convention of 1896, William Jennings Bryan warned supporters of the gold standard: "You shall not crucify mankind upon a cross of gold!" After losing the election, the so-called silver men located their defeat in the power of the "invisible empire," an "oligarchy" centered in the "mysterious money power," which had tied "the hands of the United States" and was rapidly proceeding "to enslave the human race." Although there was a vagueness in pinning down the members of the oligarchy, the Rothschilds were often mentioned.[28] But Jews were not only depicted as an internal threat; as international, rootless people, they were being imprinted on the public imagination as a worldwide financial power. The traditional anti-Jewish gallery of images was no longer confined to "mere habits of life" or religion. It expanded to accommodate fears concerning the nation itself. Jews, it was believed, endangered its institutions or threatened through greed to possess them.[29]

During these times, it must be remembered, the economic security of American Jews was neither long-standing nor assured. On the contrary, the periodic economic slowdowns in the 1880s and 1890s damaged many of their businesses, and by the mid-1880s the urban ghettos had a sizeable body of poor Jewish immigrants. In the social sphere, by the end of the nineteenth century exclusion of Jews grew increasingly rampant.[30] The affluent Jews who were part of the new moneyed class began to increasingly experience systematic discrimination. Their exclusion was part of the process, led by the business-industrial elite, of forming a new ruling class. Ridding themselves of Jews their former allies, they linked themselves instead with the old privileged strata to create an "American" ruling class. The realization of this agenda was most evident in the creation or reconstitution of exclusive institutions such as boarding schools, universities, resorts, and social clubs. In these social bases, from which Jews and other "foreign" types were excluded, it was hoped that a new and purely Anglo-Saxon national elite would be forged.

Molding a Community: Between Jew and American

Although the domestic situation was mainly responsible for shaping the response of American Jews to the mass immigration of their East European coreligionists, there was yet another important factor. The American Jewish leadership, overwhelmingly of German descent, was facing its own trauma of origin. The tide of European anti-Semitism, particularly in Germany, not only made them more conscious of their own vulnerability, it also cast doubt on their much-revered emancipation heritage. Fearing that the disease was spreading westward, some of them lost confidence in their own future in America. In an 1890 New York address, Marcus Jastrow, a highly respected rabbi and scholar of the period, expressed his concerns:

> A drop of poison has been instilled into the blood of Western nations causing a distemper contagious in its nature, and, there is no use in denying it, the contagion has reached our beloved country, and the poison, too, has been imported, and it works its way into the heart of our community, destroying the social peace.[31]

Revealing its own feebleness, the Board of Delegates on Civil and Religious Rights, a successor to the Board of Delegates of American Israelites,[32] resolved not to take any action on behalf of Jews in Germany, who in 1881 were exposed to anti-Semitic agitation aimed at revoking their rights. In defense of its position, the Board expressed its compliance with the wishes of the leading Jews in Germany, who maintained that "they were fully competent to maintain their position, having confidence in the essential justice of their cause and the returning reason of the German people."[33] We shall encounter this same rationale in both the late 1920s and the early 1930s.

Psychologically, emotionally, and politically, Jews in Germany were unequipped to defend themselves; apologetic and defensive, they opted for inaction rather than confrontation.[34] Indeed, one can argue that it was precisely these same reasons that restrained American Jews from protest or petitions to their own government.[35] The community leadership's resolve to sidestep any public action may have stemmed from its recent recognition that the distinction between individual and group rights was central to the American way of life. Given their determination to view themselves and be accepted as all other

Americans, the maneuvering room of "official" Jewish responses became increasingly limited.

As the East European Jews continued to emigrate in great numbers following the upsurge of persecution in their homelands in the 1890s, the concern of American Jews that the arrival of so many "foreign" Jews would undermine their own flimsy position in American society cannot be entirely dismissed as a figment of their imagination. It is not at all surprising that American Jews responded at first with anxiety, even rancor, and that from 1870 to 1891, "when America as a whole was pro-immigrant, American Jewry was restrictionist in approach."[36] What is rather remarkable, however, is the fact that from 1891 to 1924 when "a complete reversal of attitude prevailed" in American society, "acknowledged Jewish spokesmen . . . tried to demolish, or at best modify, every piece of restrictive legislation as it arose"; that German Jews in America soon undertook to systematically help the immigrants; that by 1891, Dr. Julius Goldman, of the United Hebrew Charities, could say that, yes, America *was* the best destination for the Russian-Jewish refugees.[37] What had transpired to bring about these changes of attitude is as much the story of America as it is the history of the Jewish American experience.

In the late 1890s, stimulated in part by the innovative ideas of Zionism, some American Jews began to reconsider the meaning of "America as their Zion, and Washington their Jerusalem." This new nationalist ideology raised to the surface the central issues that preoccupied American Jews and disturbed their host society: the charge of dual loyalty, their separatist cohesiveness, and their nation-like character that lacked territorial definition. Richard Gottheil, an early convert to Zionism and an associate of Theodor Herzl, tackled these charges. He maintained that just as Irish and German Americans retained their ethnic identity and their ties to their mother country without being accused of dual loyalty, so also could Jews. Just as the state could not "demand that the individual shall relinquish his peculiarities, his traditions, his family relationship," so too, Gottheil believed, it could not "ask of any group to give up its historic associations, its connections with other groups of the same race or of the same religion living elsewhere."[38] He was convinced that as a Jew he could be accepted just like any other American.

But what he and other Americanized Jews were beginning to realize was that whereas acceptance was extended on an individual and not on a group basis, rejection was based on collective stigmatization. Trying to avoid it, the American Jewish stewards—an intimate circle tied by business, friendship, and marriage—embarked on the task of absorbing their East European counterparts.[39] "Unprotected and undirected," they feared, "many immigrants will naturally fall into bad association and [will] disgrace . . . the Jewish community."[40] Paradoxically, it was the need to simulate the reference group's norms which served as a major catalyst in activating the better-off Jews to aid the new immigrants.[41] As Naomi Cohen has noted:

> Often praised by non-Jews for their philanthropy, Jews risked a severe loss of face if they were to dodge the responsibility of the new immigrants. Besides,

since the American public and government had expressed their sympathy for the East European victims of persecution and pogroms, the American Jew could do no less.[42]

It is difficult to gauge to what extent the Jewish communal leaders' negative image of the East European Jews reflected their own insecurity and to what extent it manifested the acceptance of their reference group's image of them as real. One thing appears more certain: in responding to particular issues that had spilled over to the public sphere, Jewish leaders relied on American culture to provide them with a menu of appropriate responses. This often proved a complicated task. For instance, although helping the destitute would be considered noble, for Jews to help needy Jews could be perceived as an unacceptable manifestation of "clannishness." Another quandary, particularly for Jews, was created by their material success. While Jewish stewards in the traditional sense of the *Shtadlan* (intercessor) accepted the American gospel that the rich were responsible for sharing with others that which the nation had so generously granted them, they were worried that distributing their wealth to Jewish causes, such as relief, would validate the venomous image of "rich as a Jew."[43] Aware of this dilemma, Reform leader Kaufmann Kohler advised in 1900 that Jews ought to become distributors of wealth, for "then will his material success, instead of rousing the envy and hatred of the foe, evoke the admiration and emulation of all for the sense of equity and righteousness of the Jew."[44]

Given the Jews' sensitivity to collective disgrace, it would have been improper to burden the general public with a particular Jewish problem. Indeed, Jewish relief and philanthropic organizations, a so-called separate welfare state, was soon to emerge to serve the needs of the impoverished newcomers. Showing the light to the "backward" masses, Jewish stewards hoped, would gain them recognition as the leaders of the entire community. "Americanizing" the newcomers would not only usher the masses into society but, more importantly for the old stock German Jews, it might succeed in preventing their own exclusion from society. For with the influx of East European Jews and the concurrent antagonistic ambience in America, Jews came to be perceived as one people, a crowd undistinguished by means or deeds, by descent or potential for ascent. Hardest hit by this undifferentiated view of Jews were not the immigrants but rather the oldcomers who, just when they thought they had "arrived" in American society, were confronted by increasingly spreading social exclusion. As Jews came closer to resembling mainstream gentility—in both their material lifestyle and their cultural refinement—they were less welcomed in their midst. Tolerated from afar, Jews were rejected as they aspired to penetrate the inner circle of American life.

Rather ironically, Jewish philanthropic organizations, which were intended to serve as absorption agencies for the largely unwelcome Russian, Polish, and Romanian Jews, constituted an alternative temple for the worship of American teachings, an altar where the Jewish elite could perform its social obligations. In these and their exclusively Jewish social institutions, Jewish stewards created a power base for their own survival as an elite. Contrary to the wish of "Americanized" Jews, this development promoted a process of dissimilation, leading them to uncover their own ethnic consciousness. But again, it was the powerful impact of changes in the American environment that induced them to embark on this inward journey.

From the end of the nineteenth century, the distinctness of American Jews was redefined in American society. Their increasingly popular designation as a racial group was vested with new meanings. One result of this mixture of nativism and racism was manifested in the nature of the opposition to immigration—it became particularistic. A sharp racial contrast was now drawn between the older immigrants of Anglo-Saxon or Teutonic stock and the newer immigrants who came primarily from Southern and Eastern Europe. Americans had to decide if they "want this country to be peopled by British, German, and Scandinavian stock, historically free, energetic, progressive, or by Slav, Latin, and Asiatic races, historically down-trodden, atavistic, and stagnant" who were inherently impossible to Americanize.[45] In a society which was becoming less tolerant of Jews, yet did not exclude them completely, partial exclusion tended to intensify the group's cohesiveness.

When the situation of Russian Jews took a turn for the worse in 1890, American Minister to Russia Charles E. Smith denied the accounts of persecution.[46] Yet information on their deteriorating situation continued to circulate. In early 1891, Secretary of State James G. Blaine drew the attention of his minister in St. Petersburg to the reality that over and above humanitarian concerns, America's interest in the conditions of the Russian Jews were due to "the difficult problem of affording an immediate asylum to a million or more of exiles without seriously deranging the conditions of labor and social organizations in other communities." While noting that those who came had been generously helped by Jewish organizations, he expressed the gravest fears "lest this resource should fail." Obviously concerned with what effects the situation in Russia might have on the domestic American front, Blaine stressed the restrictionist mood and the legislation now pending before Congress, explaining to his minister that if such policies were to be adopted, "it is only because it has been found necessary to avert the injection into the population of elements not assimilable, . . . bringing . . . the indigent and helpless to become a charge upon the community."[47] Although the plight of Jews in Russia grew progressively worse, Smith remained obtuse to their predicament.

Jewish leaders recognized that the situation, both at home and abroad, called for a different strategy. In 1891, a delegation of the community's notables, including Oscar Straus, Jacob Schiff, and Joseph Seligman, met with President Harrison. As can be expected, this politically sophisticated trio presented the problem of the Russian Jews under the guise of a humanitarian concern for "Europe's" immigrants. But since it was also treacherous for Jews to appear "international," they took pains to emphasize that their main concern was the negative impact the Jewish problem in Russia might have on

America. In accordance with their own interests, they tried to convince the administration that improving conditions in "Europe" (meaning, primarily, rights for Russian and Romanian Jews) would stop the flood of immigrants to America.[48] Harrison was persuaded to appoint a special commission to investigate the causes of European immigration to the United States.[49]

Jewish indignation gained momentum following the 1903 Easter pogrom in Kishinev. Although there was very wide public protest, the U.S. government did not respond to the cry for diplomatic intercession.[50] When a delegation of American Jews visited President Theodore Roosevelt in the White House they gained his sympathy, but he was also very candid in expressing to Oscar Straus his dislike for gestures that were not backed by power: "You know I am prepared to do anything I can for all our citizens . . . but unless we mean to do something further than simply protest it would look like an effort to catch votes."[51]

Roosevelt knew the soft spots of Jewish citizens, and when they came to him again in June 1903 with a petition which they wished to be forwarded to the Russian government through official diplomatic channels, he agreed. He was advised by his secretary of state, John Hay, that the Russian ambassador was likely to refuse to accept the petition, which he did, and the initiative was deflected, but both the administration and Jews at least received the publicity they wanted. As a "consolation prize," and by permission of Theodore Roosevelt, "the separate sheets of the petition, suitably bound and enclosed in a case provided for the purpose, have been placed in the archives of the Department of State." Secretary of State John Hay kindly commended the petition for its "language so earnest and eloquent and yet so dignified, so moderate and decorous," as to find it "a valuable addition to public literature." He assured Leo N. Levi of B'nai B'rith that it would be "sacredly cherished among the treasures of this department."[52]

Roosevelt, like most other presidents, resisted domestic ethnic pressure that sought to influence America's foreign policy. Hence, when fear of pogroms during the Easter season of 1905 again brought leading Jews to request intercession, Roosevelt, increasingly annoyed by the incessant pressure, responded to the Jews' plea as one in a pile of demands for intervention, which also included Armenians, Finns, Poles, and Congolese.[53]

Kishinev in 1903, the wave of pogroms across western Russia in October 1905, and the waning of the 1907–1908 depression renewed the stream of Jewish immigrants to American shores.[54] Close to half a million Russian Jews arrived in the United States between 1903 and 1908. A special committee of distinguished Jews was organized to undertake the problem of relief. One of the issues debated was whether Christians who had been hurt by defending Jews against the pogromists should be helped as well. Opinions were divided. Straus and Schiff, the leading spirits of this enterprise, took the broader view, claiming that nonsectarian distribution to aid the "suffering Russian people," might attract contributions from Christians. But more important, he also claimed that Jews had to be liberals. Liberalism, as Schiff explained, knew no religion.[55] Humanitarian causes had a special appeal to the more assimilated Jews. It accorded them respectability and, no less significant, it modulated their Jewishness, or so they thought. In America, East European Jews began to question the relief measures taken to aid their co-religionists, and they resented the patronizing attitude of their Americanized counterparts most deeply. "It is up to us Russian Jews to help our poor countrymen," one of the founders of the Hebrew Sheltering Society asserted, "to keep them from being insulted by our proud brethren to whom a Russian Jew is a schnorrer [beggar], a tramp, a good-for-nothing."[56]

Indeed, as the numbers of East Europeans soared and they gained more confidence, the German-Jewish "uptowners" could not disregard the potential challenge to their leadership. The ideas for a defense organization were still in the preliminary discussion stage, but the need for other than a charity organization was treated by most of the Jewish elite with disdain. However, Louis Marshall—the prominent New York attorney who was to serve as the second president of the American Jewish Committee until his death in 1929 —understood that if they did not initiate such an organization, Jews who had "objectionable" tendencies would surely do so. He thus urged that "in order to avoid mischief it was desirable that we take initiative."[57] At a May 1906 meeting, Chairman Sulzberger ended the deliberations with candid and explicit admonitions, but at the same time he clearly expressed some contempt toward their new inside opponents:

> The need for a better feeling between the native and foreign elements of American Jewry is recognized, and I deplore the license of speech that has grown among us. The suggestion that mere numbers can give rise to statesmanlike advice in matters affecting the Jewish people is unthinkable. The know-nothing element among the native American Jewish people ought to be crushed, and the unrestrained license of speech and arrogant assumption of the so-called East Siders that mere numbers give wisdom ought to be treated as nil. There is more to American Jewry than what is comprised within the Ghettos. . . . Both elements, both influences, the assumed superiority of the native Americans, and the belief of the unnaturalized that numbers should rule, ought to be nullified.[58]

It was against this wider background—the continued arrival of a huge flood of destitute Jews from Eastern Europe and the impact of their growing numbers on the American Jewish establishment—that in February 1906 a group of thirty-four elite Jews convened in New York City to consider the formation of a national Jewish defense organization. They founded the American Jewish Committee (AJC), the first ethnic-religious organization in the United States that was established for the sole purpose of defending its rights and those of its co-religionists abroad.[59] Elitist in composition as well as in approach, the founders of the AJC, mostly of German descent, wished to ensure that American Jewry would be "appropriately" represented in the outside world. They created an organization which derived its strength "not from numbers but from the quality and status of its handpicked membership." They never intended to turn the American Jewish Committee into a mass membership organization; even the broadening of its representational base was carefully controlled by its founders.[60] In its approach it combined the traditional "court Jew" strategy with the progressive notions of the American social milieu.

Insecure Citizens: The Russo-American Treaty

Between 1908 and 1911, in the anti-alien and particularly the anti-Jewish climate that permeated America, the recently established American Jewish Committee took its first steps in the public arena to tackle the issue of the Jews' inequality in the United States as reflected in the discriminatory measures that had been appended to the Russo-American Treaty of Commerce and Navigation of 1832.[61] Article I of the treaty guaranteed reciprocal rights to Russians and Americans in each other's countries. But in the last quarter of the nineteenth century the czarist government had begun to impose economic and residential restrictions on American Jews who were on Russian soil as part of its repressive measures against its own Jews. In the 1890s Russia took it a step further by refusing to issue visas on the passports of Americans in Russia.[62]

In May 1907, Secretary of State Elihu Root issued a circular with instructions to all passport applicants, announcing the new travel regulations to Russia. The directive read in part:

> Jews, whether they were formerly Russian subjects or not, are not admitted to Russia unless they obtain special permission in advance from the Russian Government, and this Department [State] will not issue passports to former Russian subjects or to Jews who intend going to Russian territory, unless it has assurance that the Russian Government will consent to their admission.[63]

The AJC was appalled by this announcement, which essentially made the Department of State an administrative arm of the Russian government's discriminatory policy against American Jews. It protested to Root that the United States "seeks to . . . apply an unconstitutional religious test to upwards of a million of our own citizens." In response to public pressure the passport directive was modified, but its amended version did not satisfy the American Jews.[64]

Until the spring of 1908 Jewish activists refrained from linking the passport issue to the abrogation of the treaty, trusting that diplomatic pressure by the United States would put an end to discrimination. Pressure on party and government leaders by prominent Jews grew during Theodore Roosevelt's first administration. They succeeded in getting both the Democrats and the Republicans to adopt resolutions in their party platforms of 1904 pledging equal protection under treaties to all citizens.[65] As the elections neared, the AJC's leadership was worried lest the Democrats would seize on abrogation as a political tool. Adhering to their traditional strategy of public political neutrality, influential banker Jacob Schiff declared that a Jewish vote should not and did not exist. But at the same time he intimated to Roosevelt that if it was revealed that the Republicans' promises were mere campaign gestures, it would cost the party 150,000 votes in New York City alone.[66]

In May 1908 the Committee submitted a lengthy memorandum to Roosevelt, suggesting for the first time that it would not be satisfied by diplomatic protest, and demanding instead that the United States terminate the existing treaty with Russia. In their brief the AJC emphasized the insult to the United States, whose passports were not being honored and whose principles of freedom of religion were being violated. As in the case of the Swiss treaty, American Jews were alarmed by the fact that inaction on the part of their government legitimized their status as second-class citizens.[67] But unlike the Swiss case, in the present situation there was an added factor: the fear that more Russian Jews might seek an escape route in the direction of America. Hence, in their brief the rationale for broaching abrogation was presented in "national" terms: Russia's bigotry against its Jews was the cause for their massive immigration to the United States, which, if alleviated as a result of the threat to terminate the treaty, would relieve America of the need to absorb so many new immigrants.[68] It was certainly an admirable performance of unqualified Americanism, but it did little to help, for in fact Roosevelt completed his term in office without any substantive accomplishments on the issue.[69]

The movers and shakers of the Jewish elite did not pass over the opportunity of the upcoming presidential election. As soon as William Howard Taft won the Republican nomination, Secretary of Commerce and Labor Oscar Straus, who was also a central figure in the AJC, briefed him on the Jewish grievances. Taft responded by arranging for Straus to meet with his nephew, Hulbert Taft of the Cincinnati *Times-Star*, a paper owned by Taft's brother. A few days later the paper published an article by Louis Marshall on the passport question and ran an editorial which suggested that Russia's discriminatory practices might cease if the United States denounced the treaty. As Naomi Cohen has noted, "The quid pro quo was obvious; the Jewish leaders would try to deliver the Jewish vote to Taft." Marshall saw to it that the Jewish press around the country reproduced the articles that appeared in the *Times-Star*. This was one of the very rare occasions on which Jews played pressure politics. However, it must be kept in mind that the AJC elite—people like Schiff, Straus, Marshall, and Sulzberger—were staunch Republicans, and for them such supportive publicity on the passport issue also meant attracting Jewish voters to their party. Briefing the president of the AJC, Judge Mayer Sulzberger, on the meeting with Taft, Straus was not abashed to admit: "As good Republicans and friends of Mr. Taft I feel we have done our full duty."[70]

Although Jewish spokespeople such as Jacob Schiff insisted that the granting of equal rights "was not a favor to the Jew, and hence did not saddle him with an eternal debt of gratitude," they remained circumspect in their behavior. Jewish officeholders were feeling increasingly frustrated by their failure to bring about a change. In early 1910 Schiff chided his associates, "We were simply licking the hands of the President. We do not respect ourselves sufficiently to come out boldly and demand our rights."[71]

But resorting to a public campaign was not an obvious choice for them. It was fraught with dangers: it could mean open conflict with the administration and a possible loss of future bargaining power; it could inflame anti-Semitism; and the prestige of the AJC could shrink considerably if the AJC lost after a public struggle.[72] In private, even the most influential among them expressed apprehension and bitterness regarding their insecure status in American society. Mayer Sulzberger was expressing more than futility regarding the specific Russian situation when he plaintively asked Oscar Straus in June of 1910:

> At what stage or period will we be free to use the public press without just offense to the Administration? In any event, is there a time when a notice of such intention to the Administration would be construed otherwise than as a threat, and, as such, be held a good cause to refuse further negotiations?[73]

However, there were a few, like Marshall, who had to reject such arguments if they were to uphold their emancipated self-image. Responding to the Taft administration's warnings that a public campaign might stir up anti-Semitism, he replied:

> If insistence upon rights of citizenship and of protection and equality with every other citizen can be productive of such a consequence, then we must bear it. We will have at least acted the part of men, and will have at least indicated that we no longer possess the cringing Ghetto spirit.[74]

As the months passed Jewish leaders realized that not only were they not gaining any ground in their struggle, they were losing the sympathy of the administration. When in May 1910 news came of the expulsion of Jews from Kiev, American Ambassador Rockhill called the reports exaggerated and claimed that in fact Premier Stolypin was distinctly "friendly to the Jews." Later in the month when an AJC delegation met in the White House with President Taft, Secretary of State Knox, and Ambassador Rockhill, they encountered opposition to their demands. Although the president promised to study the subject further and Republican intermediaries forwarded material by the AJC to the White House urging abrogation, months passed without any reply being received. The AJC soon learned that the State Department had prepared a memorandum for the president that spelled out its case against abrogation. The Jewish leadership was left with essentially two options: either arouse public opinion which might jolt the Republican president to act or, if that failed, redirect the campaign to the House of Representatives, which had a Democratic majority.[75] For the Jewish leaders, who had always tried to maintain a political neutrality with regard to Jewish issues, the latter was less preferable. Since most of them were themselves ardent Republicans, such an act would have meant giving up strong political affiliations, which, although bringing little advantage, had for many years provided legitimation for their leadership position within the Jewish community.

The AJC, although still wary of publicity, was advised by Taft's secretary, Charles Norton, that a public airing of the issue might spur the president to take action. With this clear signal the public campaign on the passport issue —by now tied with the abrogation of the treaty—was initiated.[76] Louis Marshall took the opportunity to launch the public campaign when he was invited by the Union of American Hebrew Congregations, the organization of Reform Jewry, to address their convention on the passport issue.

Marshall's address set the style, both in content and form, for the entire campaign. He opened with an appeal to American national pride, making the case that Russia's discrimination against American Jews was an insult to America. The Jew, he impressed upon his audience, "is now more than a Jew—he is also an American citizen, and the hand that smites him inflicts a stain on his citizenship. It is not the Jew who is insulted; it is the American people. And the finding of a proper remedy against this degradation is not a Jewish, but an American question."[77] One consideration was noticeably absent from Marshall's presentation: the miserable plight of Russian Jewry.

Thirty-two thousand copies of Marshall's address were distributed to members of Congress, state legislators, the press, clergy, judges, and other public leaders. However, it did not make an impression on the State Department. Secretary of State P. C. Knox continued to regard the passport issue as a strictly Jewish question and abrogation as serving "the interests of the Jewish population of the United States." Of greater significance, abrogation was regarded as harmful to the American national interests both in the commercial realm and because of its international political implications in the Far East, where Russia was viewed as an increasingly important curb to Japanese expansion.[78]

Although Marshall's address placed the issue on the public agenda, mainly through the press, much of the effort of the Committee continued behind the scenes. The Committee made some headway in Congress, but not enough to bring about a change.[79] The press, on the other hand, reported that the czarist government had removed restrictions on American Jews seeking to enter Russia for business purposes. The Committee attempted to refute what it considered false information. But there were other American Jews who were quick to express their congratulations to the president for allegedly succeeding to convince the Russians to remove restrictions on American Jews who wished to go there on business. Referring to his co-religionists, Marshall wrote with dismay:

> They are always ready to be patted on the back, to crawl on their bellies, to be
> undignified, and to seek an excuse for communicating with the powers that be,
> even though as a result of it they gain nothing but the contempt which they
> deserve.[80]

The Jewish stewards knew the rules of the game, but they rarely dared to make use of them. This time they did. After encountering the unyielding position of Taft in a meeting with Jewish representatives in February 1911, the leadership decided to step up the campaign in Congress, but on a non-partisan basis. Jewish leaders approached the most prominent political figures in the House and Senate, and by early November a change in mood was clearly perceptible. Since 1912 was an election year, the administration could not disregard the seriousness of the pressure for abrogation. Indeed, on December 4th, William Sulzer, the new chairman of the House Committee on Foreign Affairs, reintroduced his resolution to terminate the treaty. The House voted in favor of abrogation 301 to 1, and on December 19th the Senate endorsed unanimously a somewhat softer version. One year later, on January 1, 1913, the treaty of commerce and navigation between the United States and Russia ceased to exist.[81]

The abrogation of the treaty was a uniquely successful episode in American Jewish politics. In its campaign the AJC brought to bear every weapon of pressure group politics: the recruitment of public opinion by using the press, attempts to gain favor with the executive branch (and even hints that Jews might withdraw political support), and when all else failed, direct appeals to the representatives of the American people in Congress. But what set the groundwork for success was the increasing realization of the public that the Russian policy of discrimination against Jews became an American problem when it drove millions of them to emigrate to the United States. In a narrow sense the interests of the AJC and the American government coincided; both wished to see the new immigration come to a halt. Choosing to disregard its commercial and political interests in Russia, America's decision to abrogate the treaty points to the fact that immigration restrictionism had become a matter of national interest. Ironically, the burgeoning popularity of these sentiments in American society was a vital factor in the success of the AJC campaign.

After all had been said and done it became rather clear that, unlike the proclamations of its early rhetoric, alleviating the distress of the Russian Jews was not the main objective of American Jewry when it launched the struggle for abrogation. Indeed, the Jewish elite was sufficiently sophisticated to know that national interests could not become subservient to humanitarian considerations for a minority in a foreign land. When its actions are viewed within the wider context of intensifying social discrimination against American Jews and the continuing influx of their East European counterparts, it appears that what induced the AJC to embark on this public crusade were these two domestic factors. The Jewish "uptowners" preferred to believe that they were losing favor in American society because of the continued influx of pauperized Jewish newcomers. Improving their lot in their own countries, they thought, would stop the "foreign" breed of Jews from coming. This was a shared aim of the Jewish and the American establishment, and Jews realized it could work to their own advantage. Hence, at the end of the Second Balkan War in January 1913, Louis Marshall asked President Taft to introduce the question of the treatment of Jews in Romania before the peace conference, pointing out that if their conditions did not improve, they would seek refuge in America.[82]

While the stewards of the Jewish community were not indifferent to the misery of East European Jews, the ramifications that the abused rights of their distant co-religionists had on their own status as American citizens activated them to embark on a public campaign, as was the case with the passport issue.

By 1908 the East European Jews already constituted some three-quarters of the Jewish community in America[83] and the "uptowners" were becoming increasingly aware, with growing discomfort, that for American society as a whole the "oneness" of Jews by far transcended any of the differences that they perceived between themselves and the "downtown" Jews. Realizing that "a minority is always judged by its lowest representative," one uptown spokesman concluded that "our great duty therefore is to raise our race." Indeed, assisting the newcomers was more than an act of philanthropy. For the Jewish oldcomers it was "a question of self defense."[84] Philanthropy became imperative if the old elite was to safeguard its status both within and outside the community. But Americanizing the East European Jews was not a simple task. Just as the American nationality did not emerge from "a melting pot that functioned automatically," so also it was not clear "who would melt whom."[85] One thing became clear, though: a new Jewish order was in the making.

Part Two

A Growing Divide: "We" and "They"

3

Hard Times in the *Goldene Medine*
The Jewish Question in the American Context

> We suffer primarily not from our vices or our weaknesses,
> but from our illusions. We are haunted, not by reality,
> but by those images we have put in place of reality.
> —Daniel J. Boorstin, *The Image*

By the turn of the century American Jewry had been transformed from a rather homogeneous group united by common historical experience and culture into a community riven by deep schisms. A proliferation of multifarious ideologies and movements—Reform Jews and Conservatives, Zionists and anti-Zionists, international socialists and Bundists, ethnic newcomers and assimilated oldcomers—reflected the growing fragmentation in the American Jewish experience. Jews seemed to be united by little more than the plurality of adversities they collectively encountered on the outside.

Globally as well, the beginning of the new century did not augur much harmony. Resurgent nationalism, economic instability, the Great War, and a revolution in Russia revealed new elements of disintegration in Europe. The majority of the world's Jews were located at the heart of this political and economic earthquake zone. They were eager to escape, and their preferred destination was America. But their most natural absorbers, the American Jews, were experiencing their own setback from what they had believed would be an undisturbed march forward.

The more than one and a half million Jews who emigrated to America from Eastern Europe between 1900 and 1920 arrived at the peak of a nationalistic and xenophobic campaign. A general loss of confidence induced the resurgence of nativist sentiments in the early twentieth century. Fed by class differentiation and alienation from the new immigrant elements, Anglo-Saxon superiority was professed ever more fervently, both racially and culturally. A new nationalism took its hold on the American imagination. Although its federally sanctioned consequences were to culminate in the years following

World War One, its ideas and deeds were already widely articulated during the decades preceding the war.

The old motto proclaiming America a haven for the oppressed was changing to the dictum that hyphenated Americans were not welcome. The fact that despite strong adversities the new Jewish immigrants advanced economically faster and higher than any other immigrant group, that already by the first decade of the twentieth century some of them were becoming prosperous as clothing manufacturers and real estate speculators, served only to deepen the dislike of the Jews as a whole and to promote the parvenu stereotype.[1] The distinction between the new and the old Jew faded in actuality and almost vanished in the popular imagination.

The American Jewish "uptowners" felt that the arrival of the "Caftan" Jews revived the negative stereotypes of Jews which they were trying so hard to dispel.[2] Rabbi Stephen Wise had a far more sober view of the American Jewish condition:

> The German Jews [in America] are stupid enough to think that, if it had not been for the coming of the latest immigrants, namely the East European Jews, in the last thirty years, their own foreignism would go unnoticed and unchallenged, that they would have been able to get away with it as Simon Pure native Americans. They somehow felt that they were not the fellow-Jews of these more obviously Jewish aliens.[3]

Wise was not blind to the essential dissonances that existed between Judaism and Americanism. He preferred to confide these thoughts to his very close Christian friend, Reverend John Haynes Holmes, in the hope that they would not be published until "long after both of us shall be dead." "We Jews," he confessed,

> have infinitely much to learn in the way of tolerance to one another, and until that time, I wonder whether we have the right to count upon the understanding of the world, which sees a minimum of difference between Jew and Jew and lumps us all together with very much more justice than we Jews separate ourselves from one another.[4]

Wise's critique of the Jewish oldcomers of German origin was rooted in the recent experience of American Jews. It questioned the likelihood of total assimilation and acceptance by the majority culture. Furthermore, it alluded to the weakening of the Jews' cohesion; to their ethnic and cultural fragmentation. More immediately, it uncovered his disdain toward the old elite's estrangement from the so-called foreign Jews from Eastern Europe, and his insistent denial of the existence of a separate *Ostjudenfrage*.

Indeed, while the mass immigration may have served to aggravate anti-Jewish sentiments, these attitudes, although periodically repressed, had never been fully eradicated from the American mind. Since anti-Semitism indiscriminately targeted all Jews, shifting the blame to the "foreign" Jews was, perhaps, one way for the Jewish elite to avoid admitting its disappointment in American enlightenment.

It was therefore somewhat ironic that in view of the prejudicial and racist uses to which nativist Americanism was put, the Jewish establishment embraced rapid Americanization (the social process of becoming Americans) as the only solution to the Jewish question in America. But what was indeed remarkable was not only the fact that the "downtown" Jews showed little resistance to Americanization, but that they also reframed the myriad Jewish ideological options that emerged at the turn of the century as being compatible with American ideals.[5]

The Jewish elite reasoned that the greatest service they could provide for the entire Jewish community was to help the immigrants to become good Americans by hastening their integration as quickly as possibly. The result was thriving philanthropic activities.[6] Eager to make the Jewish immigrants over in their own image, the Jewish establishment showed little regard at first for their cultural heritage. For Minnie D. Louis (1841–1922), an "uptown" writer and educator active in settlement house work in New York,

> To wear the yellow badge, the locks,
> the caftan-long, the low-bent head,
> To pocket unprovoked knocks
> and shamble on in servile dread—
> 'Tis not this to be a Jew.[7]

"There is no room for Ghetto Judaism in America," Kaufmann Kohler, one of the leading exponents of Reform Judaism in America, declared in 1911. Echoing the Americanizing consensus of his German Jewish milieu, he viewed American Judaism "as an inspiring message to the new humanity that is now in the making, *not as a mere memory of the past* and a piece of Orientalism in the midst of vigorous, forward-pressing Occidental civilization."[8] But perhaps the most significant element in Kohler's pontification was his assertion of mutual compatibility between Judaism and Americanism:

> American Judaism! What a power of inspiration lies in these two words! They spell the triumph of the world's two greatest principles and ideals, the consummation of mankind's choicest possessions, the one offered by the oldest, the other by the youngest of the great nations of history, the highest moral and spiritual and the highest political and social aim of humanity.[9]

Jews went to great lengths to convince American society of their loyalty. The erudite Jewish elite resorted to popularizing their "ancient" American roots and their contribution to the American nation by what could be described as apologetic literature. Its intent was to prove that as early as colonial times Jews had contributed to the welfare of the nation and demonstrated their loyal patriotism in times of conflict far beyond their numbers in the general population. This defensive tactic was institutionalized in 1892 with the founding of the American Jewish Historical Society. Headed by Oscar Straus, himself an author of a book of this genre, the society welcomed non-Jews, explaining that its activities could benefit all Americans by informing them of the significant contributions of Jews to American society. Historical research, it was believed, would prove beyond doubt the right of Jews to claim equally with any other white man that he was an American.[10]

In American society, as has been aptly observed, "the conclusions of the apologists were not refuted, they were simply ignored."[11] But, as historian Eli Lederhendler noticed, among the Jewish sub-group the rhetoric of Americanism signified the extent to which the political allegiance of the Jewish citizens to their country was the basis for a new American Jewish politics. Though much of this rhetoric was employed for effect, and thus, perhaps, revealed only partially the real issues at stake, it was significant in that it reflected the context of the debate, one in which loyalty to America and its system of government was a key to legitimacy, even in the internal political setting.[12]

Loyalty above All

Wars have always been a favorable ground for acting out loyalty and patriotism. Indeed, the wars Americans fought in the nineteenth century generally served as integrative agents and for the most part mitigated nativist sentiments.[13] But the experience of the Great War was different. It was America's first European conflict—a war between the Old and the New, a battle between ideologies and ways of lives. A fervent tide of nationalism and flag-waving chauvinism stirred America to "100 per cent Americanism."

It was during this era that the entire spectrum of the dilemmas of Jews as Americans came into full view. In 1914 the majority of American Jews were newcomers from Eastern Europe. Their Old World background, their desire for the political and economic emancipation of their European counterparts, the Zionist impulse, and the impact of socialist ideology were all vital factors in shaping their attitudes toward the European conflict. Because most of the world's Jews lived in the war zone, America's national interests were bound to be inconsistent with particular Jewish interests. An ideological dimension was now added to the rhetoric of anti-Jewish sentiments, casting even further doubt on the Jews' Americanism.

Because Germany was the enemy, the suspicion of all things German became highly pervasive. It did not bypass the prominent American Jews of German background. Some dark rumors circulated concerning German Jewish influence in high places. Henry Cabot Lodge, for instance, whispered about secret ties between President Wilson and Germany through the offices of Paul Warburg, who had only recently (in 1911) became an American citizen and already had a chair on the Federal Reserve Board.[14] It was therefore only natural that the Jewish leadership was concerned by widespread expressions of support for Germany in the Yiddish press based on particular Jewish

interests.[15] One editorial in a Jewish paper, for example, expressed the hope
that Germany would conquer Romania, reasoning that

> with the conquest of Romania a brighter future opens for Romanian Jews.
> While Germany is supreme in that country, we can rest assured that just as in
> the case with Poland, the Jews will not suffer more than the rest. With the
> conclusion of peace Germany is pledged to secure humanity rights [*sic*] for the
> Jews in Romania as in other Balkan states.[16]

Even Jacob Schiff, the influential financier of German descent and one of
the leaders of the AJC, expressed strong pro-German sentiments, at least at
the outset of the war.[17] As Louis Marshall explained, for him (and for many
others with similar personal histories) there were two Germanys. One evoked
"evident unfriendliness to the German Government." Such feelings had been
imbibed from their parents, "whose experiences in Germany were of the most
bitter kind, such as were little calculated to inspire love or tender recollec-
tions."[18] But there was the other Germany, the one they had been brought up
to admire, the Germany of culture, which inspired "love of German literature, and especially its poetry."[19]

However, Jewish leaders were particularly alarmed by the intense suspicions that were being expressed toward East European Jews in America that
confirmed their deep-seated anxieties. Indeed, many of the non-Zionist newcomers had great difficulty in accepting the Russia remembered as a possible
ally of the United States.[20] This was true until the revolution of 1917, after
which a change of sentiments took place and a majority of American Jews
came to support the cause of the Allies. But during the early years of the war
many of the Jews who had recently arrived from Eastern Europe thought that
"compared to the Russian brand of anti-Semitism, the German gave the illusion of being innocuous."[21] Not yet initiated into the subtleties of the American political culture, they showed little restraint in giving vent to their emotions: "We were persecuted in Russia, forced to leave . . . and we have a full
moral right to hate our oppressors and to desire their defeat."[22]

The prevailing confusion was reflected in a letter written by Stephen Wise
in November 1914. While confessing to be personally "strongly on the side
of the Allies," at the same time he could "understand," however much to his
regret, "the attitude of those American Jews who cannot hope that the victory
of Russia will redound either to the advantage of civilization or to the betterment of the Jewish status." Wise thought that Jews could side with the Allies
only if it was certain that France and England would exert a liberalizing influence upon the Russian government—although he was not hopeful that this
would be the case. "What right have the Allies even to expect sympathy of
any American Jews with their cause as long as Russia fails to make any pro-
nouncement with regard to the Jewish question?" he asked.[23]

However, other than the AJC leadership's concern that the public expression of such opinions, if permitted to continue unchecked, would cast a dark
shadow over the loyalty and patriotism of American Jews, it was engaged in

its own great war over hegemony within the Jewish community. The new-comers were opting for greater democratization of Jewish institutional life. They were becoming increasingly loud in demanding a voice for themselves in shaping community life and were seeking to establish a Jewish Congress movement.

Much vigorous rhetoric was employed in a clash between "democracy" and "plutocracy." Spearheaded by Louis D. Brandeis (who was elected chair-man of the Provisional Executive Committee for General Zionist Affairs in August 1914, was a lifelong liberal, an icon of American progressivism, and a trusted adviser to President Wilson) and Rabbi Stephen Wise, the man who more than any other of his generation came to symbolize the new American Jew, the fight for the American Jewish Congress (AJ Congress) was nonethe-less inspired less by ideological reasons than by the hope of the gains to be achieved by furthering the objectives of the Zionists.[24] Unlike the AJC, when the AJ Congress was established in 1916 its declared purpose was to gain the mass support of East European immigrants and thus lay a claim as the repre-sentative of the majority of American Jews. But although it was more demo-cratic in approach, the AJ Congress would have remained relatively small had it not been for the American Zionists who understood the need to espouse some popular cause that would attract new members. The proposed Con-gress was the perfect structure for this purpose.[25]

It is rather instructive about the American Jewish experience that in the ensuing conflict over the establishment of the Congress movement and Zion-ism, both the pro and the anti factions were moved to Americanize the de-bate. Louis Marshall did not hesitate to articulate most condescendingly what he thought about the East European Jews and their leaders when he said: "There is no way to guide them or advise them, or to instill into them a sane view on any subject. They do not hesitate to pass judgment on the most deli-cate questions of diplomacy without a moment's thought. . . . Men who should know better are carried away by this insanity."[26] But even more seriously, the AJC did not recoil from making the charge against the East European Jews that being anti-Russian and, by extension, anti-Allied, they were un-Ameri-can. Marshall charged that the German government was paying numerous agents in the United States to arouse, "among the Russian Jews especially," a feeling of antagonism toward Russia and its allies, and that they were influ-encing the Yiddish press in America to side with Germany. He claimed that the AJC prevented American Jews from supporting an anti-Allied position, while the AJ Congress encouraged them to endorse the aims of the Central Powers.[27]

The rejoinders of the newcomers became ever more vociferous. To wage the struggle for equal rights, or for that matter for national rights, called for assertiveness. It could not be entrusted to the hands of the *Yahudim*, as the Jews of German descent were disdainfully designated, whose commitment, it was felt, appeared to be limited to parting with their cash. At the Kehillah convention of 1915, which was called to decide upon the establishment of the

Congress movement, the growing militant mood was very much apparent. One speaker, Isaac H. Hourwich, aimed his reproach at his own people when he said:

> It is time to set aside the Jews' traditional policy of meekness in matters of grave concern to them. . . . We have nothing to lose. What are we afraid of? Will one more rabbi be hung without trial or a few more women violated? Why have we not a right to cry and weep against the outrages perpetrated against our brothers and sisters on the other side? It is a question of maintaining the dignity and rights of the Jewish race.[28]

Writing to Louis Brandeis, Jacob Schiff charged that the AJ Congress "means the establishment of a new government, a government for the Jews by which the Jews are to be bound." He expressed his concern that its program would endanger the gains already made, since it implied "nothing less than a decision . . . that we are Jews first, and Americans second. . . . We will become a people by ourselves. We will become a compact mass of Jewish Americans, and not of American Jews."[29]

Schiff was expressing here more than a fear of the traditional anti-Jewish charge of "a state within a state." The main threat, as he perceived it, was to the citizenship status of the Jews, their most significant gain from emancipation. He was struggling to uphold the Reform principle, as proclaimed in the Pittsburgh Platform, which defined the Jews as "no longer a nation but a religious community."[30] But, writing less than two weeks after his letter to Brandeis in a more pragmatic tone to his colleague Marshall in the AJC, Schiff revealed what really underlay the Jewish establishment's strong opposition to the Congress:

> I am very much convinced that unless we do something very positive and very promptly to revive the proposed convention, those who are making a Golden Calf of a Congress will very soon say: "This man Moses is dead, these are your Gods, O Israel!," substituting the American Jewish Committee for Moses and the proposed Congress for these are your Gods.[31]

Schiff and those like him were well aware of the growing appeal of that newly imported religion called Zionism, which began to gain converts during the war years. As early as 1907 he had made public his denunciation of political Zionism, explaining that "as an American, I cannot for a moment concede that one can be at the same time a true American and an honest adherent of the Zionist Movement" which aims for the "restoration of Jewish political life and the reestablishment of a Jewish nation." If Jews were to be freed from the prejudice from which this generation was suffering, Schiff believed that they needed to feel "that politically no one has any claim upon us but the country of which, of our own free will, we have become citizens."[32] It was particularly threatening to the old elite that a resurgence of Jewish nationalism and an emergence of "separatist" tendencies within the community were taking place when American Jews were not united in supporting America's choice of allies. Indeed, the Zionist movement was the most natural habitat for these "dissidents," and it was during this period that it began to expand.[33]

The timing was somewhat perplexing, for at the peak of the highly charged crusade for 100 percent Americanism the opposite could have been expected. Two factors may serve to explain this seemingly illogical development. The first can be located in the person of Louis D. Brandeis, who lent respectability and legitimacy to American Zionism by asserting its compatibility with the American ideals of equal justice, political democracy, and economic opportunity.[34] Brandeis was very much attuned to the Zeitgeist and was aware that patriotism was the burning issue both inside and outside the Jewish community. In his oft-quoted formulation he maintained that

> multiple loyalties are objectionable only if they are inconsistent. A man is a better citizen of the United States for also being a loyal citizen of his state . . . and city. . . . Every American Jew who aids in advancing Jewish settlement in Palestine, though he feels that neither he nor his descendants will ever live there, will . . . be a better man and a better American for doing so.[35]

When in March 1916 Stephen Wise addressed the preliminary conference for organizing the American Jewish Congress, held in Philadelphia, he also resorted to the American theme:

> We have chosen the name ["Congress"] because it is the American name, because its American associations have endeared it to us, native and adoptive children of the Republic alike . . . because it is an inclusive, all-American name, with no implication of partisanship or factionalism.[36]

If Brandeis's conversion to Zionism accorded it respectability, President Wilson's idea of (national) self-determination granted it legitimacy.[37] In the Zionists' interpretation, America was more than a "haven of refuge"; its ideals and democratic education "strengthened our own movement for self-emancipation."[38] And more pragmatically the *Maccabaean*, the journal of the Federation of American Zionists, deduced that "the war implicates the Zionist cause. . . . President Wilson has made it clear that we are fighting for the rights of democracies and nationalities. . . . Only in a free world will the Zionist cause have an opportunity to be heard and to be dealt with justly."[39]

For those whose sense of self-esteem stemmed from their survival as Jews, there was nothing to lose and much to gain by safeguarding their Jewish dignity. Their Jewishness held a "tradition-nurtured attachment to Zion," an ancient past now dressed in modern Zionistic political garb.[40] Zionist ideals offered emotional support for a depressed sense of self in the increasingly hostile American environment. For those still experiencing the shock of displacement from the Old World and a sense of estrangement from the New World, the spiritual content of Zionism was a significant mediator between the past and present of the Jews in America.

The Jews with more to lose—who increasingly included East European Jews as well—expressed their insecurity by fervently rejecting Zionism as anti-Americanism. Following the Balfour Declaration, when the spiritual "love of Zion" (*Ahavat Zion*) was transformed into a realizable "return to Zion" (*Shivat Zion*), the threat was perceived as more real. The Reform movement's Central Conference of American Rabbis (CCAR) led the reaction to the Balfour Declaration. Its president, Rabbi Louis Grossman, restated the opposition to the "idea that Palestine should be considered *the homeland* of the Jews," for in fact Jews in the United States were an integral part of the American Nation.[41] Rabbi David Phillipson tried to convene a conference to discuss means of combating Zionism, but he failed to obtain the support of the AJC, which for its own political reasons was reluctant to engage in a public dispute with the Zionists.[42] Waging a rearguard battle to keep its endangered position at the top, the AJC demonstrated a compliant attitude toward its contenders. The statement it issued expressed qualified endorsement of the Balfour Declaration: still opposed to Jewish nationalism, it supported Palestine as a Jewish religious and cultural center. Yet, lest we view this as a complete change of heart, the statement, which demonstrated a shift from an anti-Zionist to a non-Zionist stand, began with a more categorical declaration:

> The Committee regards it as axiomatic that the Jews of the United States have here established a permanent home for themselves, . . . have acquired the rights and assumed the correlative duties of American citizenship, and recognize their unqualified allegiance to this country which they love and cherish and of whose people they constitute an integral part.[43]

The frequency and intensity with which Jewish spokesmen reiterated their loyalty to America revealed more than immediate insecurity; it disclosed a deeply imprinted historical lesson which held that Jewish survival depended on submission to the ruling authority. In its Americanized version it was rendered as "allegiance," which essentially denoted a conformist Jewish citizen. Public expressions on national matters that deviated from consensus opinion were to be a rare privilege extended only to the "court Jews."[44] In return, Jewish spokesmen grew extremely dependent on official authoritative sanctioning, linking even issues that properly belonged within the autonomous private domain of Jewish communal life to national affairs.

Such was the case, for instance, with regard to setting the date for the founding convention of the American Jewish Congress. It was originally scheduled for November 1917, but President Wilson, the first Democrat to break the Republican hold over the Jews in half a century,[45] intimated in a meeting with Rabbi Wise in June 1917 that he wished the date to be postponed because of America's entry into the war in April. Notwithstanding some vocal opposition from within, Wise complied.[46] Indeed, he was elated by the outcome of this meeting, for not only was Wilson persuaded that the new organization would serve Jewish interests, but, more significant for the Jews who yearned for the blessings of their "protector," he sanctified it as an American organization. Wilson allegedly told Wise that he regarded the

American Jewish Congress as being "in accord with and helpful to the aims and policies of the American government."[47] Other than to reciprocate the president's support, there seems to have been yet another reason why Wise felt he had to submit to Wilson's wishes to postpone the founding convention. In a letter to Louis Brandeis he explained that such a move might prove useful to neutralize the "very unfortunate impression" made by vocal Jewish pacifists who opposed America's entry into the war.[48]

Among the Jewish leadership, both in Wise's camp and among Marshall's followers, Jewish pacifists caused deep concern. Nonconformist public conduct was viewed as an ill-afforded luxury for a distrusted minority. "[T]here is but one course for an American citizen to take," Marshall wrote in a reproachful tone to the vocal pacifist Dr. Judah Magnes, "and that is, to stand wholeheartedly behind the Government." But it was clear that Marshall did not regard Jews as ordinary American citizens. "Do you believe," he asked Magnes rhetorically, "that the American people will not attribute to the Jews generally adhesion to a policy which runs counter to that of our Government," when a leader in Jewry is presiding "at meetings at which doctrine are avowed which are generally regarded as treasonable?"[49]

Even the most devout Jews who were faithful to the American dream of equal rights could not be blind to its limitations. By perceiving the opinions and actions of individual Jews as a threat to the entire community, the Jewish leaders were essentially accepting the majority's image of the Jews as true. In the name of protecting the Jewish collective, individual Jews—whether they identified with it or not—were expected to renounce their individual rights. "What right have you, merely for the purpose of voicing your personal views on a matter as to which the overwhelming opinion of America is opposed to you," Marshall wrote to Magnes in a reprimanding tone, ". . . to injure the Jewish people of America with whom you are so actively identified?"[50] Ironically, it was Marshall, one of the most astute interpreters of America's social and political cultures, who advocated that Jews must renounce their right to act as individuals.

The Legacy of Statelessness

Preoccupied with sustaining the gains born of conformist behavior, American Jewish leaders often chose to overlook the price tag that it carried. The legitimacy accorded to Jews as an interest group by the power holders was a way of administering control. And control from the top meant, of course, a certain loss of autonomy for the governed who could not oppose those who provided them with the license to exist. That predicament was part and parcel of Jewish life. It is safe to assume that for many of the influential Jews, convening the American Jewish Congress against the advice of the president would be

> the height of indiscretion and even run the risk of incurring the *charge of disloyalty* on the part of the Jews toward America. It is no time for us Jews to clamor for our rights apart from the right we have of manifesting our devotion to the

nation *under whose protection we live.* I trust none of the zealots will so forget their loyalty to America as to suggest a convening of a Jewish Congress when our chief business now as a nation is to join our allies and crush Germany.[51]

This response was not a manifestation of recently learned lessons, but rather of a second nature born of deeply absorbed historical experiences. The Jews of America, especially those who had not been exposed to the European emancipatory experience, had yet to fully absorb the meaning of citizenship rights. These observations are, of course, applicable to any religious or ethnic minority. However, there was one factor which set the Jewish people apart. More than the fact of statelessness, what seems to be unique in the Jewish experience was the profound effect that statelessness had on the collective Jewish psyche. The prolonged dispersion of the Jews seems to have evoked two principal reactions. The romantic sentimental response focused on Zion as a phantasm for a home—as a common fountain of religious spirituality and a shared mythical past. If only as a symbolic object of continual yearning, Zion attested to an unsettled existential consciousness. The other reaction was a pragmatic one. As a stateless and scattered people, Jews had understood ever since the *Haskalah* that a new social compact was in the making between themselves and the societies in which they lived. The modern state, whose ideology took its cue from the absolutist political theory that emphasized state sovereignty over the power of particular corporations, was celebrated by the *maskilim.* The medieval doctrine of *dina de-malkhuta dina* (the law of the kingdom is the law) provided the historical rationale for Jewish loyalty to the state. Although Jews had always recognized the importance of practical alliance with political authority, it was only in the modern period that they came to regard the state as their prime object of loyalty, and they opted for citizenship status primarily as a means of protection.[52] This was a sensible solution to their anomalous condition. As a result they developed as a group what may be described as a "citizenship passion"—their secular form of redemption. American Jews viewed citizenship not only as a guarantee of civil liberties and equality before the law, but also as protection against prejudice. As in the case of all infatuations, having become so deeply infatuated with their citizenship, they were often seduced by its pleasures and blinded to its shortcomings.

When one looks at the conduct of German Americans during the First World War one is struck by the contrast between their confidence to exert pressure, even pugnaciously, on behalf of German national interests and the careful attempt of the Jews to Americanize their particular agendas. Highly assimilated and well respected, German Americans campaigned openly to influence American foreign policy during the winter of 1914–1915, when they launched a massive drive for an embargo on the export of war supplies to the Allies. Because they transgressed the "morality of nationalism," German Americans were charged with disloyalty. The fury that they evoked in 1915 was the most dramatic reversal of judgment in the history of American anti-immigrant sentiment.[53]

But it was more than their status as "one of the most assimilable and reputable of immigrant groups" that explains the confidence of German Americans to act so flagrantly against their government's policies.[54] For even though the specter of German militarism and autocracy that since the turn of the century had cast a shadow on the image of their *Vaterland* in America, its geopolitical and economic importance, not to mention the reverence for its culture, were factors that America could not disregard. As a result, it was not long before German Americans returned to favor in their adoptive land.

The Jews, on the other hand, lacked such a psychologically protective alternative, for theirs was an imagined homeland. Only in the apologetic literature was their statelessness evaluated as an asset. In the *Patriotism of the American Jew*, Samuel McCall contended that, unlike other minorities, "the Jew can have no hyphenated citizenship because he has no motherland except that in which he lives."[55] Indeed, the Jews' primary sense of security was external, emanating from the nation's protection, and only after that was in place did they begin to draw the link between protection and the guarantee of rights.

When the future of European Jewry was up for discussion after the cessation of hostilities, the American Jews' sense of insecurity emerged in full force. Not entirely absent from their considerations were the possible effects which the various problems faced by their European co-religionists might have on their own future in America. Opinions in the Jewish community differed along much the same lines that divided it on its own internal issues.

Already during preliminary discussions in July 1916 the debate revolved around group rights versus national rights. The "uptowners," as could be expected, favored the concept of group rights, claiming that among non-Jews the demand for national rights was understood to mean that Judaism was a nationality and not solely a religion.[56] The controversy did not abate when the delegates to the American Jewish Congress, meeting in Philadelphia in December 1918, linked the debate on national rights to the resolution on Romania. Opponents of the resolution argued that Romanian Jews had no right to demand special privileges as Jews, only those rights that were accorded to every other person in that country. Supporters of the resolution contended that national rights were essential for Romanian Jews since they implied acceptance, because "when people come to the United States, they become, by virtue of being *inhabitants* of this land, Americans."[57]

The American Congress, as the delegation representing the different factions of American Jewry to the talks was named, arrived at the Paris Peace Conference carrying these two basically irreconcilable worldviews. Although after many trials and tribulations an ad hoc unity was reached, it did not obliterate behind-the-scenes disagreements.[58] When the official delegation of the American Jewish Congress met on April 2, 1919, with Secretary of State Robert Lansing and other members of the American Peace Commission, it encountered skepticism about the feasibility of obtaining "special rights for minority groups." In response to the not-so-innocent inquiry about whether the demands of the AJ Congress would not cause resentment and anger among the native populations, Julian Mack, an AJ Congress and Zionist activist, emphasized that without such guarantees the Jews in Romania and Poland would continue to be second-class citizens. Lansing remained wary, for he feared that the Jews in these countries were close to declaring themselves a national political party, which would further alienate them from the native populations, but he agreed to reconsider his position. The Jewish emissaries were asked to submit a brief on the Jewish case, only to have it diluted by the American commissioners.[59]

But even in its compromise version—as Herbert Hoover told Cyrus Adler in late April 1919—there was not the slightest chance that a national minority clause would be inserted into the peace treaty with Germany.[60] Secretary Lansing continued to have misgivings about the Jewish proposal.[61] In any event, and whether the action was done intentionally or not cannot be determined, David Hunter Miller, the legal adviser to the American Peace Commission, submitted the revised version after the deadline for the presentation of conditions of peace to the Germans. Hence it was decided that the Jewish question should be dealt with in the separate treaties between the Great Powers and the new or enlarged states, which would include such clauses for protection of minorities as deemed proper by the Great Powers.[62]

In Paris the American Jewish delegation presented its case as an *amicus curiae* brief, but unofficially some influential Jews contacted Wilson to air their opinions as "friends in court."[63] People like Henry Morgenthau (an early financial supporter of the Wilson campaign who became chairman of the Democratic Finance Committee and was later awarded an ambassadorship to Turkey) and other prominent anti-Zionists, while losing ground as Jewish spokesmen, could still claim the attention of President Wilson.[64] Morgenthau and others of his persuasion came to Paris not only to fight the Zionists but also to register their opposition to the concept of national rights. They prepared a petition for the Peace Conference which claimed that apart from the fact that not all Jews could hope to emigrate to Palestine, those remaining in the Diaspora would face a precarious position as a political group with dual allegiance.[65] As befitting a zealous American, Morgenthau remained adamant that Jews would enjoy the benefits of Polish and Romanian citizenship if they cooperated with "their fellow countrymen in bettering for all its inhabitants the land of their common citizenship."[66] For those who had yet to acknowledge their unequal status in American society, loyalty to the nation was regarded as a sufficient guarantee of the welfare of its inhabitants.

Although in the case of both Poland and Romania, Jewish rights (equality before the law and civil and political, but not national, rights)[67] were incorporated into the peace treaties—their inclusion was possible only under duress by the Great Powers.[68] The American Jewish delegation viewed the Paris Conference as a success; having participated in an international forum as representatives of the Jewish case, they returned to America believing that perhaps they could have a say in national policy as well.

But not all the Jewish leaders viewed the outcome of the Peace Conference as beneficial for the Jews of Eastern Europe. Leo Wolfson, the president of the Federation of Romanian Jews of America, for example, was not hopeful about the potential effectiveness of the League of Nations.[69] His assessments of Eastern Europe were not colored by the optimistic spirit of the age. As a realist with a first-hand knowledge of this region, Wolfson maintained that the written guarantees to the Jews were nothing more than "paper rights, and they are practically worthless." Moreover, what had been accepted as a legal *Diktat* of the victors could not guarantee observance of the spirit of the law.[70] A report by Julian Mack also left little room for optimism. He informed the executive committee of the AJ Congress that the chief of the minority rights division of the League of Nations was critical of the imposed nature of the minority treaties and excused some of the excesses against Jews on the basis that the countries involved "were told to sign the document and to accept it as it was, not as in the light of its history it might be interpreted."[71]

Yet it appears that many in the Jewish leadership had refused to understand or to acknowledge that the *Diktat* by the victors, especially by the United States, on minority rights had been intended to limit both discrimination and the forced emigration which generally accompanied it—particularly because it concerned those minorities who were potentially to remain stateless.[72] In this respect the minority treaties can be viewed as a supplement to the restrictive immigration laws that were enacted from 1917 and throughout the 1920s, especially in the United States. These two steps were taken essentially to serve the same goal: to prevent massive emigration from traditional countries of origin to traditional countries of destination.[73] Indeed, new winds were beginning to blow in the rapidly aging New World.

From Disillusion to Dissimilation

Every age has its illusions. Eras end when disillusions set in, when popular assumptions shift about what is normal, possible, and desirable. In postwar America the tide was turning toward reaction. Wilsonian idealism had culminated a reform spirit which had begun with Theodore Roosevelt. However, its extension into international affairs as a crusade "to make the world safe for democracy" had proved disappointing. Immediately after the war the pendulum that had swung so far to the left shifted back toward the right. "Europe was devastated by war," observed the liberal progressive Brandeis, "we by the aftermath."[74]

The postwar American mood was inward-looking. "Entitlement"—though a term popularized only in recent years—best captures the collective American mindset after the Great War. Americans felt entitled to a quick return to normalcy, domestic peace and prosperity, global economic pre-eminence, and much more. The previous slogan of a "world safe for democracy" was replaced by new pillars of faith: a belief in the greatness of America and in the power of prosperity.

The millions of new Jewish immigrants eagerly joined the crusade to spread the new gospel. Chasing the American dream was a traditional bonding agent in American politics—a religion that could be practiced by everyone regardless of differences in personal creed and background. But during the 1920s three elements combined to foil the aspirations of American Jewry. The aggressive nationalism of the war years endured as the springtime hope for a better world began to fade. The America-for-Americans mood renewed anti-foreign sentiments which were conspicuously exhibited in the movement to restrict immigration. And American anti-Semitism, albeit of a different variety than the dark cloud that began descending on Germany, cast its own shadow on the American Jewish dream. In 1922 Louis Marshall, president of the AJC, shared his despondency about these developments privately—and probably not by chance—with a peer who lived across the ocean:

> It is sad for those of us who have hitherto been proud of our fine [American] traditions, which have enabled the worthy immigrant to take up his home here, to note what a change has occurred since the armistice. Chauvinistic nationalism is rampant. The hatred of everything that is foreign has become an obsession.[75]

All three Republicans who were to occupy the White House in the 1920s echoed this xenophobic message. In a campaign speech in 1920, Warren G. Harding alerted America to the dangers inherent in "racial differences" and advocated that in the future the United States should admit only those immigrants who could be assimilated and whose background demonstrated that they could develop "a full consecration to American practices and ideas."[76] Calvin Coolidge, then vice-president-elect, maintained that "biological laws show us that Nordics deteriorate when mixed with other races."[77] Herbert Hoover, as secretary of commerce, declared that "immigrants now lived in the United States on suffrance [*sic*] . . . and would be tolerated only if they behaved."[78]

America's vision of the world contracted. In his 1921 inaugural address President-elect Harding articulated America's desire to work out its own destiny and jealously guard its right to do so. Pointing clearly to a return to isolationism, he added, "We seek no part in directing the destinies of the Old World. . . . We do not mean to be entangled. We will accept no responsibility except as our own conscience and judgment may determine."[79]

It is in this context that the Anglo-Saxon decade produced the most restrictionist immigration legislation in American history. It had its roots in 1907, when Senator William P. Dillingham of Vermont sponsored the creation of a Senate commission to investigate the entire immigration question and make recommendations to Congress.[80] After deliberating for four years and publishing a forty-one-volume report, the Dillingham Commission essentially endorsed the view that the new immigration was on the whole inferior to the old. The AJC had concluded at the time that "the reports . . . evidence but slight desire to adhere to the time-honored tradition that has made this country a refuge for the oppressed of all lands." Marshall's attempt to solicit support for a liberal immigration bill had been futile, as was his later attempt to suggest a clause that would exempt victims of persecution from taking the literacy test. However, it was indeed remarkable that in 1917, when under the surge of wartime nationalism Congress had succeeded in passing a literacy test over the president's second veto, the AJC was successful in securing exemptions to the law which modified its more objectionable features.[81]

In 1920, the Congressional Committee on Immigration noted with alarm the swelling stream of postwar immigration from Central and Eastern Europe that was overwhelmingly of "the Semitic race" and recommended "temporary suspension of immigration." The Committee's report to Congress included as an appendix a State Department memorandum (signed by Wilbur J. Carr, whom we shall encounter again in the 1930s and 1940s) that listed the objectionable characteristics of the Jews from Russia and Poland which made their further immigration disagreeable: they were classified as "the usual ghetto type . . . filthy, un-American, and often dangerous in their habits." They were diagnosed as physically and mentally "deficient" and economically and socially "undesirable."[82]

The notion of Americanism had been recast in social Darwinist terms. Its reification as a fixed model of cultural and racial attributes that were markedly different from "alien" ones rendered East European Jews as inherently unfit to become Americans. This was the mindset that produced the quota law of 1921. Although adopted as provisional legislation, the 1921 law constituted a turning point in American immigration policy because it meant that within a generation the foreign-born would cease to be a major factor in American society.[83]

The Emergency Immigration Restriction Act of 1921, the so-called Johnson Act, was the first to establish the principle of the quota system. It assigned each nation an immigrant quota consisting of 3 percent of the number of its nationals resident in the United States, using the 1910 census as the base year. As one Congressman remarked in 1924 to the applause of his colleagues, God had intended America "to be the home of a great people: English-speaking—a white race with great ideals, the Christian religion, one race, one country, one destiny."[84]

These racial undertones were quickly revealed when in 1924 Congress passed the National Origins Immigration (Johnson-Reed) Act. In this new law the quota was reduced to 2 percent, but, more significant, it changed the base year from which the quotas would be calculated from 1910 to 1890. Using the 1910 census as the base year, it was soon realized, permitted the entry of too many immigrants from Southern and Eastern Europe, while using the 1890 census stung most deeply Jews, Italians, and Slavs.[85] Whereas the intent of the February 5, 1917 immigration act was to "regulate" immigration of aliens, this new act aimed "to limit the immigrations."[86] Indeed, it was the Johnson-Reed Act that established the permanent administrative machinery that was to implement the immigration policy of the United States in the next decades. It also provided for the control of immigration by U.S. consular officers in foreign countries by strictly regulating the number of emigration visas which could be issued by their offices. In its final form, the 1924 act established a yearly quota of 150,000 for the European countries. This system was further modified by the National Origins Plan of 1927, which computed the quotas on the basis of the national composition of the total American population in 1920, as determined by a special executive board. However, it only took effect in July 1929, after the difficulties of arriving at a formula for establishing the basis for determining national origins were resolved.

The writing on the wall was clear, but it seems that not many American Jews took notice of the new developments. The most faithful Americans among them were also the most disappointed. Louis Marshall was cognizant of the American mood as it related specifically to the Jews. It was not the proper time, he reproached British Jewry, for foreign Jewish organizations to publicly urge the United States to relax its immigration restrictions. Insinuating the community's own feeble position, the grand steward of American Jewry attributed "to a large extent" the anti-Jewish mood on Capitol Hill "to the unfortunate idea that European Jews have, that they can with impunity engage in propaganda in favor of assisting immigration into the United States." A veteran in combating the charge of the international Jewish conspiracy, Marshall demonstrated his assimilation into American political culture when he pleaded with his co-religionists for a *"Hands off!"* policy.[87] It was time to lie low. As Cyrus Adler admitted, "The forces that are operating toward . . . restriction are too numerous and powerful to be overcome."[88]

These forces steered anti-Semitism in a new direction. If prior to World War One it was mobilized against those Jews who were particularly successful capitalists, after the war it became a weapon against liberalism and Progressive reform. The greedy Jewish capitalist was transformed into the menacing Jewish Communist. The anti-radicalism that evolved during the war years and peaked in the postwar Red Scare allowed conservative forces to exploit anti-Semitic sentiments in their fight not only against Socialists and Communists, but also against the labor movement and liberal reform. Although short-lived, the Red Scare had a significant impact upon American politics. On the one hand, it was a factor in the introduction of the 1921 immigration quota system based on national origins; on the other hand, it undermined the coalition between Jewish and non-Jewish Progressives, for the native-stock liberals became uneasy about too close an association with urban immigrants and organized labor.[89]

However, another element was needed to amplify anti-radicalism to the scale of a full-blown Red Scare and present it as a foreign threat to the American way of life. This element was provided by Henry Ford—a symbol of the American rugged individualism that breeds success—and the Ku Klux Klan, who added the image of the abhorrent international Jewish capitalist to that of the international Jewish Bolshevist and thus created the grossly unreal stereotype of Jewish power.[90] As publisher of the *Dearborn Independent*, Henry Ford launched his war against the Jews in May 1920 in an article named "The International Jew: The World's Problem," the first in a series entitled "The International Jew," which drew widely on the notorious forgery, *The Protocols of the Elders of Zion*.[91] Ford's supporters were mainly farmers of the Midwest who, like other agrarians, were traditionally deeply hostile to banks, money-lenders, and bond holders. He presented the campaign against the Jews as a struggle between the two great forces of the modern world: "creative industry" and "international finance."[92] The Ku Klux Klan added a special emphasis on vice that reflected the strain of evangelical morality in the organization. The Jew was described as a subversive radical, a Shylock seeking power through money, and a "Christ-killing" monster of moral corruption—the total negation of the American creed.[93]

However severely American Jews were jolted by domestic anti-Semitism, generally speaking it generated much despair and little action. Louis Marshall was among the few who supported an open fight. He was instrumental in publicizing the case of Leo Frank, who was accused of violating and murdering an adolescent girl in his employ in Atlanta and was sentenced to death. Although his sentence was commuted to life imprisonment, in August 1915 a mob removed him from prison and lynched him. Ten years later another inmate confessed to the crime.[94] In a rare feat, Marshall succeeded in rallying the support of Adolph Ochs, the Jewish owner and publisher of the *New York Times*, who avoided crusades for any cause or issue that involved Jews.[95]

But when Marshall proposed an assertive response to Ford his views were initially overruled by Jacob Schiff, who thought it would be advisable to temper the reaction.[96] In one of the last letters before his death, Schiff clearly expressed the rationale that guided his behavior. "If we get into a controversy," he warned, "we shall light a fire, which no one can foretell how it will become extinguished, and I would strongly advise therefore that no notice be taken of these articles and the attack will soon be forgotten."[97] Cyrus Adler's reaction to Ford's campaign revealed the extent to which Jews accepted the majority's image of them as real. Over and above his opposition to publicity and his insinuation that the resurgence of Jewish nationalism triggered anti-Jewish bigotry, Adler indirectly conceded the charge of excessive Jewish power:

> We have made a noise in the world of recent years . . . far out of proportion to our numbers. We have demonstrated and shouted and paraded and congressed and waved flags to an extent which was bound to focus upon the Jew the attention of the world and having got this attention, we could hardly expect that it would all be favorable.[98]

The problem of anti-Semitic propaganda was discussed at the annual meeting of the American Jewish Committee in November 1920, attended by representatives of all the major Jewish organizations. The mood was gloomy.

Although there were calls for action, they were no more than the traditional pleas for unity and cooperation with Christian America and for maintaining trust in enlightened American opinion.[99] Responding to a suggestion to use propaganda to counter anti-Semitism, Marshall declined gently and instead referred the speaker to a position paper issued by the AJC, which read in part:

> We have entire confidence in the justice, fairness and righteousness of our fellow-citizens and are convinced that nothing that Henry Ford can say or do would lead them to depart from those high-minded principles that have so greatly contributed to the glory of our country.[100]

In the public sphere giving expression to the Jews' deep faith in America was the norm. However, in more private surroundings it was not uncommon for Jewish leaders to express fear that pro-Ford elements who were well connected in the White House "may yet move [President] Harding to say something unwise and even disastrous about the Jews."[101]

Whether we consider these manifestations as an extraordinary form of anti-Semitism, which historian David Gerber finds during periods of intense social crisis, strain, or change, or view them, as Higham does, as "political or ideological anti-Semitism" ("a power-hungry agitation addressed to the entire body politic, which blames the major ills of society on Jews"), it appears that the bulk of American Jews during the early 1920s were most disturbed and intimidated by "ordinary" "social anti-Semitism" and its "pattern of discrimination."[102] In 1922 Stephen Wise, for instance, reckoned that Harvard University's proposal to establish a quota system for admission of Jewish students was "much more serious than the [Henry] Ford campaign."[103]

Although after much bickering Ford issued a formal apology to the Jews which was featured prominently in the nation's leading newspapers on July 8, 1927, for the most part the public response of Jews to the anti-Semitism during the 1920s can be described as silent acquiescence. The less anti-Semitism was regarded as an issue, popular wisdom seemed to have dictated, the less it would become an issue.

Jews in America wished to cling to their noble dream. Nonetheless, they were aware that, in the words of the influential religious and social reformer Rabbi Emil Hirsch, "as long as the Jew is, there will of necessity be Jewhating."[104] Indeed, the Jews had learned throughout their history to distinguish between the possible and the desirable, to take in their stride whatever came their way. The attitude that things could be worse became a central element in the Jews' psychology. There was much in the domestic situation in America to convince the leadership that Jews were not the only ones singled out during the nation's crusade for Americanization; what Ford did to the Jews the KKK did to the Catholics, and there was little love lost for the Slavs. And if they looked at the situation of their co-religionists in Eastern Europe and in Germany, Jewish leaders in America could only "count their blessings" more gratefully. From the Jewish elite's perspective it was not untenable to perceive the anti-Jewish mood as a temporary maladjustment to a new post-war order. The generosity that American life extended to them could contain their disappointments and sustain their hopes.

For most newcomers, however, the anti-Jewish animus was their first major disillusionment with America. The more eagerly they sought to escape from their isolation and climb up the social ladder, the more the majority culture sought to exclude them. Most threatening were the growing limitations in employment opportunities. As second-generation sons and daughters of immigrants began to enter the white-collar sector, they would encounter reluctant employers.[105] In housing as well, the "No Jews" signs became increasingly prevalent.[106] Even more disturbing were the discriminatory practices in higher education, for in that sector they were fused with quasi-scientific assumptions about the survival of the fittest and with 100 percent Americanism.[107] Prior to the First World War, when the number of Jews attending colleges was still relatively small, discrimination was limited to campus activities and social organizations. When their number increased in the postwar period, the object was to curb their enrollment altogether. Over and above the fear of competition in the job market, it was "the very ambitiousness and concern for achievement of the Jews," as Gerber has observed, that bothered the Protestant elite, "who continued to see higher education . . . as a maker of men, rather than as a credentialing mechanism for careers and professions."[108]

The Great Depression that began in 1929 only exacerbated the economic conditions that had been bred by the 1920–1921 recession. The short-lived golden days of the Roaring Twenties only made the fall more devastating. No American was immune, yet as a group, American Jews during the 1930s were faced with a dual challenge: an economic setback and a resurgence of anti-Semitism.[109] Just as they were becoming for the first time a predominantly native-born group, just when they expected their hopes for personal advancement to materialize, the Depression aborted their race to achieve affluence and acceptance in their own lifetime.[110] The Great Depression did not crush their hopes entirely, but for a significant segment of American Jews it fostered deep uncertainties and anxiety about their future.

Economic insecurity and increasing social discrimination combined to reinforce the growing tendency of Jews to separate themselves in an all-Jewish social environment. The renaissance of Jewish ethnicity in the1920s, although fueled almost entirely by the East European newcomers, affected the old Jewish elite as well. Moreover, it represented a fusion of interests: the Jews wished to remain Jewish—and Americans wished them to do the same.

"Jewishness" became institutionalized in the Jewish Centers, which had originally been established to serve as Americanization agents for the German Jewish immigrants and then as settlement houses serving the same purpose for the East European Jews.[111] Beginning in the 1920s, however, the popularity of the Jewish Center synagogues, which focused on social and educational activities, reflected the need, if not always the desire, for a specifically

Jewish milieu.[112] Jews, as Ira Katznelson accurately observed, "sought to preserve their distinctiveness not only as an end in itself but as a strategic resource" with which they could best advance their contact with America "on
terms as favorable and as secure as possible."[113] This trend toward exclusive-
ness was extended to all walks of life: from Jewish employment agencies to
professional clubs, from Jewish fraternities in colleges to a renewed emphasis
on Jewish education.[114]

Granted, the tendency to preserve an exclusive social life gained momentum at a time when the climate for "aliens," and especially Jews, was generally
unfavorable, yet it was supported by the most basic existential wish to survive
as a people.[115] The fear of intermarriage was a central factor that induced dissimilation; seen from this perspective social segregation appeared as obviously desirable.[116] Because the Jews had been socially and economically segre-
gated for much of their historical past, it was certainly only a minority who
thought that complete assimilation was possible or even desirable. The more
traditional East Europeans regarded separatism as the only way of guaran-
teeing their survival as Jews. Even their short experience in America, albeit
under improved circumstances, seemed to have validated their stance.

The case of Jews of German origin in America was far less clear-cut. These
descendants of Jews who had been emancipated during the first decade of the
nineteenth century in the autumn of the German Enlightenment had inherited, as George Mosse points out, "their optimism, a certain faith in themselves and in humanity." America, for the most part, had fostered their belief
that assimilation was attainable by *Bildung:* that the individual's inherent ability for self-education and development transcended all differences of religion
and nationality.[117] But not unlike the experience of Germany's Jews, such
noble aspirations were reshaped by the social and political reality in America
as well. The recent American past invited skepticism about the ideals of Enlightenment. Hence, while the convergence of Jewish social life around Jewish institutions beginning in the 1920s was not the outcome of a common
tradition, it did provide an answer to a growing common need.

For many American Jews, the first thirty years of the century were the
painful unraveling of a dream. Certain that life in America would erase their
distressing historical past, they were nevertheless haunted by that past. Promised equality and prosperity, they experienced exclusion and privation. Yet
few of those who assimilated were willing to admit to a total crisis of faith.
Domestic anti-Semitism was rationalized as a temporary aberration born of a
society readjusting itself to peacetime conditions. Social and economic discrimination was explained as part of the general climate of anti-foreignism.
Many of the more established Jews linked their changed fortune to the arrival
of their East European kindred.

However, the more recent Jewish immigrants could not remain oblivious
to the fact that their new pillars of faith were now crashing around them. A
few converted to Zionism—not really as an alternative to Americanism but

rather as an ephemeral emotional support. But the majority returned to "Jewishness," which under the prevailing circumstances lured many of the assimilated as well. Shielding themselves behind the walls of their new, self-created ghetto, they began to contemplate whether perhaps they had been willing to pay too much for too little.

But just when it had reached its weakest and most precarious state American Jewry was summoned to an unprecedented task. Neither rich nor powerful, the Jews of America were soon to confront their most urgent challenge: how to thwart the impending doom of German Jewry. As they witnessed the looming threat to their European counterparts, Jews became ever more attached to their Americanism. Their greatest disillusion with America was yet to come.

4

A Crisis of Faith
Anti-Semitism in Weimar Germany

> One must always tell what one sees. Above all, which is more difficult,
> one must always see what one sees.
>   —Charles Péguy, *Basic Verities*

So overwhelming were the two chasms of the Great War and the Great Depression that radical solutions appeared fitting to many who endured those two events. The hope of regaining faith in a future based on a continuation of the recent past was preposterous. In Germany, the war gave birth to a republic which did not survive the crisis of peace. A sense of total loss nurtured the harbingers of apocalyptic National Socialist dreams. Americans' belief in self-reliance and a laissez-faire economy began to waver after the crash. Gone, or at least muted, was the old fear that Big Government or Big Business invariably impinged on individual liberty. Indeed, what Americans had previously viewed as responsibilities belonging to the private sphere they were willing, though somewhat reluctantly, to consign to state and federal institutions in the 1930s.

Although the vision of the postwar future was never laid out explicitly in manifestos, both victors and vanquished alike tacitly shared the belief that restoring economic prosperity was imperative for the preservation of peace. In America—over and above any differences between old and new, Christians and Jews, Democrats and Republicans, Wilsonian idealists and disillusionists—all were anxiously waiting to share in the pie of affluence that postwar America promised. Few took notice of the ingredients that went into its making. Indeed, the three Republican presidents during the 1920s concentrated their efforts on fulfilling the great economic promise.

Jews in America were no less attentive to their own economic future, which indeed showed some remarkable progress during the early 1920s. Like most Americans, they were largely apathetic about political issues and expected prosperity to become the social and political equalizer. The draconian immigration act, for example, which was signed into law by President Harding in 1924, did not cost the next Republican presidential candidate Jewish votes. Calvin Coolidge ran ahead in most Jewish districts in 1924. Except for the ever-present Socialist minority, Jews were no less Republican, and no less uninterested in foreign policy, than the rest of the country.[1]

Political leaders were infused with cynicism and confusion about America's global role. They excelled at proclaiming worthy goals but refrained from setting standards of accountability and obligation. These proclivities were manifested in a new form of a "non-policy" of "involvement without commitment."[2] It was a pragmatic solution to bridge the gap between the professed desire for political isolationism and the pronounced need for economic internationalism.

In a profound mood of disarray, organized American Jewry had to place on its agenda yet another problem, that of anti-Semitism in Germany. The precarious climate of the Weimar years created a growing sense of unease among Germany's Jews. Heretofore self-reliant, they somewhat reluctantly began seeking closer ties with their American Jewish co-religionists.

While bearing in mind the circumstances of America Jewry during the 1920s, this chapter will explore the level and extent of receptiveness of the American Jewish leadership to the plight of German Jewry. More precisely, it will seek to delve beneath the surface to uncover the elements that aroused as well as tempered the particular Jewish response to the emerging German peril during the later Weimar period.

Between America and Germany

After the Great War, America sought to capitalize on its new position as the uncontested world power. The United States planned to rewrite its entire trade policy to take advantage of its new dominance in world markets and viewed the re-establishment of worldwide economic equilibrium and the revival of international trade as central to its foreign policy objectives. Indeed, soon after the war ended the United States became convinced that the key to achieving these aims was the economic recovery of Europe, to which Germany's own recovery was essential.[3] In 1922, Secretary of Commerce Herbert Hoover explained this interdependence in a memorandum to President Harding: "Currencies cannot be stabilized," he noted, "until inflation [is] stopped," but inflation could not be stopped "until government budgets are balanced," and this could not be achieved "until there is proper settlement of reparations[,] . . . for chaos here is defeat everywhere."[4]

A year later Secretary of State Charles Evans Hughes presented these views in a major policy speech before the American Historical Association. The United States, Hughes stated, did not "wish to see a prostrate Germany." He made clear that "there can be no economic recuperation in Europe unless Germany recuperates. There will be no permanent peace unless economic satisfactions are enjoyed." To implement America's involvement without commitment, Hughes proposed the establishment of a committee of independent—that is, non-governmental—experts of the countries involved to reach a solution to the reparations problem. With clear reference to France, he indicated that the United States, "would view with disfavor measures which instead of producing reparations would threaten disaster." The establishment of an expert committee, he concluded "would open a broad avenue of opportunities. . . . And, once this is done, the avenues of American helpfulness cannot fail to open hopefully."[5]

America, assured of its course, continued to court the German government. At the very peak of the Ruhr crisis, when French and Belgian troops occupied the area, it offered Germany a "treaty of friendship as well as of commerce and consular rights." Secretary Hughes explained to the German ambassador to Washington, Otto Wiedfeldt, that the treaty was intended "to promote the friendly intercourse between the peoples of the United States and Germany."[6] But in fact, America's prime motive was to launch its new trade policy on the basis of the unconditional most-favored-nation principle. Germany appeared to be the ideal initial target for such a policy, for not only was it a potential market for U.S. exports, it was also in no position to insist on concessions in the form of tariff reductions.[7] For the Germans this was an excellent opportunity to open the door for German exports to the United States and to secure the much-needed legitimacy to re-enter the world community as an economic equal.

Washington, so it seems, evaluated its achievements in figures only. Little notice was taken of the marginal Nazi movement. Robert Murphy, the American consul in Munich, recalled in his memoirs that Washington did not even acknowledge his eyewitness account of Hitler's putsch in 1923. His frequent reports, he recorded, "were accepted in total silence. . . . The only real American interest in Germany at that time was concerned with money."[8]

Yet before America's intentions were translated into deeds, the situation in Germany worsened. The runaway inflation of 1923, the widespread unemployment, and the French occupation of the Ruhr presented enormous economic and political problems to the young republic. During the same year political unrest became rampant: first came the Communist uprising in Saxony and Thuringia in October, followed in November by Hitler's abortive putsch to unseat the legal government by violence.[9] Before long the deteriorating conditions in Germany unleashed a backlash against the Jews. Sporadic riots intensified during the summer and autumn of 1923, reaching their peak in Berlin on November 5th and 6th of 1923, when a mob of some 30,000 assaulted Jews and looted close to 1,000 Jewish-owned stores.[10]

In response to these violent attacks, in which one bystander in Berlin was killed, the *Jüdische Rundschau*, the German Zionists' press organ, reacted with fervent rhetoric. While in early 1923 the Zionistische Vereinigung für Deutschland (ZVFD)—representing the small but vocal Zionist minority—had still maintained that "antisemitism is not a matter of concern as far as the continuation of Jewish life is involved," arguing that the fight against it "has therefore no Jewish content"[11]—the message now was very different. Published on the front page under the title "Die Schicksalsstunde des deutschen Judentums" (The Fateful Hour of German Jewry), it read in part:

> A pogrom has taken place in the streets of Berlin. . . . The Jews in Germany are no longer secure in their persons or their lives, equality which has always been praised as a hallmark of Jewish existence, is shaken. . . . The fruits of Jewish emancipation are called into question. The politics of assimilation, the politics of systematic abrogation and dissolution of Judaism have suffered shipwreck. Today, German Jewry faces the fact that its policy of the past one hundred years is completely bankrupt.
>
> German Jewry must understand today that *only we Jews can help ourselves*. German Jewry must maintain solidarity. The call "Death to the Jews" affects all [of us]. The common enemy—if nothing else—binds us together. . . . Irrespective of our ideological and political differences, we rush to set aside all that separates us, provided the German Jews are equally ready to rebuild with us German Jewry as a powerful organism.[12]

These strong denunciations demonstrated a more activist approach on the part of the Zionists, who in face of the anti-Jewish attacks called for cooperation with the non-Zionists despite ideological differences. However, the Zionist minority condemned those Jews who, outwardly at least, maintained unqualified faith in the concept of full assimilation as a solution to the Jewish problem. Not least, the Zionists in Germany, as elsewhere, were certainly not unaware that the re-emergence of the Jewish problem carried with it the greatest potential to gain new converts to their cause. Their outcry was intended not only to give expression to their own doctrine, but also to discredit their ideological foes, mainly represented by the Centralverein deutscher Staatsbürger jüdischen Glaubens (Central Association of German Citizens of the Jewish Faith), known as the C.V. Founded in 1893 as a response to a burgeoning anti-Semitic movement, the C.V. proclaimed that "while we find it necessary today to organize, nothing is further from our mind than the spirit of isolation." Rather, its aim was to defend the rights of Jews within Germany, based upon the principle of "civil self-help," as well as to "help them to cultivate their German-mindedness (*deutsche Gesinnung*)."[13]

Yet the Zionists and non-Zionists did meet in their shared desire to restore their greatness as German Jews, "to rebuild . . . German Jewry as a powerful organism," as the *Jüdische Rundschau* put it.[14] Paradoxically, they were also brought closer together by their collective sense of the shame they had been subjected to during the Great War. In 1916 a *Judenzählung*—a census of Jews enlisted in fighting units—was ordered by the German Army to determine the extent of Jewish dereliction of duty.[15] Having to reassert their patriotism separately from other Germans had been an emotionally traumatic ordeal which had affected all of Germany's Jews. It had been especially distressing for the nationalists among them, who had urged their co-religionists to volunteer for the war effort *"over and above the call of duty,"*[16] and who had truly felt that "it is not difficult to shed one's blood for one's country," sincerely believing that "in this war [we Jews] will at last obtain equality in all respects."[17] But it would be wrong to conclude from such assertions that German Jewish leaders did not realize that the very act of insisting on their equality revealed just the opposite. Indeed, it was the Great War that first impelled the German Jews to embark upon a *voyage intérieur.*

However, it was within the traumatic climate of the early years of the Weimar Republic—the grief over Germany's defeat, the blame placed on the Jews for the November Revolution and much more—that even the most pious devotees of *Deutschtum* began to experience an existential crisis and to undergo a change of consciousness. With their traditional belief in *Deutschtum* being attacked by both German nationalists and Jews who yearned for Jewish national revival, even the C.V., as the main defender of the faith, was spurred to search for a synthesis between *Deutschtum* and *Judentum.*[18]

As with the case of the highly acculturated integrationist American Jews during the early 1920s, the external and internal forces—nationalism that outlived the war years, anti-Semitism, and the presence of a growing community of East European Jews promoting Jewish nationalism—were yet to "penetrate the deeper layers of vital convictions" of German Jews.[19] Most of the latter, along with an important minority of American Jews, were both mentally and emotionally light-years away from recognizing that "emancipation and assimilation," as Max Horkheimer was to write almost four decades later, "do not yet mean complete identity."[20]

The German Zionists had an ideology that could explain the present situation, for it took into account the inherent limits of emancipation and assimilation. The non-Zionists, on the other hand, could only identify their future with that of the Republic. But it was precisely the lack of a foreseeable future for the Republic, especially after 1928, that inhibited a long-term view of their own prospects.[21] Thus, it becomes less astonishing that during the last years of the Weimar Republic, the C.V. failed to perceive the general breakdown of the system and, by extension, usually translated any electoral loss for the Nazis, however slight, as a gain for the Jews. In fact, in the early 1920s, when the desire to maintain faith in the future of the Republic was still predominant, it was plausible to render anti-Jewish rowdyism as yet another manifestation of the general "teething problems" that the young Republic had to endure.

For the majority of German Jews the "Jewish problem" during the Weimar years peaked and ebbed along with the fortunes of the domestic social and economic situation. Indeed, when the economic situation improved, anti-Semitism, along with the "Jewish question," seemed to recede. Although it was never entirely eliminated from their agenda, most of Germany's Jews relegated anti-Semitism, consciously or unconsciously, to the sidelines. After 1924, sharp disagreements concerning defense strategies made cooperation between Zionists and the Centralverein less likely.[22]

In both Germany and the United States, Jewish consciousness, as enig-
matic as it was ambiguous, was a major force in shaping the perceptions of the
situation in Germany. Among German and American Jewish leaders similar
pragmatic and psychological factors—be it their respective refusal to admit
to their declining position of authority, their shared reluctance to call attention to their otherness, or to abandon their faith in the American or German
dream—inhibited their receptiveness to their changing terrains.

The reaction of the American Jewish Committee to the increasing anti-
Semitic agitation in Germany in its annual report of 1922 denotes no particular alarm. Instead, we sense an unerring faith in the categorical imperative of
Enlightenment; an optimism, nurtured by trust, that the irrational, once ex-
orcised, would render reason and humanity supreme. "It would be a confession of the bankruptcy of civilization," the report asserted, "if these manifestations of barbarism and stupidity were to prevail for any length of time.
Good sense and the plainest dictates of humanity and decency are certain to
triumph."[23] Like their German counterparts, these American Jews presumed
that civilization determined politics, investing the political life of a nation
with a high moral purpose. Although the common assertion that in Germany
Staat and *Volk* were perceived as distinct entities is correct,[24] it did not mean
that the two domains had no impact on each other.

American Jewish leaders were well informed about the political upheavals
in Germany; the AJC even contributed $5,000 in 1922 to challenge the trend.
Yet their own growing sense of being strangers at home in America placed a
considerable damper on their public reactions to the spread of anti-Jewish
agitations in Germany. Even the murder of Jewish Foreign Minister Walter
Rathenau in June 1922, for instance, hardly elicited a response from American Jewish organizations. But for the Jews in Germany, it was a sign of the
coming storm, as Max Warburg wrote to his brother Paul in America.[25] In
America, on the other hand, mainstream opinion—both Jewish and non-Jewish—held, as Louis Marshall observed in 1924, that there was "not the slightest likelihood that their [the Nazis'] plan will ever be carried out to the slightest extent."[26]

Neither alarmed by nor convinced of the accuracy of the reports about the
anti-Jewish riots in Berlin in November 1923, Marshall, in his capacity as
president of the AJC, nonetheless contacted Secretary of State Charles Evans
Hughes and informed him of the Nazi threats against Jews.[27] However, there
are no indications that he thought that the situation in Germany warranted
official intervention by the U.S. government. Overall, Marshall's conduct can
be viewed as a display of civic responsibility. As a leader of the major Jewish
defense organization, he was obligated to his constituency to present the Jewish case to the authorities, and as a patriotic American he was no less obligated to share information with his government concerning developments
within the sphere of its national interest.

The more outspoken Stephen S. Wise, president of the AJ Congress, also
expressed his concern to the Department of State. In reply, Secretary Hughes

promised that the reports "from United States officials in Germany" concerning anti-Jewish agitation would receive "careful attention." Referring to the plight of those Jews in Germany who were American citizens, he wrote, "we are making suitable inquiries to ascertain the facts." The implications were clear. The U.S. government would not intervene, even on behalf of American citizens, based on reports of non-official, that is, Jewish, sources; the information would be independently verified. But when responding to problems affecting Jews who were not American citizens, on whose behalf, as Wise emphasized, the government was not authorized to intervene, Hughes disclosed that the United States would not be "oblivious to the demands of humanity." American diplomats, he reassured Wise, would endeavor on "proper occasion" to express in an "informal and appropriate" manner the "humanitarian sentiment" of the American people.[28] In hindsight, Hughes's letter can be seen as a succinct statement of American policy throughout this period. As the world's superpower, the tradition of humanitarian diplomacy in nineteenth- and early-twentieth-century America had been relegated to the history books. The sentiments may have survived but the sense of commitment was fading.

Wise, in the name of the AJ Congress, also dispatched a telegram to the German ambassador in Washington, Otto Wiedfeldt. He had expressed shock at the anti-Jewish riots in Berlin, and asked that his message be conveyed to the German government in the name of the "great masses of the American people" because of what had been inflicted upon "our fellow Jews." Wise spoke as an American who "in common with most American citizens" hoped that Germany could resume its life as a "great country."[29]

A difference in Jewish response—more in style than in substance—can be discerned between Marshall, the spokesman of the old Jewish elite, and Rabbi Wise, who claimed to represent the new majority of the East European Jews; the former provided information, the latter asked for action. Nonetheless, these reactions reveal a fundamental sameness. The unwritten rule of American political culture prescribing the acceptable mode of behavior for a minority group had been well internalized by both the old and the new elites. Both recognized that particular interests—be they of a separate religious, ethnic, or national group—could be accorded legitimacy only by being presented as the opinion of the general American public. American Jews thus advanced the Jewish case as Americans on behalf of other Jews. In this the American Jewish leadership displayed a high level of integration, for it thereby showed its acceptance of the notion expressed in 1915 by the oracle of liberalism, Woodrow Wilson: "America does not consist of groups. . . . A man who thinks of himself as belonging to a particular national group in America has not yet become an American."[30]

But the sound of fury was not heard for long. As in Germany, where a period of stabilization was a source of contentment, in America, the Jews, like everyone else, were relentlessly and optimistically bent on seizing their chance to taste American affluence during a period of prosperity.[31] Notwithstanding anti-Jewish attitudes which thrived in the United States in the early 1920s, for the majority of Jews this era still offered the first golden opportunity to leap over the last hurdle barring their access to the American dream.

It may be an irony of history or, rather, a manifestation of the innate flaws in human nature, that those same Jews who only some decades before had pleaded in the name of Jewish solidarity to be redeemed from their oppressors in Eastern Europe had grown somewhat callous to the plight of others in need. When Rabbi Stephen Wise, for example, was approached in March 1925 to organize a protest against the persecution of the Jews in Poland, he viewed it as pointless, bitterly admitting that

> the chief fact that stands out in Jewish life is not so much the indifference of the world to injuries done to the Jews, but the indifference of the Jew to the welfare of world Jewry. . . . The sins of Jewish omission are greater by far at this time than the sins of Christian commission.[32]

The promise of riches preoccupied people everywhere. Affluence was colored with a noble aura as the guardian and redeemer of world peace. Economic rehabilitation was the declared American agenda, and the means used for its realization were subjected to minor critical examination. Hence, when in October 1924 the Dawes Plan loan, offered to Germany to help meet her reparation payments, was floated in New York by J. P. Morgan & Co, more than half the total of $110 million was subscribed within fifteen minutes. Indeed, not many in America noticed that it was only with the support of forty-eight members of the German National People's Party (Deutschnationale Volkspartei, DNVP), attained under pressure of economic interests, that the Plan commanded a majority in the Reichstag (on August 29, 1924). Fewer realized that the DNVP had campaigned against the Plan with the slogan "No new Versailles!"[33] What made America's policy towards Germany that much more attractive and marketable at home was the seeming absence of government involvement. Since it was implemented by non-official, semi-autonomous agencies, the U.S. government could continue to play detached (isolationist) and act attached (internationalist). But America was back in Europe, although convinced that it was risking only its dollars.

So deeply grounded in mutual interests were the relations between the two countries that they survived a number of potential storms without damage. Paul von Hindenburg's election as president in April 1925, for instance, aroused only an ephemeral revival of world war antagonisms. Within days President Coolidge, confidentially and without solicitation, assured Germany of continued sympathetic relations between the two nations, expressing his trust that Hindenburg would be a positive force in creating the necessary inner unity of Germany. The Treaty of Berlin, which reconfirmed and expanded the arrangements formulated in Rapallo between Germany and the Soviet Union, also failed to cause much alarm in the United States.[34] Ignoring the dark shadows being cast by Germany's past, America preferred instead to focus on the light emanating from its policy to ban war as an instrument of national policy. When Gustav Stresemann signed the Kellog-Briand Pact in Paris in August 1928 in the name of Germany, America was convinced of a new spirit of cooperation. The U.S. ambassador to Berlin, Jacob Gould Schurman, became quite carried away in expressing the American appreciation of Germany's action. A self-admitted Germanophile, he told a distinguished audience of German elites that the two nations "were marching forward together in a noble venture for the civilization of mankind."[35]

The ultimate test of the increased trust and cooperation was yet to come, however. The renewed negotiations on the reparations issue were scheduled for 1929. But by 1928 it had already become clear that soon after the Dawes installments reached their maximum level, Germany's foreign exchange would incur a deficit. Hence, it would be impossible for Germany to make the annual reparation payments and also meet its other commitments of interest and principal payments on outstanding loans, primarily to the United States. Harsh reality was knocking on America's doors. Its "non-policy" policy called for a revision of the Dawes Plan.[36]

As the new committee of experts under the chairmanship of Owen D. Young began the negotiations, it became apparent that the interests of the major debtor and the major creditor no longer coincided. While the Germans aimed at a settlement based on their ability to pay without damaging their economic development, the United States insisted that the legitimate claims of the former Allies be met. More of an anathema to Americans was Germany's insistence on linking fulfillment of its reparations obligations to certain territorial adjustments. During the talks, some discordant sounds began to be heard.[37] Nonetheless, when the terms of the Young Plan are evaluated, they clearly appear to have favored Germany: total reparations were fixed at the low figure of 112,000 million Reichsmarks, and for the first time a time limit was set for Germany's obligations. Annual payments were decreased and during the first three years they were to be substantially lower than under the Dawes Plan. But above all, the Allies agreed to evacuate the whole Rhineland by June 30, 1930, five years earlier than the date laid down in the Versailles Treaty.[38]

Not all Germans were happy with the results. The Nazis fulminated against "Three generations of forced labor!"[39] The nationalist right's opposition to the Young Plan culminated in submitting to a referendum the Freedom Law (Law against the Enslavement of the German People) on December 22, 1929. These reactions did not appear to raise many eyebrows in Washington, nor did the fact that in the fall and winter of 1929 the Nazis scored their first considerable successes at the polls. Indeed, the results of the referendum could be seen as reassuring, for only 13.9 percent of the electorate voted in favor of the Freedom Law. Thus, imprisoned by its own misconceptions, Washington could interpret the campaign against the Young Plan as an insignificant expression of anti-Americanism. But it ignored the implications of the show of unity of the nationalist right. In fact, this campaign, organized by the press tycoon Alfred Hugenberg and supported by the DNVP, the militant right-wing Stahlhelm, and the National Socialist German Workers' Party (NSDAP), made the Nazis the prime beneficiaries of the Young Plan by breaking their isolation in the political sphere.[40]

Facing the Threat: German Jews Look to America

As with the case of the Dawes Plan, German Jews believed that an improved economic situation would alleviate their plight, but the Young Plan remedy also came too late. Even the *Centralverein Zeitung* (*CVZ*) did not remain impervious to the danger of anti-Semitism. As early as 1925, it began to devote much of its space to attacking *völkisch* anti-Semitic theories and practices, the NSDAP, and Hitler's speeches. Almost entire issues of the *CVZ* were dedicated to refuting attacks against the Jews.[41] While the NSDAP lost seats in the 1928 Reichstag elections, it made considerable inroads into local, rural areas like Thuringia. These developments did not go unnoticed by some of the leaders of German Jewry. Shortly before those elections, Dr. Alfred Wiener, secretary-general of the Centralverein, addressed a meeting of the executive committee and warned against the Nazi propaganda campaign in such rural districts. Most of those present rejected what they perceived as his excessive pessimism, arguing that it was untypical for Germany as a whole. However, after the elections this optimism waned somewhat, and the C.V. decided to investigate the basis and origins of the National Socialists' support. Their findings confirmed the irrefutable fact of at least limited success on the part of anti-Semitic forces.[42]

However, the overwhelming majority of Germany's Jews were reluctant to confront the implications of these developments.[43] The C.V. interpreted the Nazi gains in the local elections as merely another manifestation of traditional anti-Semitism, which German Jews had seen wax and wane throughout their history. This attitude was exemplified by the reaction of one Jewish member of the Reichstag: "No!" he exclaimed, "It would be false to take these people [Nazis] seriously politically."[44]

Yet something was happening, and that something, although not yet defined, felt sufficiently different to warrant a special response. Alfred Wiener, a typical representative of his constituency, adamantly believed that, above all, the situation called for a campaign to remind the general public of the contributions of Jews to the German nation.[45] One such symbolic effort was begun in 1927 by the Reichsbund jüdischer Frontsoldaten, which produced a volume in commemoration of the Jewish war dead that was solemnly presented, along with a "beautiful flower piece," to Reich President von Hindenburg on his eighty-fifth birthday in 1932.[46] But Wiener, the politically astute and legally trained Jewish leader, seemed to have realized that with politics being transferred to the streets, it was the power of the discontented masses that had to be checked.

Starting in the mid-1920s, the American Jewish leadership kept a close watch on the situation in Germany as well as in Eastern Europe.[47] In 1926, following a year of increased anti-Semitic propaganda, desecratory acts, and sporadic physical assaults, the American Jewish Committee assigned Jacob Landau, the director of the Jewish Telegraphic Agency (JTA), to undertake a survey of anti-Semitism in Europe. His report emphasized the growing strength of anti-Semitic movements, particularly in Poland and Germany.[48] The AJC was troubled by the findings, but apparently even more so by the potential effects of their publicity on their own position in America. It decided to "distribute only the relevant sections to responsible Jewish leaders in the countries concerned."[49]

The C.V. had established regular contact with the AJC in 1928. In the same year a confidential report, probably initiated by the C.V., arrived from Berlin, containing detailed information on international anti-Semitic activities. The report, manifestly intended to solicit the cooperation of the AJC for the Centralverein's defense activities, emphasized that if left unattended, the problem of anti-Semitism would not be arrested and might well reach the United States.[50] Yet other Jews in Germany were adamant, as Max Warburg wrote in June 1929 to his youngest brother Felix in America, that "under all circumstances . . . an international battle against anti-Semitism" must be avoided, "since we will otherwise naturally be accused of mixing foreign elements in domestic German relations."[51] Felix must have understood, for in America as well Jews often rushed to present their patriotic credentials.

It is clear that the Jewish American leaders of German descent were well informed about the situation in Germany. It also may be considered rather natural that they would be approached by their own for advice and assistance. However, our understanding of how they absorbed this information is more nebulous: in what way did their past and recent American experience facilitate or hinder their understanding of the situation which their German counterparts were facing?

In July 1929 Dr. Alfred Wiener came to the United States to raise funds for a defense campaign to combat the surging anti-Semitism. It was no simple task for German Jews, either psychologically or financially, to face their predicament on their own, nor was it a matter of course for them to seek help among their descendants in America or elsewhere.

Under normal circumstances an encounter with their German past would have evoked sublime memories for the American Jewish elite, but under the stressful present conditions it also conjured up some old rivalries. Some of the elements in this complicated relationship between American and German Jews figured in the cool, if not hostile, reception that Wiener, the envoy of the largest Jewish organization in Germany, was accorded by his American co-religionists. To begin with, Louis Marshall, the chief officer of the American Jewish Committee, was far from eager to meet with him, alluding to the traditional contest for pre-eminence when he noted that the German Jews were "sufficiently satisfied to believe that they cannot be taught anything." In a rather provocative tone, Marshall cautioned his associates that "what these gentlemen [of the C.V.] are after is not advice but money."[52] The American Jewish luminaries had hoped their German counterparts would seek their counsel.

At first, Marshall did not take the situation in Germany seriously. It was Morris Waldman, the executive secretary of the AJC since 1928, who in an intensive correspondence with Marshall in July 1929 alerted him to the menace of Nazism.[53] Scheduled to attend a meeting to organize the enlarged Jewish Agency in Zurich, Marshall agreed to discuss the situation there with the German leaders. In what was probably his last letter before he died in Zurich in September 1929, Marshall admitted to Waldman that the situation was "graver than he had believed."[54] But, like the majority of Americans, the "one real remedy," he believed, was in an "early restoration of Germany's economic prosperity." As a Jew whose survival as the "other" depended in no small part on self-serving rationalizations, Marshall and people of his milieu interpreted anti-Semitism, be it of the American or the German variety, exclusively within the social and economic spheres. He thus concluded that "the persecution of the Jew as the historic scapegoat would naturally cease" once affluence was restored. And drawing on the contemporary experience of American Jewry, Marshall reminded his colleagues that in American society as well, "ten years ago" there were those who would have looked with favor upon "this kind of an [anti-Semitic] outburst."[55]

Like most American Jewish observers of the German peril, Marshall was caught within an insoluble double bind. On the one hand, knowing the history of the Jews in Germany, he marveled that the Centralverein was acting "as though this were something new," castigating its leadership for their "deficient memories." But on the other hand, he claimed that the animus was not widespread; it was directed toward "the banker, the capitalist"—revealingly drawing on negative Jewish stereotypes—"the portion of a community which is numerically weakest." Marshall confidently pronounced that the plight of German Jews could be alleviated in part through "the condemnation by Jews [like himself] of those [other Jews] of the profiteer and codfish aristocracy classes who flaunt their wealth and make themselves generally obnoxious. Alas, they are to be found everywhere."[56]

Like most American Jewish leaders, Marshall maintained that "nothing can be accomplished by hysteria or by taking alarm." In their reshaped consciousness, the American Jewish elite had come to view anti-Semitism as an ongoing experience associated predominantly with the Old World. But to conceive that Germany, the enlightened, cultured, modern state of their forefathers, could be anything like Russia or Romania was beyond their emotional and intellectual comprehension. Indeed, they initially interpreted the specific state of affairs in Germany as comparable to their own recent experience of social exclusion in America and, hence, they advised their counterparts to deal with the situation as they themselves had. For Marshall, the solution lay in adopting an attitude of "ridicule and derision, and even more in exemplary citizenship."[57] Mocking the seriousness with which his German co-religionists regarded Hitler, Marshall was of the opinion that "if they had the gift to reduce stupidities of this character to the ridicule of which they are susceptible, just as we treated Ford and the K.K.K., they would have easier sailing."[58]

As to the ways and means proposed by the C.V. to combat anti-Semitism, the chief American Jewish steward "doubted from the beginning the efficacy of the [defense] methods," adding that "the state of mind that now exists cannot be overcome by printer's ink or by public meetings addressed by Jews or by scientists." Waldman concurred, scorning the educational objectives of the C.V. as "a waste of money and energy . . . an exaggerated optimism." Even if such meetings were to attract the *goyim* in great numbers, he asked rhetorically, "how much effect can the apologetics of the Syndicus of the Central Verein [*sic*] have on them?"[59]

Although critical of the proposed defense program of the Centralverein, Waldman, like Cyrus Adler, who was shortly to become the president of the American Jewish Committee following Marshall's untimely death, was "deeply impressed by the gravity of the situation" and "its pernicious effects—through 'export'—in fortifying and intensifying existing anti-Semitism in other countries."[60] At this point, but not for long, American Jews were still wary of admitting to fear of anti-Semitic "export" to their own country. But their discussions about whether to extend financial aid to the C.V. do point to their own apprehensions. Waldman, for example, advised that "the matter [of financial help] should not be officially handled by the Committee, not even become a matter of record. . . . Obviously a public effort to raise this money is out of the question."[61]

The "largest and most powerful Jewish community in the world"—a characterization so often used frivolously to chide American Jewry[62]—was itself not secure enough to publicly admit to the spread of anti-Semitism in Germany and the need of fellow Jews in Europe for help. These issues reflected too closely upon their own situation in America, the contempt they aroused as Jews, and their fear of "displaying" their wealth in support of other Jews. In fact, similar inhibitions restrained the AJC's response to domestic anti-Jewish sentiment: their motto was "Ignore it and it will disappear, treat it as a problem and it will turn into one."

The comparison Marshall drew between the situation of Jews in America and Germany made Waldman uneasy. The humiliation experienced by the Jews in Germany had apparently enhanced the already exaggerated sense of veneration which the Jews of German ancestry felt toward America. A proud American, Waldman emphatically denied any basis for such a comparison. Neither the KKK nor the attacks of Henry Ford, he maintained, could be seen as an organized anti-Jewish movement. Moreover, he was convinced that "the cosmopolitan character of America, due to the diversified racial elements combined with the English sense of fair play which our culture here has inherited from our English mother culture, is much more impervious to anti-race propaganda than the less sportsmanlike temper of the German people."[63] As a liberal social activist, Waldman could not have been oblivious of the

American version of bigotry and racism. Yet, during an "Anglo-Saxon" decade fraught with strong anti-Jewish sentiments, there was little else for an American Jewish apostle of integration to do other than to maintain faith in the greater decency of American culture.

The Demise of an Illusion

The belief that a people's culture and spirit determined its good and evil deeds —an idea very common in the nineteenth century—was eagerly accepted by American Jews. At least initially, this conviction seems to have provided the psychological shield to sustain their faith that Nazism could not be replicated in the United States. For as long as events in Germany were understood as a result of the Germans' particular *Geist* and national character, fair-playing America could be viewed as immune to such developments.

But what underlay the indignant response of the American Jewish establishment to their German co-religionists was far more complicated. These community leaders, mostly of German descent, had not fully shed their cultural origin. Their Americanism mostly meant addition, but not much in the way of subtraction. The resulting compound of identities inevitably included contradictory impulses. Rabbi Bernhard Felsenthal's description of his tripartite identity fitted most members of this milieu:

> Racially I am a Jew, for I have been born among the Jewish nation. Politically I am an American as patriotic, as enthusiastic, as devoted an American citizen as it is possible to be. But spiritually I am a German, for my inner life has been profoundly influenced by Schiller, Goethe, Kant and other intellectual giants of Germany.[64]

For American Jews to have recognized the dire plight of their German counterparts would have involved a loss of their own exalted referential past. In May 1933, Rabbi Wise wrote to Albert Einstein that "American Jews of German descent believed that they owe it to their German past to disbelieve in the stories of Hitlerish barbarism and brutality,"[65] but his observations seem to be even more applicable to the years before Hitler's ascension to power, when these Jews negated such a possibility altogether. And there was another psychological impasse that was difficult for the American Jewish elite to overcome: whereas their struggle on behalf of East European Jews testified to their own superior position, the deteriorating plight of their own kindred in Germany narrowed the gap between themselves and the "inferior" East European Jews.[66] Perhaps then, the anger vented on the representative of the C.V. and the critical remarks directed at Germany's Jews in general were the expression of a painful awakening from a dual illusion—that of their glorious German past and that of their present status in America.

The tension between the leaders of American and German Jewry was not ideologically based, for both the C.V. and the AJC defined Jewishness in religious terms, encouraged the integration of Jews into the majority culture, and stressed the importance of their unwavering loyalty to the nations of their citizenship.[67] However, the interaction between the two communities during these early stressful years suggests that their shared heritage was inadequate to bridge the gap created by their diverse particular experiences. Paradoxically though, they both experienced a somewhat similar change of consciousness. The deep infatuation of both groups with *Deutschtum* was now tempered, and they began to re-anchor their identity deeper in their Jewish roots. But to render the Jews' new *Weg nach Innen* (inward journey) as their final and complete divide with *Deutschtum* would be inaccurate.

The emancipation of German Jews had inspired in them a deep attachment to German culture and a strong bond with the progressive and liberal forces in Germany. As historian Leni Yahil has noted, "As long as German liberalism and nationalism were connected, and the vision of a united Germany was a democratic one, Jews had no difficulty in professing identification with this German nationalism."[68] Although after 1848 anti-liberal nationalism had incited anti-Semitism, the Weimar spirit and its constitution had restored faith that justice and reason would be the basic creed of the new Republic. Indeed, during the Weimar period, Jewish integration into German society reached a peak—bringing about an almost perfect correlation between their political and cultural affiliations. Yet, within a mere fifteen years, Germany's Jews both came closest to achieving unequivocal acceptance as Germans and were drastically deprived of it. It was perhaps this sudden and bewildering shift from close identification to total alienation that prevented them from seeing how radically different the newly emerging situation was. In their understandable desire to maintain above all their niche in their beloved fatherland, both the Zionist leader Kurt Blumenfeld and Alfred Wiener of the C.V. still thought it feasible (in September 1930 and April 1931, respectively) to persuade the German government to issue a public declaration to condemn the anti-Semitic excesses and assure the German Jews of their civil and political rights. A number of Zionists, among them Robert Weltsch and Gustav Krojanker, were even inclined to ferret out the "positive" goals of National Socialism that would permit a modus vivendi between the two nationalist ideologies. They referred to National Socialism as *Neuer Nationalismus*, a *Volkstumsbewegung* and *Jungdeutsche Nationalbewegung*, in order to emphasize elements of renewal rather than highlight the excess of its institutions.[69] The chauvinistic racial character of Nazism was generally overlooked, but a minority that espoused "purification of the Jewish species" found these ideas attractive. It was not only Zionists who erroneously assumed that Nazi ideology would allow a distinction between *Staat* and *Volk*. This distinction had been an essential tool in the survival kit of all German Jews since German unification, fostering their identification with the Germanic spirit and allowing them to ignore its "national home."[70]

So unsuspecting were the German Jews that nationalism could be linked to anything but liberalism and its counterpart doctrine, democracy, that even the Zionists among them "who know the value of *Volkstum* and *Volksideale*" refused to believe that any nationalist movement, even of the Nazi type, could "nourish its constructive forces on feelings of hatred."[71] Their naive perception of Germany's new nationalism and their misconceived notion of their own sense of nation and nationality were two important factors that obfuscated their initial assessment of National Socialism.

Business as Usual? Reactions to the September 1930 Reichstag Elections

The National Socialist German Workers' Party (NSDAP), with 107 seats, became the second largest party after the Reichstag elections of September 1930. A victory of this magnitude was unprecedented in German parliamentary history.[72] George Gordon, the American chargé d'affaires in Berlin, interpreted the results for Washington as "a body blow to Republican form of government," viewing them as "a clear indication of the dangerous mentality possessed by a large proportion of the population."[73] However, Washington showed no particular concern, and its policy toward Germany was not perceptibly altered.[74] The New York stock market crash of September and October 1929 and the ensuing depression overshadowed, if not entirely obliterated, a possible rethinking of American policy in view of the volatile political situation in Germany. In fact, what was developing into a global financial crisis made it all the more urgent to implement the policy America had pursued since the end of the war—to restore economic stability.

The natural partner for pursuing this national interest, and an essential political backer of any administration, was the American business community. It was strongly supported by three successive Republican administrations. During the "dollar decade" of the 1920s it was Germany that offered ample attractive opportunities for American investors.[75] Bankers provided the capital for the more important German cartels, and American corporations bought some of the largest German plants.[76] If one was to judge by the American business press, the economic establishment was overwhelmingly opposed to the Fascist and Nazi ideologies, and even to war. But in practice few, if any, of the American industrial magnates were disturbed by the broader political and social issues that threatened democracy or capitalism.[77] In fact, one may argue that as the potential spoils increased, the importance of ideology decreased. Alfred Sloan, Jr., chairman of the board of General Motors, for example, adhered to the prevalent philosophy that seeking profits was a legitimate aim, irrespective of political circumstances. In a letter to a stockholder in April 1939, he supported rather bluntly the idea that "an international business operating throughout the world should conduct its operations in strictly business terms, without regard to the political beliefs of its management, or the political beliefs of the country in which it is operating."[78]

Already in his campaign slogan—"Four more years of prosperity"—Hoover had expressed his belief in the primacy of economics over politics in achieving world order. As president, his plan for a moratorium on both war debts and reparations was intended as a partial solution.[79] "The essence of the problem," Hoover told his delegates in July 1931, on their way to London to negotiate a "standstill agreement" on certain privately held German short-term credit, "is the restoration of confidence in Germany's economic life, both in Germany and abroad."[80] Indeed, military force was discounted as an instrument to maintain the world order, and economic prosperity draped in noble principles was accepted as the solution. In the era between the two world wars, the United States sustained the Wilsonian belief that moral force and enlightened public opinion were the principal ingredients for world order. "My ambition in our foreign policies," President Hoover wrote several years after he left office, "was to lead the United States in full co-operation with world moral forces to preserve peace."[81]

This optimistic mindset helps to explain how the American public remained largely oblivious of the political changes in Germany in the late 1920s and early 1930s. Even Sol Bloom, a member of the House Foreign Affairs Committee, could believe as late as 1932 "that Germany was truly emerging as a democracy."[82] In fact, until the late 1930s the most prestigious newspapers only rarely devoted editorials to the Hitler movement and its potential threat to world peace, or for that matter to anti-Semitic rowdyism, notwithstanding the constant flow of information from their own reporters in Germany, as well as from American Jewish organizations.[83] While it may seem tenable to argue that in the early 1930s the Jewish problem appeared minor in comparison with the outstanding economic problems between the two countries, the omission appears to have stemmed from a more basic reason—Hitler and Nazism were simply not taken seriously.

In February 1930, the *New York Times*, in one of its first references to the German situation, noted that the "former menace" was becoming a "burlesque." In the same vein, it editorialized after the September 1930 elections that "if it is true that a watched pot never boils, the menace of Adolf Hitler has been grossly exaggerated."[84] Hans Morgenthau has claimed that since the First World War American perceptions of Germany had been "decisively influenced by emotions, sentiments and utopian notions."[85] Whichever Germany dominated the American imagination in the early 1930s—whether that of Frederick the Great and Bismarck, of Beethoven and Goethe, of a vanquished nation excessively punished by the victors, or a mixture of them all—it was perceived as incapable of "delivering herself over to a madcap Austrian."[86]

The general American ambience at the time no doubt had a significant effect on the initial reactions of American Jewish leaders to events in Germany. Not only were they exposed to the prevailing public mood but, as recent converts to Americana, their faith was boundless. Yet an additional and less easily recognized element shaped the leadership's response—its European Jewish heritage.

A First Warning: Waldman's Report

Much like in the general press, in Jewish publications the reactions to the election results of September 1930 were generally subdued and reflected an essentially positive German image. The *American Hebrew*, the organ of the American Jewish Committee, for example, was of the opinion that "the success of anti-Semitic parties in Germany possess[es] no quality of permanence." It viewed the Reichstag's riots as no cause for panic among German Jews, assuring its readers that "Hitlerism cannot prevail in the Reich." The basis for this assertion was yet another conviction—that Germans were "not a people who love revolutions."[87] The *American Jewish Congress Index*, expressing the views of the more traditional Jews, conceded that Hitler's success would constitute a calamity for German Jewry, but was confident that this was "not very likely."[88]

Regardless of how the changes in Germany were appraised, the Jewish leadership in America could not afford to ignore them. As Cyrus Adler made clear, the outcome of the September 1930 elections created an "unusual situation" which warranted "a rather unusual step." It took the form of a special conference which was called for November 1930 by the American Jewish Committee to discuss the situation in Germany. "This is not part of our formal program," declared President Cyrus Adler at the opening of the special executive session, "nor of our regular record." By reiterating the private nature of the meeting, and defining it as a mere "consultation among ourselves," he clearly revealed the sense of unease that prevailed among the organizers.[89]

Morris Waldman was invited to present a report entitled "The Anti-Semitic Menace in Germany," which he had drafted following his June to September trip to Germany.[90] Apart from providing most incisive insight into the situation, Waldman's report was the first to elicit a response from a group of the most prominent Jewish leaders. It raised many of the issues that American Jews were destined to face and pointed to some of the inherent paradoxes in Jewish life in America. The audience, whether religious or secular, was predominantly composed of inveterate integrationists who regarded the Jewish problem as mostly a history and memory of other Jews.

A careful reading of the report reveals that Waldman was very much aware of his clientele's mentality and constructed his arguments accordingly. He emphasized universal principles rooted in the Enlightenment tradition and de-emphasized Jewish particularism. No less important, he ventured to bring the problem of the Jews in Germany closer to home. The report was brief on facts—for these people certainly did not lack information. It appeared that his goal was rather to strike a deeper emotional chord: to awaken the Jewish consciousness that many of them had labored so hard to suppress.

His presentation began with a brief summary of the results of the September elections in Germany, followed by a dose of "shock treatment"—reading from the program of the National Socialist Party those paragraphs concerning the proposed solutions to the "Jewish problem." Having set the mood, Waldman embarked on winning over his skeptical listeners by declaring that what was transpiring in Germany was "of greater significance than any pogroms committed in Eastern Europe." Hitler's party, he went on to explain, was "determined to destroy what the Jew has gained through emancipation— his equal status as a citizen." In his interpretation, "should the Jewish position in Germany break down, automatically the Jewish position throughout Eastern Europe will suffer the same fate."

Waldman's analysis and insight merit serious consideration for a number of reasons. Apart from recognizing the uniqueness of the situation in Germany, he also located the threat within the political sphere and not, as it was usually depicted, in the social realm. Moreover, Waldman was among the few who believed that "the Fascists, once in power, would not hesitate to carry out their anti-Semitic program." While his presentation was draped in universal garb, he understood the threat as being aimed specifically at the Jews.

Waldman's primary goal was to alert the American Jewish elite to the seriousness of the situation of the European Jews. He did not recoil from tapping his insider knowledge of their mentality, although it should be borne in mind that his arguments did not necessarily reflect his real convictions regarding the position of the Jews in America. Aware of the importance that citizenship status played in the construction of the Jews' psychological shield, he did not hesitate to jangle their most sensitive nerve by predicting that "if anti-Semitism gains strength in Europe, if the anti-Semites succeed in putting through anti-Jewish laws, if the outlawing of the Jews by the *numerus clausus* and other measures becomes a permanent feature . . . it will have a suggestive influence on public opinion in the United States and adversely affect the position of the American Jew." Intimately aware of the highly acculturated integrationist sensibilities of his cohort, Waldman did not take the particularistic route. "There is . . . more at stake," he explained, "than purely Jewish interests. If the Fascists should obtain the control of Germany, the peace of the world would be seriously menaced." He could therefore conclude that "the Jewish situation in Germany is . . . not one of purely local concern."

Like a master weaver Waldman continued to interlace the threads on his loom. But to create the desired fabric, one persistent knot had to be untangled—the disappearing threads of memory had to be retrieved. "We Jews frequently forget," he said as he began to deconstruct the emotional chaos of the disciples of emancipation, that in many countries it "is only 50 or 60 years old . . . [that] it has not yet penetrated the sub-consciousness of the average non-Jew that the Jew should be an equal." And having raised doubts about the realization of their expectations, he sought to undermine yet another pillar of their faith by identifying their spiritual role models, the German intellectuals, as "the most bitter foes of the Jews" today.

Waldman's objective was to provoke a broadly based response to the Jewish problem in Germany. On this particular occasion, he targeted the Jews who hitherto had not been involved on behalf of Jewish causes, seeking to enlist their moral and financial support. He understood that by describing the situation as utterly bleak, or as particularly Jewish, there was a risk of alienating them even further. Thus, in making his plea, Waldman reverted to using this milieu's own universalist lingua franca:

> This fight is the duty of all, Jews and non-Jews alike, who wish to safeguard the principles of liberalism and tolerance and prevent the establishment of an order in which men are deprived of human rights because of their national or religious differences.

Although his presentation of the struggle was de-ethnicized and de-Judaized, the Seligmans, the Sulzbergers, the Guggenheims, and their like were nowhere to be seen or heard on such matters. Sophisticated as Waldman's stratagem was, it was far from successful, for, as he noted afterward, most of his audience reacted to his assessments as "excessively alarming . . . and unduly pessimistic."[91]

The spread of anti-Semitism in Germany, Waldman explained in his report, posed a double danger, to which he offered two separate solutions. In Germany, the "possible infringement of the rights of the Jews" should be dealt with by the C.V., but unlike in 1929, he now recommended that they should be "morally and financially encourage[d]." In America, however, the Jews were endangered by the "extension of the [anti-Semitic] movement in a virulent form to Western countries including the United States." Because he was an astute observer of the American scene, Waldman's strategy called for enlisting general (i.e., non-Jewish) public opinion against Hitlerism as the solution on the domestic front.

However, when examining the steps that he suggested to combat anti-Semitism in America—interestingly, the only part of the report missing from his published memoirs—it becomes apparent that the loss of faith of the Jews in their own status in the New Zion was greater than their still-existing faith in America's morality. Eager to project an image of self-assured Americans, they dreaded the fact that the image of the victimized Jew in Germany would deflect attention to their own already vulnerable state. Hence, "both from the practical point of view and the consideration of the importance of keeping the Jewish bodies inconspicuous," it was suggested that the JTA be employed to mobilize "general public opinion against Hitlerism." With growing uneasiness and rapidly spreading illusions, it was rationalized that the JTA would be perceived as a regular news agency. Even more appealing was the fact that since the JTA was not "an official Jewish body . . . the Jewish community would avoid being involved." Waldman concluded his presentation by "emphasizing that such propaganda as may be carried on in this way, should clearly avoid doing anything which is likely to embarrass or injure the interests of Germany as a whole."

It is difficult to gauge to what extent the Jewish leadership's universalist approach was grounded in a deeply held ideological conviction—a by-product of its European heritage and its subsequent American acculturation—

and to what extent it was a pragmatic reaction to the current predicament of American Jews. It appears more plausible that the latter was the predominant factor which, ironically, only confirmed the somewhat pitiful state of American Jews. For the Jews who had exchanged Berlin and Frankfurt for Washington and New York, the memories of their past were becoming increasingly discordant. Notwithstanding their disappointments in America, it was unacceptable for them to publicly herald their Jewishness and even their Germanhood above their Americanism. Waldman's warning in November 1930 did little to touch those Jews who felt too proud of their German past and/or too insecure about their American present to express doubts about the future of either one.

Thirteen years later, in a 1943 survey report, Waldman still recalled his disappointment at the response of the Jewish audience in November 1930. "I solemnly warned of the impending danger," he said, but "only a few of the hundred men present seemed deeply impressed and concerned."[92]

Repression and Denial

The verbatim report of the discussion following Waldman's address indeed bears out this impression. However, to merely conclude that the meeting "was dominated by men who refused to take alarm"[93] is to overlook important nuances in the responses which may shed light on the elite's initial perceptions of the Jewish problem in Germany and its projection onto the condition of the Jews in America. The deliberations, which took place among a rather homogeneous group with a similar cultural background and social status, nonetheless exhibited many divergent opinions and reactions. The historian's task is therefore made more complex, since not only is it difficult to identify a unified response of American Jewry as such, but even an examination of a more controlled group unveils substantial differences of opinion. Notwithstanding, certain categories of response can be discerned and linked to the participants' ambiguous identity—whether it stemmed from their Jewish historical consciousness or from their American experience.

The opening remarks of the AJC's new president, Cyrus Adler, reveal these leaders' incongruous reading of the German situation. Characterizing Germany as "one of the most enlightened countries in the world . . . [and] forward-looking," Adler lamented that what was taking place was "a recrudescence of something that we never believed would be witnessed in that land." Having declared the meeting as informal and closed, Adler also limited its agenda by making clear that "as Americans" there was no room for interference in the politics of another country, and "particularly, not to discuss their political parties."[94] Hence, the new reality, that almost six and a half million Germans had voted for the Nazi party, was both present and absent at this special meeting.

Not unlike the American administration, most speakers at the meeting brought an economic interpretation to the events in Germany. Few cared to recall that anti-Semitic sentiments were neither new to German history nor active only in times of social dislocation or economic hardship. Adler set the tone when he explained the present situation in Germany in the context of the "hardships and miseries" resulting from the war. Felix M. Warburg, scion of the famous family of German bankers, analyzed the NSDAP's gains in the last election as being "to great extent, the vote of the dissatisfied unemployed." German-born industrialist Ludwig Vogelstein, president of the Union of American Hebrew Congregations and chairman of the American Metal Co., Ltd., was certain that "with an improvement in the economic conditions, there is apt to be a considerable reduction in the antisemitic feeling in Germany." Alexander Marx, a Jewish historian, was certain that "once the economic conditions have improved," the present wave of anti-Semitism "will die down as its predecessors have died down."[95] The "Review of the Year 1930" published by the American Jewish Committee presented the same analysis and hence supported President Hoover's declaration of an intergovernmental debt holiday.[96]

But other voices could be heard as well. Leo Wolfson, the ex-president of the Federation of Romanian Jews of America, reasoned that anti-Semitic excesses in Germany and elsewhere were not so much a manifestation of hatred of Jews as of conditions which drove people to adopt "certain attitudes." To combat these attitudes, he urged the Jews in Germany and elsewhere to see it as their "business, as citizens of each country, to contribute towards the solution of these problems" instead of

> whining and . . . protesting . . . and telling what hurts—everybody knows that, and we are almost callous to anything we hear about these things. . . . It would not be amiss to have the German Jews devote a great deal of attention towards solving the inner political and economic problems of Germany . . . and a study of these problems, instead of their own immediate problems, would bring about a quicker solution of the problems than merely the recital of them at meetings. [Applause][97]

This kind of attitude was not new. Both Marshall and Henry Morgenthau had argued with regard to previous crises that Jews could enjoy the benefits of citizenship if they acted in full cooperation with their compatriots in improving the nation of their common citizenship.[98] Indeed, an activist-participatory stance was the traditional advice given to Jews when confronting hardships in their host societies. In ancient times the prophet Jeremiah wrote to the Jews in exile: "Build houses, settle down, . . . work for the good of the country to which I have exiled you; pray to the Lord on its behalf, since on its welfare yours depends."[99] But in modern times these viewpoints communicated far more than adherence to a new civic faith and criticism of Jewish separateness. They also provided ample testimony to the somewhat fictitious nature of Jewish solidarity—a precept that increasingly was practiced on the rare occasions when empathy with the victim was cost free, or when its expression was advantageous, or at least not harmful, to the empathizer. Cyrus

Adler must have been aware of this collective change of heart. He followed his greetings with the admonition that perhaps "we have been accustomed, maybe even gotten a little hardened, to statements and difficulties in the situation of the Jews in various countries."[100]

Indeed, in trying to explain their failure to gain the desired acceptance into their host society, it was not uncommon for Jews to place the blame on those "other" Jews themselves who, they maintained, had not invested sufficiently in their country and hence were partly responsible for their own adverse conditions. The more Jews wished to identify with those who labeled them as different, the more they adopted the values, attitudes, and opinions of this reference group, including its anti-Jewish myths. The charge of Jewish power is but one example that illustrates how fiction was treated as fact. Vogelstein, for example, approvingly cited Professor Carl Becker, the former Prussian minister of culture, with whom he had discussed the situation in Germany, who had advised that for the moment the only thing people outside Germany could do was to "lie low," since any outside agitation would be construed to mean that "international Judaism" was asserting itself. For these distinguished Jews the "international Jew" was an uncomfortable reality that had to be dealt with. A warning was issued "not [to] do anything here that would . . . create the impression that 'International Judaism' was coming together" and, that any fund-raising activity on behalf of German Jews "should be done in absolute confidence, and not with any publicity."[101]

Including the hostile imaginary perceptions of the nemesis in the definition of the self is self-defeating. Jews had embraced what Sander Gilman has called the "liberal fantasy." They had become convinced that by demonstrating "good behavior," conforming to and abiding by the rules and mores that defined the reference group, they would gain acceptance as well as access to the power and status of that group.[102] Thus, if the German Jews would only identify with Germany's problems instead of with "their own immediate problems"—if they would forgo their own particular needs, abandon their difference, and out of inner conviction bind their fate solely to that of the nation, they would become an accepted part of it. The anti-Zionists among both German and American Jews based their opposition to Jewish nationalism on these very same notions.[103] But this seemingly fair contract contained some loopholes, not all of which the Jews recognized. The more they expressed their desire to become like their reference group and the closer they came to attaining acceptability—to becoming German or American— the more the Germans and Americans realized the value of their power and the more reluctant they became to share it with outside contenders. But this "conservative curse," another of Gilman's terms, "is not merely an artifact of marginality" existing within the fantasy of Jews or other minorities.[104] Indeed, the Germans' own sense of superiority depended on the existence of the Jews as outsiders. Thus a precarious balance had to be maintained between allowing the Jews to integrate (thereby erasing German shame at excluding the "inferior" Jews out of fear of losing power to them) and keeping

the Jews marginally present in German society in order to highlight and preserve the Germans' "superior" position.

The discussions at the special conference reveal that confronting the plight
of the German Jews fostered a deeper level of self-awareness among American Jews concerning their own situation as Americans and as Jews. Even
James N. Rosenberg, a prominent lawyer who took a strong interest in the
protection of the rights of individuals under law, was compelled to acknowledge that anti-Semitism was present in America in "devious and many ways."
Rhetorically he asked, "I would like to know what [sic] one of us doesn't encounter it [anti-Semitism]." When contemplating action with regard to Germany, Ludwig Vogelstein alerted his audience that "as Americans . . . we have
to be careful" not to "expose ourselves to ridicule" by demanding others not
to restrict immigration, and to remember that the United States had its Ku
Klux Klan. Former congressman Nathan Perlman reminded his listeners that
Hitler's propaganda concerning the Jew as an inferior race was not "a new
thought." Recalling his days in Congress, he reminded the assembled group
that it was "a school of thought that has been in existence even in this country
. . . the National Origin Plan, the Quota Law, was in part based upon the idea
that we must keep out an inferior race, or other inferior races, if not our
own." And Dr. Samuel Schulman, of the Central Conference of American
Rabbis, acknowledged that "even here in this country we have people who
think that a man can't be an American unless he is 100% of Anglo-Saxon
blood."[105]

It may appear perplexing that this group of very proud Americans appeared almost "eager" to concede that neither anti-Semitism nor racism was
unique to Germany and to emphasize their existence in the United States. Yet
this admission of their own experience evidently enabled the American Jewish elite to downplay the Nazi threat, and provided emotional legitimation
for their indignant and callous response to their "whining" German counterparts. Deflating the particular Jewish aspect of the Nazi menace was another
way of justifying responses such as Vogelstein's, who thought that "it must be
stated, in justice to the situation . . . that the Hitlerites did not confine their
attacks to the Jews only; they also belabored other people . . . all those who
were opposed to the Fascist ideals." While Vogelstein was factually correct,
he certainly knew, even in 1930, that the harassment of Jews was not primarily due to their anti-Fascist stand. In fact, he himself recognized that the
situation had to be viewed "historically," recalling for his audience that Germany had been "for many years a hotbed of anti-Semitism."[106] For those of a
similar mindset these arguments provided a rational shield against an irrational reality, behind which times and memories past could be put to rest.

The speakers suggested a wide spectrum of solutions for dealing with the
crisis, many displaying an ambivalence resulting from the fusion of the "Jew
of the Ghetto with the Jew of the emancipation."[107] The one who epitomized
the modern split identity of this group was Reform Rabbi Dr. Samuel Schulman. Although proud of the emancipation movement which had done "won-

derful things," Schulman nonetheless held it responsible for the fragmentation in Jewish life, "which could not but have repercussion in the house of our enemies." And at the same time, out of "very serious conviction" and not as a "rhetorical phrase," he believed that when facing an "extraordinary situation" and when seeking help, a Jew must first "think of the God of Israel."[108] But Schulman was also in agreement with those—in particular Felix Warburg, Cyrus Adler, William Liebermann, Nathan Perlman, and Jacob Kohn—who proposed using scientific arguments to combat the German so-called scientific racial theories. Felix Warburg reported that a "foremost student of anthropology"—probably German-born anthropologist Franz Boas, although he was not mentioned by name—had offered his services to repudiate such doctrines.[109] Schulman, while conceding that racial ideas could be scientifically fought, "beg[ged]" the group to acknowledge the larger issue: Hitler's real aim—which racial theory was intended to serve—was to impress upon the German people "that a citizen can only be a Teuton." Although Hitler used the term "German," Schulman explained that he preferred "the term Teuton" "because I myself am so much a child of the thought of the emancipation. . . . I deny the right of anyone to read the Jew out of the German people." Although the Jew "cannot become a Teuton," this Reform Rabbi insisted that the Jew "belongs to the German people" and that the battle waged on his behalf ought to be directed at keeping him German. This meant a universal war to eradicate the "poisonous philosophy . . . that States and peoples . . . should be based upon unbroken and unmixed continuity of blood."[110]

A confluence of two memories shaped the intuitive and emotional perceptions of the American Jewish power brokers with regard to the German menace: that of the glorious heritage of the German past which still suffused their vision of the present reality, and a Jewish collective memory whose master narrative unfolded the story of Jewish survival. They thus continued to depict Germany as the "country in which science, art and music flourish,"[111] a view that reinforced their trust that "these outbreaks in Germany are not the expression of the German people or the German Government," that "Hitler is not the master of Germany," and that his ideas attracted "only a fraction" of the German people.[112]

Drawing, like Schulman, on the source of their identity, the memory of the Jewish people and the faith in the power of the Almighty added another opaque coating to the lens through which American Jews perceived the events in Germany. Retrieving from the historical memory such adversaries as Pharaoh, Haman, and Torquemada (and more recently Adolf Stöcker and colleagues) and remembering that "the whole crew have disappeared, and the Jewish people are still here," served the acclaimed historian of the Reform movement, Rabbi David Philipson, as proof that "the God of Israel still lives."[113] Cyrus Adler resisted the traditional representation of Jewish history as a continuing saga of persecutions, "separate" from world history. As a child of the Enlightenment, he resented the image of the timid and forsaken Jew and urged his listeners to remember that "[there] was also a Mordecai and an

Esther . . . a Moses . . . and coming down to modern time, it is true we had a Dreyfus trial, but there was Zola and other people to stand up against it."[114]

Although he attempted to eradicate the traditional notion that "the entire world is against us," Adler's thinking was rooted nonetheless within the Jewish traditional paradigm which understood catastrophes in terms of martyrology.[115] Yet, overall, he was among the very few who came out against the prevalent inclination to minimize the serious and unique nature of the events in Germany, expressing concern that they had not "realized the depth of this particular thing."[116]

Even those few who acknowledged that the situation in Germany was unprecedented were hampered by their own insecure position in America from undertaking a serious effort to aid German Jews. As Rabbi Philipson admitted bluntly: "I don't think we can do anything here, except to deliberate and to sympathize and to discuss."[117] Understandably, it was the better integrated American Jews who were cognizant of the limitations to any independent particular Jewish action on behalf of Germany's Jews. Hence, President Adler made clear in his opening remarks that "as Americans" there was little that could be done by way of political intervention, but, he added "we felt that at least we ought to sit down and take counsel together to see what, *if anything*, we could do by way of aiding in the solution of the difficulty which . . . impends upon . . . Jews in the German life."[118] Both Philipson and Adler, while in no way minimizing the seriousness of the situation in Germany, were unable to offer more than a rhetorical expression of Jewish solidarity.

At the end of the session, Judge Gustav Hartman proposed a resolution to deplore the anti-Semitic outbreaks in Germany and at the same time express confidence in the ability of the German people and their government to suppress them. The proposition was withdrawn on the ground that this was just a meeting of friends, to which Judge Hartman replied, "If you really didn't want to be overcautious, we could very well adopt it."[119]

"Inactive in the Face of Danger": The Assimilationist Dilemma

It was not only the AJC leadership who could be described as overcautious. Rabbi Stephen Wise, leader of the American Jewish Congress, was equally equivocal in his reaction. He too considered the political dimension as marginal, and his appraisal of the situation was decisively swayed by his high regard for German *Kultur.* Wise, writing in *Opinion* in 1932, was certain that Hitlerism was not "the last word of the German people. . . . Schiller and Lessing more truly express the soul of Germany than do Hitler and Goebbels." And "above all," he reassured his readers, "whatever political and partisan changes may for a time threaten the peace of Germany, the . . . Jews . . . will not be physically exiled from the Germany of Heine . . . nor be doomed to the spiritual fate of eviction from fullest sharing in the life and status of German citizenship."[120] Not much had changed in Wise's opinion since his explanation after the September 1930 elections that "it is not Germany at its best and highest that is indulging in anti-Semitic riots, but only rowdyism . . . not the Germany of Rathenau and Stresemann, but the Germany of Hitler."[121]

But despite the confidence expressed in public, in early 1931 the AJ Congress decided to send Dr. Joseph Tenenbaum, the future leader of the boycott movement, on a fact-finding mission to Germany. He reported that the German Jews were destitute and that "Jew-baiting and Jew-beating are the order of the day."[122] So bleak was the report that AJ Congress Executive Director Bernard Richards feared it would persuade the readers "that the whole situation is utterly hopeless and that nothing can be done to improve conditions." But Richards's real concern seems to have been that the gloomy report would in fact undermine the willingness of Jews to pledge financial support to the American Jewish Congress.[123]

Jacob Landau, the managing director of the Jewish Telegraphic Agency, presented an equally alarming report to the American Jewish Committee. He assessed the situation of the Jews in Germany as more serious than in Poland, Romania, and Russia combined, concluding that "[i]f in such a country as Germany where the Jews have been thoroughly assimilated in language, manners, and culture, there could arise such anti-Jewish fanaticism then the situation is extremely serious." He advised that the Nazi policies and actions be presented as "un-American" in order to solicit the protest of non-Jews.[124] In May 1931, he met with the leaders of the C.V., most of whom considered that protest abroad would make it easier for the Nazis, should they come to power, to "take drastic measures against the Jews, by arousing the belief . . . that the Jews are enemies of Germany." Dr. Bruno Weil, one of the most outspoken members of the group, insisted that the German Jews should fight their own battle and accept financial assistance only if it was a considerable sum. In fact, he was skeptical about whether Jews in other countries were "a sufficiently important factor to bring about effective intervention."[125]

Neither the accessibility of information nor the increasing realization of the seriousness of the situation was sufficient to impel the American Jewish establishment to develop a course of action. Bernard Deutsch of the American Jewish Congress suggested that the Joint Foreign Committee in London be contacted to ascertain the attitude of German Jews toward outside help. His proposal did not create much interest and it was shelved.[126] In December 1931 Wise recommended that one or two AJ Congress representatives go to Germany "to determine what . . . is to be done in the event of Hitler's coming in," or to get President Hoover to send a "distinguished non-Jew" to discuss matters with Hindenburg and Brüning.[127] These ideas were also not acted upon.

Following some preliminary contacts that lasted for almost a month, representatives of the AJC and the AJ Congress met at a joint conference in January 1932 to discuss the situation in Germany. As both David Bressler of the Committee and Deutsch of the Congress admitted, neither group had a clear vision of how to respond to the situation.[128] After much deliberation, it was finally resolved to approach some leading German Jews, whose names were not easily agreed upon, to ask them what kind of help would be most effective. The reply from Dr. Ludwig Hollander, the Centralverein's executive director, was diplomatic: he agreed to bear in mind the offer for assistance, if the situation should require.[129] Practically speaking, this was the sole result of the conference.

The diversity of opinions and suggestions that were aired provide some further insight into the dissimilar public stances that were taken by the AJC and the AJ Congress concerning the situation in Germany. These diverging approaches seriously impeded the chance for any action, whether joint or separate. Furthermore, they clearly reveal that to think of American Jews as a unified group defined by basic shared interests and opinions is an imaginary construction that tricks historians into writing history as they wish it to have been. Indeed, American Jewry was no more than an imagined community. Not only did it lack a clear hierarchical structure, it was virtually anarchical. This was a highly differentiated community, sponsoring a proliferation of activities representing multiple opinions and interests.[130] Hence, when analyzing the American Jewish reactions to events in Germany, one must attempt not only to distinguish between the different voices and styles that were used, but also to determine the intended audience. Those targeted at the general non-Jewish public usually differed in style and content from the messages transmitted to the policy makers in Washington; just as the opinions expressed by a particular leader to his specific constituency did not necessarily match the views he voiced before leaders of other Jewish organizations.

Most of the AJC members considered that any action on the part of world Jewry would be detrimental to the Jews in Germany. Felix Warburg warned that the German Jewish leadership should not "expect more from us in the way of cooperation than we are ready and able to give them." Perhaps, by way of rationalizing the Jewish leaders' own limited ability to act, he believed that "if the Hitlerites should get into power . . . they will sober down, just as much as the Communists have in Russia and the Laborites have in England."[131] Warburg, so it seems, perceived Nazism as another historical discomfort, certainly not as a potentially unique disaster. Even Adler, who was "not so optimistic"—and reminded Warburg that "the Germans are neither Russian nor English, but German and therefore very thorough . . . thoroughly bad as thoroughly good"—objected to any public action by Jewish organizations and gave priority to the importance of fighting Nazi propaganda in the United States.[132]

Baruch Zuckerman of the Labor Zionists, however, feared that silence on the part of American Jews might arouse the suspicion that they were engaged in some deceitful activities because "no reasonable person will be able to believe that the Jews of America are inactive in the face of the danger." His recommendation did not go further than suggesting that propaganda work be carried out by some influential publicists. He did, however, caution that if nothing were done to counteract Hitler, mass action such as protest meetings and demonstrations "may be necessary later." Lewis Strauss of the AJC reasoned that propaganda would be ineffective because the Germans were not only anti-Jewish but anti-American as well. He suggested instead making every effort to strengthen the Brüning government. But when Nathan Perlman of the AJ Congress proposed that a delegation go to Washington to meet with Senator Borah and other members of the Senate Foreign Relations Committee, Strauss rejected the idea, claiming the time was not right for such action.[133]

But among the more ethnic-oriented Jews there was pressure from below for immediate action. Rabbi Wise, in his attempt to placate his constituency, explained the inaction by claiming that "our hands are tied" until the response from Germany's Jews arrived.[134] Wise, venturing into "high diplomacy," went to Washington in March 1932 to meet with Senator Borah, seeking to solicit from him a statement of protest against Hitler's anti-Semitic program. Ironically, this attempt almost resulted in a complete rupture of relations between the two recently united Jewish organizations. Borah, the influential Republican and "friend" of the Jews, was far from anxious to come forward himself. Instead, he proposed that it would be more effective—and, one may add, less realistic—to aim for a presidential statement, to be given in an interview with Adolph Ochs of the *New York Times*. Ochs, the editor of the most prestigious newspaper in the country, and a distanced Jew, declined the honor.[135] Borah even offered to accompany both Wise and Adler to the White House, but Adler felt that Hoover should be spared the embarrassment of being obliged to refuse the request.[136] The presidential election year of 1932 —which normally would have provided a favorable opportunity to exert pressure—proved inopportune.

For the American Jewish power brokers there was little else to do other than hope that as Americans they would awaken their nation's conscience. Yet however Americanized this group had become, claiming, in Wise's words, that "the Jews of the world, no more than the Jews of Germany, do not demand exceptional treatment or privileged position or favored status for themselves," they had also remained "inflexibly self-insistent as Jews."[137] This dissonance would be manifested in the way they conceived their expectations as well as in the manner in which they endured their disappointments.

Part Three

A Fragile Political Voice, 1933–1935

5

Jewish Leaders versus the Voice of America, 1933

Values alter facts
The moment we love an image,
it cannot remain the copy of a fact.
—Gaston Bachelard, *Poetics of Space*

Although the pogrom of Kishinev had aroused widespread indignation in America, anti-Semitism of the Nazi type kindled little interest. This difference in response may be attributed to several factors. The Great War and the Red Scare that followed created in America what historian Paul L. Murphy has described as a "new permanent dimension of intolerance."[1] In 1922 John Spargo sadly noticed a "whole library of books" devoted to discussion of the "Jewish Question."[2] With the onset of the Great Depression many social critics came to realize that the climate of intolerance was a culmination of three generations of economic, social, and moral crises.[3] Bad times always provide a catalyst for emotions that are better concealed in good times. It is therefore not remarkable that in an overwhelmingly Christian society the practice of blaming the Jews for the nation's misfortunes gained popular support.

It was within this unsettling American context that in 1933 the German Jewish issue was placed on the public agenda by American Jewry. However, that did not mean that events in Germany dominated or had a uniform impact on American Jews—a community with varying levels of integration and acculturation and, more basically, with divergent self-perceptions. Nor did the evolving situation become a critical psychological or ideological factor that altered the values or modes of behavior of the Jewish community or its leaders. This point may require further elucidation, for in attempting to decipher behavior, one is tempted to make assumptions about human nature. In the context we are dealing with here it seems to be presumed that an extraordinary situation will elicit an equally extraordinary response. But as research in other areas has demonstrated, the response of individuals and collectives to crisis situations is governed by pre-existing patterns. As Nathan Wachtel has observed, "Every event occurs in a context already there, made up of institutions, customs and practices, meanings and patterns which both resist and sustain human activity."[4]

It seems that for the contemporaries, more than for historians, it was easier to accept the flawed reality of human nature as normal. James N. Rosenberg, for example, a member of the executive board of the American Jewish Joint Distribution Committee (JDC or Joint) and an AJC activist, expressed shock at the failure of the world, both Christians and Jews, to sense the implications of the German outrage, but he was not surprised. Sharing his indignation with the discouraged high commissioner on refugees, James G. McDonald, who was about to resign, he reflected:

> But I suppose it has always been that way in the world; people are concerned with their own immediate affairs and when it comes to the sufferings of other people, especially when the people are far away, most people . . . have not the imagination to be concerned.[5]

It should also be acknowledged that deciphering and interpreting the meaning of human action is a rather demanding task for the historian, which carries its own limitations. The narrators, at best, can only metaphorically work their way into the minds of their subjects in an attempt to reconstruct their thoughts, beliefs, and behavior. Moreover, the penchant of historians for imposing excessive order upon intractable materials may attenuate their awareness of the inevitable presence of contradictory impulses. Indeed, their desire to create a harmonious presentation may numb them to the existence of multifarious voices and opinions. And another factor must be acknowledged. The writing of history is commonly affected by a moral and ideological position. While this is not only unavoidable but even desirable, it can lead to one-sided readings that might encourage misunderstanding, distortion, and even hypocrisy. Although recognizing these limitations is a far cry from overcoming them, it should at least serve to sensitize historians to the shortcomings of their craft and to their personal prejudices.

With these observations in mind, the present discussion will probe how the Jewish leaders attempted to awaken the voice of America as a source of moral potency to influence the general American discourse on the German Jewish problem, with what stock of political wisdom and life experience American Jews formulated their response to the crisis, and what promoted and what hindered their campaign to awaken mass consciousness among Jews and non-Jews to the fate of German Jewry.

Americanizing the Protest

Throughout their American experience, Jews had rarely admitted overtly that a "Jewish problem" existed in their New Zion. But by the early 1930s they could no longer ignore its existence, only minimize its weight. Thriving right-wing sentiments fostered a gamut of anti-Jewish allegations, which ranged from accusations against the powerful "international Jew" to the charges of Jewish communism and Jewish solidarity. The growing popularity of Zionism among American Jews—which was a timely solution for the Jews who rejected total assimilation but at the same time refused to identify with any of the religious forms in the community, thus enabling the secular Jews to be considered "good Jews"—added a new dimension to an old reproach, that of questionable national loyalty.[6] Moreover, the mushrooming of avowedly anti-Semitic organizations at home could not be disregarded. Almost non-existent in early 1933, they sprang up in the latter half of the year following Hitler's accession to power and rose to a peak of membership in the summer of 1934. Although organizations like the German American Bund, the Silver Shirts, and the White Shirts were more formidable in voice than in action, their propaganda echoed the jarring rhetoric of Nazi anti-Semitism loudly enough to jolt American Jews out of their relative complacency concerning their own situation.[7] Rabbi Stephen Wise was probably not alone in feeling that the year 1933 marked nothing less than the "disintegration of quasi-emancipation."[8]

It was only natural that under such harsh circumstances the prime concern of American Jewish leaders was with the impact that this "eccentric decade of right-wing extremism" would have on their own community.[9] AJC President Cyrus Adler, who at no time "considered the Jews of America in danger," nonetheless advised them to be careful against the very "determined foe operating in this country" as well. Julian Mack of the AJ Congress also warned that the danger of Hitlerism was present everywhere.[10] However, since most Jews were still fighting for acceptance as Americans, they were reluctant to openly acknowledge the existence of a domestic threat. In tune with their ambitions they were advised "not [to] concede for one minute that Hitlerism can ever, or will ever get a foothold in a country which is dedicated to the principles of Washington, Jefferson, Lincoln." Moreover, Jewish popular opinion was prone to believe that giving vent to such fears would be "a disastrous error," since it would "be saying and proclaiming to the rest of our fellow citizens that we have so little confidence in the American ideal," and prove "our own lack of Americanism."[11]

Morris Waldman was afraid that fighting anti-Semitic propaganda in America might have harmful repercussions. It might, for example, give credence to the charge of corrupt use of Jewish money. But more pivotal to his argument was the concern that by attempting to suppress anti-Semitic groups, American Jews would be "undermining the fundamental rights of free speech and assembly" thereby destroying their "basic safeguards." Waldman thought these tactics unwise, "in view of the age-long unpopularity of the Jews."[12]

The fear that European fascism—the term used at the time—might triumph in the United States was not, however, limited to the Jews in America. As the Depression deepened, liberals and radicals became overtly concerned that fascism would have great appeal to the discontented middle classes. "The usual complacent assumption that we cannot become fascist, simply because America is 'different' or too large," Raymond Gram Swing of *The Nation* wrote, "does not bear analysis."[13]

Feeling ever more vulnerable, American Jewish leaders were cautious to evade the charge of dubious patriotism and its antipode "Jewish solidarity." Under these circumstances it was hardly surprising that from the beginning of the crisis they felt reluctant to appeal for support on behalf of Germany's Jews qua Jews. To circumvent this condition, two main options seemed to have been viable: either the particular Jewish problem had to de-Judaized, that is, reformulated as a universal human issue, or, if presented as a distinctly Jewish concern, Jewish official involvement had to be concealed. But circumstances prevented an either/or course of action; rather, they seemed to conspire to create a neither/nor situation. American Jews neither launched the protest as a Jewish issue, nor were they successful in persuading the American political powerhouse and general public opinion that what was at stake was an ecumenical concern. Rabbi Stephen Wise recognized this tragic double bind, and it evoked in him anger and frustration. He pointed to the heart of this dilemma when he lamented:

> If we are not strong and brave and wise enough to meet together in the sight of men to consider what can be done to lighten the burdens unjustly laid upon our people, then, in truth, we do not deserve a better fate. . . . If, too, our status as citizens of the nations in which we dwell is as precarious as some Jews imagine it to be, then, indeed, we have nothing to lose.[14]

But for the American Jewish masses, about half of whom were first-generation immigrants, such rhetoric was not enough to mobilize them to action. They were mostly too preoccupied with their own existential crisis, not least of which was maintaining or finding a job in an economy which in 1933 had an unemployment rate of 26 percent.[15] That is not to say, however, that American Jews lacked empathy for their fellow Jews in Germany. Harry Simonhoff has described the "sorrow, fear, anger, and compassion" felt by the Miami Jews. "Of course," he opined, "the victims of Nazi savagery must be helped to leave their harsh, stepfather land."[16] But where to? Not many American Jews seem to have contemplated a solution in their own backyard. Fearing that Jewish refugees would aggravate their own insecure social and economic status, a growing number of them began to wonder about "this thing called Zionism[.] There might be something to the idea of a Jewish state in Palestine. If it is a matter of money, then here is a check."[17]

Indeed, as in 1930, it was no easy matter for the leaders of Jewish organizations to activate Jews and non-Jews to combat an emerging Jewish crisis in faraway Europe. Julian Mack, for example, expressed his concern to Stephen Wise about the silence of business leaders who were missing from "the list of those who have expressed themselves publicly." Wise was realistic enough not to expect support from this sector. When Mack urged him to recruit the Jewish financial moguls through one of their own, he answered, "[I] have no confidence in the capacity of [Felix] Warburg to act with vigor on Jewish questions."[18] The best Wise could promise was to try to contact directly two of the top Jewish tycoons, David Sarnoff and Bernard Baruch, neither of whom at the time had much to do with Jewish affairs.[19]

In explaining the silence of the business community, Wise was not unaware of the "national interests."[20] Judge Joseph Proskauer, an AJC activist, adhered to a similar opinion much longer. In a press interview given in 1935 he insisted that American Jews had "no moral right to bind [themselves] as a separate group inside the United States, to disturb the economic and diplomatic relations between America and a country with which America is at peace."[21] The aptness of such "patriotic" views was confirmed by 100-percent Americans who served as guides to the Jewish leadership, people such as James G. McDonald, the president of the Foreign Policy Association and the future League of Nations' first high commissioner for refugees. During a discussion with Bernard Deutsch, the AJ Congress president in 1932–1933, McDonald frankly explained that the United States had "larger fish to fry in Germany" (than the Jewish problem), by which he meant, according to Deutsch, "that the economic situation and the American policy with respect to it were more important." He clearly concluded that "any American Ambassador who goes to Germany must fail from the standpoint of dealing with the Jewish question."[22] Others as well, such as Federation of Jewish Charities activist Jacob Billikopf, who traveled in Germany in the summer of 1933, also encountered the same opinion. Talking with representatives of the American press he was told that Wall Street bankers were bringing all sorts of pressure on the American press "to go easy on that Jewish stuff in Germany. . . . [The bankers are] eager to salvage as much of their investments in Germany as possible." And in view of that, Billikopf lamented, "What weapon has our ambassador?"[23]

It was not only the traditionally conservative business milieu that was not easily persuaded to place a ban on Nazi Germany. Lay and religious liberal circles in America clung to their illusions about Hitler's intentions well into 1934. The liberal Washington-based National Council for Prevention of War, while opposing the general oppression and denial of freedom of the Nazi regime, saw its "constructive side" and "much that has already been accomplished in the way of moral, social and political reform."[24] Similar optimism can be found in a report on "Understanding Hitler's Germany" which Robert Dexter, a Unitarian minister who spent the summer of 1933 in Germany, presented to Secretary of State Cordell Hull (it was also published in *Church and Society*). Dexter said that "instead of to condemn its [the German regime's] policies because of certain elements involved," it was important to "realize the new hope and the new spirit which Hitlerism with all its defects has brought to the German people . . . a gain not only for them but for western civilization as a whole." The *Christian Century* enthused with even greater pathos that "Hitler has been able to do something that even Bismarck did not do. Besides, unemployment is decreasing, life is more hopeful, the youth are more virile and filled with a higher motive than mere sentimentalism. Germany is awake!"[25]

On the Jewish front there was also cause for frustration. Following the first anti-Nazi rally that took place at Madison Square Garden in March 1933, the New York *Evening Post* published a letter by a "Hebrew," as he designated himself, who described the gathering as "worse than useless." He derided the "professional" Jewish speakers as "nonentities" and demanded to know where the "representatives of the Straus, Marshall, Guggenheim, Warburg, or Schiff families on the program" had been. The response came from another Jew: "American Jewry can only echo an ashamed and humiliated 'Where?'"[26] Among members of the American Jewish Committee there was deep resentment that a conference called in May 1933 to discuss the German situation drew few participants. Sol Stroock, a member of the policy committee, deplored that people were simply not interested and quoted one person who wrote, "I have too many other things that take my time and attention."[27]

Indeed, the leadership of the AJC found it extremely difficult to bring about a change of consciousness among its followers. Giving vent to his frustrations at the conference, Stroock pointed out that "It seems strange that we should have to beg people to come to help us save whom? Save themselves— and I mean save themselves, without any qualifications whatsoever." Apart from stressing that Nazi anti-Semitism had a direct bearing upon the lives of American Jews, Stroock called for a new self-definition that would reject "the fallacy"—which Nazism had made emphatically clear—"that there is something different between Jews who happen to come from one country and those Jews who happened to come from another country." He also addressed the growing cleavage within the American community between the German Jews and the *Ostjuden*, himself confessing to having "sinned" with the rest by not having given those people a fair chance in leadership.[28]

Voicing the fears of those who maintained that "going public" with a particular Jewish issue somehow violated good American behavior, Cyrus Adler wrote of the need "to create a public opinion in this country against Hitler and his party absolutely without reference to the Jews at all, because . . . we cannot be constantly thrusting ourselves before the public without danger to ourselves."[29] One year later, in June 1934, Sol Stroock again called attention to the domestic repercussions of Jewish public protest against Germany, but this time his concern had a different focus. While accepting that the situation had "naturally" turned the American Jews into "a very emotional people," he feared that it was "possibly" leading to "an exaggerated" view of the situation, which made the American Jews become "not only Jewishly conscious . . . which is very desirable," but also "terribly Jewishly assertive, Jewishly voluble." Stroock warned that keeping the German Jewish problem "in the forefront and in the public eye," had made the American Jews "nuisances, and to those that are going to follow us we have become more than nuisances, we have become menaces."[30]

By contrast, Rabbi Stephen Wise continued to maintain, at least publicly, that only through protest and boycott could the forces of morality be aroused against Nazism. Such an attitude, he insisted, would not escalate anti-Semitism, for he wanted to believe that "America and Americans . . . respect the Jew who is unafraid and unashamed, who has the power of wrath against injustice, rather than the Jew who is nervous and fearful and who has little faith in the justness of the American people."[31] Of whatever mind, American Jews did not fail to profess on every occasion their faith in America.

It seems that in 1933 Hitlerism was not perceived by the general American public as a serious threat to the Jews in Germany. Moreover, for the community leaders, challenging the Nazi excesses against the Jews was intertwined with their own dilemma of being Jewish in America. It is in the context of this collective and particular set of circumstances that the American Jewish leadership perceived and reacted to the news from Germany. Before going any further, it is therefore important to assess what exactly the leadership knew.

Voices from Germany

Among historians the desire to dispel the ambiguity that surrounded the early perceptions of the Nazi regime is not entirely innocent. Not least because of the cataclysmic aftermath, we tend to expect "knowledge" and "understanding" to coincide. Hence, the question "What did they know?"—they being the victims *and* the witnesses—has never been a purely scholarly question. Indeed, in its updated version—"Had they known more, could they have done more?"—the query is even more loaded, for it implies, as Elizabeth Janeway has observed, that "understanding and action are *expected* to connect."[32] In the existing historiography this assumption often leads to judgment instead of critical analysis of the period, particularly regarding the behavior of the witnesses and the issue of rescue. The implication is that lack of information exonerates inaction, or, conversely, availability of facts can serve as grounds for condemnation if action did not result. Notwithstanding such issues, which give the moralist an entrée, the question of how much they knew is relevant on another level. Reconstructing the information that was available at that time provides the historian with the raw material that fed the perceptions of contemporaries. When examined in the particular context of a specific group of witnesses, it may reveal the complex circumstances and motives behind the response or the lack thereof.

Having "read diligently whatever had been published about Hitler in the press of many languages," Rabbi Stephen Wise reacted to Hitler's appointment as chancellor with "a minimum of surprise."[33] Other Jewish leaders as well testified publicly that for thirteen years they had watched "with dismay and the gravest apprehension the rise of a monstrous anti-Semitic movement," but as they had in the late twenties, in early 1933 they confessed that with Hitler's accession to power, they had "kept silent," hoping "that Hitler and his followers would come to realize that their conduct was unworthy of the great tradition of culture of the German nation."[34] Indeed, as we saw in the previous chapter, the captains of Jewish organizations had kept a close watch on events in Germany during the Weimar years.

It is reasonable to assume that immediately following Hitler's accession to power the extensive coverage in the general press was the main source of information for the Jewish leadership in America. Apart from providing daily updated information, its editorials reflected the general mood of the nation, which certainly played a role in establishing the parameters for the particular Jewish reaction to the situation. This may partially explain the fact that Jewish leaders deciphered the situation in Germany within the interpretative framework that prevailed among the general American public. In early 1933 there was a consensus among liberals that the reason democracy had failed in Germany was "in large part the result of the lack of fair play to Germany, and the short-sighted slighting of German rights and needs by other nations, including our own."[35] Likewise, Rabbi Wise linked the victory of the Nazis and the wrongs it inflicted upon the German Jews to the unjust treatment accorded to Germany following the Great War. He demanded for Germany "justice and even magnanimity from her erstwhile foes . . . and the right from Germany for the Jewish people."[36]

For the first five weeks or so after Hitler's appointment, the American press, while not ignoring the Nazis' actions against the Jews, emphasized the regime's fierce campaign against Communists and Socialists. It was only after the March elections and the intensified attacks on the Jews that it began to pay explicit attention to their situation.[37] In these early months information was not as tightly controlled as the regime would have wished. For the most part the coverage was accurate and rather extensive. Yet it was not uncommon to encounter skepticism. "Terrible things may be happening," the *Los Angeles Times* opined, "but not as terrible as the reports from Germany would have you believe."[38]

It stands to reason that there was a gap in perception between those who reported from the scene, whatever their leanings might have been, and those publishers, editors, and commentators who were trying to interpret these events at a distance. The difficulties of synchronizing the deeply embedded vision of Germany as a civilized society with the emerging image of bestiality were evident in the perception of all observers, be they diplomats, journalists, or Jewish activists.[39]

The Jewish leadership was privy to first-hand information through its direct contact with the victims. The American Jewish Joint Distribution Committee, for example, had a permanent representative in Europe. Its Berlin office, at whose disposal an emergency fund was placed in March, was in close contact with needy Jews.[40] In May, Rabbi Jonah B. Wise, chairman of the 1933 campaign of the JDC, returned from Germany and reported that the conditions of the Jews there were hopeless. The American Jewish Committee was briefed by Dr. Maurice Hexter who traveled to Germany in late May. He reported categorically that the news which had already filtered out had "by no means been exaggerated. . . . The reverse is rather the case."[41] Jacob Billikopf of Philadelphia visited Germany in August. His trip generated two very detailed reports, one of which FDR's successor as governor of New York

Herbert Lehman considered sufficiently important to refer to President Roosevelt, who described it as "intensely interesting."[42]

But assessing the situation was difficult for even the more astute observers on the scene. The future president of the World Jewish Congress, Nahum Goldman, reported from Berlin in early February 1933 that "no immediate dangers are in sight." Goldman felt that if the Nazis were to win in the March 5th elections the prospects would be "very bitter." But his final analysis was based on the reverse supposition: "If the Nazis will not gain a majority, a turbulent few months will follow, in which case the Nazi regime will not last for years."[43]

Stephen Wise himself spent the summer of 1933 in Europe. Discouraged from entering Germany by U.S. Ambassador William Dodd, who claimed his safety could not be guaranteed, he and his wife toured the surrounding countries and met with scores of homeless refugees. Wise was deeply touched by these encounters with Hitler's earliest victims. Writing to his daughter, he appeared to have been horrified, convinced that "the Jews of Germany are finished" and, as Justice Brandeis had already told him in early February, that "their only recourse is '*heraus.*'"[44] However, at about the same time (summer 1933) he still thought it possible that "effective action by the League of Nations through a commission and economic pressure by enlightened public opinion," if brought to bear immediately, "might bring about the end of the Nazi government and its policy of persecution."[45] This apparently contradictory vision was soon dispelled. On October 14th, Hitler announced his decision to withdraw from the Geneva Disarmament Conference and the League of Nations.

The authentic voices of the anguished were brought to the leadership's ears through many letters that were sent to relatives and to various Jewish organizations in America. Many of these letters are filed in the archives of the AJC and the AJ Congress.[46] It was most upsetting for proud Germans to admit to their radically diminished status, perhaps even more so than to endure the tangible hardships. They preserved their sense of self by insisting that "the Jews retained their dignity despite the fact that they were ruined, their goods appropriated, and themselves suppressed in all ways."[47] Indeed, the American Jewish leaders who visited Germany were "impressed" with the "rare and beautiful dignity" of the German Jews' "attitude toward the whole problem," by their willingness to "sacrifice themselves in every possible way."[48]

For those whose lives had turned into nightmares, it was inconceivable that the facts could be known and not acted upon. Believing that the problem was lack of information, many German Jews apprised their co-religionists across the ocean of the situation. "I cannot imagine that people abroad know how much desperate our situation is," a certain Ilse wrote, asking that her letter be made public after she had apologized for writing "all this." Already in a somewhat "safer" place in Germany, she described to her American relatives the anti-Jewish excesses following the March elections. "If the foreign countries do not help us soon," she pleaded "we are lost." In a postscript to her letter she added: "I just read the papers and found out that our situation is known abroad. Thank goodness!"[49]

It must be emphasized that it was only after the promulgation of the Nuremberg Laws in September 1935 that mainstream German Jewry—under the leadership of the "National Representation of Jews in Germany" (Reichsvertretung der Juden in Deutschen)—sought contact with the *Yishuv* (the Jewish community in Palestine) and with British and American Jews. But even then they continued to evade the image of "poor relations passively waiting for salvation from their wealthy cousins" in America and elsewhere. It is rather revealing that when the German Jews expressed thanks for the financial and psychological support extended to them, they stressed that it enabled them to continue to bear the heavy burden of their efforts to help themselves.[50]

Hope and despair, belief and skepticism were dual perceptions that were shared by all, whether impartial observers or involved witnesses. Few saw through the masterful deception that the Nazis perfected to an art. The new regime made every effort to maintain a peaceful, civilized atmosphere—the Nazis were "sickeningly" courteous. This form of propaganda was expected to work favorably for the Nazis, especially with foreign tourists, some of them American Jews.[51] In August 1933 the *Christian Science Monitor* ran a two-part series entitled "A Traveler Visits Germany" which described that country as a heaven on earth where trains arrived on time, traffic ran smoothly, and the street cafés were lively. *The Nation*, on the other hand, griped that it was nearly impossible "to restrain the silly people who after a week or two in Germany, during which they have seen no Jews beaten up in the streets, go back to their own countries and declare that the stories told in the papers about Germany are all untrue."[52]

Even those who came genuinely seeking to uncover the truth needed solid proof to believe it. "Is it possible that these people could be so cruel?" marveled Mrs. Ruth Billikopf, who accompanied her husband on his trip to Germany. "One can hardly believe the things one hears about them," she reflected. Jacob Billikopf admitted that if his wife had not heard so many first-hand reports from the "lips of Jews," she might have come back "with the impression that the picture, especially with reference to the Jews, was frightfully overdrawn."[53]

Michael Williams, the editor of the Catholic publication *Commonweal*, was among the few who were not beguiled. Addressing his plea to the leaders of the American Jewish Congress, he wrote from Europe in late May:

> The present situation of the Jews in Germany is deplorable beyond any words of mine to describe. . . . I beg you not to be deceived nor to let your people be led astray by the false denials concerning the Jewish persecution. . . .
>
> Either muffle your ears to the weeping and wailing of the children of Rachel, and harden your hearts to the cry of humanity itself and thus let the worst crime of our age proceed to its ordained end in the deliberate extinction of nearly a million men . . . or else come quickly and strongly to the rescue.[54]

One could hardly claim that American Jewish leaders lacked factual information concerning the events in Germany during Hitler's first year in power. Nor could it be argued compellingly that what transpired in Germany during 1933 was accepted with equanimity. In Rabbi Wise's understanding, for example, "the frontiers of civilization have been crossed . . . the beginning of a world-wide movement against us, a world-wide conflagration, a world-wide undertaking against the Jews."[55] Cyrus Adler described the situation in Germany as "indescribably bad and absolutely unparalleled in modern times."[56] Judge Julian Mack concluded that "the Jewish people at least in Germany is up against a fate more terrible than the Spanish Inquisition and expulsion."[57] And for Felix M. Warburg, what the Nazis' takeover had precipitated in their first year in power was enough for him to declare that "one feels ashamed for the century."[58]

Although these opinions were more than just rhetoric, they failed to tell the full story. Not unusually, American Jewish leaders were prone to hold two separate and contradictory convictions about the situation. While recognizing the unprecedented nature of the German situation, they were predisposed, at the same time, to accept the interpretation that Nazism was a temporary aberration that outside intervention would only exacerbate. Moreover, the tension between the self-appointed leadership of the so-called uptown and downtown Jews was also reflected in the way they dealt with the German problem. *Opinion*, the chief organ of the AJ Congress, expressed the tensions which the struggle for power within the community provoked. Eagerly awaiting the "beginning of the end of the Bavaro-Prussian Jewish regime in the American life," it bitterly attacked those "willful and tyrannical Prussians who are Germans first, some sort of Americans second, and no sort of Jews third except as they use the Reform Temple as a shield wherewith to guard themselves against the contamination of brotherhood with all non-German Jews."[59]

The uptown leaders, much like their German co-religionists, were also profoundly imbued with the idea that protection by the public authorities was "the moral duty of the State."[60] For them, Hitler's radio address of March 12th, in which he commanded his cohorts "to exercise the strictest . . . discipline," warning against "staging isolated operations," was adequate proof. Referring to this address, the editorial in the *American Hebrew* condemned the American Jewish Congress for "formulating a program for anti-Hitler condemnation," while Hitler was "attempting to slay the anti-Semitic beast with unequivocal warning to his followers." Furthermore, they interpreted the Nazi anti-Semitic racial ideology as instrumental rhetoric—opium for the masses intended "to help them [the Nazis] come to power." But having achieved power, it was reasoned, that "beast is no longer of value, but of harm to their state."[61]

There may also be a more experiential reason why the Jews in Germany and elsewhere failed to believe the Nazis' intentions. Amos Funkenstein, for example, argued that this was less the result of a historical mentality of passivity than of a thoroughly modern faith in the state.[62] While this observation is valid, it is somewhat exaggerated. For as much as the Jews had acquired a sense of trust in the state, they also sustained a deep suspicion of it. In America, for instance, equal political rights had not removed for many Jews the feeling of being "strangers at home." Although some would argue that such faith led to "Jewish passivity," in that Jews rarely acted qua Jews, in fact the American Jewish leadership became extremely active in attempting to solicit the support of non-Jews on behalf of Jewish interests. Was the effort to mobilize Gentiles to shoulder the anti-Nazi struggle a manifestation of Jewish timidity, a prudent tactic, or perhaps evidence of maturity in coming to terms with reality? It was probably all three.

The Dilemma of Jewish Particularity

While American Jews were well aware of the adverse conditions of their German co-religionists, this did not erase earlier tensions between the two communities, strains that were exhibited in the response of the leadership in America. In the late 1920s, as we saw in the previous chapter, the power brokers of the AJC had already expressed deep resentment toward the independence of their German counterparts. In 1933, it was the agents of the downtown Jews who took the lead in criticizing the Jewish children of the German emancipation, accusing them of refusing to see the events in Germany in their true light. Writing in the left-liberal weekly *The Nation*, Ludwig Lewisohn voiced a deep estrangement from these Jews: "[Are] they of the Jewish faith?" he asked sarcastically. "They are not even that. They whine that they are Germans, Germans."[63] Rabbi Stephen Wise was particularly outspoken on this issue. The German Jew, he charged, was not only "unrooted and unanchored in the best of his own tradition," but now "at last denied a place in Germany." For Wise, as we have seen, the primary lesson of 1933 was the failure of emancipation.[64]

Outspoken Jewish leaders were vehemently attacked both domestically and abroad, first by those who believed that Hitler *"wird nie zur Macht kommen"* (would never come to power) and, once he did, by those who had hoped that the new regime was "only a temporary insanity."[65] Wise and the AJ Congress encountered harsh criticism from German and American Jews for backing public protest against Hitler's anti-Jewish policies. The decision to hold a mass rally at Madison Square Garden generated strong pressure to cancel it or at least defer it. Wise and his associates were charged with being incompetent to judge the effects that such a meeting could have and were warned that they would be held responsible if any harm was done to the Jews in Germany as a result of it.[66] Wise was not easily moved. On more than one occasion he expressed his contempt for German Jews. "I do not give a penny for the counsel of the Berlin people," he wrote to his close associate Julian Mack. Because they had said for years that "there is no *Gefahr* of Hitler coming to power," Wise concluded that "they have no judgment." A couple of months later he reiterated that "the German Jews did not ask our judgment while they were fighting in the German front and they made a hideous mess of it. I do not know that we can afford to be governed by their counsels now."[67] Addressing the rally in Madison Square Garden, Wise declared quite bluntly that the German Jews "who have virtually been silent throughout the years of anti-Jewish propaganda cannot be followed by us as the wisest of counsellors."[68]

Notwithstanding this criticism, the dire situation of German Jews undoubtedly sensitized American Jews to their own situation at home. It induced them to begin searching their souls—to doubt whether their history in the *goldene medine* was "a tale of progressive emancipation in a liberal society."[69] For indeed, by the 1930s, anti-Jewish sentiments among Americans were no longer rooted in a dislike for the stranger who spoke a foreign tongue and believed in an alien God. Rather, it was an animus directed against people who were similar to themselves and who aspired to participate in the life of the nation, to enjoy not only equal rights but also equal opportunities, to compete for the same jobs, and to contribute to the national culture.[70]

However, of all the failings that were ascribed to Jews, none, perhaps, stung more than the accusation that they kept themselves apart from their "host" society. During this period the charge of Jewish separatism was continuously aired in the public discourse. The most important American Protestant weekly, *The Christian Century*, criticized the "persistent separation of the Jewish community as a self-contained racial and religious group in a society predominantly Christian."[71] In the same publication, which was particularly critical of Jewish nationalism throughout the decade, Joseph McAfee, a lay official of the New York Community Church, ascribed the cause of the "Jewish problem" to the practice of "Jewish Solidarity in America"—the title of his article. The issue was not a religious one; the sacred American doctrine of religious liberty was not questioned. Rather, it was a "social problem which persistent Jewish solidarity precipitates in American society." At its core, the argument went, was the self-contained and impervious social nature of the Jews as a group, which makes for a "self-consciousness [that] is socially baneful."[72] American Jews had no right to be "different."[73] Protestant liberal opinion, at least as reflected in McAfee's article, contended that for those who claim "hospitality in the American community," being different "is nobody's right . . . except as that difference may redound to the common good." But the Jew who adhered to group solidarity, it was claimed, was unable to contribute to the enrichment of the American nation, since "he is holding back. . . . He is confining his priceless ointment in a sealed container. He is unwilling to lose his Jewish life that he may find it in the larger American life."[74]

Christian America viewed the dilemma facing American Jews as irreconcilable: as a "futile effort to preserve a solidarity which is rebuked by its own professions of loyalty to common American aims and values."[75] Liberal Protestants cautioned their Jewish compatriots that "even Christianity," despite what its most devoted advocates might claim, "cannot produce a social consciousness" that would guarantee a well-adjusted permanent coexistence of the two cultures. They reached the rather grim conclusion that "the Jew cannot hope to dwell permanently in the midst of alien cultures and maintain his own insulated cultural stream except at the risk of a social tension which is constantly threatening to break into overt tragedy." It is "a delusion" to imagine that a tolerant mindset could eliminate such tension. "It expects too much of human nature."[76] Indeed, even T. S. Eliot, the chief exemplar of modernism for many New York Jewish intellectuals, thought in 1933 that "a spirit of excessive tolerance is to be deprecated." In Eliot's "ideal Christian society" the population "should be homogeneous," and what was "still more important" was "unity of religious background; and reasons of race and religion combined to make any large number of free-thinking Jews undesirable."[77]

Indeed, even among the more liberal public, tolerance of the Jews tended to be conditional. An editorial in *Harper's Magazine* on "The Nazis and the Jews" employed the usual philo-Semitic rhetoric to praise the Jews for their contribution to Western culture, which made them worthy of defense against Nazi accusations. The writer nonetheless chose to attribute the success of Jews in England, for example, to the fact that the country had "never been overrun by crowds of them as has happened in southeastern Europe and elsewhere in localities not necessary to specify." Like any other group that "seems to be getting more than its share of what is accessible," Jews should expect to "be disliked by observers who are less fortunate."[78]

More forthright in his attitude toward Jews was Newton D. Baker, the former secretary of war. The fact that Baker was co-chairman of the National Conference of Christians and Jews, an organization dedicated to improving the relationship between the various faiths, did not mean that he trusted Jews. Writing to the Reverend Everet R. Clinchy, the director of the Conference, he argued that "if Jews elect to be different, they must sometimes take the consequences of being the out-group. Moreover, they need to understand Gentiles' feelings on the question of Jewish divided loyalty and their affinity towards Communism."[79]

When consulting with his Jewish associates about the advisability of holding public protest meetings, Baker was rather more subtle but no less revealing. Using, unconsciously perhaps, a typical anti-Semitic line of argument, Baker wondered if the Jews were not placing "too much emphasis on their special case." After all, he wrote to Rabbi Brickner, "the world is full of cruel and foolish programs affecting large numbers of minority peoples." As a non-Jew, Baker thought he could provide his Jewish friends with a "more detached view" of the situation. As he reasoned, "one of Hitler's foolish claims is that Jewry has a world consciousness and a set of community sensibilities which are superior to their national obligations." He wondered therefore, "whether these exclusively Jewish protests will not be used as lending color to his belief."[80] Opinions that Baker could communicate to Clinchy as his own he attributed to Hitler when writing to a Jewish friend.

Jewish leaders were well aware of the latent and overt messages of this discourse, and its resurgence in such critical times was reflected in their response to Hitler's tyranny. Rabbi Stephen Wise, for example, was quite shocked to learn of the letter from Baker, someone he considered an ally of the Jewish cause.[81] The allegations of communism—so frequently stressed by German propaganda—were particularly alarming to the Jewish leadership. Following the March elections in Germany, Wise, for example, thought that to "deny an allegation about German Jewish relations to Communism" would be "incriminating and also *verletzend* (insulting)."[82] In a similar vein, the Carl Schurz Memorial Foundation cabled its affiliates in New York, some of whom were prominent Jews, that the campaign waged by the German government was against communism, not against Jews, and "by reason of this point measures against Jews in individual cases unavoidable."[83]

On the domestic front the phobia that linked Jews and communism was mainly reflected in the anxiety about public protests and the boycott against German goods. Anxious not to antagonize American anti-Communist public opinion, the AJ Congress was "nervous" about the participation of Jewish Communists in its public events. Rabbi Wise removed one such Jew from the list of speakers at its parade in May 1933 in protest against the Nazis' book burning, confessing to Judge Mack that "we cannot afford publicly to side with Communists or give sympathy and support to them."[84] The AJC also made use of the Communist scare in its attempt to counter the increased popularity of the boycott campaign, warning that "if the boycott should bring Communism to Germany, the Jewish boycott would be blamed for it and it would even be charged that the real object of the boycott was to bring about the success of Communism, as part of a carefully premeditated international Jewish plot."[85]

Notwithstanding the great sensitivity of Jewish leaders to the charge of being sympathetic to communism and their occasionally unwise particular decisions in this regard, the political reality was such that they had to maneuver around strong anti-Communist sentiments, a fact that any responsible leader had to take into account or be charged with gross incompetence. Moreover, this Jewish milieu was naturally and spontaneously strongly anti-Communist, and their ideas in this respect coincided with the norms of American society.

The mode of response of American Jews to anti-Jewish defamation during the 1930s roughly reflected two predominant kinds of self-definition: there were those who identified themselves as Americans and considered Judaism as primarily a spiritual legacy, not a peoplehood with its implication of dual loyalty; and there were those who wished to be accepted into American society as Jews with a particular ethnic affiliation and identity. Whether apologetic or assertive in their approach, Jews shared a common desire to distance themselves from the traditional, unflattering image of the Jew. Above all they wished to avoid committing the offense of *shanda fur de goyim*—embarrassing themselves before the Gentiles.[86]

Keenly aware of the prevailing mood, American Jews attempted to explain their particularity in ways that would be acceptable to Gentile society. Typically, the author of an article in the *American Hebrew* entitled "The Psychology of the Jew," while reiterating his faith in the liberal-progressive credo that all human beings were essentially alike, made an exception for Jews based on the uniqueness of their collective historical experience. As a "stranger in strange lands," the Jew represented "everywhere the small defenseless minority" on which it was the easiest to "vent one's hostile aggression." The common charge of Jewish clannishness expressed in the contemptuous stamp of "Jewish solidarity" was explained as the result of "continuous strife, struggle, and persecution" which had made Jews "naturally timid," and unwilling to "obtrude" themselves. As a result, the Jew had "adhered to his own group." This had been true, however, only in the distant past. The modern progressive edict, he argued, was based on "co-operation and renunciation," the "two great pillars of civilization." Its basic doctrine advised the Jews that "in order to live, we must let live, we must co-operate with our neighbors; but, to do so, we must renounce or give up many of our most primitive impulses." To appeal to the Gentile—the true object of this discourse—the Jews' image had to be recast. Hence the writer endowed the "new" Jew with attributes that were the very opposite of those imputed to him by the Christian majority. His "most outstanding" trait was his "flexible adaptability." Although of necessity the Jew had developed certain "protective" traits which were "not quite in harmony with the ideals of his neighbors," there were grounds for optimism, since "most of them he gives up as soon as he finds that he can trust his neighbors."[87] But would his neighbors trust him?

"The gentility of Gentiles" appeared limited, as pointed out by a 1933 article of that name in *Harper's Magazine*:

> My summer neighbors cannot be accused of anti-Semitism in the ordinary sense of that word; they are as indignant as anybody at the behavior of the Hitlerites; they abhor the idea of persecution of Jews, of discrimination against Jews. . . . But they will not have Jewish neighbors, even if the Jews are in all perceptible respects like themselves.
>   The one imperceptible but decisive difference is that Jews are Jews, whatever that means, and we are Aryan Protestants.[88]

These potential allies of the Jews were willing to accept those Jews who were "virtually indistinguishable from their Gentile neighbors." But as to the "fanatical Jewish super-patriot who goes around with a chip on his shoulder . . . who sees people as anti-Semitic merely because they do not like him personally—where is the difference between him and the Nazi?"[89]

For the millions of Jews who had come to America from Eastern Europe, such sentiments could not have helped them feel at home. Faced with economic hardships and social rejection, many of them turned in their disillusionment to Zionism, a modern substitute for their scorned ethnic otherness.

Rabbi Stephen Wise was the most illustrious spokesman for this Jewry. Speaking in late 1934 to his own congregation he dared to raise the question "Is the American Jew Safe or Unsafe?" Pointing out that there were currently over 200,000 industrial jobs available in New York which Jews could not "hope to occupy," he acknowledged that this fact made life "unsafe for them." He was painfully honest with those who may have been tempted to adopt the affluent Jewish elite as a role model: the handful that had been admitted to "places" were "tolerated . . . rather than welcomed." The perspective of the fortunate few was false, he argued, and it "proves nothing with respect to the general status of the Jew in America."[90]

While Wise's rhetoric may not have been entirely innocent—it was part of the struggle to oust the traditional Jewish leadership—his rendition of the "Jewish condition" in America was far from fanciful. What amplified his sense of alarm was the plight of German Jewry. While he did not draw parallels between America and Germany, he did identify a common danger: the willingness of the privileged and the powerful to surrender their Jewish consciousness and to entrust their security to the tenets of emancipation. Nazism, in his view, had proved them wrong. Wise interpreted the current situation of German Jews as "inwardly safer" than in the pre-Hitler days, when their lives had been "a most unconvincing sham and pretext."[91]

Like many contemporary American Jews, Wise had first traveled down the road of assimilation, only to despair of its achievements and return to Jewish ethnicity. Using a negative dialectic, he argued that the American Jew was not safe "if he must feel that he dare not be as completely and unequivocally and rejoicingly Jewish" as others who take pride and joy in their heritage; if he "imagines that it is necessary for him to surrender his Jewishness, to pretend to be other than what he is." "The mere fact" that American Jews "are bidden by their own and sometimes by those outside of our own life to be careful lest we give offense to the possessing and powerful groups in American life is a pitiable sign of Jewish insecurity."[92]

But Wise himself had adopted the very same rules of behavior for which he castigated his fellow Jews. As an appointee serving on the New York City Affairs Committee, a non-partisan body for civic reconstruction, he was alarmed by the fact that three of its four members were Jews. In a letter to his close friend John Holmes, who was a member of the Committee and a church leader, he wrote that it was "a very great mistake" that official communications were signed by three Jews. This created the impression, he added, that the Committee was "Jewishly controlled" or a "Free Synagogue Auxiliary." Wise suggested it would be best if Holmes signed all communications alone. "The names Guggenheimer, Goldstein and Wise are too much even for me," he concluded.[93] Those who analyze the psyche would probably diagnose his behavior as "counterphobic."

These painful truths found their way into Jewish folklore as well. The following lyric, written for a 1934 stage show, is narrated in self-mocking imagery:

> The Brotherhood has for its aim,
> A Rabbi with an Anglo-Saxon name,
> Whose application we'll have to decline,

If his name ends in -vich, or -sky or -stein.
In addition to being an Aryan,
He must be a Parliamentarian,
Who can table a motion and squelch hubbub
And who'll represent the Temple at the Rot'ry club.[94]

Indeed, even in the particular Jewish sphere there were "rites of passage." One had to become more like "them," to be acceptable to "them"—to the various establishments of the majority culture. To gain recognition, if not acceptance, meant tempering the particular Jewish voice to make it moderate in tone and inoffensive in substance, a voice that could harmonize with the political and cultural tune of the majority.

Yet there were also Jews who spearheaded the idea of cultural pluralism, advocating the fostering of minority cultures and group differences as a basis of the American nationality. Rabbi Abba Hillel Silver, the zealous Zionist leader, used this argument to counter the charge that excessive Jewish solidarity was detrimental to the American social fabric. Silver linked the current criticism directed at the Jewish community to its activities on behalf of the German Jews and rhetorically asked whether the desire of American Jews to organize in defense of their persecuted fellow Jews in Europe created a threat of "rebellion against common and wholesome social tendencies," and interfered in "the common life of the community," as Joseph McAfee had concluded.[95]

Indeed, the attempt to comprehend the meaning of Nazi anti-Semitism was making American Jews increasingly convinced that to yield all "differences" in the name of total assimilation was not a panacea for the anti-Jewish disease. On the contrary, as Rabbi Silver argued, "the most virulent anti-semitism developed in Germany, and in place of a self-willed 'difference,' a legal, proscriptive and discriminating 'difference' was forced upon them [German Jews] as a mark of shame." In light of the German case, "social unity" or "cultural unity" as advocated by the spokesmen of America's majority culture appeared to be "just as dangerous a slogan" as "racial unity." Carrying this view to extremes, Rabbi Silver wondered whether in America there was not, albeit unconsciously, a similar craving for a "social and cultural *Gleichschaltung* after the model of Nazi *Deutschtum*, an American species of 'national concentration' of the variety which was devastating the free life of Europe" at that time.[96]

Ostensibly American Jews were continuing the vehement debate that had originated with the struggle for emancipation. But by the 1930s the traditional polemic of "to be or not to be"—to assimilate into Gentile society or to preserve a separate Jewish identity—had lost much of its relevance as it became more and more apparent that neither option was acceptable to the surrounding society. That the dispute raged on only proved that consciousness always lags behind reality. However, the quest for unequivocal acceptance was pursued fervently by all American Jews, regardless of whether they wished to be accepted as "similar" or as "different." As elsewhere, their quest entailed remolding the Jews' image, purging it of the common stigmas historically attached to it and endowing it with virtues respected by all nations.

"Jews Calmly Await Hitler's Policies"

The yearning to nullify the image of Jewish powerlessness often generated a rhetoric of Jewish might that had little in common with reality. The editorial in the *American Hebrew* of January 20, 1933, for example, condemned as "enemies of the Polish Jews" those Jewish opinion makers who portrayed their situation as "deathly." Having been "accustomed to hardships and struggle" it was certain that the Polish Jews "will not surrender." As courageous fighters who are "not resignedly waiting for the undertaker," they were proclaimed worthy of American Jews' help.[97]

Upon Hitler's appointment as chancellor, the Centralverein issued a statement in which it expressed its conviction that "none will dare to infringe upon our [German Jews'] constitutional rights. Any attempt to the contrary will meet with our most determined position for the defense of our constitutional rights. Our slogan today is: 'We calmly wait.'" The *American Hebrew* accordingly titled its first editorial following Hitler's accession to power, "Jews Calmly Await Hitler's Policies."[98] Regardless of whether the C.V.'s declaration was a true reflection of the mood among Germany's Jews, the Jewish community leaders in America took pride in their response since it was poised, rational, and above all assertive. These self-appointed leaders felt uneasy with the traditional paradigm that made heroes of victimized Jews. It wished to abolish this Jewish uniqueness and make the Jews *ke-khol ha-goyim* (like all the other nations). The extent to which American Jewish leaders were anxious about the image of Jews is further demonstrated by Rabbi Stephen Wise's fear that under the pressure of Nazism the Jews "may be moved consciously and deliberately to surrender their ideals" such as democracy and liberalism, peace and cooperation. Invoking the metaphysical conviction that although the Jew was "a victim in every generation," he was a "victor through the ages," he pontificated to his German counterparts that "to battle and even to die for these things is not to make a vain sacrifice," regardless of the suffering and torture they may have to endure. "Better that Jews nobly perish," Wise moralized, "than ignobly survive."[99] These reactions reveal that new elements were beginning to mold the behavior of Jews. A religious tradition coupled with humanistic and liberal thought was now merging with twentieth-century nationalism to create a "normal" collective personality, one that, in addition to asserting moral superiority, would also demonstrate physical endurance.[100]

The interpretation of Nazism by this Jewish elite—the grand beneficiary of the American dream—did not deviate much from that of its American counterpart. As expected in times of uncertainty, these conservatives hoped for the restoration of the status quo, principally in the form of law and order, for disorder was believed to be a temporary phenomenon. Following the September 1930 German elections, the *New York Times* portrayed Hitler's so-called magic spell over the German people as exaggerated and posited that "the net result" of this escapade "should be to bring together the parties and elements in Germany standing for sobriety and the existing political order." A month later, as we saw in the previous chapter, it still maintained that "Germany has no idea of delivering itself over to a madcap Austrian."[101] Resistance to internalizing the metamorphosis that Germany was undergoing ran so deep that even after the March 1933 elections, the voice of reason continued to adhere to its earlier convictions that Hitler would not survive or "invite trouble."[102]

In this spirit the *American Hebrew* took pains to reassure its readership after Hitler's appointment. Citing from the Nazi Party's official bulletin, it reported that Hitler's cabinet was unanimous in its determination to eschew "all policies of suppression, economic adventure and financial experimentation," and was imbued with confidence in the power and institutions of the German state to restore order. The writer could even find parallels within the American experience. President von Hindenburg and his collaborator Franz von Papen had taken "a leaf out of the book of Abraham Lincoln, brought their enemies into the camp where they can watch them, perhaps control them, possibly bend them into the twig that shall make the newer German tree." "Upon analysis," he further reflected, "the possibility of carrying out the dangerous Nazi international program, or the violent medieval Nazi threats against the Jews of Germany in particular, seems to have been checkmated by the manner in which the Cabinet was carefully constituted."[103]

This editorial reflected the Jewish elite's desire to believe that rationality would prevail among German conservatives. They wished to assume that the leader of the DNVP, Alfred Hugenberg, for instance, would not support the Nazi anti-Jewish program; and they were confident that "von Papen and the rest of the Conservatives certainly will not."[104] These observers seemed to have been persuaded by von Papen's assertion that *"wir haben ihn uns engagiert"* (we [the conservatives] have roped him [Hitler] in). In fact, most of the prominently positioned onlookers accepted von Papen's evaluation that "in two months we'll have pushed Hitler into a corner."[105]

The results of the March 5th elections, when analyzed from a particular perspective, did little more than to "agitate the mind" of the uptown American Jews. In its March 10, 1933, issue, the *American Hebrew* sought to placate those Jews who experienced "apprehensions" about the results of the elections. Anxiety, it argued, was the result of being "unmindful" of the wider historical perspective of anti-Jewish persecution. In their thinking it was imperative to remember that in spite of the "machinations of Haman the Persian there are Jews in Persia," and so, it deduced, after the "cunning of Hitler the Prussian," one could "vision the time beyond Hitler."[106] The eve of Passover 1933 provided an occasion to contemplate the history of Jewish redemptions with "a sense of awe and inner excitement of promise." This year, the whole catalog of Pharaohs, from the unnamed tyrants of the Exodus to the latest madman in Germany, will pass in an unholy panorama on Seder night. Each will make his bow . . . and recite his piece of passion, fury and fanaticism and fade onto the limbo of forgetfulness.

We are strengthened in the faith that even the steel helmet of Hitlerism will not for long grind our brethren into dust.[107]

It is of particular interest that in times of distress even the most assimilated Jews clung to the traditional faith in the eternity of the Jewish people. Those who did not wish to rely on religion or on the idea of a Jewish national state had no choice but to turn to Jewish history in search of an explanation for the Jewish people's past and as a source of faith in their future.[108] But the mythohistorical spirit, other than providing hope, may also have encouraged hazardous illusions. Such were the "half a dozen possibilities" that were described in the *American Hebrew* after the March 5th elections, "from which can be deduced conditions that may work out favorably for the Jews of Germany." In the editor's reading of the situation even a Reichstag in name only was better than an absolute dictatorship; should it adjourn, anti-Jewish legislation would be less likely to originate with a dozen responsible cabinet members than in an assembly of 650. Even if these reputable conservatives were dismissed, there would still remain the option of an appeal to President von Hindenburg. Subjugating the German Jews economically would appear to be the height of folly and would retard the process of national reconstruction. Finally, the editors concluded, German *Kultur*, free now to work out its destiny on the Nazi platform, would not descend to the low level of Poland. It was "within reason to believe that the anti-Jewish agitations . . . will now decline, if they do not cease altogether. The inspiration that provoked the resuscitation of the medieval lies and libels against the Jews . . . were meant [as] a scapegoat to the . . . depressed populace; to arouse pre-election hysteria and bring Nazi victory. This objective was achieved March 5th."[109]

It is not so surprising that the Nazi regime was initially perceived by some American Jewish opinion makers as manageable, evoking reactions that entailed options. Those elements that were deemed most threatening, such as the economic restrictions imposed on the Jews, were dismissed as totally untenable and irrational. That was not always the case among German Jews themselves. Some of them endorsed the economic program of the right-wing parties and wished to participate in its implementation, cognizant of the fact that "in a completely illogical way" they were prevented from joining the national reconstruction effort, since these parties "associated their economic and political goals with a fight against Jewry."[110] The significance of the racial elements of the National Socialist ideology as a blueprint of Hitler's rule eluded American Jewry for quite some time. They were thus able to construe the situation in Germany as a temporary anomaly, even finding parallels in American society. The fact that there would be no Jews in the German public service, for instance, was not a cause for alarm, since after all there were "no

Jews in the Nazi political party. And even in the United States the political spoils still belong to the victor." In the same vein it did not seem far-fetched to surmise that when the German government did begin to attend to its serious problems, it would "sober up on the Jewish question" since "after all, Germany is not a backward nation."[111]

In general, the American Jewish establishment's initial perceptions of Hitler's accession to power were rooted in a universalist weltanschauung whose spirit was the German Enlightenment and whose incarnation was American democracy. From this dual perspective the German Jewish problem qua Jewish dissipated, allowing the leading American Jews to "guess" that the German government and the German people would "make the portrait of new Germany on the design and the pattern of Britain and America." The writer of these words was quite clear about his identity, asserting that these assessments were those of "an American and are written from the point of view of American democracy."[112]

"We protest not for our own sake"

Arguing the Jewish case on the basis of universal-American principles (read also, interests)—although at times interpreted differently—was the strategy of both the AJC and the AJ Congress. Their recommended actions as well as their expected effectiveness were linked to the "approval" of the government and "the American people as a whole."[113] In an absorbing exercise of collective preservation, Jewish power brokers demonstrated mastery in walking a tightrope over an abyss. By viewing themselves as part of the civilized world, they could claim its power as their own while at the same time admitting their powerlessness as Jews. A suggestive version of this self-deceptive narrative appeared as follows: "We, as Jews must protest again and again. But . . . in harmony with the protests that have gone out . . . from other parts of the world. . . . Not a useless threat by a minority group that could not and would not frighten the Hitlerites in Germany."[114] Similarly, AJC President Cyrus Adler called on the Jews to speak out not "solely because Jews were being oppressed in Germany but because human liberty was being taken away from people, from Jews and from other people." Not until such a position was adopted, he warned, could American Jews expect to "get the real sympathy of the larger part of our fellow citizens." Although Adler acknowledged that his views might be interpreted as cowardly, he believed that his was "the decent attitude."[115]

When pressured by the State Department to oppose the economic boycott against Germany, the Jewish apostles of Americanism reacted even more vehemently. In a newspaper interview in early 1935, Proskauer called on his coreligionists "to do everything in our power to relieve the distress not only of the oppressed Jews of Germany but of the oppressed non-Jews." As to the duty of American Jews, they were expected to "conform with absolute fidelity and loyalty to our primary obligations as American citizens."[116] As Jerold Auerbach deduced, this in effect amounted to asking the Jews to accept second-class citizenship in return for acceptance as first-class Americans.[117]

The behavior of the AJ Congress leaders in response to the German crisis reflected the attempt to maintain the rationale of being "a man in the street and a Jew at home."[118] The lead advocate of this behavior was Rabbi Stephen Wise. As a Jew at home we have already heard him preach against surrendering Jewishness. But in the street his organization reacted to Hitler's rise to power in much the same way as did the ostensibly more Americanized American Jewish Committee. The Congress's press release of January 30, 1933, praised the German people for being "noteworthy among Europeans for their firmness of character, natural justice, and intelligence" and appealed to the "sober common sense" of the parties cooperating with Hitler and of President Hindenburg.[119] Wise still held to his earlier perception that Hitler was "more formidable in partial defeat" than in triumph. He expressed optimism that a sense of governmental responsibility would prevail upon the actions and policies of Hitler and his party.[120]

On March 27, 1933, during the first major mass protest meeting against "anti-Jewish wrongs," held at Madison Square Garden, Wise appealed to the "Conscience of the World."[121] This took place some three weeks after Hitler had obtained, together with his nationalist allies, 51.9 percent of the votes and had formed a majority government, and after the endorsement of the Enabling Act, which effectively put an end to the authority of parliament and the constitutional organs of control. Yet, as a noted civil libertarian, Stephen Wise, like most other Jewish leaders, did not reproach the German people. "This protest tonight," he proclaimed before the huge crowd,

> is not against the German people whom we honor and revere and cherish. . . . [It] is not against the political program of Germany, for Germany is a master within her own household. . . . It is an unforgivable calumny to declare that we are *"Deutschfeindlich."* . . . Because we are the friends of Germany . . . we appeal to Germany in the name of America which has been stirred as rarely before against wrongs perpetrated upon Jews.[122]

Jewish leaders were yet to discover that to arouse the voice of America on behalf of Jews was not an easy task. It was certainly far from a foregone conclusion that they could do so.

The struggle against Hitlerism impelled Jewish leaders to contemplate their own situation as Jews in America. The image of America they cherished was no longer a faithful copy of reality. Those who could face the disillusion painfully admitted that for Jews in America who wished to help their German counterparts "it hurts to be muzzled." Yet, as the speaker here, Judge Irving Lehman, confessed, "When I have an impulse to speak, I do not feel that I can speak as other American citizens; I feel especially responsible for the first time because I am a Jew."[123] Although the leaders of the Committee had often

explained their hush-hush response as a demonstration of their sense of responsibility—be it toward their own constituency or toward their German
counterparts—playing the diplomatic ostrich was dictated by their American
reality.

The AJ Congress leaders were scathing about the "conservative responsible and thoughtful" Jew. In Julian Mack's portrayal, he was "more fascistic
than the government and . . . the first to blame all the anti-Semitism on the
liberal, radical, and, of course, the communistic element in Jewry. These conservative Jews . . . are dead scared of anybody who risks standing up for his
rights and saying what he thinks."[124] But here again action did not necessarily
follow from perception. When the Provisional Committee for Protest against
German Fascist Atrocities was formed under the sponsorship of a group of
liberals led by Professor James Shotwell, Mack was invited to join. As an exemplary American, a former professor at Northwestern University and the
University of Chicago, and a judge of the U.S. Circuit Court of Appeal since
1911, Mack declined. "Much as I should like to join the committee," he explained, "it seems to me best that Jews who are at all prominent in Jewish
matters would better keep off of the committee. It is, of course, not a matter
of logic; it is just a question of the best practical way of dealing with the
terrible situation."[125]

And terrible it was. It made clear the precarious status of the Jews in America. While recognizing the cowardliness of his decision, Mack admitted that
as a prominent Jew his behavior was circumscribed by the fact that in America he was judged first and foremost as a Jew. Lest it be suspected that his refusal to join was proof of a narrow particular Jewish worldview, he added that
"of course" his sympathies and those of every liberal "are as strongly against
the Fascist views as they are against the anti-Semitic phase of the Hitler
crowd."[126]

Indeed, while anti-Nazi Jewish protests were inhibited by disapproval on
the right, they were also criticized by the left for confining their battle to
sectarian interests—a view that was paradoxically also the prevailing ideology
of the conservative Jewish elements. Shortly after the Madison Square Garden protest rally, *The New Republic* voiced regret in its editorial "that whether
accidentally or by design they [the Jews] have said hardly a word about the
suffering of other German groups which are feeling the iron heel of a bloody
tyranny even more severely." Similarly, Dorothy Thompson and Benjamin
Stolberg criticized the American Jewish Congress for confining all protests
to the persecution of the German Jews.[127] Rabbi Wise seems to have anticipated these reproaches but evidently thought that a grand gallery of Christian speakers would constitute a shield. In describing to Mack the radio
broadcast that followed the Madison Square Garden rally, he called his attention to the fact that "we put only Christian speakers on the air."[128]

American Jewish leaders, whatever their ideology, were quick to realize, if
not to admit, that "the destiny of the Jews, a small and scattered people, is in

the hands of larger forces." Not only were these to be supported, but, in order to ensure that the plight of the Jews would find its way on to the agenda of the civilized world, it was necessary to "observe restraint in behavior that will evoke respect and goodwill instead of aversion and irritation." Summing up the bleak status of the Jews, Morris Waldman, added, "We cannot with impunity ignore the question '*Ma Yomru Ha-Goyim?*' [What will the nations say?]."[129]

The need to enlist non-Jewish public opinion was the first challenge. It was based on the assumption that, as Felix Warburg put it, "While it is useless for the Jews to talk for their own *pro domo*, protests coming from people of standing, non-Jews, make a deep impression."[130] Judge Julian Mack was no less convinced that "the remedy—if there is one—seems . . . to be an aroused public opinion—non-Jewish." In fact, only if that "cannot be done," he advocated, "as a last resort, Jewish meetings and protests."[131] Keenly aware of the Jews' dilemma, the *American Hebrew* concurred with the prevailing opinion that "if the few million Jews of the world are too weak to obtain justice for their German brethren . . . we shall continue to demand it from the conscience of Christendom."[132]

In America of the 1930s, if Jews were to be only catalysts rather than public agitators against the Nazi menace, the campaign had to be publicly de-Judaized. But even those who cooperated with the Jews, their so-called allies, were not necessarily willing to grant them more favorable treatment. Newton Baker, co-chairman of the National Conference of Christians and Jews, for instance, reiterating previous views he had expressed, wished them to be reminded that "other nations have troubles, too, and that the Jews must not merely think of themselves."[133] He therefore refused to take part in Jewish protests. The American Jewish leadership did not necessarily view adapting to the prevailing mood as an act of compromise. For some it was an inherent part of their ideology, for others it had always been a permissible tool of survival.

In March 1934 "The Case of Civilization Against Hitlerism" was presented under the auspices of the American Jewish Congress. Bainbridge Colby, the former secretary of state under Wilson, opened this public "trial" at Madison Square Garden by declaring that tonight "America is speaking" to express its abhorrence of Nazi cruelty and oppression, and exhorted "America [to] detest it." The drift toward non-sectarianism was made even clearer on this occasion by Stephen Wise's proclamations that "we [Jews] are not the only victims of Hitlerism." The Jews were suffering along with other groups, including "the great Catholic Church and the Protestant churches." Hence, he emphasized, "We protest not for our own sake."[134]

The American Jewish Committee also counseled the Jews to stress the broader aspect by arguing "principally that Naziism threatens to destroy the fundamental values of Americanism," and as such "to appeal to Americans for their own protection."[135] But a year later, in 1934, the Jewish leadership was prepared to admit that American Jews had failed to obtain Christian support with regard to the German problem.[136] However, from the beginning of the crisis American Jewish activists were concerned with far more than mobilizing public opinion. Indeed, their major efforts were carried out in the political sphere, both on stage and behind the scenes, where they attempted to gain a hearing on the German crisis with the nation's power holders. It is to these activities that we now turn.

6

Co-optation of Protest
Trying to Break Through, 1933

We are reassured almost as foolishly as we are alarmed;
human nature is so constituted.
——Victor Hugo, *Les Misérables*

Franklin D. Roosevelt's promise to remember the forgotten man and his adamant conviction that national government had a responsibility for the welfare of all of its citizens had a tremendous appeal for American Jewish voters.
Not only did it provide hope in their present dire conditions, it also echoed
with their general liberal-progressive social credo. Though it was less emphasized because of domestic considerations, the fact that the new president
was an internationalist who was committed to the American role in safeguarding the world order was also extremely attractive to American Jews.[1] It was
therefore not surprising that 82 percent of them voted for Roosevelt in the
1932 elections.[2]

The new president became the "master of ethnic politics."[3] He responded
to the millions who feared that the American dream might never become part
of their reality by making them feel accepted as steadfast partners in the national effort to redeem America. For Jews, Roosevelt's promises were visibly
fulfilled as he ushered them in unprecedented numbers into the national halls
of power.[4]

For Jewish leaders who were terribly worried about the conditions of German Jewry, the presence of so many Jews in and around the Roosevelt administration—as official appointees and unofficial advisers—was a source of hope
that their plight would gain a favorable hearing in the nation's capital. Indeed, it was through the Jews who became part of the "Roosevelt court" that
American Jewish leaders tried to mobilize the decision makers to act with
regard to the German situation. The story of how they fared is a multi-lay-
ered story: it tells of the opportunities and limitations for pressure-group
politicking in American political culture; of inter- and intra-Jewish ethnic
politics; and of the impact of integration on a particular group's solidarity.

This chapter will trace the various routes that Jewish leaders explored in their attempts to influence America's policy with regard to Germany's Jews during the first year of Hitler's rule.

The "President's Jews"

There is no doubt that for many American Jews the Roosevelt administration and the New Deal programs provided an unprecedented window of opportunity to enter the ranks of the nation's elite. The fact that Roosevelt and the Democratic Party he led were opposed by much of the nation's established elite had much to do with enabling individual Jews to advance their professional and social status and to establish successful careers in government. Indeed, it was the new regime's diverse needs and the limited opportunities for the talents of Jews in the private sector that linked the two in an unprecedented close association. More than 15 percent of Roosevelt's top-level appointees—attorneys, economists, statisticians, and other professionals—were Jews, at a time when they constituted barely 3 percent of the nation's populace.[5] But of course, for Roosevelt the fact that many of the new recruits were Jews was incidental.

Felix Frankfurter, a Harvard University law professor and a close adviser of FDR, was in effect running a "one-man employment office," as Arthur M. Schlesinger, Jr. described it.[6] With access to a rare pool of much-needed talent, Frankfurter recruited many "happy hot dogs," as the novices he brought to Washington were called, to serve in the new administration and work for the various New Deal agencies and programs.[7]

One of the most important among these New Dealers was Benjamin (Ben) Cohen, who was central to the team that drafted the Securities Exchange Act of 1934, the Public Utility Holding Act of 1935, the Communications Act, the Tennessee Valley Authority Act, the Wagner Act, and the Fair Labor Standards Act. Cohen was considered "the intellectual leader" behind the New Deal legislation, and "even Felix Frankfurter would call him for advice."[8] Other Jews who played significant roles in the Roosevelt administration included Isador Lubin, who was commissioner of the Bureau of Labor Statistics and in effect served as FDR's chief economic advisor, and David Niles, who in later years became White House special assistant. Jews also held a number of prominent positions in the Department of the Interior: Abe Fortas served first as director of the Division of Manpower and later as undersecretary, Saul K. Padover was assistant to the secretary, Nathan Margold served as department solicitor, and Michael Straus as director of the War Resources Council. Charles Wyzanski served as the Department of Labor counsel, David Lilienthal chaired the Tennessee Valley Authority, and Nathan Straus administered the U.S. Housing Authority. Many other Jews staffed important positions in the Justice Department, the Securities and Exchange Commission, the Social Security Administration, the Agricultural Adjustment Administration, and other governmental agencies.

In yet another circle one could find the Jewish experts who were called in on special assignments—men like James P. Warburg and Bernard Baruch, the conservative financiers who offered advice on monetary issues. Baruch, who despite his earlier conservative bent heavily underwrote the Roosevelt campaign, seemed intoxicated by being asked for counsel by the president of the United States. "Apparently," he confided to a friend, "I am to be responsible for the economic side of this whole thing."[9]

In yet another tier of nouveaux powerful Jews were some political supporters. They included such figures as the Lehman brothers—Irving, a judge on the New York Court of Appeal, and Herbert, a prominent banker and Roosevelt's former lieutenant governor and successor in Albany; Henry Morgenthau, Jr., FDR's Dutchess County neighbor who was to become the secretary of the treasury;[10] and Sidney Hillman, president of the Amalgamated Clothing Workers, who played a major role in molding the unions into effective political forces.[11] And there was Samuel (Sam) Rosenman, the New York State judge who is credited with coining the term "New Deal." Active in Democratic Party politics, he was picked from Al Smith's circle and became much more than a speech writer for Roosevelt. His Jewishness was essentially a denominational identity, and like many of this circle he associated himself with the AJC.[12] By his own admission, Rosenman never approached FDR directly on matters pertaining to Jewish issues.[13]

Not all Jews felt comfortable with the growing visibility of their co-religionists as active participants in shaping America's future. Fearing a backlash, the *American Hebrew* played down Jewish participation in government. "There could hardly be fewer Jewish appointees" in the New Deal, it reported, with only one Jew in the Cabinet and none among the undersecretaries of the executive departments. "The Department of Commerce," it reassured its readers, "has not a Jew at its helm."[14] Jerome Frank, the general counsel of the Agricultural Adjustment Administration, for example, wished to limit the number of Jewish lawyers on his staff. An assimilated German Jew from Chicago, Frank viewed the Jewish origin of staff attorneys as an unfortunate "disability," and advised his assistants "if possible to recommend lawyers who are not Jews."[15]

These anxieties about "over-representation" were not groundless. Before long Roosevelt's enemies took to expressing their dismay by evoking the stereotypical image of Jewish power. The New Deal was soon re-labeled the "Jew Deal," and FDR was not insensitive to this criticism. Ben Cohen, for instance, was refused a seat on the Securities and Exchange Commission allegedly because the president feared some possible anti-Semitic backlash from the business community. Some years later, when Harold Ickes asked the president to consider Cohen for assistant secretary of the treasury, the president thought it would be a mistake to place a Jew under Morgenthau.[16]

Yet at times Roosevelt did prove to be more courageous in handling anti-Semitism—particularly when it involved the services of a needed advisor. In the midst of the 1936 presidential run, for example, Sam Rosenman suggested to FDR that he and his wife should stay off the campaign train as it moved through the Midwest Bible Belt. Roosevelt insisted they come along. "That's no way to handle anti-Semitism" he chided his aide; "the way to handle it is to meet it head-on."[17] The Rosenmans went on the train ride, undoubtedly convinced that the Jews had a friend in the White House. A short addendum: When FDR offered Rosenman the post of director of the office of economic stabilization in 1945, he declined, fearing anti-Semitic criticism.[18]

Undoubtedly, however, the first row in the presidential gallery of Jewish advisers was occupied by Louis D. Brandeis and Felix Frankfurter. Both Brandeis, who was appointed to the Supreme Court in 1916, and Frankfurter, who was the only tenured Jew on the Harvard faculty for twenty-five years, can be considered part of the nation's elite. However, the term "outside elite" would more precisely define their status. Indeed, in one of his letters to Roosevelt, Frankfurter portrayed himself as an "outside insider."[19] It is therefore not surprising, perhaps, that when the president invited him to join the administration as solicitor general in March 1933, he replied that he could be of best service as a professional freelancer.[20] On the same occasion, Roosevelt acknowledged that Frankfurter "ought to be on the Supreme Court," but added that among other factors—which could be mitigated by serving as a solicitor general—his "race" might work against his appointment.[21] We do not know if, or what, Frankfurter answered FDR. What we do know, however, is that when his name began circulating as a likely candidate to replace Benjamin Cardozo on the high court in late 1938 and a number of Jews petitioned against his appointment, he could hardly contain his anger about

> prominent Jews who are unwittingly embracing Hitlerism by actually sponsoring a position of political inferiority and second-rate citizenship for Jews. For their suggestion that Jews should not be called to public life because they are Jews is for me completely undistinguishable from Nazism.[22]

Frankfurter seemed understanding when fear of an anti-Semitic backlash originated with Roosevelt. But he was "shocked out of his boots" when it came from one of his own.[23] Whatever the source of his drive to become an insider—whether to justify his primary loyalty to America or to overcome the anti-Semitism that he encountered throughout his career—Frankfurter, like the rest of the Jews who struggled for acceptance, adhered strictly to the rules of survival he knew so well.[24] Thus, although, and perhaps because, the Oval Office and FDR's private ears were so accessible to him, he seldom permitted himself to directly approach his benefactor to further Jewish interests.

An entry visa, however conditional, to America's elite circle required a certain demeanor. The following incident, although extreme, is rather telling about the price some Jews felt they had to pay for conditional acceptance. When it became known to Frankfurter that his aged uncle, a renowned scholar with the national library in Vienna, had been placed in a concentration camp, he turned to Lady Nancy Astor, who was known to dislike Jews and to be friendly with some of the leaders of the new Germany, to secure his release.[25] In late 1941 the uncle died and the New York press reported that his release back in 1938 had been secured through the State Department. Appalled by such an "allegation" which might have embarrassed his friend the president, Frankfurter, wishing to set the record straight, wrote to Roosevelt:

> Precisely because I wanted to avoid criticism even of the evil-minded and hard-hearted against any charge of favoritism by your administration, I did *not* invoke the good offices of the State Department. On the contrary, I secured his release through the kindness of Lady Astor's intervention with her then German friends.[26]

When the president replied that "even a Justice of the Supreme Court is entitled to ask his own Government to help out persecuted people, even though they be his own close relatives, in any part of the world," Frankfurter thought it was "most sweet" of "Frank" to write to him, adding about his uncle that "he kept his soul free."[27] Frankfurter could not and did not make such a claim for himself.

Judge Louis L. Brandeis—"Isaiah," the "old prophet," as he came to be known by Roosevelt's inner circle—was "neither insider nor outsider," but "poised always at the boundary."[28] In Washington he was held in the highest awe as the moral voice that spoke out of a stark and formidable rationalism. Rexford Tugwell, a member of Roosevelt's early "Brains Trust" and one of his future biographers, attributed Brandeis's impact on the president to two factors: the first factor was Brandeis's "disciples"—the first in his hierarchy, he noted, was Frankfurter—and the second, his ability to advise the president on the constitutionality of his legislative enactments.[29] Yet no matter how successfully Brandeis prevailed over social and professional barriers, his ongoing concern with defining what constituted loyal Americanism and his eagerness to conflate Jewish values and American ideals seem to reveal his unease with calling attention to Jewish distinctiveness.[30] Observing his position as a Supreme Court Justice most punctiliously, Brandeis employed Frankfurter as a conduit to communicate his ideas to the president. In October 1938, on the single occasion that he met with FDR while on the bench, he tried to persuade him to keep the gates to Palestine wide open for German refugees. The president, as always, was "sympathetic."[31]

In a collective portrait of this "inside-outside" elite, two main features stand out: an impeccable record of solid Americanism and a virtually eclipsed Jewish identity, which together might deflect the charge of dual loyalty. When assuming the mantle of Zionist leadership, Brandeis was honest enough to confess, "I have been to a great extent separated from Jews. I am very ignorant in things Jewish."[32] Indeed, he defined Zionism in a way that robbed it of Jewish content. For him Judaism was meaningful as a source of American ideals, and Zionism was most valued for its identification with American patriotism. "Let no American imagine," he admonished, "that Zionism is inconsistent with Patriotism."[33] For Frankfurter as well, his Jewish origin was not an inconsequential mark of identity. He struggled to elude the particularities of his Jewishness, as when he insisted, for example, "I was not a Jewish professor at the Harvard Law School, but I was a Harvard Law School professor who happened to be a Jew." In the same vein, as he once explained to President Wilson, his commitment to Zionism expressed his feelings as "a passionate American."[34]

These prominent Jews, although often criticized within the Jewish community for their alienation from Jewish life, were perceived as most powerful on the "outside," and therefore as indispensable. Throughout the German crisis and the Second World War, most of them were approached by various Jewish leaders for some sort of help. In 1933, when Rabbi Stephen Wise was nearly "a solitary voice crying out in the wilderness"[35] against the Nazis' madness which crisis-ridden America largely ignored or dismissed, he chose to turn to none other than Brandeis and Frankfurter, in the hope that they would usher him into the Washington halls of power.[36] The heads of Jewish organizations had mistakenly believed that the president's Jews, as I call the influential Jews in and around the White House, would enhance Jewish power on the national political scene. This hope was misplaced. Whether it was based on the proverbial legacy of Jewish solidarity—commonly resurrected during times of crisis—or reflected a misconception about the nature of power, it resulted in the anomalous situation where a handful of citizens in the service of their nation, who happened to be Jews, were expected to act in the name of a particular group. But the reality was different. The Jews who "arrived" in the nation's capital did so on the basis of their drive and talent and the administration's need for them. For their part, these experts came to serve, first and foremost, the big "R" and his three little "r's"—relief, recovery, and reform. Not only did they not necessarily identify with the Jewish collective "we," but the few who did felt very reluctant to use their influence to advocate particular Jewish causes. On the contrary, as servants of the American government the president's Jews often tried to bring the actions of the Jewish leadership in line with the administration's interests. Yet the Jewish presence in and around the government and the Oval Office played a role in occasionally facilitating, but mostly hampering, the efforts of the Jewish leaders to engage the concern of decision makers for the plight of German Jewry.

Groping for Influence

During the early months of the German crisis two objectives dominated the American Jewish agenda: to persuade the United States government of the need for official representation to Germany concerning its anti-Jewish declarations, and to solicit a public statement of condemnation, preferably by Roosevelt, concerning Jewish persecution. While these two matters were obviously related, they in fact entailed an attempt to influence what in the 1930s were two nearly separate domains: foreign and domestic policy. Pursuing the behind-the-scenes routes that the Jewish leaders explored as they attempted to break through the political enclave and alert the administration to the Nazi menace may provide an important perspective from which to understand the predicaments which the American Jewish leaders had to face in these dire times.

The AJC had traditionally supported the approach of backstairs diplomacy. Trusting that its leadership was sufficiently well connected to Roosevelt's "court Jews"—many of whom were affiliated with the Committee—it relied on them to serve as go-betweens with the Washington power brokers. In early January 1933, Cyrus Adler urged Irving Lehman to approach the president-elect and impress upon him the need for official diplomatic intervention. Adler did not accept the State Department's position, which considered the plight of German Jews to be a domestic German affair and hence above intervention. He pressed instead to return to the pre–World War One American policy of supporting representation on humanitarian grounds.[37]

But Irving Lehman was not just a member of the American Jewish Committee. He was also a judge on the New York State Court of Appeals; a brother of the newly elected governor of New York, Herbert Lehman; an activist in New York Democratic politics; and an old friend of Roosevelt. Lehman's response demonstrated his various interests and affiliations. While expressing understanding and sympathy for Adler's request, Lehman had reservations about whether the State Department could make any representation to a foreign government unless American interests, "however widely defined," were directly involved. Hence, he reasoned, under the present circumstances,

> a representation on any other ground other than the protection of American interest is in itself an insult to a foreign nation which would be justified only under extreme conditions. . . . Frankly, my opinion is that if the American Jewish Committee desires to present to the new administration a plea for a more extreme attitude than I have outlined, that plea would, I think, not meet with a sympathetic reception and a conference would serve little purpose.[38]

To avoid being considered a nuisance and to give the new administration time to adjust, Lehman suggested waiting until May or June to approach the White House with regard to diplomatic intercession.[39]

In February 1933, Rabbi Wise and Bernard S. Deutsch, the titular head of the American Jewish Congress, met with the German ambassador to the United States, Baron von Prittwitz. To approach directly the top representative of a foreign state was apparently easier and less fraught with diplomatic or psychological barriers than to reach one's own political elite. Attempting to placate the first Jewish notables to approach him, Prittwitz opined that Hitler's pronouncements before his appointment were no more than campaign propaganda and added that Hitler would not win the upcoming elections. Wise asked the ambassador to express his opinions publicly so as to reassure the concerned American Jews, which he naturally refused to do.[40] Reporting on the meeting to Wilhelmstrasse, von Prittwitz wrote in a somewhat self-protective tone—perhaps justifying his meeting with Jewish representatives—that it had not been an attempt to intervene in the internal affairs of Germany, but an effort on his part to appease Jewish fears in order to prevent the emergence of negative American public opinion toward Germany.[41] Recalling this meeting in his autobiography, Wise wrote that while he felt "anger," the ambassador projected "chiefly sorrow" and "slightly concealed shame" over the conduct of his country.[42]

Neither of these first two independent forays into the domain of foreign affairs bore any fruit. These early failures may have been instrumental in convincing the leadership of the need for a united Jewish front. In early 1933 Alfred M. Cohen, the president of B'nai B'rith, suggested that together with the American Jewish Committee and the American Jewish Congress, the "Big Three" should convene to discuss the establishment of a unified front to deal specifically with the German situation. The meeting took place on February 22nd. It was decided to establish a Joint Conference Committee (which was re-established in June as the Joint Consultative Council) that would discuss and coordinate the response of the participating organizations. Other ideas that enjoyed a general consensus were the essential need to recruit non-Jewish cooperation in the fight against Hitler and the importance of a united effort to gain a hearing with the president-elect concerning the appointment of a sympathetic American ambassador to Germany.[43] However, this attempt at building a unified front lasted a mere three weeks. When the AJ Congress began its preparations for the much-opposed protest rally at Madison Square Garden, the almost inevitable split occurred.[44] It is not unusual, of course, for rival groups to have some degree of common interest. However, the ability to translate common interest into a powerful tool depends on a willingness to overcome differences and pool resources together for an ad hoc coalition. And it is usually at this juncture, where the powerless may advance their position by unity, that the powerful regain the upper hand—for it seems that the closer one comes to realizing a chance for power, the less willing one is to share it.

Historically, American political culture has encouraged its citizens to participate in the political process, provided they recognize the primacy of national interests. Yet in America of the 1930s Jewish support of a particular interest, even when clad as a national interest, was not only politically naive but daring as well. However, it appeared that the self-appointed Jewish leaders, using different means for essentially similar ends, were ready for the challenge.

Revealing political acumen, the heads of the American Jewish Committee did not wait for Roosevelt to take up occupancy in the White House. They searched for routes to touch base with the president-elect with regard to Germany's persecution of the Jews, hoping that during the interregnum period the more relaxed atmosphere that normally characterizes a lame duck administration would work to their advantage. Through the good offices of the New York financier Lewis L. Strauss, President Hoover was approached on his last day in office with a request that the State Department check press reports concerning a German anti-Jewish plan.[45] In fact, American Ambassador Sackett had conferred with German Minister of Foreign Affairs Konstantin von Neurath regarding this matter some hours before. But Strauss's original plan was to have Hoover and Roosevelt dispatch a joint message to the German government. It did not materialize, for the president-elect chose to remain silent.[46]

Containment of Protest

On March 4, 1933, Franklin D. Roosevelt took the oath of office. His inauguration speech was addressed to a nation in despair. Stating his priorities on the domestic front, he declared that "this nation asks for action, and action now. . . . Our greatest primary task is to put people to work." In the sphere of foreign relations, America remained dedicated to the "good neighbor" policy. But as for international economic relations, while acknowledging their great importance, he made clear that they were "secondary to the establishment of a sound national economy."[47]

The next day, March 5th, the election results gave Adolf Hitler a right-wing majority in the Reichstag. "Contrary to his usual habit, he refrained on this occasion from issuing a triumphant proclamation to his party comrades, the SA and the SS." Instead he gave his loyal supporters the opportunity "to stage revolutionary-styled operations throughout the country—to hoist swastika and black-white-red flags on buildings, to arrest undesirable persons." At the same time, "Hitler was preoccupied with installing Reich Commissars in all of the non-National Socialist Länder."[48]

Although it was a Sunday, Roosevelt did not take time out to celebrate his victory. According to his diary, which he abandoned after two days, he kept a busy schedule on his first day in office. After attending church and having lunch with his family and friends, he met in the Oval Office "with all members of the Cabinet, Vice-President, and Speaker Rainey, outlining banking situation." This was followed by a meeting of members of both houses of Congress. After dinner he met with Professor Warren and with members of the press and gave a five-minute radio address. Close to midnight he received the secretary of state.[49]

FDR's attention during his first week in office was dominated by the domestic economic predicaments, but the sphere of foreign affairs was not neglected. His first priority on the international agenda was to rescue the Geneva Disarmament Conference, which seemed on the verge of collapse. Shortly after, he began his efforts to create a favorable mood for convening an international economic conference. After receiving British Prime Minister Ramsay MacDonald's agreement to come to Washington to reach "some fundamental understanding," Roosevelt issued invitations to ten nations in "good standing" in the international community. France, China, Japan, Italy, and Germany were among them.[50]

Preoccupied with domestic crisis and wary of political opposition to bold foreign policy initiatives, Roosevelt's new administration did not respond to the "spontaneous" anti-Jewish outbursts following the March elections in Germany.[51] However, American Jewish leaders could not remain indifferent. Because of their faith in FDR, reaching the Oval Office was their primary aim. Their course was fraught with obstacles as they learned to walk the tight-rope of trying to balance their Americanism with their Jewishness. Not un-like Adler's quest for representation which had been checked by Lehman's intervention, the steps of the American Jewish Congress representatives were also closely controlled by their own Jewish agents in Roosevelt's court. In-deed, as soon as the new president took up occupancy of the White House, the rules of behavior for the leaders of Jewish organizations vis-à-vis the ad-ministration became more stringent. To approach their own American po-litical establishment on particular Jewish issues was historically a most un-comfortable matter for the Jewish power brokers. In the case of Roosevelt —surrounded by many Jews who were helping him to deal with the calami-tous national situation—it had become an even more delicate task.

A variety of tactics was employed to overcome the discomfort of present-ing particular Jewish demands. One tactic was to approach the president of the United States on behalf of a third party. This is precisely what Governor Herbert Lehman did in early March when he conveyed to Roosevelt an ap-peal on behalf of British Jewish leaders to "consider appropriate means of urging German Government to take . . . steps . . . to reassure foreign Jewish opinion by ensuring fullest protection for all peaceful and law-abiding citi-zens and residents without distinction of race or creed."[52]

On March 8th, three days after Roosevelt took the oath of office, Nazi Germany celebrated is own electoral victory with anti-Jewish riots that re-sulted in bloodshed. That same day Stephen Wise pondered whether to "try to break through" and see the president, "or whether it was not quiet [sic] fair to trouble Roosevelt at this time."[53] Wise was not free to decide on his own. Conforming to a strict hierarchical structure, he called on Brandeis for a rul-ing. The justice was of the opinion that "it would make a bad impression on Roosevelt, in the midst of his overwhelming responsibilities . . . to trou-ble him with our, in a sense, lesser problem."[54] Frankfurter agreed with this ruling.

The president's Jews increasingly emerged as FDR's task force, shielding him from what they or he may have considered unwarranted or untimely pressure. These loyalists—Brandeis, Frankfurter, Lehman, and Rosenman— in effect functioned as a defense cordon, blocking or at least controlling the access of Jewish leaders to the White House. Even Wise, who in the eyes of the rank and file was the commanding general of the anti-German protest movement, behaved as a regular obedient soldier in his dealings with the president's Jews. In this instance, as we have seen, Brandeis did not approve approaching the "Chief" but consented to Wise's "trying to get to [Senators] Borah and Pittman" to accompany him on a meeting with Secretary of State Hull to convince him "to communicate with Berlin." Two days later Wise was off to Washington to confer with "LDB." and "FF.[55]"

The fact that Wise's exertions were tempered by his "superior" was not enough to check the mounting grassroots pressure on the AJ Congress from its constituent organizations and the Yiddish press (particularly from Samuel Margoshes, the editor of *Der Tog*) to protest against conditions in Germany. During the national executive committee meeting of March 12th, a resolution was proposed to sponsor a series of meetings "to voice the protest of the American people against the outrages committed against the Jewish citizens of Germany and to call upon the civilized peoples of the world to express their disapproval of the tacit conduct of the German Government in the face of attacks upon peaceful citizens."[56]

The resolution was carefully worded; it did not call on the U.S. government to act, and spoke only on behalf of German Jewish *citizens*. But even this watered-down agenda must have felt excessive to Wise and Deutsch, for they attempted to block its passage. But they failed. In accordance with the resolution, an emergency conference of national and local Jewish organizations was convened by the AJ Congress on March 19th, attended by over 1,500 frustrated representatives. Aware of the antagonism of the masses to the "counselors of inaction," the AJ Congress's Bernard S. Deutsch informed the audience that demands for protest action had "flooded" the offices of the Congress. "We are here today," he proclaimed, "to translate this popular mandate into responsible, vigorous, orderly and effective action."[57] The appeal was designed to play on the two most sensitive nerves of his audience:

> This tragic hour in Jewish history calls imperatively for the solidarity of the Jewish people. And we American Jews are resolved to stand shoulder to shoulder with our brother Jews in Germany. . . .
> As Americans who believe in the brotherhood of man, we invite [you] to join with us in a demonstration of American faith in the sacredness of human rights and sanctity of human fellowship.[58]

But rhetoric alone, even if adorned with such catchphrases as Jewish solidarity and human rights, was no longer adequate. J. George Fredman, the commander in chief of the Jewish War Veterans (JWV), proposed an amendment calling for action in the form of a boycott of German goods. The AJC was adamantly against such an idea. One of its spokesmen, Judge Joseph Proskauer, supported his own criticism of a boycott by reading a letter drafted for this occasion by Irving Lehman, who could not attend due to pressing business in Albany. His message was characteristic of the thinking that prevailed in the more assimilated camp. "I implore you in the name of humanity," he admonished, "don't let anger pass a resolution which will kill Jews in Germany."[59]

Nonetheless Fredman's amendment for an organized boycott gained wide support on the floor, but Wise and Deutsch, while backing the resolution for a day of national protest, managed to defeat this amendment.[60] Jews in public life had developed what Stephen Isaacs has perceptively described as "a sophisticated, subterranean scanning system," with regard to what was acceptable and what was not.[61] Under the banner of a purely abstract faith in

"Americanism" it was permissible to voice protest in the name of values sanctioned by the general consensus. An official declaration of a boycott against a "friendly" foreign government was not only contrary to the sacred principle of "national interest," but could also be interpreted as a separatist act that implied distrust in the system. It was understandable that the Jewish establishment was reluctant to authorize such a program. What may on the face of it seem more puzzling is that this "unpatriotic" idea originated with a veterans' group. But the inherent instrumentality of the rhetoric of patriotism has many facets, and American Jews were not unique in enlisting it for their own purpose.

Although mass demonstrations can be delusory as social action, as Earl Raab has aptly pointed out, they can also be therapeutic in times of frustration.[62] And Rabbi Wise, who was increasingly reproached by the masses for lack of action, could do little else than preach Jewish activism. Using the occasion of his fifty-ninth birthday to deliver a sermon designed to arouse Jews to action, he said.

> The time for caution and prudence is past. We must speak up like men. How can we ask our Christian friends to lift their voices in protest against the wrongs suffered by Jews if we keep silent? . . . It is not the German Jews who are being attacked. It is the Jews.[63]

Delivered some five days before the scheduled mass rally at Madison Square Garden, Wise's sermon should also be read within the wider context of Jewish politicking. In part it was an attempt to offset the impact of the intensifying activities of the JWV, which on March 20th endorsed the boycott movement and announced a plan to hold a protest parade three days later. It was also intended to garner public support to counter the harsh criticism of the boycott that was being voiced by Jews in Germany and their AJC sympathizers.[64]

Both the Congress and the Committee, as well as B'nai B'rith, continued to impress upon the State Department the need for an official diplomatic intercession with Germany. Although it was the one area where basic agreement existed among the various organizations, the growing division over the boycott precluded coordinated action even on this issue. On March 21st, Undersecretary William Phillips, a veteran career diplomat, met with delegates of the AJ Congress. In the press conference that followed he made clear that "humanitarian diplomacy" was not about to make a comeback, for "it would be very difficult for us to make a protest unless Americans were involved. . . . When it comes to the matter of German nationals . . . the comity of nations must be considered on the one hand and the sympathy of our citizens on the other."[65]

The next day Secretary Hull added the politician's touch to that of the civil servant by attesting to the State Department's interest in gathering "the *actual* facts about the situation in order that we might understand first of all *accurately and authoritatively* just what the conditions in Germany are."[66] One would have thought that a gloomy mood would have prevailed among the participants in the aftermath of the meeting with Phillips. But such was not the case. Reporting promptly to Brandeis, Wise first assured him that his advice had been followed and reported that Phillips had been "most helpful and understanding. He did exactly what we wished him to do. . . . I telephoned to the White House and Colonel [Louis McHenry] Howe was most friendly but thought it would be a mistake for me to see the President at this time. I told him that we had followed your advice for weeks in not trying to gain access to FDR."[67]

In Wise's perception of the State Department meeting, failure was turned into success: Phillips had been most helpful; powerlessness was transformed into power. Phillips had performed to order; rejection became acceptance. Howe had advised him not to see the president, but had been friendly.[68] Safeguarding himself against criticism, Wise reminded his "boss" that they had followed his advice.

Having entered the meeting with the aim of petitioning for official representation, Wise came out feeling that Phillips had been ever more forthcoming. Phillips "did one thing more," Wise reported; "he promised to telephone to Norman Davis [chairman of the U.S. delegation to the Disarmament Conference in Geneva] to put the situation before him and move him to urge the German government in the name of sanity to end this awful business [of persecuting the Jews]."[69] Wise seemed to have interpreted Phillips's "promise" as compliance with his request, while actually he had agreed to defer his goal of obtaining official intercession.

It is somewhat puzzling that Wise, not a total amateur in diplomatic affairs, misread polite, yet empty, gestures as a sign of a change in policy. In great part his assessment of the situation was obstructed by pressure from all sides. To the president's Jews, like Brandeis, Wise needed to demonstrate that he was the rational, responsible leader who could be trusted to present the "Jewish case" before the nation's decision makers. But to his traditionalist-oriented rank and file a temperate approach to the problem was far from satisfactory. They were much more impressed with the idea of the boycott movement. Wise was trying to maintain his power base but at the same time not compromise his image as a responsible leader. On March 20th, the day the JWV endorsed the boycott movement, he urged that "something must be done" to contain "the feeling that rages through the country" among his fellow Jews. Somewhat ironically, he was worried about a potential misuse of the power that the powerless did not have. "There are all sorts of things being spoken of, such as boycott of goods, the avoidance of German steamers, and, after all, four million Jews in America have a real purchasing power."[70]

But Wise was beginning to face a more insidious dilemma. To be taken seriously by his contacts in government, and to be granted continued access to them, he had to act in a manner which *they* would consider responsible. Hence, when talking to the *New York Times* about the plan of the JWV to hold a mass protest parade on March 23rd, Wise was careful to disassociate himself and his organization from their agenda. "We want Jewish meetings," he said, "and as soon as we take our hands off we are going to have Communist, Marxist, and Revisionist demonstrations."[71] Whether intuitively or from experience, Wise knew the worth of a timely response in the right place to reinforce his credibility. It was in this tense atmosphere that on March 23rd he rushed to meet with Phillips again, assuring him that the boycott movement was not being endorsed by "responsible" Jewish organizations.[72] In May, Wise also reminded Roosevelt of his success "in averting an organized boycott of German goods by American Jews and in postponing discussion in the Senate of the proposed Hitler war of extermination against Jews."[73]

Being alone at the top and withstanding the pressure from below was yet another imagined accomplishment that Wise took credit for. "I have so few in the [AJ] Congress who are of any real service in the way of counsel," Wise lamented to Julian Mack. Moreover, he continued, "You cannot imagine what I am doing to resist the masses."[74] In the context of consolidating his power both inside and outside Jewish circles, such sentiments not only intimated the extent of his authority and endurance, but also expressed his willingness for loyal cooperation with the political establishment.

Indeed, the proximity to the powerful and the quest for their approval tend to distance the leader from the discontented masses he represents. As he grows increasingly sympathetic to the elite's point of view, the leader may begin "to wonder if the impatience of his followers is not due to their imperfect appreciation of the facts of life as he now understands them."[75] It is likely Wise was not entirely aware that he was being co-opted. As Michael Parenti has observed, the nature of co-optation is such that those being co-opted are neither aware of the role they play in the process nor do they believe that it is happening to them.[76]

Since the AJ Congress, more susceptible to pressure from below, maintained a high public profile with its protest activities, the AJC evidently felt obliged to explain its public silence. Although the two organizations represented different constituencies, they competed for the crown of leadership of the entire American Jewish community. The battle was being waged more over image than content, however, for even though neither group could demonstrate tangible gains on the German front, the American Jewish Committee could ill afford to lag behind its publicly aggressive competitors in the American Jewish Congress. Indeed, the special meeting on the German situation called by the AJC in early April was essentially a response to its problem of image. As Judge Horace Stern, chairman of the executive committee, explained, "It was impossible . . . to make any public statements of what the Committee was doing; and I am afraid an impression has been prevalent . . . that the Committee has not been as active as our emotional natures might have wanted us to be under the present situation." The meeting had essentially been called on the premise that "at least our own membership ought to know what the Executive Committee has been doing."[77]

It seems that the rivalry between the different Jewish organizations was what at times prompted action by their leadership. At the same time, by allowing selective contacts with those in power in Washington, the Roosevelt administration often played one organization against another. A potential troublemaker like Rabbi Wise, for example, was sequestered. Not only was he unable to gain access to the White House, within the State Department his admittance did not pass beyond Phillips. But three days after this meeting, on March 24th, representatives of the AJC and B'nai B'rith gained an invitation to meet with Secretary of State Cordell Hull. Adler had wished for a meeting in the White House but Judge Lehman had suggested that the president not be approached until May. Under the circumstances Dr. Adler could not wait for the "first prize" and agreed to settle for a meeting in the State Department, joined by Lehman and Alfred M. Cohen, president of B'nai B'rith.[78] What loss of prestige the American Jewish Committee may have incurred by lagging behind the American Jewish Congress was more than made up for by meeting with the secretary himself. Those more acceptable to the political establishment were generally rewarded for their support—provided certain conditions were met. In his report to the special meeting, Judge Stern stressed that Hull had "requested and granted the interview on condition that it would not be made public."[79] Indeed, in the diplomatic sphere it was not uncommon to be sworn to secrecy. But the way Stern justified this stipulation was most revealing of the underlying insecurity of Jews which hampered their every step. "It is obvious," Stern explained,

> that if a statement were to have been given out that these gentlemen were going to see Secretary Hull, that even if the American Government then did something as a result of that visit, it being known that the Secretary had been seen by prominent Jews, the value of the action taken by the Secretary would have been largely dissipated.[80]

Yet even the need to forgo the benefit of publicity did not detract from the delight experienced by those who were granted the opportunity to interact with the powerful. Adler was "profoundly impressed" by Hull, finding him the "superior of most" that he had met in this office during the past thirty years.[81] Hull, according to Adler, was very compassionate in his response. He was also impressed by the presentation. What had happened in the last few weeks in Germany, he said, was "so staggering . . . that he hardly could comprehend it . . . it almost made him despair of the human race." Although the expressed aim of the meeting was to "question whether this administration would return to the older theory" of humanitarian diplomacy, Adler appeared to have been most impressed by the fact that the secretary had been "particularly courteous" and had told the participants that they "could always have access to him whenever we felt that there was anything we wished to bring up to his attention."[82] These demonstrations of courtesy and sympathy, along with promises of accessibility, were all enlisted to neutralize the pressure that was being exerted on the administration. If they felt flattered by the serious attention extended to them, there was a good chance that Jewish leaders would modify their demands and be encouraged to display goodwill and a sense of responsibility.[83]

Hull not only accorded his callers all of these things, he also proved reliable. Having promised to ask the American Embassy in Berlin for an update on the situation, he telegrammed the reply on March 26th, only two days after the meeting. It was addressed to the presidents of the AJC, the AJ Congress, and B'nai B'rith, and its conclusions were reassuring:

> Whereas there was for a short time considerable physical mistreatment of the Jews this phase may be considered virtually terminated. . . . Hitler . . . issued an order calling upon his followers to maintain law and order. . . . The feeling has been wide-spread in Germany that following so far reaching a political readjustment . . . some time must elapse before a state of equilibrium could be reestablished. In the opinion of the Embassy, such a stabilization appears to have been reached. . . . I feel hopeful . . . that the situation which has caused such wide-spread concern throughout this country will soon revert to normal.

Hull ended his message with a promise "to watch the situation closely with a sympathetic interest."[84]

On March 26th, the same day that Hull transmitted his optimistic message to the American Jewish leaders, Goebbels recorded in his diary Hitler's own promises:

> In the night I go to Berchtesgaden, whither the Leader has summoned me. Up there in the mountain solitude he has pondered the whole matter fully and has come to a decision. We shall make headway against the foreign lie only if we get our hands on its originators or at least beneficiaries, those Jews living in Germany who have thus far remained unmolested. We must, therefore, proceed to a large-scale boycott of all Jewish business in Germany. Perhaps the foreign Jews will think better of the matter when their racial comrades in Germany begin to get it in the neck.[85]

Most of the victims were not oblivious to their worsening situation. But none have recorded it in the thick of experience with such immediacy and poignancy as Victor Klemperer. The son of a reform rabbi who became a Protestant when he was thirty-one years old, Klemperer was first and foremost a devoted son of his German homeland. After serving at the front during World War One he was appointed a professor of Romance languages at the Technical University of Dresden in 1920, a position he held until the Nazis forced him to retire in 1935. His survival in Germany had nothing to do with his love for the *Heimat*, but rather with the fact that his wife, whom he had married in 1906, was considered an "Aryan" by the regime. Painstakingly recording the gradual transformation of German Jews from insiders to ultimate pariahs, on the evening of March 27th, Klemperer wrote in his diary:

> The government is in hot water. 'Atrocity propaganda' from abroad because of its Jewish campaign. It is constantly issuing official denials, there are no pogroms, and has Jewish associations issue refutations. But then it openly threat-

ens to proceed against the German Jews if the mischief-making by "World Jewry" does not stop. Meanwhile there is no bloodshed in the country, but oppression, oppression, oppression. No one breathes freely anymore, no free word, neither printed nor spoken.[86]

The next day, on March 28th, Hitler's ideas were implemented as an order that called for the immediate formation of action committees to plan and execute "an organized boycott of Jewish businesses, Jewish goods, Jewish doctors, and Jewish lawyers." The committees would be responsible "for ensuring that the boycott does not do any harm to innocent parties but instead does all the more harm to the guilty parties." Item number 11 of the order commanded committee members to "refrain from harming a single hair of a Jew's head. . . . We will come to terms with this smear campaign simply by the drastic force of these measures cited."[87] On March 29th Hitler informed his cabinet members that he himself had called for the boycott and described the alternative as spontaneous popular unrest.[88] Despite opposition from his national ministers, the boycott was scheduled for Saturday, April 1st. But a day before the scheduled boycott Hitler suggested the possibility of postponing it until April 4th if the British and American governments were to declare immediately their opposition to the anti-German agitation in their countries. On the evening of March 31st both governments were prepared to make the necessary declaration, but Foreign Minister Konstantin Freiherr von Neurath made it known that it was too late to change course.[89]

The AJC linked Hitler's decision on the boycott to mass protest meetings that had taken place on March 27th at Madison Square Garden and in other places around the country. Its reading of the situation was likely to have been based on the fact that on March 25th Hermann Göring, the number two in the Nazi hierarchy and the new Prussian interior minister, summoned several leaders of German Jewry and requested that they send a delegation to meet with Jewish leaders in London and America and convince them to stop the anti-German propaganda about atrocities against Jews, for otherwise he would not be able to guarantee the safety of the Jews in Germany.[90] On March 26th, the day the delegation arrived in London, a cable reached the AJC in New York. Signed by Kurt Blumenfeld, president of the German Zionist Association, and Julius Brodnitz of the C.V., it read: "We protest categorically against holding Monday meeting, radio and other demonstrations. We unequivocally demand energetic effort to obtain an end to demonstrations hostile to Germany."[91] That the meeting with Göring had had an immediate effect on the Jews he summoned is borne out by the fact that only two days before a "Confidential Report" by the German Zionists had reached London, which was totally different in tone and substance. It read: "It must be clear that the protest movement against the persecution of the Jews in Germany is totally justified. Not only do the press reports abroad not exaggerate the seriousness of the situation, they understate it."[92]

Rabbi Wise could not remain impervious to the pressure of the German Jews who telephoned him from London. On the day of the Madison Square

Garden rally the British Zionist Federation cabled him to confirm the seriousness of the request for moderation, advising him to assert in his speech that the present German government both wanted and was trying to stop the atrocities and urging him to avoid the wild exaggeration that appeared in the sensational press.[93] Indeed, in describing the event to Mack's daughter, who lived in Vienna, Wise reassured her that "not a bitter word was spoken against Germany." To Mack he wrote that "the easiest thing in the world would have been to arouse that audience . . . to murderous rage" but he proudly reported that the Jews acted with "absolute self-restraint." But in response to the allegations that were being voiced in America about the linkage between the protest movement in America and Hitler's decision about the boycott, Wise was adamant that "no matter what the Hitlerites do now, it will be nothing more than the overt commission of acts that would have been covertly performed, protest or no protest."[94]

The Nazis' plans for a boycott brought Wise and Deutsch back to the State Department, where they conferred again with Undersecretary Phillips on March 30th and 31st. In the next few days Wise conveyed his observations to his three closest associates. Writing "in confidence" to his friend, Minister John Haynes Holmes, he confessed that the "change of administration has been bad for us [Jews]."[95] In assessing the situation for the sake of Frankfurter, the insider-outsider, Wise was more circumspect, merely writing that, "our State Department did its best." He did acknowledge some problems, which he attributed to the inexperienced new personnel.[96]

Wise's most authentic voice could be deciphered in his letter to Mack, whom he briefed first. Again, he reiterated that the changes in personnel were what made the path in the State Department more "delicate" and "difficult" for the Jews' advocates. Tacitly conceding the intrinsic weaknesses of people in his position, Wise chose to believe that if Frankfurter "could have handled things" the results would have been different. "I think," he wrote to Mack as a matter of fact, that Frankfurter "feels a certain disinclination to step out into the open at this time." "Perhaps," he rationalized, Frankfurter's "very great influence with the Administration ought to be reserved. He knows best." As if attempting to avoid his own insights, Wise added, "it may even be" that Frankfurter "is exerting" influence "just as Herbert [Lehman], who I know has phoned twice to the White House in recent days."[97] Frankfurter, writing by chance to Wise on the same day that Wise briefed him about his meetings at the State Department, was uncharacteristically complimentary. "It seems to me," he wrote, "you have been most effective in the discreet exertion of the weight of our government on behalf of elementary decencies. More power to you."[98] Among the president's Jews the voice of discretion set the tone and Wise was becoming a virtuoso performer.

Being drawn closer into the labyrinth of government often caused Jewish leaders to identify with its agenda and lose sight of their own aims. Wise's presence at the State Department during the two days prior to the declared

German boycott was partially responsible for producing this undesirable effect. He observed the efforts of Phillips, who "practically lived on the Berlin telephone line"; it is hardly astonishing that in Wise's perception it was the State Department's "intervention" that "no doubt . . . moved the Nazis to see that they could not afford to continue to affront civilization by continuing the boycott." Moreover, the fact that the boycott lasted only one day and involved little violence was credited to the pressure of public protest. From there it was but a short leap to adopting the State Department's view that "the one-day boycott was a concession to the wilder members of the Nazi group."[99]

The Slough of Despond

On April 1st the *Völkischer Beobachter* reported that members of the Jewish race had been barred from the Superior Court at Köningsberg as well as from the district and county courts. To avoid a "discontinuity of the administration of justice," Jewish lawyers who could provide proof of service as frontline soldiers during World War One were permitted to enter the court and settle the "case of members of their race." On April 3rd the same newspaper reported that teachers who had Jewish blood were to be immediately dismissed from all schools in Berlin and that all Jewish physicians employed by Berlin's social services were also to be discharged. These local initiatives were forerunners of the Law for the Restoration of the Professional Civil Service, which was enacted on April 7th.[100]

Wise could no longer sustain much optimism. On April 3rd he began to exert pressure on his "agents." He wrote to Frankfurter: "If things start up again today and tomorrow" in Germany, "then LDB cannot be spared. Unless, dear FF, you were to let me know by wire that you would be ready to step into the breach and see FDR if it becomes necessary to do so."[101] Two days later he confided to Mack: "Acting in accordance with the suggestion of Phillips we have been silent for days." But he added, "I won't be able to keep the Congress from making a statement today."[102] The next day, April 6th, the AJ Congress published a strong condemnation of the German government's continued discrimination against Jews.[103] In view of America's national interests and the attitude of Brandeis and Frankfurter, it was a rather bold step to take. Yet Wise must have understood that as long as he continued to play by the rules, neither one of them would offer to intervene with the president. Hence, he decided to sound an alarm by making a public statement.

The tactic worked. Impelled perhaps by his own discomfort, Frankfurter was quick to contact the president and to alert him to a possible embarrassment. The next day, April 7th, the two met. After consulting with Brandeis, Frankfurter telephoned Wise with the following report:

> I have seen General Headquarters [FDR] . . . and I feel sure that he is watching the thing [situation of the Jews in Germany] with understanding and sympathy.

> Action followed very speedily upon our talk. Florence Court [Brandeis's resi-
> dence] and I think that neither you nor Irving [Lehman] should go down for
> the present.[104]

Wise was "very happy about this because it means that at least someone has
talked straight to General Headquarters." He had little choice but to express
full trust in his own "chiefs," adding "no one could put the case for us better
than F. F. excepting possibly L. D. B."[105]

Yet the fact remained that in early April the problem of the Jews in Germany was not Roosevelt's top priority in world affairs. His energies were focused on organizing the preliminary economic talks which were to open in
Washington on April 21st. To create a favorable mood for American interests
at the planned world economic conference in London, FDR recruited the
best men to plan it: Bernard Baruch and James P. Warburg were called in as
advisers on monetary issues, Frankfurter was assigned the task of making contacts for the president with a Soviet spokesman in the United States, and
Henry Morgenthau, Jr., was asked to investigate the possibility of selling farm
surplus to the Soviets.[106]

Stephen Wise undertook to attend to yet another "national interest." In
early April rumors began circulating that Hitler might attend the planned
economic talks in Washington as Germany's chief of state. The Jewish community became terribly agitated by such a prospect, and Wise tried "desper-
ately to avert bitter criticism of the administration because of this news."
Denied direct access to Roosevelt, Wise managed to send "word to the White
House in other ways" to inform the "Chief," as he often addressed him, that
"we [Jewish leaders] know that it is inevitable and that he [Hitler] cannot be
treated as an outlaw quite yet, seeing that we are in friendly relations with
Germany, one of our debtor nations."[107] To gain credibility it was important
for Wise to impress upon the president that he, the leader, did understand the
broader national interests, even if at times he was forced to act otherwise
under pressure of the masses, who were becoming more restless. Such times
were nearing. "It will not be long," he wrote to Mack, before the Jewish
masses would "insist that something more meaningful come from the Administration . . . to the embittered souls of American Jews.[108]

Cyrus Adler may not have been less frustrated and despairing, but he seems
to have maintained a calmer front. "I know," he wrote to Judge Lehman on
April 10th "that the Jewish problem is an infinitesimal negligible factor in
the affairs of the world and I do not expect it to remain in the minds of the
President or the Secretary of State any length of time, but they must not
be allowed to forget it."[109] Adler did not make much headway, since Lehman
remained reluctant to use his influence with the president. "Any attempt
to bring pressure on the government," he replied "would be ill-advised, un-
necessary and ungracious," adding confidently that the United States government was "doing more in that direction than appears on the surface."[110]
The more the "excluded others" appeared determined to assert their Jew-

ishness, the more the "integrated others" displayed a need to assert their Americanism.

Wise, who was more assertive than Adler, forced Frankfurter into action. FDR was well aware of the delicate predicament his loyal servant was faced with. Whenever possible and if the price was reasonable Roosevelt would make an effort to return a favor. In the cabinet meeting of April 7th, following his meeting with Frankfurter earlier in the day, Roosevelt instructed Secretary of Labor Frances Perkins and Secretary of State Cordell Hull to study the refugee problem and make recommendations. According to Frankfurter's own account, the president agreed to a "moral gesture" of admitting a small number of prominent individuals persecuted by the Nazis.[111] Apart from the satisfaction of being able to deliver results to his own people, perhaps even more important for Frankfurter personally was the fact that the president was responding to his counsel.

Among Jewish leaders, though, there was hardly a sense of accomplishment, but rather feelings of self-doubt and even despair. Cyrus Adler confessed that although all of his time was devoted to Germany, he "accomplish[ed] nothing."[112] "I wish I could go on fighting," Wise wrote in early April, "but for the first time in my life I feel that it will be good when the fight is over, seeing that one can do so little."[113] Some three weeks later, the leader of the anti-Nazi protest grew even more despondent:

> It is no exaggeration to say that as I see and hear the news [from Germany] from day to day, I am looking into the deeps of hell. Sometimes I feel as if I could hardly live through it and as if I hardly cared . . . as if release from it all would not be unwelcome—if death meant release.[114]

These expressions of pessimism by the Jewish activists could be viewed as a recognition that they had been living with delusions that had been intensified by their frequent contact with members of the administration as well as by their seemingly blind trust in Roosevelt's "court Jews." This new insight into their position, painful as it may have been, held the potential of spurring the Jewish leadership to more resolute action. Wise was ready for an offensive; however, having been partly co-opted already, his options, as we shall see, no longer seemed clear-cut.

As they took stock of their efforts to bring about diplomatic intervention, Jewish leaders became increasingly aware that the White House and the State Department would continue to avoid any action. In fact, it was not until after *Kristallnacht* in November 1938, when the U.S. government recalled its Ambassador Hugh R. Wilson, that a diplomatic initiative was used to protest events in Germany. Secretary of State Hull was opposed to the recall even then.[115] Moreover, the attempt to gain influence in the sphere of foreign affairs could have laid American Jews open to the charge that they were conducting their affairs as a "state within a state," an allegation they could ill afford.

With the battle on the diplomatic front essentially lost, the Jewish leadership appeared to have reconfigured its priorities into what it thought would be more attainable goals. Unlike his Washington-accommodating colleagues, Wise had to remain attuned to the voices of the masses, with whom he was beginning to lose ground. The grassroots movement to formalize the boycott of German goods and services was gaining momentum, notwithstanding the objections of the "responsible" leadership.[116] American Jews were also agitated by the fact that the British political elite—Foreign Secretary Sir John Simon, Lord Reading in the House of Lords, Winston Churchill, and some influential backbenchers who had taken up the matter in the House of Commons—was protesting against Germany's injustices to the Jews, while in their own country silence prevailed.[117] The pressure to break the silence, especially of President Roosevelt, became overwhelming.

Two primary goals emerged: to ease the immigration restrictions for German refugees and to obtain a public expression of sympathy from the president on behalf of the German Jews.[118] Both can be described as symbolic gestures, intended mainly for domestic American Jewish consumption. A trickle of German refugees to American soil would reinforce the Jewish rank and file's faith in their leaders, while a presidential statement would Americanize their cause. But Roosevelt had rarely made the blunder of exposing himself to direct Jewish pressure; he continued to utilize his Jewish associates as his buffers.

Wise, however, could no longer afford to remain silent. "Silence is acquiescence," he wrote to Mack.[119] With no direct access to the White House, his only option was to try to convince his connections of the seriousness of the situation. Provided this could be done, there was a chance, he thought, of triggering a reaction which could eventually reach the president and bring about the desired response. On April 15th Wise wrote to Frankfurter:

> I have been waiting, I confess, day after day in the hope that you might send me some further information about your talk with Headquarters [the April 7th meeting with FDR]. I do not want to ask your sympathy but I do want you to know that I am having an awfully hard time of it with the Jewish masses who cannot be expected to understand why no word has come from the Administration in all these weeks.[120]

Wise also confided in this letter that he was very troubled by being denied access to the White House, a state of affairs that he perceived as harmful to the cause. "Roosevelt ought to know the story," he wrote to Mack on the same day, and quickly added, "Of Course F. F. must have told Roosevelt much, but there is still much to be told. Very much."[121] It appears that Wise was beginning to sense a growing distance between his views and interests and those of his contact. Indeed, Mack was informed that Wise needed him badly for he did not have "complete confidence" in Frankfurter, "or anywhere approaching it." The same source, the Zionist activist Lawrence Berenson, who knew both Wise and Mack, also indicated that while Wise "feels a lack of proximity" to Brandeis, "he trusts him 100%."[122]

Wise permitted himself to voice his true feelings of frustration and exasperation where it would be least harmful. "I am sick over the whole thing," he wrote to Mack on April 15th. Daring for the first time to express his disappointment with Roosevelt, he confided to Mack that the AJ Congress would "have to do the very lamentable thing of crying out against the President who has not by a single word or act intimated the faintest interest in what is going on." Yet even here Wise tempered his criticism of FDR by expressing his understanding for "the difficulties, perhaps the political impossibilities of doing anything."[123]

When communicating with Frankfurter on the same day Wise was more circumspect, realizing perhaps that in order to gain influence he needed to demonstrate a certain level of trust in the system and a willingness to partially relinquish his autonomy.[124] Wise was apparently prepared to pay the price:

> I would be guided by that [the President's] judgment if at all possible and I could [changed in Wise's handwriting to "might"] make that judgment dominant if only I knew it! . . . I do not think we can stand out against a formal and organized boycott [of German goods]. I would be willing to stand out against it to the end, and I might prevail if I had a word from Headquarters that would strengthen my position. . . . An organized . . . boycott would be very much graver and more damaging to German interest[s] and anything that damages Germany by indirection damages us [Americans] and lessens Germany's capacity to import, that is to say, to buy from us.[125]

This approach also manifested the extent to which co-optation inevitably modifies the leader's behavior. Wise was prepared to obey FDR's judgment as if it coincided with his group's interest—he came to view an anti-Nazi boycott as first and foremost detrimental to American interests, abandoning in the process any thought about the possible impact it could have on Germany's economy and its treatment of the Jews.

Jewish leaders, already entangled in the net of the powerful, were left with a rather ineffective and uneasy option. Although they were becoming increasingly disappointed with the Roosevelt administration, psychologically they were becoming increasingly reluctant to act as an opposition. On the contrary, the more despondent they felt about their own helplessness, the more they sought to understand and identify with their chosen protectors—whether the president and his administration or their agents in FDR's court.

This predicament fostered peculiar incongruities. They revered Roosevelt as "king of the Jews" and at the same time felt greatly disappointed by him; they perceived the situation of the Europeans Jews as cataclysmic and concurrently felt self-conscious about being the center of attention. Cyrus Adler gave vent to some of these frustrations. "I am afraid we Jews must maintain our perspective," he chided those Jews who criticized the leaders of the world; as "important as we are to ourselves[,] the whole world cannot be allowed to go to smash on our account."[126] Similarly, Adler also seemed willing to accept without demur the fact that he had had "no direct relations with the President since he came into office and this at his request," since "because of the large interests that he was taking up with various foreign nations," the president "did not wish anything to intervene."[127]

Judge Samuel Rosenman strengthened this line of reasoning with "authoritative" backing. Appearing together with Adler before the executive committee of the AJC, he reassured "on the basis of direct information" those already inclined to believe that FDR was "deeply concerned over the German situation." The president kept a public silence, he explained, only because of his great concern about the economic and disarmament conferences. He went on to explain that FDR would not do anything that could jeopardize those conferences "because if they fail, the result for the world at large and for the Jews in particular would be extremely unfavorable."[128]

Let us bear in mind for future reference that as early as 1933 there were influential Jews in America who accepted the existence of a linkage between the fate of world Jewry and the welfare of America and its allies, long before it became the rationale for abandoning particular "Jewish interests" in favor of "victory first."

The masses under Wise's guidance had yet to attain the level of worldliness that would enable them to adopt the stance that what was good for the world was good for the Jews. They were more skeptical and therefore more demanding. Hoping to move Frankfurter to act, Wise deployed the few available weapons in his depleted arsenal. In his letter of April 15th he informed Frankfurter that Senator King wished to introduce in Congress a resolution of protest and "I begged members of the Senate to say nothing up to this time because I felt . . . that any congressional utterances now would seem to be a deviation from the silence of the Administration." With a proven record of loyalty and compliance, Wise made an effort to reclaim his honor and position of leadership when he added, "I cannot feel that I have the right to stand out any longer against the possibility of the *American people* making their voice heard in the halls of Congress."[129]

Wise continued to perform a balancing act between being a loyal American and being a committed Jewish leader. If at first he expressed his willingness to be guided by the president's judgment if only he knew what it was, as the silence continued he came to listen more closely to his Jewish constituency. He began to talk about the conference that the AJ Congress had scheduled in Washington for April 19th and informed Frankfurter that during the conference he intended to influence his "insatiable" constituency "in accordance with the judgment of Headquarters," but now not only on condition "that judgment be ascertainable," but with the added stipulation that it would be "acceptable from the viewpoint of obligation to Jewish interests." He made clear his plan to arrive two days early in order to mobilize congressional opinion. Having stated his terms, Wise left his door open, requesting an immediate reply.[130] This was a quantum leap, for not only had Wise exerted pressure on his main contact to FDR, but he had also pressed for a word from the White House with the added provision that acceptance depended on its compliance with Jewish interests.

This time Frankfurter reacted quickly. Was he worried lest his friend the president would find himself in an awkward position, which by extension might reflect negatively upon his own effectiveness vis-à-vis the Chief? Upon receipt of Wise's letter on the next day, he immediately contacted him by telephone.[131] Following this conversation, Wise dispatched a day letter to Frankfurter:

> Last Sunday [April 9th] you telephoned me that you and LDB [Brandeis] were persuaded that the President was alert to the meaning of events in Germany *especially* in relation to the *peace of the world* and further that in his own wise way he would at the *right moment* give effective evidence of his concern over the occurrences in Germany *which must* have aroused his moral nature and have evoked his constructive statesmanship. However the presence of wide popular demands for mass demonstrations organized boycott etc is becoming increasingly heavy and all but impossible to resist.
>
> This pressure will undoubtedly be reflected in resolutions in Congress voluntarily offered and insisted upon by Senators.
>
> Once this process is initiated and reflected on the hill [Capitol Hill] the action may *seriously embarrass* the White House because of the possible ineptitude and irresponsibility characterizing such action which in considered and responsible form the President might give assent.
>
> Thus far have succeeded in getting Senators to refrain from action. Fear the accumulation of continued and growing pressure because of action in British Parliament especially utterance of British Foreign Affairs . . . and because of Holland facilitating entries refugee Jews. Receiving abundant confirmation . . . from escaped survivors of Hitler outrages.
>
> Time is of the essence prayerfully hope for *some word* by the President in *whatever* form he may choose to express his own deep feeling and that this word will be spoken at once.[132]

It may at first seem puzzling why Wise dispatched the day letter, since it contained essentially the same basic arguments as his letter of the day before. Moreover, upon a closer reading, it does not sound authentic; the voice does not seem to be Wise's own. In his letter to Mack written on the same day Wise himself provided the answers, confiding that the "telegram was written by Felix through dictation to me over the telephone as well as addressed to him."[133] However, he did not reveal what considerations had led to this semi-clandestine operation.

A plausible explanation may run as follows: Frankfurter must have been disappointed that his April 7th meeting with Roosevelt had failed to yield any clear results, especially since he rarely approached the president on sectarian matters. Moreover, he was extremely careful not to overstep recognized boundaries. Having drafted for his old acquaintance Secretary of Labor Frances Perkins two executive orders which would have helped German Jews to qualify for American visas, Frankfurter assured Assistant Secretary of State Raymond Moley that the proposed changes would not lead to mass immigration or constitute interference in Germany's domestic policies.[134] Still, no action had followed.

His inability to "deliver the goods" to his co-religionists may indeed have caused Frankfurter some discomfort, but it seems that he was no less affected by what it revealed about his personal influence on FDR. As the insecure outsider-insider, Frankfurter constantly sought reassurance about his status, and he was particularly sensitive to how rapidly and to what extent his ideas were acted upon by the president. Yet, well aware of his delicate position, he could not conceive of expressing to the president his own frustrations as a Jew; the clear divide between his views and those of the other Jews had to be maintained.

Armed with the message he had dictated to Wise on April 16th, Frankfurter thus renewed his plea, disguised as a message from a "professional" Jew, to the president. He telegrammed FDR on the same day, enclosing, of course, the dictated day letter by Wise, which at last reached its intended destination. Asking for "some word of progress" on plans for assisting refugees, Frankfurter cautioned the president that Wise might go public and embarrass FDR politically.[135] Frankfurter's messages were not answered by Roosevelt. A reply was issued by Secretary Hull, upon the president's request, that expressed appreciation for the "courtesy in bringing Rabbi Wise's wire to our attention."[136] Frankfurter's craving for an acknowledgment of his loyalty to the "Chief" was recognized, albeit indirectly.

Another telling example of how careful Frankfurter was to maintain his pure Americanism before FDR can be found in his response to the Jewish leaders' suggestion that he request a meeting with the president to discuss the easing of visa restrictions for German refugees. Officially the request for the interview was to be made by Irving Lehman. When consulted by Joseph Proskauer, Frankfurter made clear to him that he was not to be used "as conduit," for it "would carry wholly unwarranted implications" about his "relations to the President and to the Administration." Lest we misread this as a streak of modesty on Frankfurter's part, he quickly corrects this impression. Although he informed Proskauer that he would be willing "to accompany" (not join) a delegation headed by Irving Lehman, he added a condition which reveals how he perceived his role and status. In an unusually convoluted style, which reflects perhaps his deep-rooted uneasiness in both worlds, he stipulated:

> But my presence should be the result of an expression of desire on the part of the President, in response to a suggestion in Irving's communication to the President that it would be also desirable, if it be agreeable to the President, to have me present at the interview to be set by the President.[137]

Frankfurter, the chief Jewish agent in the White House, was prepared to join the Jews only if his own "Chief" would deem his presence desirable beyond any doubt. For as he wrote to Secretary Hull, "I am attached to the welfare of the Administration of Franklin D. Roosevelt more than I have been to that of any other President."[138] Indeed, it was Frankfurter's total devotion to FDR which made his failure to produce results all the more difficult to bear. But in fact there is no evidence that he pressured either the president or the secretary of state to act.[139] In Frankfurter's view it was the "formal timidities of the Bill Phillipses," the conduct of the State Department's bureaucrats, that prevented the president's wishes from being implemented.[140] It was only further down the power pyramid that Frankfurter dared flex his muscles. Protesting to Assistant Secretary of State Raymond Moley, he appeared to have been provoked more by the compromise of his president's honor than by the inaction. "It really is disheartening," he wrote, "that the humane and courageous determination of the President taken two weeks ago last Friday [the cabinet meeting of April 7th] should have failed of execution somewhere along the route. . . . Can't you have the wise and brave determination of the President vindicated promptly?"[141]

Frankfurter, so it appears, felt more at ease placing the blame for derailing the train of action on his co-religionists. Criticizing in particular the accommodationist leadership of the AJC, he angrily reproached Judge Proskauer:

> Now I don't give a damn about the internal rows among New York Jewry. But they have much significance to something about which I care profoundly, namely, the realization by this government that there are no real divisions among the ranks of American Jewry in their anxious desire, *as Americans*, to have the government speak out on . . . "fundamental human rights."[142]

It is hardly likely that the sophisticated Harvard professor and friend of the president could have been so naive as to think that the silence of the administration was in any way linked to internal divisions among the Jewish ranks. Frankfurter confided his real predicament to Secretary of State Cordell Hull. In the troubling days of late May 1933, he wrote to him: "For once in my life I wish that, for a brief period, I were not a Jew. Then I would not have even the appearance of being sectarian."[143]

What unavoidably emerges from the sad saga related here is the weakness inherent in an ambivalent identity, which not only inhibited the exercise of power but also the testing of its potential. The failure to influence cannot be taken as conclusive evidence that there was no potential to influence or that defeat necessarily implies lack of resources.[144] Yet, somewhat paradoxically, it was the very proximity of individual Jews to the centers of power that blocked Jewish activists from exerting pressure on the decision makers. For it was precisely the Jewish outsider-insiders who were most careful to avoid walking through the corridors of power in broad daylight with their Jewish hats on public display.

It is only those who enjoy the dubious benefit of hindsight who can categorically claim that "American Jews should have refused to be coopted by the system."[145] Those, like Rabbi Wise, who paid the price exacted by co-optation were more perceptive about the painful dilemma. "We have been put in the terrible position," he lamented to Mack, "of seeming to do nothing about Washington when F [Frankfurter] and I [Irving Lehman] and Bernie B. [Bernard Baruch] and Sarnoff and all of us have felt that we *could not afford* even to seem to try to break in on those supremely important Washington negotiations of what, from an American point of view, is a lesser matter." Giving expression to his utter sense of futility, Wise concluded:

> Perhaps at the head of this job at present there should be one who feels that nothing else counts, that nothing else matters and who is ready to smash through all barriers.[146]

Summing up Hitler's first six months in power, historian Rafael Medoff concluded that while "Wise and his colleagues had hesitated," Hitler had consolidated his political power, and thus, "a crucial moment of historical opportunity for the American Jewish leadership had passed unexploited."[147] But Medoff does not even hint at what this missed opportunity was, or how and with what power it could have been exploited; both assertions are treated as axiomatic.

7

The Demise of the Myth of Jewish Power

> The worst pain a man can have is to know much and be impotent to act.
> —Herodotus, *The Histories*

Many factors shaped the response of Jewish leaders in America to the Nazi menace. On the immediate level few would contest that the combined impact of social apprehensions born of strong anti-Jewish sentiments and economic insecurities generated by the Depression contributed to temper the organized Jewish response and to hamper a broader grassroots involvement among American Jews.

However, the Jewish political posture in America, as elsewhere, was molded by something more distant and evasive—the primacy of Jewish survival. With the exception of the extreme Left, assuring Jewish continuance has been the basic substance that informs the political behavior of Jews. Since the *Haskalah*, Jews had viewed the modern nation-state as the best guarantee for their survival, and "identification with the state," as David Biale aptly noted, became "the modern version of Jewish politics."[1]

In America, particularly during the insecure decades of the 1930s and 1940s, survival was understood mostly in economic and psychological terms. Securing it was understood by most Jewish leaders to involve a display of unqualified American patriotism. In line with America's political culture, survival entailed going to great lengths to deny the existence of a Jewish vote or any particular political interests and to profess complete trust in the liberal state's institutions as agents of necessary reforms. The liberalism and opposition to political parochialism that were prevalent among American Jews for most of their history were undoubtedly part of their genuine political gestalt, but they were also part of their survival strategy. It is more than likely that most American Jews would have been delighted if their Gentile friends had viewed them as Edward S. Martin did when he wrote in 1933:

> American Jews are fervent supporters of government, take a moderate interest in politics, do not organize as the Irish sometimes do. . . . They are seldom troublesome in politics. When we got into War there was no complaint of any lack of Jewish support.[2]

Such, however, was not the case. American Jewry, to be sure, was shaped by the society with which it had cast its lot, but it neither fully shed its ethnic origin nor disconnected itself from its separate history. Jews everywhere continuously felt emotional allegiances and particular obligations to their co-religionists. Their connection to K'lal Yisrael (the Nation of Israel), their belief that all Israel are responsible for one another, is rooted in rabbinic law. It mandates a hierarchy of obligations that differentiates between groups of claimants on the basis of moral stature, dependence, social intimacy, and communal solidarity. In their particular world Jews are instructed to provide for family members before non-relatives, neighbors before more distant townspeople, and distant townspeople before the Jewish poor of other jurisdictions. These ordered priorities of responsibility stem from the conviction that political obligations are not derived from abstract principles but from the lived connections forged by shared lives and common identity.[3]

But in a society that claimed to uphold universalist ethics and insisted that we treat the whole world as our brothers and sisters, loyalty to the nation and loyalty to a separate tribe were seen as incompatible. Eager to negotiate the terrain between their American patriotism and their particular commitments, American Jews were compelled to narrow the expressions of both. Their patriotism lost its critical edge and their particular solidarity, though constantly evoked as rhetoric, was rarely affirmed in more than a token manner. Lacking a philosophical justification for particularism, the American Jewish community sought to resolve the conflict by identifying its specific interests with the broader dictates of liberal universalism. Such was the case during the Nazi era. Jewish leaders presented the struggle against anti-Semitism as part of a larger struggle against fascism and all assertions of national and racial superiority. But Americans were not easily convinced. While most of them must have recognized that the forces of modernization and acculturation were reshaping the consciousness and behavior of American Jewry by diluting its group cohesion, enough of it remained to regard them as somewhat a people apart. Indeed they were, although it was not always by their own choosing.

To be sure, not all American Jews subscribed to a consciously particular ethics of obligations. Wide disagreements existed about what order of priorities and agendas should guide them. But intuitively, most Jews embraced the notion of "oneness" as a source of power, especially when dangers loomed. In January 1933 this notion was expressed in the following form:

> Jewish unity is not of yesterday, not of thirty years ago. It was not created by any organization. It is a fact and has always been a fact. It is cemented by common sanctities and common sorrows. It is a real power in the world.[4]

In late February 1933 an officer of the Joint expressed these ideas more subtly when the Committee launched its campaign for the relief of the destitute Jews in Eastern Europe. "Let us face this situation honestly and in all frankness," he said,

> Our situation here at home is such that it is futile to think of coping adequately
> with this problem. But simply because we have our own problems and a first
> duty at home is no reason for ignoring this other obligation. For we can do
> much. We can keep alive the bond of brotherhood. . . . We can save them from
> hopelessness.[5]

Of course, there were also many American Jews who wished to be "normal,"
to be relieved of the burden of a particular identity and obligation. Jewish
leaders and politicians alluded to this throughout the period of crisis, although perhaps no one expressed it as candidly as the editor of the *Menorah
Journal*, who wrote in early 1943:

> There is a strong pull, for the faithful, to regard Jewish life and interests as
> being always in the center of the world. To be sure, our enemies have been
> doing their cruelest to make them so. . . . Yet, as free men and women, our vital
> concerns with national and world politics, with social and economic problems,
> with science and literature, art and music, transcend—however intensely they
> include—our Jewish devotions. There must be a sense of proportion.[6]

Notwithstanding the cacophony that characterized the discourse of
American Jews, they nonetheless maintained a sentimental attachment to the
notion of universal Jewish solidarity. But its public organized expression, as
governed by Jewish leaders, was restricted by two permanent and deep commitments: securing the well-being of American Jewry and averting any suspicion of questionable patriotism. However, no fair assessment of the conduct
of American Jewish leadership can be made if we confine our inquiry only to
questioning the soundness of their priorities, choices, and will without taking
heed of the actual parameters for influence. Jewish leaders did not operate in
a vacuum, nor were they free agents to act upon their wishes, whatever they
may have been.

"Power," as Michael Parenti has noted, has "an elusive, almost intangible,
quality."[7] However difficult to define, it is too tantalizing to discard, and historians often let it creep into their narratives in disguise, using such terms
as "influence," "control," "pressure," and the like. Yet when treated as little
more than catchwords, these notions lead to moral judgment rather than a
sound historical critique. In order to overcome the emotional overtones that
have often obstructed the assessment of the response of Jewish leaders to the
crisis in Europe, it is not enough to consider what they could have done. It is
just as important to address realistically what they could *not* have done because of the power relationship that existed between Jews as a sub-group and
the political context in which they operated. In that regard, it must be kept in
mind "that power is used not only to *pursue* interest but *is a crucial factor in
defining interest or predefining the field of choice within which one must then define
one's interests.*"[8] Yet interests are rarely defined autonomously—they are de-
limited by broad social and political forces.

In America of the 1930s, whatever political power Jews developed was
mostly in the arena of big city politics. But as in the economic sphere, where

individual Jews had amassed considerable wealth but had never come close to controlling the financial and corporate structure, so in politics local power mavericks rarely succeeded in extending this power to the national arena.[9] Even if the weapon of delivering a voting bloc had been available to the Jewish leaders, Jewish voters were in no position to decide presidential elections. While American Jews were free to decide four times not to vote for FDR, his Republican opponents held even less hope for them. In real terms, Jews could have done little else than register their protest, but their voting power did not have the leverage to affect the national agenda.[10]

But the Jewish response was further mitigated by the American paradox. While wishing to remain part of *K'lal Yisrael*, the abounding rights and opportunities allured many American Jews to exploit the many options that came their way, as individuals, to become Americans. As a result, and especially during the bad times of the 1930s and 1940s when the struggle for acceptance suffered a setback, action on behalf of Jews overseas, while not abandoned, became increasingly qualified by two provisions: publicly it had to conform with American national interests, and parochially it was not to endanger the hard-won yet tenuous status of American Jews. Nowhere were these restrictive conditions more apparent than in the issue of immigration.

This chapter will continue to follow the reactions and modus operandi of Jewish leaders. It will consider in detail the remaining months of 1933, as well as 1934 and 1935, addressing the major events in Germany that became an issue for and affected the lives of American Jews either directly or indirectly.

Immigration and Jewish Solidarity

To avoid the pitfalls that reading history backward may occasion, a number of facts ought to be recalled. While it is often emphasized that in 1933 only a very small minority of German Jews thought of emigration, to America or elsewhere, as an immediate course of action, the fact that not all those who desired and had sufficient means to do so were granted permits to immigrate to the United States is generally downplayed.[11] Also, by the early 1930s immigration policy was a dead issue for most immigrant groups in America, including Jews.[12]

In view of the deepening economic upheaval which was exacerbating an already intensely anti-foreign and isolationist mood, it is hardly surprising that when the "likely to become a public charge" (LPC) clause of the 1917 Immigration Act was further restricted by Hoover's directive of September 13, 1930, it did not evoke any particular protest among American Jews. Although Jewish leaders were not indifferent to the results of the Reichstag elections that took place a day later, when the Nazi Party became the second largest party, it is not surprising that they did not view with special alarm Hoover's new provisions which called upon the consular officers to "pass judgment *with particular care* on whether the applicant *may become a public charge;* and if the applicant cannot convince . . . that it is *not probable,* the visa will be refused."[13] Nor is there a record of a particular reaction when Hoover proclaimed in October 1932 that "with the growth of democracy in foreign countries, political persecution has largely ceased. There is no longer a necessity for the U.S. to provide an asylum for those persecuted because of conscience."[14] Although it is clear that America's gates had been closed since the 1920s out of racist motives, this policy had been in force a decade before Hitler's accession to power made it detrimental to the European Jews.

It was more than reasonable, perhaps, that under the strenuous circumstances prevailing in America, protecting its own—increasingly more broadly defined to include both Jewish and non-Jewish Americans—became the priority of American Jewry. In April 1933 Max Kohler, the legal expert of the AJC on immigration matters, viewed the enforcement of the Hoover Executive Order of 1930 as "sensible," because "to allow other bread winners to come over here in numbers would make our own position even more acute."[15] Another telling testimony to this state of affairs was voiced by Joseph P. Chamberlain, the American advisor to League of Nations High Commissioner for Refugees James G. McDonald. Feeling discouraged by the apathy of the members of the non-Jewish community who failed to contribute to the cause of the refugees, he had to admit that he was "not very much surprised" in view of the fact that "even in the Jewish community here, many . . . believe that their responsibilities to people in this country should be more fully considered than they have been in the past. . . . Furthermore, there is an unwillingness among many people to subordinate their interests in welfare work . . . to the work for the refugees."[16] A similar critical view, depicted as a "classic dictum of many of our leading Jews," was aired in *B'nai B'rith Magazine*. "We . . . Americans," it charged "are greatly and increasingly overburdened by our responsibilities toward those of our brethren among us who are in distress and we decidedly do not want any more immigrants who are likely to become public charges."[17]

Not only did American Jews view the incoming of refugees as an economic burden, but many of them perceived immigration as a destabilizing factor that had a direct impact on their position in American society.[18] While some of the Jewish leaders tried to work behind the scenes to relax the interpretation of the Hoover decree, most of them were extremely uneasy with any congressional initiative, particularly when led by Jewish representatives. Such was the case when on March 22, 1933, Representative Samuel Dickstein, a Democrat from New York, and since 1931 chairman of the House Committee on Immigration and Naturalization, introduced a resolution for the repeal of the Hoover decree of 1930. Dickstein, representing a district of East European Jews on the Lower East Side, and himself of the same background, was a steadfast opponent of restrictive immigration.[19] But considering the negative mood in Congress toward lowering immigration barriers, it is not at all clear whether it was a serious proposal or a grandstanding act for the benefit of his constituents.

All the same, although the resolution gained the backing of the Jewish members in the House, the leaders of the Jewish organizations were much more reluctant to support it.[20] Cyrus Adler refused outright by citing the high rate of unemployment as the reason for his opposition. His reply to Dickstein, however, gives us an insight into the underlying rationale of the Jewish response. Commenting on the wording of the resolution, Adler was opposed to "*directing* the Secretary of State to issue certain new instructions to Consuls." Coaching the congressman in the art of politics, Adler noted: "I assume that you did not introduce such a Resolution before because you thought that you could not move the last Administration." Was he alerting Dickstein to the importance of using political expediency as an alibi for introducing the resolution at this hour, on the assumption that otherwise he would be charged with serving his group's particular interests? Perhaps, but Adler certainly revealed prudence when, although he knew better, he emphasized to the Jewish congressman that the secretary of state was sympathetic to the cause and therefore deserved the courtesy that "all steps taken which affect the Department of State should have his concurrence in advance if possible." For those who accepted Adler's view that discretion is the better part of valor, his argument was convincing.[21]

Dickstein also sought the support of Max Kohler, the recognized authority on immigration law. Interestingly, Kohler based his opposition not only on economic grounds, but also on more particular fears. "You create a situation," he warned Dickstein, "where it will be charged with force that American Jews want to sacrifice America's obvious and essential interests on behalf of their German Jewish co-religionists!"[22] Paradoxically, Kohler, the assimilated American Jew, chose to define Dickstein's responsibilities first as a Jew and only second as a member of the House of Representatives. As we shall see, this was not the only instance in which Jews, acting prudently, denied themselves the right to participate in the democratic process for fear of being accused of acting out of particular Jewish interests.

When Rabbi Stephen Wise took the stand to testify on the resolution before the House Immigration Committee, his views were grounded in much of the same Americanized sensitivities and Jewish insecurities. He opposed any public political action on behalf of German Jews which would necessitate "special amendments to American immigration laws," or "new legislation with respect to the victims of persecution." Wise further affirmed that all Americans "accepted without demur the philosophy of immigration which now seems to obtain in the halls of Congress."[23] He was for the revocation of the Hoover decree, provided it was done "without reference to the German [i.e., Jewish] situation, but purely with respect to the general immigration restrictions."[24] Although these kinds of testimonies by Jewish leaders were merely tactical, they nonetheless reflected the position of Jews in America in the 1930s.

The lack of support from the Jewish establishment did not seem to discourage Dickstein. Congress resumed hearings on the measure in May, and Max Kohler again testified on behalf of the AJC and B'nai B'rith. Kohler made clear that he was not challenging the propriety of the executive order, and asked for a very limited gesture involving "nonlaborers and some exceptional persons" whose admission may have been barred by "haphazard action of the consuls abroad." He was prepared to support the Dickstein bill if it were designed to "simply allow in a few particular cases review of the refusal of visas by the head of the State Department," provided the applicant in question was not likely to become a public charge or compete with American laborers. Kohler was not ambivalent about stating his interests: "I am chiefly interested in the situation as it exists in Germany," he declared, "though I would not recommend special legislation for them [Jews]."

None of the Jewish moguls who had been invited to testify were to be seen, and it was left to Elias A. Cohen and Nathan Perlman, junior officers of the AJ Congress, to lead the retreat from Wise's earlier "daring" position. Cohen echoed much of Kohler's views and stressed that he was not asking for a change in the immigration laws, but urged that "before making any attempt to revoke the Executive Order . . . those committed to helping the victims of Nazism should try and persuade [the Administration] to interpret the 'public charge' clause as leniently as possible."[25]

When Dickstein first approached Jewish leaders to support his House resolution, Kohler had begged him to let it "die a natural, quiet death."[26] It died, but not quietly. In a highly dramatized performance on Capitol Hill, Jewish spokesmen scored high marks for their recitation of the patriotic theme. But not all were impressed.

Felix Frankfurter, the rather cautious and somewhat sycophantic Jew, was dismayed as an American by this spectacle. The Jews' policy "in regard to asylum for religious and political persecution must be in the light of day and not 'surreptitious,'" he insisted. "It is the utmost confusion of the whole history of the United States and the concepts of international law to suggest that adherence to our traditional policy in welcoming the persecuted is even remotely an infringement upon the internal affairs of another government."[27] Jews in public life were particularly sensitive to displays of disapproval from Jews who feared that their "influence" with the president, for instance, would "hurt the Jewish people," as Wise put it in a letter to Frankfurter. Frankfurter immediately countered with the protest that "to make any concessions to fears about misuse on the part of others of exercise of one's rights and duties as an American citizen is to introduce and accept for this country the Nazi doctrine of citizenship and helotry."[28]

However, these candid exchanges were carried out among intimates. They were more in the nature of private group therapy for people who were experiencing similar anxieties. Seldom did Frankfurter, or his colleagues, publicly claim with such assertiveness their rights as citizens. At most, and not too frequently, the president's Jews, after thorough consideration, would approach the policy makers on behalf of Jews far from the public limelight.

"Does he not know? Does he not care?"

At the end of April 1933, representatives of the AJC and the AJ Congress were granted separate interviews with the secretary of state, which elicited yet another, and by then redundant, assurance of "careful and sympathetic interest."[29] The demand of the two organizations was basically the same: to liberalize the interpretation of the 1930 executive order that restricted the immigration of German Jews to America. In their report on the meeting Stephen Wise and Bernard Deutsch emphasized that their proposal would be acceptable since Secretary of Labor Perkins had indicated that the matter was "not far from the mind of the President." Wise reassured Hull that the request would be phrased "carefully" in order to not be "too offending to a government with which our own was nominally in friendly relations." To display their total allegiance to the president, they casually remarked that a number of senators had been ready to speak out for weeks, but had been "held back from public utterance" by the Jewish loyalists. Nonetheless, in his memorandum on this meeting, Wise admonished his associates that Jewish leaders should "not be satisfied with the vapid and meaningless declarations from the State Department. These can be had day after day. They mean nothing. They stand in the way of action if they are blandly and stupidly accepted as a substitute for action."[30]

A month later Wise would confess that if FDR had consented to any slight modification in the strict interpretation of the LPC clause, it would have been "accepted" as an "adequate gesture."[31] But it took Roosevelt a while longer to respond. This was an established ritual. Jewish leaders would ask for a supporting gesture from the administration, which would usually be granted because, as one historian has noted, "it entailed no political price while it earned political points."[32]

Cyrus Adler may have been equally frustrated by the idleness of the State Department, but when he wrote to the secretary he was guided by other considerations. Although he tried to impress upon Hull the need to hear "some expression of feeling" from the government, using the word "feeling" advisedly, as he put it, Adler was aware that when addressing the champion of economic internationalism the argument had to be presented in ecumenical terms. He therefore made the case that Germany's present actions with regard to "a section of its citizens" was a "challenge to the economic security of the world."[33] But when daring to press for an easing of immigration regulations, American Jews could only resort to a steadily depleted arsenal of moral imperatives. "It would be a fine and generous thing for America to do," Adler wrote to Hull, for it "would not only earn the gratitude of the four million and a quarter Jews of America"—understandably not an adequate incentive— "but . . . the respect and admiration of the entire world."[34]

It was left to a Gentile to speak the truth in public to a Jewish audience. James McDonald delivered a confidential address in early May 1933 in New York. Sharing with the participants his pessimism about the practical value of their actions, he said:

> I am sure you can do many things which will satisfy you [*sic*] own love and affection which will give you a feeling that you are protesting, that you are upholding the Jews in Germany—I venture a doubt. I personally know nothing which the Jews can do en masse publicly as a group, which will help Jews in Germany.[35]

It was a harsh reality to digest. Although McDonald was suspected by Wise, Frankfurter, and others of being "pro-German," his views carried much weight with Jewish leaders because he was well connected in Germany as well as in Washington, and they often made use of his prestigious position. Moreover, rumors circulated that he was being considered as the next ambassador to Germany.[36]

In the month of May, as the mood grew more desperate, the envisioned solutions became more chimerical. "If L.D.B could talk for half an hour to F.D.R. and Hull," Wise fantasized, "and bring the impact of . . . that mighty conscience upon their souls, I really believe something can be done." Wise was almost ready to believe that with Brandeis in the lead it would be "not a battle won but half the war." However, the justice guarded the neutrality of his position jealously and refused Wise's "mild request" to make a public statement.[37] Brandeis, not least, perhaps, because his power to influence remained untested, continued to be regarded as the only potential redeemer. Even years later, in September 1940, Wise was still lamenting "If only L.D.B. had taken hold in 1933, when some of us begged he should!" Speaking about the "one and only," Wise even dared to subtly dispute Frankfurter's judgment, adding, "Were you not among those opposed to his doing so that time?"[38]

Under considerable pressure by Wise, Frankfurter engineered a meeting between Hull and Brandeis at the justice's home in May 1933. Although it was suggested that Hull be given a "dispassionate presentation of the German problem," Brandeis urged for a statement by the president of "the kind W.W. [Woodrow Wilson] would have made," and a relaxation of the curb on immigration. As a good American he passionately expressed to Hull that he "felt more ashamed of [his] country than pained by Jewish suffering" and lamented the difference between the present American attitude and the nation's "nobler past."[39]

Although nothing resulted from the Hull-Brandeis meeting, Mack thought that a similar meeting with Undersecretary Phillips "would be most helpful."[40] Indeed, so despondent was the mood that the mere fact of a contact with a member of the administration was viewed as something of an achievement. A meeting with Assistant Secretary of State Raymond Moley, for example, although it netted little more than "information that Felix Frankfurter was the person in whom the President put the greatest confidence" and advice that it might be worthwhile for him to get in touch with FDR, was also considered "important."[41] But Frankfurter, who knew that friendship and politics were an odd couple, was reluctant to exert direct pressure on the president.[42]

Making no headway with their own government and desperate enough to disregard even a stern warning from Brandeis, a group of influential Jews met on May 12th for a private dinner with Dr. Hjalmar Schacht, the president of the Reichsbank who came as Hitler's representative for the Washington economic talks.[43] The dinner was hosted by David Sarnoff who had befriended Schacht at the Young Plan Conference in 1929. Other guests included Wise,

Proskauer, Irving Lehman, Baruch, and others. What transpired in the meeting remains unclear, but Schacht reported to Hitler that he had told the Jewish leaders that in the Third Reich no economic difficulties were foreseen for Jews in Germany.[44] Brandeis and Mack were "keenly awaiting the report" from Wise, but they were to be disappointed. Apparently Wise never reported on this abortive attempt at a direct dialogue with the Germans.[45]

The only dubious benefit that American Jews accrued from Schacht's visit was communicated to Judge Irving Lehman by Roosevelt who, after meeting with Schacht, informed him that "at least the German Government now knows how I feel about things." The president gained more; he used this opportunity to send a message to American Jews that he preferred the informal approach, reasoning that it would be less dangerous for Jews in Germany.[46] This opinion put just about the final damper on the Jews' hopes for official diplomatic intercession.

Bitterly disappointed by his president, Wise could only turn to Frankfurter and cry out in bewilderment, "He [FDR] has saved the world from war. In heaven's name, why can't he be moved to save the Jews of Germany? Does he not know? Does he not care?"[47] Wise's relationship with FDR, especially his "fatal attraction" to the president in later years, was far from a foregone conclusion. In fall 1932, before FDR secured the nomination of the Democratic Party, Wise had considered "[going] through the country . . . in order that people who believe in him and trust him may know . . . that he is a man of no moral courage whatsoever and of no political integrity."[48] This deep mistrust had its origin in the so-called Walker scandal. Corruption in New York's magistrate courts and the city administration were probed by the Seabury Investigation Committee in the summer of 1932, whose recommendation was to remove from office the mayor of New York City, James Walker. Roosevelt, then governor of New York who was campaigning to win the Democratic presidential nomination, procrastinated in his response. Indeed, Walker was shortly thereafter forced to resign. Rabbi Wise and his close associate John Hayes Holmes, both active in New York City social politics, were extremely critical of the governor's behavior and they caused FDR great political embarrassment.[49]

Upon learning of Roosevelt's nomination as the Democratic candidate for the presidency, Wise had expressed his disappointment and sense of outrage to many of his friends. "There is no basic stuff in the man," he complained to Frankfurter, "no deep-seated convictions. . . . He is all clay and no granite."[50] But Wise, like others among the Jewish leaders, was also realistic. Knowing that practical possibilities to exert influence were extremely limited, he was reluctant (perhaps, in hindsight, more reluctant than he ought to have been) to do anything that might threaten the tenuous links of prominent Jews to the administration, which seemed to him their only hope for action.

While Wise could console his daunted associates that "if we cannot achieve anything we can comfort ourselves that we are doing what we can," by temperament he was determined to follow a more militant course.[51] Encouraged by Senator William E. Borah, the ex-chairman of the Foreign Relations Committee, to activate the "power of numbers," he resolved to take part in the American democratic ritual: "to bring all the pressure" of Jews around the country by letters and telegrams "to bear upon the President, the State Department and Congress demanding action." Unfortunately this proved to be yet another abortive campaign with no troops to fight it. Feeling "a little guilty in restraining such action up to this time," Wise pledged not to do so any longer. "I have no right," he wrote in a tone of self-reproach.[52] But were the Jewish leaders free to exercise their will?

Representatives of Jewish organizations, not to mention those Jews serving in and around the Roosevelt court, had rarely taken the liberty to publicly air their disappointment in America. Apart from trying to avoid any situation in which they could be suspected of disloyalty, they were reluctant, perhaps, to reveal their powerlessness and to publicly admit their country's indifference to the fate of the German Jews. They displayed public-spirited patriotism in order to avoid accusations of having particular interests, but they often resorted to more sophisticated rationalizations to conceal their own powerlessness in the face of that apathy.

For instance, how could Jewish leaders reconcile total devotion to the president with the fact that he did not "as yet lift a finger to save the Jews of Germany from Hitler!"?[53] One solution, which was adopted for quite some time, was to believe that it was "the State Department [that] has not played the game along with FDR's mind."[54] Indeed, when it came to the plight of the Jews in Germany Roosevelt, conveniently, preferred to trust his State Department and not to intervene. Jewish leaders did not question too much the fact that he was very involved in other foreign policy issues.

Until June 1933, Roosevelt's fear of disrupting the London World Economic Conference was considered the "great factor" in explaining his continued silence.[55] The trust that he "was going to pull the nations of the world out of their economic difficulties"[56] made it much easier to be persuaded that failure of the Conference would cause "nationalistic intensification in all countries" which "in all likelihood" would lead to "Hitlerite action against Jews elsewhere than in Germany."[57] In fact, even after the Conference had taken place and failed, Rabbi Wise listed it as a principal reason for his having opposed the public declaration of a Jewish boycott.[58]

The president's Jews also played their part in fostering this view. On June 5, 1933, Judge Samuel Rosenman reported to the executive committee of the AJC that "the President is deeply concerned over the German situation . . . but he had withheld any public statement because his present greatest concern is with the economic and disarmament conference and he would not do anything that has the slightest possibility of doing injury to these conferences." Most important, he impressed upon his audience that "if they fail, the result for the world at large *and for the Jews in particular* would be extremely unfavorable."[59] When Raymond Moley ventured to weaken the Jews' explanation for their cautious behavior by suggesting that the Conference was not an "insuperable obstacle in the way of a direct statement from the White House," his opinion went unheeded.[60]

Wise was even able to derive some "extras" from the Conference. If before it convened it provided him with a rationale for behaving with self-restraint, when it "prove[d] to be a fiasco" he used it as proof for his own foresight and wisdom. As he reported to the AJ Congress's administrative committee upon his return from Europe in September 1933, he had opposed a call by Samuel Untermeyer, the moving spirit behind the boycott movement, to hold a boycott conference in London concurrently with the World Economic Conference, and he noted with satisfaction that "it is a mercy from heaven that the Boycott Conference was not held in London for we might have been held as contributory to the disaster which ensued and to the disaster in which the whole World Economic Conference developed."[61] This kind of rationalization, born of continual efforts to negotiate between the constraints of reality and his desire for action, was probably what enabled him to endure the many humiliations that came his way. But at the same meeting he also noted more soberly that "the Government's name is taken in vain almost as often by English Jews as by American Jews. When Anglo-Jewish leaders do not want to do a thing, they attribute their disinclination to the inspiration of the Government."[62]

Between Patriotism and Anti-Semitism

Especially in times of crisis Jews were careful not to call attention to what the majority construed as their otherness. Judge Joseph Proskauer, one of those who most consistently followed this course, cringed at the idea that Jews would sponsor an anti-Nazi protest, arguing that "for Jews in America, qua Jews, to demand any kind of political action, is a negation of the fundamentals of American liberty and equality."[63] Addressing a conference of the AJC on the German situation in May 1933, Proskauer was more pragmatic, warning American Jews not to make public demands—which in any case could not be accommodated in the present "complicated situation of foreign affairs" and would only "cause a repercussion on the Jews of America for interfering in these larger concerns." Rather, he proposed to trust those in charge of American policy and to remember "that we are Americans and must be loyal above else, above all else, to America, and to keep quietly and earnestly at that process until the impact of American public opinion is fairly registered in Germany."[64] The feared repercussion, although it was not always publicly admitted, was anti-Semitism.

Yet for a people whose concern for survival had always informed both their doctrine and practice, seeking protection from the state, however indifferent, was the sole option. Indeed, as anti-Jewish sentiments became more vehement, open, and widespread—most historians agree that anti-Semitism in America began to escalate in the late 1930s, reaching its peak in the early 1940s—Jewish leaders seemed to feel an ever greater need to express their patriotism.[65] Although at no time did anti-Jewish prejudice constitute a serious threat to the Jews' civil and political rights, their behavior in the public sphere was nonetheless framed by its existence. From the early 1930s the twin fears of anti-Semitism and charges of disloyalty constituted a significant factor in informing the response of American Jewish leaders to the crisis that befell their beleaguered fellow Jews in Europe.

Indeed, it was not a simple matter for American Jews to negotiate between their deep allegiance to and affection for America and their awareness that this very soil was a breeding ground for anti-Jewish hatred. As one of the finest minds of his generation, Rabbi Milton Steinberg, wrote in 1934, the Jews of his day stood between two worlds, one in which they could no longer live, the other which they could not fully enter. Perhaps "only a people of acrobats could preserve a semblance of poise on a footing so unstable."[66]

But keeping poised was not always easy. Sol Stroock, chairman of the AJC, undertook to ease the American Jews' sense of "recreancy," as he put it. Explaining the course pursued by the AJC with regard to the German situation, he pointed out that "we do not believe . . . that whenever a claim is made by a Jew or Jewry that we must immediately rally to the cause of that Jew, irrespective of whether it is the right thing to do."[67] Addressing on the same occasion the "peculiarly difficult position" that the German crisis occasioned for American Jewry, Max Kohler assured his audience that the curbs on immigration met with the overwhelmingly strong support of the country at large. In return, "as patriotic American citizens . . . [we] do not want to do anything which will really jeopardize and injure the interests of our country, however dear the cause may be of the German Jewish refugees."[68] But dissolving the emotional collective "we" was not that simple, making the solution of the "loyalty equation" that much more complicated.

To circumvent the virtual taboo of pressing for particular Jewish interests, the burden of obligation was shifted to America. In its redrafted version, the problem became, in Kohler's words, that of *"our country"* which under "abnormal conditions" must scout "for a path which will . . . do deference without real injury to our country to the principle of asylum for refugees and at the same time accord with the needs and wishes of the great majority of the country, that our enormous army of unemployed should not be materially increased by admitting refugees."[69]

Similar sentiments figured prominently in the initial opposition of the Jewish establishment to a public boycott of German goods.[70] "I find an overwhelming objection among my Christian friends to action by Jews which may adversely affect the interests of this country," Judge Proskauer wrote in June 1933 to Samuel Untermeyer, who headed the boycott movement. He could "conceive of nothing that would more foment antisemitism here in this country than organized boycott."[71] Proskauer's fears were not groundless; one only has to examine the *Christian Century* in the 1930s to ascertain that even the Jews' friends thought they had a long way to go to become "real" Americans.[72]

Ostensibly Brandeis thought differently. Meeting with the Jewish leaders, he argued that if the boycott was to be "continued and extended," it was Jews "who must head it." Brandeis conceded that to expect the American Federation of Labor or Christian clergy to lead the struggle was "an utterly mistaken policy" since their interest was "polite, but still lukewarm." Well aware that fear of increasing anti-Semitism lurked behind the reluctance to join the boycott, he said: "I am not afraid that what we are doing will evoke or create anti-Semitism. The American is an essentially manly being and he admires nothing more than courage."[73] But even Brandeis had to admit that the Jew was not entirely free to act, since, as he wrote to Wise some months later, "his wrongdoing is apt to injure the whole Jewish people. We must make all see that each is constantly in the show-window; and that because of existing prejudice each must act as trustee for the whole people."[74]

The Roosevelt administration itself was not averse to playing on the Jewish leaders' fears of anti-Semitism, which only reinforced their inclination toward prudent behavior in the public sphere. The well-orchestrated pressure to which they were repeatedly subjected had a clear connotation: demands to liberalize the immigration laws and regulations were liable to increase anti-Semitism. This warning was highly effective, not least because the Jews' primal insecurity disposed them to experience potential danger as actual danger and to react accordingly. It is likely, as W. I. Thomas asserted, that "if men define situations as real, they are real in their consequences."[75]

In late October 1933, Judge Julian Mack held a series of meetings with administration officials in Washington. On his agenda was one central item: to call attention to an overlooked provision of the 1917 Immigration Act that would permit the secretary of labor to accept bond as a guarantee that a potential immigrant would not become a public charge.[76] This matter involved both the Departments of State and Labor, which occasioned open tension between the two. The conflict was negotiated and the Labor Department, and by extension American Jews, won the legal battle. But it was an ineffective victory, since Labor Department officials could not agree on the number of bonds they could politically afford to accept and how forcefully they could press the issue.[77]

The more bitter pill to swallow, perhaps, was the strategy that Roosevelt administration agents employed on this occasion. Daniel MacCormack, the commissioner of immigration, forewarned Mack that any action in the direction of liberalizing immigration regulations would increase anti-Semitism, which would in turn lead to adverse congressional action that might result in reduction of the quotas to 10 percent of the present number. Mack responded by expressing confidence that a public statement by Roosevelt could avert hostile action by Congress and swing public opinion to favor the admission of "qualified" political and religious refugees.[78]

To "explain his position more fully" MacCormack asked Mack out for lunch. In this more intimate setting he first "emphasized his pro-Semitism" by telling Mack of his recent "personal selection of Judge Thacher" (a Jew) as head of the legal committee of the commission investigating the Ellis Island situation. MacCormack, himself a naturalized citizen, then went on to describe the recent encounters he had had around the country with "many non-Jewish liberals," none of whom had spoken in favor of admitting refugees, and some of whom had even expressed themselves against it. The commissioner's first order of business seemed to have been to impress upon Jews that their natural potential allies could not be counted upon. He then extended his warning to the political sphere, telling Mack that he had not the slightest doubt that "if the Germany quota were filled during these times of depressions and especially if it were filled largely by Jewish refugees, nothing could stop Congressional action against it." MacCormack emphasized repeatedly that he was reporting facts, that he had no sympathy with this position, but that it was important that the Jewish leadership appreciated this "factual situation."[79]

Because he was being subjected to a seemingly "positive" form of co-optation, Mack could hardly disregard MacCormack's warning. Indeed, when powerful insiders undertake to alert the powerless of an impending danger—not only acknowledging the existence of prejudice, but demonstrating their sympathy by offering advice—they can easily come to be regarded as allies. A dual goal was realized by making use of such tactics: not only were Jews made ever more grateful for their country's protection but also, convinced that the threat was real, they curtailed their pressure on the administration. While Mack had hoped to influence the system from within, the system managed to work its way into him. Indeed, on that same afternoon he told Labor Department Solicitor Charles Wyzanski—one of Secretary Perkins's *Yiddish kopf*, as she fondly referred to the socially concerned Jews who came to Washington during the New Deal period—that he was anxious to keep the issue out of Congress.[80]

Mack's reaction was not an isolated incident. Wyzanski, who had won the legal case for the labor department on the bond issue with his "excellent" opinion, duly urged Secretary Perkins to exercise judgment and selectivity in accepting the bonds, to avoid exacerbating domestic anti-Semitism.[81] Like many other Jewish New Dealers he too was reluctant to use his position for what might be interpreted as sectarian purposes. As a reaction, perhaps, he was overly concerned about the political damage the bond issue might inflict on the president, especially if he were to make a public statement about the new policy.[82] Indeed, concern over repercussions from publicity was rampant. When journalist Edwin Mims showed Mack the proofs of his forthcoming article on "German Refugees and American Bureaucrats," which sharply criticized the Old Dealers for their opposition to the ruling on the bonds issue, Mack advised against publication on the grounds that a "red hot diatribe" would do more harm than good.[83]

Cyrus Adler feared that anti-Semitism would only be aggravated by "the constant airing of their [the Jews'] wrongs and their sorrows and the showing of their sores, wearying people . . . giving the impression that in the world they wish to put themselves forward as the only problem."[84] Such an assessment of the Jews' behavior, which was assiduously promoted by certain sectors of American Jewry, may perhaps explain why "the German problem" was regarded as "much over-stressed."[85]

MacCormack met with Judge Mack again in June 1934, this time to alert him as well to the "tremendous growth of anti-Semitism" in America. He informed Mack that if in 1933 the number of refugees admitted was 1,200, in 1934 it would total 3,600. Presenting his position as that of an ally, MacCormack warned empathically that "our enemies will cry out" at an increase of 200 percent. He further confided in Mack that when the German quota had been set in 1924, it had been based on the belief that the immigration would be "almost entirely Teutonic or Nordic, and that if Congress had believed it would be ninety per cent Jewish they would have taken some steps at that time to avoid this." In view of the situation and out of what one may suspect was less than genuine concern for the future of American Jews, he suggested that there were two alternative courses of action: either protect the nearly five million American Jews from an intensification of anti-Semitism that would result from an influx of refugees, or aid "at the best, a comparatively small number of the five hundred thousand German Jews to come over here."[86]

Judge Irving Lehman was rather agitated when he received Mack's report of this last meeting. Although he was aware of the general feeling in Washington that anti-Semitism was on the rise and that some "sincere liberals" believed that the situation was "fraught with danger," Lehman did not "share these fears." He pinpointed the reason for the present mood in the new administration's practice of introducing "into the official life of Washington men of a different type . . . a considerable number of Jews." But as far as Lehman was concerned,

> More important is the fact that those who wish to discredit the Administration program insist that it is un-American, and they stress the participation of Jews in the formulation of the program for the purpose of suggesting that its inspiration comes from those who have not inherited American traditions. That is not, in my opinion, a sign of increasing anti-Semitism in this country, but to some extent it must be regarded as an appeal to latent anti-Semitism and thus may become a danger in the future. I concede that we must not be oblivious to this danger, but I do not wish to exaggerate it.[87]

This rather convoluted message displays the dilemmas that were triggered by the increased visibility of American Jews in public life. Especially for the most prominent among them, to accept at face value the existence of an anti-Semitic threat was tantamount to betraying their faith in the American creed. Because they were far more sensitive and responsive to doubts about their Americanism than to anti-Semitism, this section of American Jewry, even when it conceded that "latent" anti-Jewish animus existed, preferred to view it as an instrument for discrediting the administration's New Deal program as un-American. But their acknowledgment of the prevalent restrictionist mood in the country, even among liberals, obliged such people as Lehman to admit that "it would be hopeless . . . to combat these views at the present time. Any attempt to open wide the doors to those who suffer from political or religious persecution would be doomed to failure."[88] It was undoubtedly humiliating for a Jewish American patriot to acknowledge his country's indifference to human misery, and Lehman did not wish to believe "that there would be any widespread opposition to the admission of five or even ten thousand German Jews a year, provided it can be shown that the immigrants admitted will never become a public charge and will not cause displacement of labor here." For him, it "seem[ed] impossible" that "the admission of such a small number would intensify anti-Semitism here (in America)." Lehman was not disturbed "by the supposed danger, but by the fact that Colonel MacCormack believes it exists."[89]

It was not long before what Jewish leaders first heard behind closed doors and resented came to be espoused by the formulators of "Jewish opinion" as a correct approach. In an article in *Opinion*, the house organ of the American Jewish Congress, American restrictionism was defended as a means of protecting American Jews against anti-Semitism. Having established the "folly" and "unfair[ness]" to the "alien, his family and to us as Americans" of admitting the destitute into a country with high unemployment, the writer succinctly summarized the predicament that the German situation generated for American Jewry:

> If too many of the Jews in foreign lands were admitted here in any one year, it would arouse the bitter and positive resistance of the restrictionist as well as cause a rise in the anti-Semitic movement in this country. In essence, the question put to a number of prominent Jews was this: is it desirable to insist upon the admission of possibly 25,000 more Jews from Germany (and later from Poland, Austria, etc.) and thus give fuel to the claims of the anti-Semites here that we, the Jews, were seeking to bring all the unfortunates to this country in these unfortunate times, or is it the wiser policy to safeguard the mental, physical, and social happiness of the four million Jews now in the United States by refraining from bringing too many more Jews here?[90]

By the end of May 1933 Roosevelt still adhered to his policy of silence on the German problem, the State Department offered little more than "sympathy," and American public opinion remained indifferent. There were not many alternatives left to explore in the attempt to arouse the consciousness of America to the plight of the German Jews. In late May 1933 a meeting was arranged between key staffers of the American Jewish Congress and the Jewish members of the House of Representatives to "consider questions of policy." Stephen Wise's scornful description of the congressmen intimated that it was less a meeting of choice than an act of last resort:

Sabath, who is a thick and thin supporter of the President . . . ; Celler, who is
blatant but insignificant; Mrs. Kahn[,] who has probably the best head of the
whole crowd—though that does not mean very much; Dickstein, who can best
be characterized as Dickstein;* Sirevich, a super-articulate charlatan; Bloom,
former vaudeville manager and real estate speculator . . . ; Ellenbogen of Pittsburgh, a Viennese lad who must wait another two months before he can be
sworn in, because seven years have not elapsed since he became a citizen.[91]

The group reported a great deal of anti-Semitism in the halls of the Congress, alluding to the danger of pro-German and anti-Jewish speeches in the
House. But what seemed to have disturbed Wise the most was the timidity of
the Jewish representatives who attempted to "defend the President's inaction." He depicted them as being more "eager to support the Administration
rather than do the thing that is obviously needed in the Jewish interests." As
to the prevalence of anti-Semitism in the House, he made this barbed comment: "Much of what they imagine to be anti-Semitism in general is nothing
more than contempt and loathing for them personally, which of course they
rationalize away in self-protective terms of anti-Semitism."[92]
    One week later Wise displayed the very same traits that he deplored in
others. Speaking in the name of Proskauer, Stroock, Deutsch, and himself,
Wise informed Sabath that after their "fullest consideration" they "urge no
Jewish speeches for the present" in the House.[93] Briefing Frankfurter on the
same day, Wise revealed that the decision had been reached as the result of a
vicious anti-Semitic speech delivered by Republican Congressman Louis T.
McFadden of Pennsylvania the previous week. "We are fearful of the super-
intervention of the Jewish members of the House," he wrote, adding that in
the smaller Senate there was "less likelihood of any explosion against us,"
perhaps, as he insinuated, because it was unlikely that the issue of the German Jews would be taken up there.[94]
    McFadden, an anti-Roosevelt Jew-baiter, spoke against the administra-
tion's resolution to repeal the gold standard. The resolution was approved by
a margin of almost five to one and aimed to cancel the gold clause in all federal and private obligations and make them payable in legal tender. "Is it not
true," asked McFadden, echoing the old libel, "that, in the United States today, the Gentiles have the slips of paper while the Jews have the gold and
lawful money? And is not this repudiation bill a bill specifically designed and
written by the Jewish international money changers themselves in order to
perpetuate their power?"[95] Although McFadden continued relentlessly to lash
out against Jews at every opportunity, he remained an isolated phenomenon.
No member of Congress came out in his defense and he was in fact defeated
in the Democratic landslide of 1934.[96]
    It was not just fear of anti-Semitism that accounted for Jewish ambivalence

---

*In German "Dickstein" means literally "fat stone" or "thick stone." By extension, it
is to be read as "thick-headed" or a "fat head."

regarding congressional action on behalf of their German counterparts. Although experience had taught Jews to be skeptical and critical of political authority, they had also learned to appreciate its importance for group survival. The importance accorded group survival in Jewish tradition thus considerably restricted options for action, especially in the public sphere. When, for instance, Democratic senator from Utah William R. King expressed his intention to introduce a resolution to express sympathy with the Jews in Germany, Wise and Deutsch decided that "it seemed unwise to offer a resolution which would seem to isolate the Administration and make it appear that, while the Senate sympathizes with the Jews, the Administration was giving no indication of similar sympathy."[97]

At times the threat of anti-Semitic reaction was the overt ground for discouraging congressional action while the real reason lay hidden elsewhere. Such was the case when Hamilton Fish, the conservative Republican congressman, introduced a resolution requesting the president to "use his good offices to make friendly representation to the German government" with respect to its Jewish citizens.[98] Stephen Wise related to Fish that Jewish leaders were "averse" to pressing the resolution at present, because "in the first place" they "were afraid of McFadden," and in the "second place" the Jewish members of the House "might feel that they ought to make speeches" and they felt that "whatever is publicly said should be said by non-Jews." Knowing that Fish was about to meet with the president, Wise asked him to make clear to the "Chief" that he (Fish) was "acting of his own accord" and that "he was not being pressed" by Jewish leaders. It was not an easy decision to refuse Fish's offer; since he was a fairly well-known anti-Communist, some of the prominent Jews thought it would be "of special importance to have him speak up in the House" on behalf of the Jews.[99] Yet the dread of antagonizing the "Chief" overwhelmed all other considerations.

During 1933 there was little to encourage Jewish activists to believe that their efforts had made more than the slightest impression on those they wished to influence. On an institutional level, action by Jewish organizations was limited by domestic circumstances which made them hesitant to force the issue of the Jews in Germany into the public sphere. Furthermore, the leadership had often been subjected to "orders" from the president's Jews that echoed the interests of the White House. After all, Rabbi Wise was not left with much room to maneuver when Sam Rosenman instructed him, "You should not ask the President to make any declaration now or any public act," or when he informed him that "receiving a delegation or deputation [by FDR] . . . is out now."[100] The only thing he could do was to pour his heart out to Mack:

> I think that's a pretty bad report. It shows how vain and ineffectual all private effort has been. Had we acted publicly six weeks ago in demanding action by the President, we might have had it. Now it is almost certain that it is too late to get it, and they who, like FF [Felix Frankfurter], have dealt with him cannot force his hand now.[101]

As the list of options grew shorter, and the options that were tapped yielded but few results, Franklin D. Roosevelt's figure loomed larger and larger as the Jews' only true source of hope. Whether or not it was in order to preserve this psychological sanctuary and at the same time rationalize their own powerlessness, Jewish activists attributed the president's inaction at least partly to their own inadequacy. As Wise wrote to his close friend John Haynes Holmes, "If we are undone in the end, it will not merely be because of the effectiveness of our foes but because of the timidity and cowardice of ourselves."[102] It may therefore be less surprising that in public, a mere ten days after Wise had received the "bad report," he was able to assert before a crowd of over 800 people in St. Louis that he had "no doubt that President Roosevelt has been as far from indifferent to the horror of the situation in Germany as you and I. But for reasons which must have seemed adequate to him, he has refrained from public utterance or public action.[103]

But by midsummer Wise's sense of inadequacy was shared by most of the Jewish leaders who worked on the German case. In a "personal and confidential" letter to Proskauer in August 1933, Morris Waldman took stock of the ineffectiveness of everything that had been done by American Jewish organizations:

> In spite of the tremendous amount of energy we have expended, our efforts have been quite futile. . . .We sent an emissary to Mussolini—with, at best, dubious results. We saw Schacht with even less results. We have seen the Administration, but whatever the Administration has done has had no effect on Hitler. The public condemnation of the world has been aroused and kept alive . . . but Hitler is impervious to public opinion. . . . No government has made representations, and I am not sure that even if representations would be made . . . they would change the situation. The Jewish boycott has been futile. . . . We have asked the Government to mitigate the executive order of 1930 in re visas from Germany. With what effect? Just vague general assurances.[104]

Waldman was starkly realistic and uncommonly insightful when he perceived Hitler as a unique phenomenon for whom conventional diplomatic rejoinders would be inconsequential. He opined that neither Roosevelt nor the League of Nations was capable of mitigating the anti-Jewish measures of the Nazis. Not to mention that "to leave the destiny of the Jews throughout the world to the weak and limited powers of the existing Jewish organizations (whether they are united or not makes very little difference—weakness added to or multiplied by blatancy does not give strength) still spells ineptitude." "The only hope," he concluded in his letter to Proskauer, "is to destroy the Hitler regime."[105]

As 1933 drew to a close, Lillie Shultz, publicity director of the American Jewish Congress, prepared a memorandum on its "past performance and future action." The "confidential and urgent" report opened with the grim conclusion that "outside of the protest and propaganda movement . . . the Congress has done almost nothing to realize any of the practical plans it has announced." Among the programs of the Congress that were not realized Shultz listed petitions to the League of Nations and to FDR asking for aid on behalf of Germany's Jews, a Million Dollar Emergency Fund Drive, and the boycott. "Today" she concluded, "we have nothing but a paper program."[106]

When Wise returned to the United States in the fall of 1933 after a summer in Europe, his frustration reached an all-time high. He came back convinced that Hitler would wait only as long as it would take him to prepare for victory before he would "talk the world into war again." Writing to his zealous pacifist friend, John Haynes Holmes, Wise added, "Shocking as my word may sound, I am not sure that he ought to be permitted to wait," for Germany was looming as "a military training institute" and the treatment of the Jews was "one of the pre-products of the war spirit."[107] But this early foresight made him all the more frustrated as he failed to awaken his fellow Jews and fellow citizens to the dangers of fascism. To his intimates he began to vent his anger at Roosevelt, describing him as "immovable, incurable and even inaccessible excepting to those of his Jewish friends whom he can safely trust not to trouble him with any Jewish problems."[108]

In October 1933 Felix Frankfurter observed:

> It is idle to hope any longer for amelioration in Germany, and indeed it does not require hindsight to see that there never was any reason for hope. The Nazis had at least candor in their brutality and violence. Hitler told the whole world in *Mein Kampf*.[109]

Between Frustration and Hope

But as 1934 progressed Germany's Jews "were given a . . . powerful lift by the Röhm Revolt," as Victor Klemperer recorded in his diary. "They [the Nazis] cannot survive this blow. Especially now with the emergency of the failed harvest just around the corner, accompanied by the complete bankruptcy of the state and the impossibility of purchasing foreign food." The Nazis' defeat seemed so certain that Klemperer expressed a feeling of "almost pity for Hitler as a human being. The man is lost and *feels* it; for the first time he is speaking without hope."[110]

Back in America, Jewish leaders also became convinced that there was "a lull in the persecution of the Jews."[111] They reasoned that because of Germany's critical economic situation the government would try to improve its image abroad. Stephen Wise and other Jewish leaders also cherished great hopes that the Röhm Revolt, as the June 30th purge of the SA leadership and other of Hitler's conservative enemies was to become known, would have an impact on American public opinion. "I think we have made much progress" Wise wrote to Justice Brandeis. "The Hitler illusion will not likely be restored." Wise referred to Hitler's speech of July 14th, in which he explained the recent bloody purge against the "enemies of the state," as "that of a man cornered and conscious of his peril."[112] Brandeis seemed to have shared his premature optimism, writing to Judge Mack that "the last month of German affairs has helped us mightily."[113]

Morris Waldman's report about his trip to Berlin after the Night of the Long Knives—yet another name for the Röhm Revolt—also described an atmosphere of respite for the Jews. "There was not the slightest appearance of change," he observed, "except that fewer Jews were seen among the crowded tables in the restaurants." He emerged from the meeting with George Messersmith, the U.S. minister to Austria, to report a "positively predicted counter-revolution within two months." Waldman agreed with him that the "imminent economic collapse" was behind the foreseen changes and that without raw materials Germany "will succumb and change of government will come."[114] Waldman was concerned, however, that if Göring were to assassinate Hitler, the German public would be told that it was the Jews' doing. He therefore immediately advised the officers of the AJC in New York by cable, to "restrain comment."[115] But should change of government come without the assassination of Hitler, the Committee's expert on European affairs estimated that the

> position of the Jews is likely to become better. There will not be immediate restoration of their position or revocation of race edicts. But they will gradually recover their position up to the level enjoyed before the war—*ein anstaendiger Anti-Semitismus* [a decent anti-Semitism].[116]

These optimistic interpretations of the events in Germany during 1934, however questionable, can perhaps be understood as a counterbalance to the growing frustrations Jewish leaders endured as their efforts to influence America's policy proved abortive. Attempts to seek encouraging precedents in a more "glorious" past proved anachronistic. When Simon Sobeloff, a U.S. attorney of Baltimore and a Jewish activist, tried to mobilize reluctant Jewish leaders to support a Senate resolution calling upon the president to communicate to the German government the dismay of the American people over the treatment of the Jews, he cited the 1911 abrogation campaign of the Russo-American Treaty of Commerce and Navigation of 1832 as proof of the power of Jewish pressure, when activated.[117] In reply, however, this concerned observer was tactfully informed of the different diplomatic circumstances that had prevailed in the case of the treaty. He was also asked to bear "another factor . . . in mind":

> In 1911 there were practically no Russians, other than Jews, in the United States. The denunciations of Russia's violation of the treaty of 1832 had no opponents who were moved at attachment to Russia. Public agitation to-day against the Nazi regime would cleave the American people into two or more warring camps. I am sure that no patriotic Jew desires to bring about the dissension, even strife which would result from such an agitation.[118]

But apart from their distress at having failed to touch the soul of Roosevelt and his administration, the chiefs of the Jewish organizations were no less frustrated by their failure to penetrate the hearts of their own. In late June 1934 Zionists and non-Zionists alike could share their disillusionment, as can be seen from a letter that Cyrus Adler wrote to the Zionist leader Morris Rothenberg:

> I have been disappointed, as I am sure you have been, in the lack of heartiness in the response to the United Jewish Appeal made in the face of a situation that has not met the Jews of the world in hundreds and hundreds of years. With all the indignation that has been expressed against the Nazi Government, with all the excitement that has been created, the actual response for the maintenance of Jewish institutions in Germany, for the meeting of elementary needs of the refugees scattered throughout the surrounding countries, and for the meeting of the initial cost of the settlement of German and other Jews in Palestine has been appallingly half-hearted.[119]

The qualified optimism in 1934 that arose in part from the fact that "the Jews ha[d] not been deprived of their citizenship" did not last for long.[120] Returning from Germany in the fall, Samuel Margoshes, the vice-president of the AJ Congress and the editor of the Yiddish newspaper *Der Tag* (The Day), reported that the Jews of Germany saw no other alternative except emigration.[121] In December Stephen Wise wrote to Holmes that the situation in Germany has "taken much of the joy out of life, and I confess I have terrible fears for the future."[122]

Even the Berlin riots of July 1935, which renewed protests and requests for intercession by the Jewish organizations, failed to stir official Washington to action. For the most part they were consistently ignored.[123] On July 26th, delegates of the American Jewish Congress, the American Jewish Committee, B'nai B'rith, and the Jewish Labor Committee (JLC), an organization formed in 1934 to represent the non-Zionist Yiddish-speaking workers, met with William Phillips, who was acting secretary of state in Hull's absence. In much more militant language, the group's written protest stated that it was "inconceivable that the American Government should stand passively by and neglect to lift its voice against these assaults upon humanity, or to utter its condemnation of the violation of the fundamental principles of human rights."[124] It also summarized the recent events in Germany and the effects the reign of terror had upon "numberless Catholics and Protestants and liberals," and requested that a note of protest be delivered to the German government.[125] After giving "careful study to the views" of the Jewish delegates, Phillips wrote in his brief reply of July 29th, "I fully understand your solicitude . . . with respect to recent occurrences in Germany affecting various religious and racial groups there."[126] Both sides seemed to have tacitly agreed to present the case against Nazism on a broad liberal basis. But employing a strategy of pragmatic universalism yielded nothing except a good rating for the representatives of American Jewry. They are "rather solid citizens," Phillips recorded in his diary. "I received them sympathetically, told them I would give their appeal consideration, but promised nothing."[127] When President

Roosevelt was asked at a press conference for his reaction to the latest reports coming from Germany, he referred to Phillips's letter of July 29th, saying that it "amply express[ed] his Government's views."[128]

In August 1935, Dr. Jonah Wise of the JDC, upon returning from Germany, briefed Morris Waldman that "the situation of the Jews in Germany has reached the lowest ebb."[129]

The Nuremberg Laws: The Futility of Protest

When in the next month the Nuremberg Laws were enacted and the German Jews were stripped of their citizenship, it became clearer even to the optimists among the American Jewish leaders that emigration was the only solution. In a September 1933 letter to Albert Einstein, Rabbi Wise expressed the hope that with the "utter hopelessness of the situation" revealed, "it may at least be possible to arouse America."[130] Indeed, from the early days of the German crisis Jewish leaders had considered "dramatization—either massacres there or public demonstrations and meetings here—to be the only method of really awakening the open-minded Gentile world."[131]

But the promulgation of the Nuremberg Laws, which evoked widespread criticism in the American press, still failed to stir official Washington. Roosevelt was preoccupied with nursing his own wounds. The defeat of his proposal to join the World Court and the passage of the first Neutrality Law with a mandatory arms embargo were clear signals of congressional disinclination to take any interventionist steps.[132] The Italian-Ethiopian crisis heightened antiwar sentiments, and the sluggish economic recovery made international involvement all the more unpopular. All these overshadowed Nuremberg and made an already reluctant president remain silent.

Indeed, having so recently confronted Washington's apathy with regard to the Berlin riots, Jewish leaders refrained from approaching the administration directly and enlisted instead High Commissioner for Refugees James McDonald to argue the case on their behalf. In turn, McDonald contacted Felix Warburg and suggested to him that New York Governor Herbert Lehman should try to impress upon the president that the urgent nature of the situation justified informal representations by American ambassador to Berlin William E. Dodd. McDonald, who was experienced enough not to indulge in hopes that such an intercession would alleviate the situation of the Jews in Germany, emphasized the need for unprecedented relief measures. Indeed, he soon became convinced that "there can be no future for Jews in Germany." He urged the leadership of the American and British Jews to join together and appeal for the evacuation of at least 200,000 Jews over a period of ten years. Jewish leaders for their part discounted such a possibility, claiming that in addition to the formidable costs, there was nowhere for the refugees to go. In fact, American Jews deplored McDonald's repeated advice that their "only weapon against grave injustices is 'money'" and regarded it as an unsafe approach. In a subsequent letter to Warburg, McDonald seems to have modified his earlier suggestions. McDonald advised the Jewish leaders, perhaps reacting to their more modest expectations, to ask Dodd for informal action, which would include instructions to the American consuls in Germany to show more leniency with regard to issuing visas.[133]

It was McDonald's efforts, indeed, which awakened the "court Jews" to action—whether because they could not refuse the "other" who was pleading in the name of the Jews, or perhaps because non-Jewish support made the events in Germany a more legitimate issue with which to "bother" the president. On November 1, 1935, Governor Lehman sent a letter to Roosevelt, asking him to increase the immigrant quota of German Jews from 2,500 to 5,000. In his effort to "market" the German refugees, he underscored for FDR the difference between the new type and the old, meaning the East European Jews.

> The type of immigrant from Germany is of the highest. I have met many of those who have come over here in recent months and they have impressed me as very much the type of men like my father, Carl Schurz, and other Germans who came over here in the days of 1848 and who later were among our best citizens.[134]

In his reply, prepared by the State Department, Roosevelt claimed that "a very large majority of immigrant visas under the German quota are issued to Jewish applicants," and since many Jews from Germany were granted visas under other quotas, the 5,000 number had more or less been reached. Stated as such, the figures were correct, since visas were granted according to national origin. But, having become more skilled in the art of gestures, the president reported to Lehman that the State Department had issued instructions to its officers to grant the applicants "most generous and favorable treatment" and to waive certain document requirements. The principal consulars were briefed on the "changed spirit" during their visits to Washington.[135]

Not unexpectedly, the president was held above reproach. When Felix Warburg wrote to McDonald about this exchange with Lehman, it was more comfortable for him to believe that "every time the President promises something, somebody evidently gets hold of it and the soup becomes so watered down that the effect is nil."[136]

The memorandum prepared by the American Jewish Committee on the situation of the Jews following the enactment of the Nuremberg Laws echoed McDonald's insight, but no less that of Lehman. Not only did it acknowledge that a large part of the Jews "can no longer live in Germany and that a new home must be found for them," but rather curiously it referred to the important role that the United States would again play in providing an asylum for the Jews. Moreover, the memorandum affirmed that the "large Jewish element" in America was "prepared to assist their emigrating co-religionists in every human, mental and financial respect," noting at the same time, however, that it was almost impossible to find places for penniless Jewish refugees. But a stipulation was quick to follow: "of course the needs and interests of American Jewry must be taken into consideration." And there were further crucial provisions for Jews in every country to follow: they "must always judge all political measures according to their effect on the destiny of their own country. In the case of possible conflicts between national and merely Jewish interests the national interests will have preference."[137]

By 1935, Jews were aware that avoiding an entanglement in another war topped the list of American national priorities, and the leadership was quick to express its support for the national sentiments. Returning from a goodwill mission to Germany, Rabbi Morris Lazaron reported to his friend R. Walton Moore, the assistant secretary of state and Hull's confidant, that the fight against the threat of fascism needed to be a global one. But the essence of his message was to assure the administration that "not even to save Jews in Germany would any reasonable American Jew expect our Government to interfere in German affairs or go to war." "Responsible Jewish leadership," he reassured Moore "does not let its Jewish feeling run away with its instinctive American loyalties." Indeed, the Central Conference of American Rabbis (CCAR) declared war to be "an unmitigated evil" and urged all Americans to "abstain from all participation in it." The CCAR, representing the liberal Reform faction of American Jewry, opposed the administration's initial measures of military and naval rearmament and supported the Ludlow Amendment, requiring a national referendum before declaring a war.[138]

In retrospect the Nuremberg decrees came to be viewed as a pivotal marker on the road leading to the catastrophe. The contemporary Jewish world, however, appeared to have perceived them as much less ominous. The *Yishuv*'s leadership in Palestine thought they might provide an unprecedented opportunity for drawing new immigrants who would develop the country economically and appraised the impact of the new legislation in these terms.[139] Neville Laski, the chairman of the British Board of Deputies, was not surprised by the new legislation. Although he sought interviews with a few public officials, hoping to have them sign a letter of protest, he did not wish to appear naive. In a letter to his American associate Morris Waldman, he wrote most candidly:

> I cannot think that this will do the slightest good. I am not fool enough to think that it will procure an alteration of the legislation. It will, however, have the effect of indicating to those whom I venture to call our Storm Troopers that whatever can be done is being done. I believe even they realise that protest meetings are quite valueless, although at times they call them themselves for the purpose of exuding their excessive emotion. I am also . . . arranging for a meeting of the Joint Foreign Committee . . . again, not because we . . . think it [is of] the slightest use, but to remove a pinpoint of criticism, that we did not call a meeting at such a moment.[140]

Representatives of the major European Jewish organizations met at a conference held in London on October 14, 1935, to discuss the desirability of protest activities against the Nuremberg Laws. After "an exhaustive discussion" it was decided that such protests were "altogether inexpedient for the moment" and that it would be advisable "to wait for a while" pending, "a more complete picture of the scope of these laws, thus affording us an opportunity for convening the protest meeting . . . provided, of course, the international situation has become more favourable."[141]

As the Jews of Germany were disenfranchised, and the gains of the emancipation were nullified, the Jewish citizens of the free world were in fact incapable of forcing open the doors of their respective countries. And even if they could have, perhaps their experience as absorbing agents in the not-too-distant past made them reluctant to relive the ordeal. The desire to protect their hard-won fragile position within American society even muted at times their cries of moral indignation.

Instead, American Jewish leaders entrusted the voice of conscience to James McDonald, who in the aftermath of the Nuremberg Laws decided to resign the post of high commissioner, a step he had been contemplating since mid-1935.[142] As Morris Waldman recalled in his memoirs, he and his associates thought that to submit only a brief letter of resignation to the League would be to miss an opportunity, and therefore they "prevailed upon him to make his withdrawal a peg on which to hang . . . a sweeping condemnation of the Nazi regime."[143] The document, as James Rosenberg conceived it, was to have an "effect . . . wider than the immediate present. . . . It would stand as a permanent record of the struggle for humanity and justice." But, instead of taking this "moral or educational" task upon themselves, they typically sought a non-Jew to perform it. Melvin Fagen thought it was indeed "one of the rare opportunities for us to throw a stone at Germany through the Commissioner and not to have to fear any consequences for the Jews."[144]

When asked to appraise the situation of the Jews at the end of 1935, Morris Waldman wrote: "The Jews as a whole have only just begun to sense the real dangers. . . .They are only now beginning to realize that the events abroad are menacing their own position." Since the Nazis' "murderous assault upon the position of the Jews in Germany has not brought any punishment," Waldman concluded that "the Jews have lost prestige. The myth of Jewish power and influence has been destroyed."[145]

On the last day of the year, back in Germany Victor Klemperer summed up 1935:

> Still the Third Reich and hopes of living to see the fourth greatly diminish.—
> The most important thing however: I learned to type![146]

Part Four

Crisis and Patriotism, 1936–1942

8

FDR
"The greatest friend we have"

Friends are to be feared, not so much for what they make
us do as for what they keep us from doing.
        —Henrik Ibsen, quoted in André Gide's *Journals*

On January 11, 1936, President Roosevelt and Rabbi Stephen Wise met.
It was their first meeting since FDR had come to occupy the White House.
For Wise, it was not a simple meeting to orchestrate, nor was it "easy to go
there."[1] The air was fraught with residues of past political rivalries and the
ensuing long-standing White House ban on Wise, whose ego as a Jewish
leader and no less as a private person had been deeply bruised by this estrangement. When the president put out his first feelers for a meeting in
September 1935, the rabbi's strongest desire was to regain his badly battered
pride, and he played hard to get. Seeking support for this tactic, Wise wrote
to David Niles, an activist in progressive politics whom FDR later appointed
in 1942 as adviser on minority affairs: "If the President desires Dr. Wise to
visit him," he would have to "personally and in writing invite him. I hope you
will agree that was the only decent and self-respecting thing to do."[2] The exclusion from the Roosevelt court had been a double-edged affront for Wise;
it compromised his position vis-à-vis both the president's Jews and the Jewish organizational establishment. That Wise felt deeply humiliated on both
counts was revealed by his reaction to FDR's invitation. "I would not accept even" his "or FF's verbal invitation," he wrote to Niles. "That time has
passed. If he [FDR] could have me cheaply, that is to say, through a third
hand verbal invitation, I would not be in a position to secure that for the Jewish cause that I am resolved to ask of him."[3]

Although the meeting was arranged through intermediaries,[4] Wise was in
no position to stand on ceremony for long. He could hardly forgo the unique
opportunity that a presidential election year might present for his cause.
Those who were expected to deliver the goods were not oblivious to such
maneuvers. Indeed, Assistant Secretary of State Wilbur J. Carr was alerted in

May by the consul general in Hamburg that American Jewish leaders might use the upcoming presidential election campaign to push for modification of visa regulations. Carr thanked him for the "timely warning."[5]

Wise continued to feel troubled about the circumstances that led to his meeting with FDR. Writing some three weeks later to Holmes, his partner in the feud with FDR in 1932, Wise justified his decision by claiming that he "might help him [FDR] see the light and the right about the Nazi situation." Trying to assuage Wise's uneasiness, Holmes reassured him: "You need not offer any apology, but rather should be highly elated that you got this invitation to the White House. It means, of course, that the mountain came to Mohammed . . . with the President making his overtures to you."[6] The thought that the upcoming election campaign might have induced FDR to arrange for a meeting did not seem to have occurred to Wise. Although the Jewish vote was in no way crucial for victory, neither was it insignificant. But perhaps what concerned the president even more at this time was the conflagration of protest that might accompany withdrawal of Jewish support.

Renewing an "Old-Time Friendship"

"Had a good talk with the President yesterday," Wise wrote to Brandeis, although he could not report any results. Raising the question of the German Jews, Wise suggested that the president say a "word in personal approval of McDonald's report." Roosevelt promised to think it over and discuss it with Frankfurter, making clear whose advice he would consider (if at all). He also revealed to his guest whose counsel of inaction he had been following when he quoted from a letter by Max Warburg which assessed that "things are so bad in Germany there is nothing that can be done."[7]

Wise was not disheartened by the meeting; he thought that if pressed hard, FDR could "be moved to say or do something more." Roosevelt for his part enjoyed very much renewing their friendship and healing the breach.[8] He had reason to feel good, for Wise came out feeling "deeply strengthened" in his resolve to give FDR "the uttermost of my support in light of our talk."[9] Indeed, as early as January, Wise committed himself to "put aside . . . all of September and October in order to make such contribution as it is possible for me to make" toward the re-election of Roosevelt.[10]

As the high winds of an election year gathered speed the powerless sought to harness the energy they invested in the powerful to their own advantage. Stephen Wise did not wait long to exploit the opportunity. In March 1936, he approached Frankfurter in a "personal and confidential" letter with a rather humble demand:

> I am terribly afraid that the Republicans are going to make capital of what they, without knowing, will hold to have been F.D.R.'s inaction re Nazism. . . . It is going to make support of F.D.R. unnecessarily difficult on the part of those who, like myself, have some part in leadership of Jewish affairs and organiza-

tions. . . . Some dignified, fitting, unobjectionable way must be found in which
F.D.R. could express himself.[11]

Knowing well the sensitivities of the president's Jews, and inadvertently
revealing his own, Wise was careful not to appear as if he were trying to infringe upon Frankfurter's sphere of influence. Hence while Wise offered, and
likely had wished, to write to the president himself, reckoning he would take
it well in view of their "old-time friendship," he had to acknowledge Frankfurter's pre-eminence and the greater weight by far that he carried with Roosevelt. Wise, not obtuse to the need for flattery, suggested to Frankfurter that
he was much better suited for the role, since the president knew "how disin-
terested" and how "completely devoted to him personally and to his Administration" he was. "You and I know," he reiterated Frankfurter's own explanation of 1933, "that the State Department has not played the game along with
F.D.R.'s mind, which is the more reason for some outspoken word by him."
Wise was coming of age. He had learned to voice his wishes in a way that
would please his contact's ears, to underscore their common interests, and
to disregard their differences. "I am not for a moment thinking of any benefit to the Jewish cause. I am thinking chiefly if not solely of making F.D.R.
absolutely invulnerable in this matter," he reassured Frankfurter. Knowing
how much FDR's reelection mattered to Frankfurter, he added, "I know his
[FDR's] fine mood and spirit. I know how he abhors the Nazi things. . . . I
wish him to have the fullest benefit and perhaps the almost complete support
of American Jews."[12]

Frankfurter understood the game Wise was playing very well. But because
he was also a highly sensitive observer of the scene, he realized the time had
come for FDR to make a slight personal gesture to Wise. As could have been
expected, Frankfurter was not eager to push on his own for another Jew. This
time he recruited Raymond Moley for the task of presenting to FDR's secretary Marguerite (Missy) LeHand, "as our joint view," the suggestion to appoint Wise as one of the U.S. representatives to the intergovernmental refugee conference in Geneva. In his letter to LeHand, Moley commended Wise
as a Jewish leader second only to Brandeis because he had "greater sway over
the great Jewish masses . . . than any other person." He concluded his bid by
explaining that Wise's "appointment would hearten them [Jews] as a symbol
of interest and sympathy," not forgetting to mention that he would be "one of
the most powerful advocates of the New Deal."[13] Although the appointment
did not materialize, this did not seem to hurt the "old-time friendship."[14]

The rapprochement between FDR and Wise in January 1936 was a typical instance of the co-optive process at work. It made FDR's inaction more
easily understood and less severely judged. Notwithstanding the good intentions of Wise, the re-established relationship between FDR and Wise seems
to have contained and even weakened the Jews' pressure on the White House.
Since for Wise, and most other Jewish leaders, nothing appeared as important as keeping the Oval Office's door open to them, the cost was obvious—to

proclaim unequivocal loyalty to the "Chief." Wise, especially, offered continual obeisance to FDR and campaigned tirelessly for his re-election. The fact that domestic Jew-baiting flared to unprecedented proportions during the 1936 election campaign may have served as a catalyst to the Jews' support of FDR.[15]

The administration, on the other hand, was "a little afraid to put forth Jews too prominently in this campaign." Indeed, FDR had even insinuated "the necessity for a time of Jews lying low. He was speaking of the appalling growth of anti-Semitism in America."[16] But Jews could hardly remain impervious to the attacks against their protector, for wasn't he, in part, being harassed for giving them a chance to advance both inside and outside his administration?[17] Soon there was an exchange of roles: Jews endeavored to protect their own custodian. When it came to Wise's attention, for instance, that an exclusively Jewish fund-raising event was being organized by James Farley, the postmaster general and a close supporter of FDR, he became "concerned about what hurt it would do to R. [Roosevelt] if it leaked to the press . . . in light of all the foolish things being said about Jewish influence in Washington."[18]

In a similar vein, when addressing the Democratic National Committee, Wise underscored that his whole-hearted support for Roosevelt was "not as a Jew but as an American." In doing so he was trying to remove a double sting: on the one hand, to absolve the president of the stigma that Jews supported him qua Jews, and on the other hand, to dismiss the charge that the Jews' political support was dictated by parochial interests.[19] Even in the *goldene medine*—mutatis mutandis—while the Jews had made up their minds about America, "America" as Rabbi Jonah Wise had painfully noted, had "not yet made up its mind about the Jews."[20]

The Fruits of Re-election

Seeing no possibility of altering the U.S. refugee policy, some Jewish leaders thought that on the eve of the election they could at least elicit from FDR a critical statement about British immigration policy in Palestine. The Arabs' fears of displacement were heightened by mass Jewish immigration from Europe following Hitler's accession to power, which pushed the proportion of Jews in the total population from 17 percent (170,000) in 1929 to 31 percent (400,000) in 1936 and increased considerably Jewish land purchases for new settlements. The year 1936 saw the spreading militant reaction of the Palestinians, and in April the Arab Higher Committee declared a national political strike to enforce demands for immigration restrictions. This was the beginning of the three-year Arab Revolt.[21]

In response, the British dispatched the Peel Commission to investigate the causes of unrest. Although he was on sabbatical at Oxford, Frankfurter remained on presidential duty. Fearing that Wise would attempt to influence

British policy by pressuring FDR to intervene, he cabled Mack on May 20th: "Tell Wise we think there should be no holler against Royal Commissions [*sic*] he should lie low."[22] This time Frankfurter was duly worried, for indeed, two days before, in a rare move Wise had written to FDR without his counselor's approval to express his concern regarding the situation in Palestine. In a strictly confidential reply the president assured him that proper action would be taken to protect American interests in Palestine.[23]

The *Yishuv* leadership came to London in an attempt to negotiate with the British government, and Wise, who was in Europe at the time, hurried to join them. Reporting to Brandeis on the talks, he wrote: "It seems now as if nothing could avert suspension [of refugees' immigration to Palestine]; announcement may be postponed for a time but that is all."[24] His reading of the situation in London, coupled with the fact that a U.S. presidential election was only months away, convinced Wise that his efforts must be focused on Washington. Indeed, since it was politically expedient, FDR was ready to perform a gesture for his Jewish constituency. After consulting with Secretary of State Cordell Hull the president asked him to inform the British that the United States "would regard suspension of immigration as a breach of the Mandate."[25] Prime Minister Stanley Baldwin thought that he could well afford a small gesture to the American president which would help appease his Jewish voters. In a dramatic announcement a day before the new policy was due to take effect, the British agreed not to suspend immigration until the Commission submitted its report. Wise was eternally grateful to the "Great Man."[26] While ultimately the gates of Palestine would close, in the intervening years some 50,000 Jews, mostly from Germany and Austria, were able to come to Palestine. Yet, as Wise's biographer, Melvin Urofsky, so poignantly observed, "His success also had its price, one which in later years would have grave results. Wise failed to understand that Roosevelt had acted less out of humanitarian concern or friendship for the Jews than out of a calculated political expediency. At little cost to his administration, he made a gesture which, for reasons of British self-interest, paid off."[27]

In October, a month before the election, Stephen Wise was again invited to meet with the president, this time at Hyde Park. The rabbi extended his heartiest appreciation for the president's intervention in the Palestine issue, a service "that we [Jews] have no right to forget." When the conversation turned to Germany there was less to be thankful for. FDR cited two people who had toured Germany and reported to him that "the Synagogues were crowded and apparently there is nothing very wrong in the situation at present." Wise explained to his host the effect the Berlin Olympic Games had on the Nazis' behavior, but still came out feeling that Roosevelt tended to regard the stories of persecution against the Jews as exaggerated. In his report to his Jewish backers about the meeting, Wise suggested that a written update on the actions of the Nazis should be prepared for the president.[28] But Wise was extremely busy that autumn with Roosevelt's re-election campaign. Nearly two months after the meeting, at the end of December, he recalled the importance of presenting the "Chief" with a statement that might give him "some idea of what is happening in Germany."[29]

Roosevelt's inaction, however, was never due to lack of information. Indeed, if the time and price were right, this astute politician was not averse to gratifying his loyal supporters, some of whom had contributed heavily to underwriting his re-election campaign. The end of 1936 was the right time; national income was up, unemployment was down to seven million, and Congress had the largest Democratic majority since Reconstruction.[30] Governor Lehman, himself no slouch at deciphering the political topography, took stock of the credit that American Jews had accumulated with the president during the election year. Prepared to cash in, the governor informed Roosevelt of difficulties encountered by Jews who sought the services of U.S. consulates in Germany, complaining that the visa sections were understaffed. Implying limits to his own authority, Roosevelt nonetheless promised to "do everything in his power to be helpful."[31] Soaring rhetoric and lofty promises have been the stuff of American presidential leadership throughout its history.

With a signal from the president to go ahead, the bureaucratic train was slowly set in motion. In late 1936, the State Department dispatched Klahr Huddle, a foreign service inspector, to Germany to review visa procedures. His report concluded that the admission of German Jews to the United States did not pose a great risk due to the unusual character of the potential immigrants. According to Huddle's account, many of them "come from better-class families and . . . although they frequently have only distant relatives in the United States, these . . . have a sincere desire to assist . . . so that the likelihood of their becoming a public charge is very remote."[32] From Vienna, American Consul Messersmith added his weight to the forces calling for change. In late December 1936, the State Department notified certain consulates that they had occasionally interpreted the LPC provision improperly. On January 5, 1937, new orders were issued instructing the consuls specifically to base their decision on whether applicants were probably going to become a public charge; if they were, they were to be denied a visa. But it added the modest yet significant provision that the possibility of becoming a public charge was not sufficient grounds to reject an applicant.[33]

In terms of sheer numbers, the change was indeed dramatic. The total count of immigrants from Germany increased in fiscal year 1937 to 12,532 (40 percent of the quota) from 6,978 (26.9 percent) in 1936. But the economic recovery of 1936 was short-lived, and by 1937 the economy was back in a recession. This was a useful weapon in the hands of restrictionists, whose quick reaction had an immediate impact on the tactics of Jewish activists with regard to easing the refugee problem.

Hence, when Emanuel Celler introduced a bill in the House of Representatives in mid-1937 to exempt refugees from the LPC provision, immigration expert Cecilia Razovsky wrote the congressman that his move might be coun-terproductive, for the visa situation was "as satisfactory as it possibly can be."[34] The same approach was used by Celia Davidson of the National Council of Jewish Women. When she testified before the Senate sub-committee on im-migration in April 1937 on the Starnes-Reynolds Bill, which sought a 90 per-cent reduction in the quotas, she said: "I think there are very few of us who want to open the doors to new immigration at this time."[35]

But while Jewish leaders in America were trying to maneuver their way around a hostile political climate, conditions for the Jews in Europe were rapidly deteriorating. Not only was the situation becoming increasingly un-settled in Germany, but in Poland Foreign Minister József Beck announced in Parliament in early January 1937 that one million of the Polish Jews (out of an estimated 3.3 million) were "superfluous" and must emigrate.[36]

Rabbi Wise must have realized that after Roosevelt's landslide victory the stockpile of rewards that could be expected was rapidly being exhausted. He nonetheless took it upon himself to inform Roosevelt, just three days before his inauguration, of the latest pronouncements in the Polish Parliament. Just "one word" in the inaugural address, Wise pleaded with him, would "bring solace and perhaps healing to the hearts of millions who have been terror stricken by the utterance of the Polish government." Roosevelt could not resist an appeal to his vanity. If the cost was reasonable, he was inclined to be responsive. The president thanked Wise for the "sentence" which had been duly sent and arrived "just in the nick of time" to be included in the inaugural address. It read: "We will never regard any faithful, law-abiding groups within our borders to be superfluous."[37] One may wonder what happened to Wise's original plea for a "word" of solace for the Polish Jews and why FDR had re-cast it to apply to America's Jews. Was Roosevelt of the opinion that what really bothered Rabbi Wise was the status of American Jews?

Whereas the more overt wave of anti-Semitism in America was a year away, its leading figures—Father Charles E. Coughlin and his Social Justice movement; Fritz Kuhn, who headed the German American Bund; William Dudley Pelley and his Silver Shirts; Gerald P. Winrod of the Defenders of the Christian Faith; and Gerald L. K. Smith—had been chafing the sensibilities of Jews for a number of years.[38] It was not only Nazi diatribes that sensitized the Jews in America to their precarious position. Of much more concern were leading voices of liberal Protestantism, who, in a series of editorials in the *Christian Century* in 1936–1937, expressed in no uncertain terms the idea that Jewish ethnic identity was illegitimate and threatened the cultural integrity which, it was argued, was essential to the survival of American democracy.[39]

Although these waves proved too weak to survive an increasingly anti-Nazi shift in American public opinion, they were strong enough, when combined with the impact that the persecution of European Jews had on American Jews, to intensify the latter's sense of insecurity.[40] With these mounting apprehen-sions the Jewish leadership became demonstratively more appreciative of the

American Providence as a heaven, and of FDR as a savior. As the anxieties that permeated the lives of American Jews became more extreme, the priority they gave to their own self-preservation became more easily justified.

Thus, when Representative Donald O'Toole, a Democrat from New York, was about to introduce a bill in April 1937 to provide asylum for those fleeing Nazi persecution, Rabbi Wise effectively urged the congressman to abandon the idea. In a recent meeting of "the representatives of all the leading Jewish organizations," he wrote to O'Toole, it had been decided "that no Jewish organization would at this time sponsor a bill which would in any way alter the present immigration laws." American Jews, so it appears, were no longer employing the "national interest" argument in order to justify their inaction. Rather, as Wise's explanation to O'Toole revealed, "self-preservation" had become central and legitimate as the new course for Jews in America:

> I wish I thought that it were possible for this measure to be passed without repercussions upon the Jewish community in this country. I have every reason to believe, unfortunately, that any effort that is made at this time to waive the immigration laws will result in a serious accentuation of what we know to be a rising wave of anti-Semitic feeling in this country.[41]

The impact this profound sense of insecurity had on the attachment of Jewish leaders to Roosevelt is revealed in a note that Wise wrote shortly after to Zionist leader Emanuel Neumann:

> I do want you to know for your comfort—whether it will avail to help us or not—that in the District of Columbia we have a great, good Friend. He is thinking about us and for us. He is planning for us. We are in his mind and on his heart. Thank God for that little "*refuah*" [remedy] in a time of endless "*makkot*" [afflictions]![42]

American Jews revered Roosevelt not because he proved dependable or trustworthy and not because he could or would help them. Their exaltation of the "Chief" was grounded in pessimism more than in hope. As if struck by a fatal illness, they had little else to do than to entrust their morrow to a faith healer.

By mid-1937 both the situation in Poland and the awaited report of the Peel Commission generated grave concern among Wise and his associates. Fearing that the Commission would endorse partition of Palestine, which was indeed confirmed when the report was issued in July 1937, Wise was anxious to alert FDR "and move him to deal directly with Chamberlain." But he did not dare make a move without asking permission. Writing to Frankfurter, he asked: "Ought I go to see him now? Ought I let [James] Farley [chairman of the Democratic National Committee] arrange it? . . . Query— Am I right to go and see him?" Knowing how hesitant and reluctant to disturb FDR Frankfurter was, Wise reassured him, "I haven't asked or tried to see him since the election."[43]

Not making much headway in reaching Roosevelt through Frankfurter, and with the Jewish situation in Europe growing progressively worse, Wise turned to Mack with a new plan. The idea was to get at the "souls" of the Jewish members of Congress, "most of whom, alas, are uninformed and nearly all of whom are little concerned," to go "as Jews, or together with a group of non-Jewish members of both Houses of Congress" to the president. They were to put "the Jewish question before him and [ask] him whether something cannot be done to bring to European lands a sense of American horror, though, alas, it must be added parenthetically that there is not too much of such American horror." While Wise admitted, "I am not sure that I know what the President can do," he asked rhetorically, "Have we the right to omit to do anything which holds out the faintest promise of relief for our people?" Wise was, perhaps, getting closer to facing the bitter truth about his powerlessness, but he was still reluctant to admit his disappointment with Roosevelt. "I know the President is worried and harried," he wrote to Mack. However, when he continued, "I do not know that anyone has made a real effort to bring home to him, burdened as he is, the evil of the present world Jewish situation," it became manifest that he was terribly frustrated with the attitude of his own co-religionists. "I have not written to Felix [Frankfurter] or to anyone else," he added, "I know Felix feels that the 'Skipper' [FDR] ought to be spared." Ending this desperate letter with the observation that "the Central and East European situation is catastrophic," he pleaded with Mack: "Give me your judgment."[44]

Jacob Fishman, a member of the AJ Congress governing council and a columnist and managing editor of the *Jewish Morning Journal*, did not wait to be asked for his judgment. Unsolicited, it arrived at Wise's desk. It read in part:

> Jewish diplomacy has proven itself bankrupt in the most dangerous crisis in Jewish history, and it does not mean that only one tendency, that of the "sha-sha" Jews and shtadlonim [intercessors] is bankrupt, but even the so-called democratic tendency in Jewish diplomacy is just as helpless and powerless. . . .
> What did the American Jewish Congress learn from its five years of unsuccessful struggle against Hitlerism . . . ? What did the same Congress learn from its unsuccessful interventions with the New Deal Government which holds to its "splendid isolation" every time when there is a need of a strong word against these anti-Semitic countries?[45]

Fishman's frustrations were shared by many among the Jewish leaders who tried to bring succor to the Jews of Europe. None of them regarded their efforts as successful. Yet with so very few options available to them, one may wonder, however offensive it may be to our moral judgment, if declaring an open war on FDR and his administration would have constituted responsible behavior.

A Haven of Refuge: Not on American Shores

Hitler's dream, as recorded on the very first page of *Mein Kampf*, to return Austria to the Great German Motherland, came true on March 12, 1938. For the 185,000 Jews of Austria it was the beginning of a nightmare. The *Anschluss* hurled the plight of the Jews under Nazi control back into the headlines, since it turned the refugee problem into a major international issue. In America, the Nazis' savage brutality against the Jews of Vienna shocked public opinion.[46] In Germany, Klemperer confided in his diary: "The last few weeks have been the most wretched of our life so far. The immense act of violence of the annexation of Austria, the immense increase in power both internally and externally, the defenceless trembling fear of England, France, etc. We shall not live to see the end of the Third Reich."[47]

President Roosevelt, in his attempt to forestall expected pressure, was quick to react and "intrude into a situation in which he was virtually powerless to act, bound as he was by a highly restrictive immigration law."[48] On March 25th, he issued an invitation to thirty-two nations to send representatives to a conference in Evian, France, which was to convene in July to discuss the refugee crisis. The outcome of the conference was clearly spelled already in the invitation. It read: "No country would be expected to receive greater number of emigrants than is permitted by its existing legislation."[49] Recalling conference chairman Myron Taylor's appeal in his opening address for governments to act and act promptly, *Newsweek* provided perhaps the best one-sentence summary of the conference when it sardonically observed: "Most governments represented acted promptly by slamming their doors against Jewish refugees."[50]

Few Jewish activists had any illusions about the outcome, but none failed to applaud the president's gesture. A day after the announcement was made, Frankfurter sent a congratulatory note. Although he acknowledged that the victims of Nazism "won't find a haven of refuge here or elsewhere," he was quick to add, "What you have done will help sustain their souls in their material enslavement." Governor Herbert Lehman communicated to the president but a single word—"Splendid." It merited the reply, "I only wish that we could do more." Stephen Wise did not lag behind in praising the "Chief," nor did he miss the opportunity to voice support for his policies. "Let the anti–New Deal heathen rage!" he wrote, "The rest of us bless you!" When writing to Mack, however, Wise was more skeptical: "It is a grand gesture, but I am not at all sure it will avail."[51]

Faith was their only sustenance, since prolonged skepticism was a privilege the powerless could ill afford. For Wise "the only definite thing [was] the Skipper's firm, real desire to be of help." Similarly, Frankfurter had the "best reasons for believing" that whatever action had been taken in Washington since the *Anschluss* had had "the direct lead and enterprise of the President." And when things did not materialize since they were not really expected to and when Wise was "growing a little impatient" about the Evian Conference and "thought of stirring up the State Department," he was not abashed to admit that he "feared it might be viewed as in poor taste."[52] Not much had changed; the innocent and the culpable remained the same. Frankfurter reiterated the familiar explanation to Wise:

Yes, while F.D.[R] has his heart and will in the refugee problems, the decorous deenergizers in the State Department seem gradually to attenuate his endeavors. I sometimes think that the greatest values of civilization are being allowed to go by default these days through all these miserable "prudences" of unimaginative and timid souls.[53]

Yet, notwithstanding what the Jewish leaders thought of the president's gesture, it was with "amazement and horror" that they learned that on the same day the White House had made the plans for the Evian Conference public, Congressman Emanuel Celler of New York had announced his intention to introduce a bill calling for unrestricted immigration for victims of religious or political persecution.[54] Representative Samuel Dickstein also announced that he would propose a similar bill. "It is very bad," Wise wrote about the Celler proposal, "so bad that it almost seems the work of an agent provocateur." The ramifications were clear to him: "[It] simply means that the whole country will go down on the President's proposal with a thud." Even if Celler was thinking of nothing else "but November 8th, 1938" (the upcoming congressional elections), Wise reasoned, "he should have had a non-Jew introduce the measure."[55] Members of the AJC were just as troubled by the Celler proposal. In its executive committee meeting the drawbacks were couched in "universal" terms: the resolution, it was claimed, would "bring to the surface a great deal of illiberalism and hostility to aliens."[56]

Under massive pressure from Jewish spokesmen, both Celler and Dickstein withdrew their proposals.[57] The Jewish leadership was reluctant to make use of the legislative branch, lest it be construed as a move against the president. It was only around the Jewish kitchen table that more particular fears and sentiments could be unleashed. In private Morris Waldman warned that any statement about the immigration problem by Jewish representatives in Evian "might have an undesirable effect here by creating the impression that these Jewish organizations were trying to promote a larger immigration of refugees into the United States."[58] These timorous reactions by the leadership of the two main Jewish organizations poignantly demonstrated how difficult it was to be a Jew, even in America, during these trying years.

Commenting on the Evian Conference a few years later, Roosevelt blamed its scanty results on the "overly cautious" attitudes of most other nations. Wise also criticized "the supercaution of many nations," but chose to glorify "American generosity." For him, as could have been expected, the appalling disappointment of Evian was the "failure of the British Government to rise to a great occasion."[59] In the Jewish popular imagination, America was to remain a haven for the oppressed and they, its champions.

Kristallnacht: A Degradation Ritual[60]

When President Roosevelt was waiting anxiously in the White House for the election returns on November 8, 1938, he may not have been briefed of the incident that had taken place in Paris the day before, when 17-year-old Herschel Grynszpan had walked into the German embassy and shot the third secretary, Ernst von Rath. The next day the *Völkischer Beobachter* published a threatening editorial against the Jews. Von Rath died on November 9th at 5:30 in the afternoon. Starting immediately and continuing into the next day, a nationwide pogrom against the Jews was ignited. In his diary Goebbels recorded: "Yesterday: Berlin. There, all proceeded fantastically. One fire after another. It is good that way. . . . In the whole country the synagogues have burned down. . . . The action itself took place without the least hitch. 100 dead. But no German property damaged." The real situation was worse by far. Apart from some 91 Jews who were killed, hundreds more committed suicide or died of mistreatment in the camps, 267 synagogues were destroyed, and some 7,500 businesses were vandalized. Again Goebbels in his diary: "We now await the foreign reactions. For the time being, they are silent. But the uproar will come."[61] It did, particularly in America.

In the weeks following the pogrom, nearly 1,000 different editorials were published. There were hardly any American newspapers, regardless of size, location, or political bent, that did not condemn Germany. Even those that prior to *Kristallnacht* had been reluctant to admit that violent persecution was a permanent fixture in the Nazi State denounced Germany.[62]

American Jews were hard pressed to decide how to respond. Rabbi Stephen Wise "sitting in sackcloth and ashes over the suffering of our people" cried out "How long, oh Lord, how long?" But other than lamenting, as he wrote to Brandeis, "It is so difficult to know what we can and ought to do."[63] Wise sought the counsel of Ben V. Cohen, but he was of the opinion that the Jews "cannot again rush to Washington and ask the Bishop of Washington, who is a great friend, to go to the Skipper."[64] Not knowing what to do himself, Wise came up with suggestions for what the president could do. One idea was to have Frankfurter pen a letter for the president "to some Jewish friend, for publication"; another was to send for the German ambassador, "whose mere appearance . . . at the White House would have a very good effect." Notwithstanding the outcome, Wise "felt assured" that the president was "nauseated over what is happening" and believed that he was "acting in London and Berlin under certain possibilities."[65] Nowhere did Wise hint what these "certain possibilities" were.

The General Jewish Council, an umbrella group which had been formed some four months earlier for the purpose of coordinating the policies among the major Jewish organizations concerned with securing equal rights for Jews, gathered for a scheduled meeting on November 13th. The meeting began with a eulogy for the late B. Charney Valdeck, chairman of the Jewish Labor Committee, and was followed by a resolution in honor of the eighty-second birthday of Justice Brandeis. Among the other subjects that were discussed during the eight-hour session were Jewish unemployment, the religious question on the U.S. census, the radio campaign of Father Coughlin, and a report on approaches to the problem of anti-Semitism. No changes had been made to the agenda in view of the pogrom in Germany three days before. However, following the proposal of B'nai B'rith President Henry Monsky, the participants did agree unanimously "that there should be no parades, public demonstrations, or protests by Jews."[66] On November 18th Wise issued a report marked "Confidential. Not for Publication in Any Form Whatsoever" to clarify the AJ Congress policy with regard to the crisis in Germany. "The silence of the American Jewish Congress" he wrote, "must not be regarded either as lack of activity or vigor on our part. Both are the result of well considered policy."[67]

The Council kept to its regular schedule; its next meeting was set for December 18th. No special meeting was called in the interim. In earlier consultation with the Federated Council of Churches and the National Conference of Jews and Christians, an interfaith day of prayer was set for November 20th.[68] For once, mainstream American Jewry had reached a consensus—it was united in a policy of public silence.

For the 160,000 people who were reported by the U.S. consulate in Berlin to have applied for American visas by November 29th, the response of American Jews brought little relief. Rabbi Stephen Wise, an early critic of the "sha-sha" approach, must have felt compelled to justify his support for the silence of his Jewish compatriots. "The Jews for the first and only time have been silent," he wrote to Frankfurter, "because Christians for the first and only time since Kishineff [*sic*] have spoken."[69] As in early 1933, Wise still brandished the image of the responsible leader. Having assumed the role of controlling his reckless co-religionists "who do not understand that non-protest on our part is more eloquent and effective than any Jewish word could have been," he complained to Ben Cohen, "I have had to sit on the lid and keep my fellow Jews from unwise demonstration and protest."[70]

The Jews' public silence reflected the fears stirred up by Father Coughlin and his cohorts; it reverberated with the worry of a deteriorating economy in which unemployment had reached the ten million mark; it reverberated with insecurity and guilt. But perhaps most telling, the silence revealed a rudimentary truth—American Jews were no different from other people. They shunned any action that could have affected their own well-being. A post-*Kristallnacht* position paper of the American Jewish Committee candidly expressed these sentiments:

> While humanitarian accomplishments in bringing . . . victims of persecution to the United States and finding work for them cannot be highly enough praised, this is helping to intensify the Jewish problem here. Giving work to Jewish refugees while so many Americans are out of work has naturally made bad feelings. As heartless as it may seem, future efforts should be directed toward sending Jewish refugees to other countries instead of bringing them here.[71]

Assistant Secretary of State Pierrepont Moffat was concerned about the consequences of the gestures which he thought would have to be made in view of the mounting outcry by the American public: "The difficulty was to find ways and means of making a gesture that would not either inherently hurt us or provoke counter retaliation that would hurt us."[72] His concern was superfluous, however, since the administration was well attuned to the Jewish leaders' attitudes which, in part, were of its own shaping. Following *Kristall-nacht*, for example, the British government was willing to relinquish some of the 65,000 places it had been allocated on the U.S. immigration quota to permit German refugees to come to America. Undersecretary of State Sumner Welles had to refuse the offer, based on "objections from the stand point of [U.S.] policy." But what kept this policy essentially uncontested, perhaps, was—as Welles pointed out to the British Ambassador Sir Ronald Lindsay—the "strong impression that the responsible leaders among American Jews would be the first to urge that no change in the present quota for German Jews be made."[73]

The Roosevelt administration had attempted to divert the refugee problem from American shores even before the Austrian crisis. However, since the situation in Palestine made that country less realistic as a destination for settlement, other options had to be presented. Still "shocked" and "surprised" by a typically co-opting gesture, Rabbi Wise accepted an invitation to the White House in January 1938 to listen to something about which the president had not "talked to a soul as yet," but wanted "to unburden" himself of. Roosevelt entertained the idea of finding unoccupied territories for the Jews as a second choice. Wise was disappointed by the talk.[74] But there were others in the Jewish camp who adopted the president's line of thought, especially after the *Anschluss*. In the spring of 1938, Bernard Baruch proposed the so-called Baruch Plan which called for the establishment of a nondenominational refugee commonwealth—the United States of Africa—as a solution to the refugee problem. Baruch expressed his opposition to the revision of U.S. policies toward refugees because of the strained economy and his belief that "no discrimination in favor of any particular political, religious or racial group" ought to be pursued.[75] He did not change his mind or heart after November. In fact, the Jewish leadership was deeply concerned lest the discussions of resettlement, when linked to such ideas as "overpopulated lands and unoccupied areas," provide a "certain sanction" to the East European countries to force out their "superfluous populations" of Jews. Wise thought that such a potential influx of refugees would make the Central and South American countries reluctant to open their doors.[76] The reluctance of North America was no longer an issue.

This seeming ambivalence between the desire to encourage emigration, on the one hand, and the apprehension that such a solution might induce Poland and Romania to expel their Jews, on the other hand, became more pronounced after the November pogrom. That dilemma was revealed when the General Jewish Council attempted to formulate a statement on refugees at its meeting of December 18th:

> Although it was felt that on humanitarian grounds mass immigration of German Jews could not be opposed, it was felt with equal force that other coun-

tries, with far more semblance of right than Germany (overcrowded Poland?), might demand a similar solution for very genuine population problems. Though efforts were made to reconcile these opposing desires . . . no satisfying solution was found. . . . It was finally determined that, at least for the time being, nothing should be done with regard to this matter.[77]

The outpouring of sympathy, however sincere, did not change basic attitudes and policies of FDR and his administration or among the mainstream of American Jewry. However, as the refugee problem became more acute, and the option of America as an asylum was beginning to lose its hold even on the American Jews' imagination, Palestine came to be viewed as a sound philanthropic solution to the problem even for non-Zionists. At least, the thinking went, it would not result in increased anti-Semitism at home.

Taking their cue in no small part from the president's Jews, the representatives of Jewish organizations were becoming exceedingly prudent in public. On November 15th, Roosevelt announced that he was recalling Ambassador Hugh Wilson for consultations, but he also stated that he would not recommend modification of immigration laws to Congress. Samuel Rosenman, a senior "court Jew" and a presidential adviser, backed his chief's decision, writing to him: "I do not believe it is either desirable or practicable to recommend any change in the quota provision of our immigration law." An increase in immigration, he further advised, would aggravate the unemployment situation and produce a "'Jewish problem' in the countries increasing the quota."[78] But Roosevelt must have anticipated that unless he made some gesture, however slight, he might come in for moral criticism. On November 18th, in a second press conference, he announced that 12,000 to 15,000 visitors' visas granted to German Jewish refugees would be extended for at least six months. In this instance, the president followed the advice of Secretary of Labor Frances Perkins.[79] A few days later Brandeis cabled Wise: "Think Skipper [FDR] should not be called upon now to make suggested protest he expressed himself fully."[80] The entry of December 3rd in Interior Secretary Harold Ickes' diary was as follows:

> I spoke to him [Brandeis] of the cowardice on the part of the rich Jews of America. I said that I would like to get two or three hundred of them together in a room and tell them that they couldn't hope to save their money by meekly accepting whatever humiliations others chose to impose on them. . . . Justice Brandeis agreed with me completely.[81]

What else could Brandeis have done—tell Ickes about the Jews' long history of persecution and what it had done to their collective psyche? Or perhaps call to his attention that even the United States was reticent in its response? Indeed, Roosevelt's expression of shock and indignation over the November pogrom went a long way with the American Jewish establishment.[82] Since he was their only hope, they drank *l'chaim* in their synagogues and recited special prayers for the welfare of the president. Rabbi J. Konvitz, the president of

the Organization of Orthodox Rabbis, waxed lyrical in expressing his gratitude: "The greatest friend we have, who lights up the darkness of the world,
is our President, Franklin D. Roosevelt. His words are like balm for the bro-
ken Jewish hearts. . . . Traditional Jewry will engrave, with the blood of our
holy martyrs, the names of our President and his people in the annals of Jewish history for generations to come."[83] "America Has Spoken," was the title of
an article by Stephen Wise in *Opinion* of December 1938. "This loathing of
Germany's shame," he effused, "has been embodied in the protest of him who
is in truth not merely the President of the United States but the voice of
America's conscience."[84]

In November 1938, a few days before the pogrom, Morris Waldman
summed up his impressions of a recent trip to Europe in a confidential memorandum to Cyrus Adler. "The prevailing respect for alleged Jewish influence
and money," he noted, had been "undermined, if not destroyed, by the apparent impotence of the Jews of the world to protect their fellow-Jews in any
degree against the growing cruelties of the rulers of Germany." With an all-
too-accurate prophecy he warned that if Hitler were permitted to "pursue his
aims in the East," the position of the Jews would be "little less than cataclysmic."[85] Waldman was not the only one with such prescience. The editorial of
the *Congress Bulletin* of December 16, 1938, which commented on the spread
of Nazism to Eastern Europe and the proposed independent Ukraine, deduced that this meant "Nazi domination over a Jewish population of some six
million people. It means the total ruin of the Jewries of Poland, Ukraine,
Rumania and others—the actual extermination of European Jewry."[86]

These insights failed to translate into action not only because of the Jews'
inability to influence policy, but also because of a trait that Waldman, in the
above communication with Adler, so perspicuously identified among his fellow Jews:

> Eager to avoid suspicion of lack of patriotism (Hitler and Mussolini have re-
> cently added war-mongering to the other charges against the Jews) they are
> prone to support the policies of their respective governments with great zeal,
> mistakenly identifying in their minds support of the contemporary government
> with patriotism to the country as such.[87]

Although this criticism was directed at French and British Jewish leaders for
their support of appeasement, Waldman's observations were painfully applicable to his own leaders. He reiterated here what he had already stated in
1935: "Hitler destroyed the myth of Jewish power." Indeed, it had only been
a myth.

Rescue or Sympathy?

After *Kristallnacht*, Consul Raymond Geist wrote a private letter from Berlin
to George Messersmith: "The Jews in Germany are being condemned to
death and their sentence will be slowly carried out; but probably too fast for

the world to save them."[88] Though few probably shared Geist's foresight, many in America felt the time was ripe to attempt a major rescue effort. In February 1939, Senator Robert Wagner of New York and Representative Edith Rogers of Massachusetts introduced identical bills calling for the admission of 20,000 refugee children over a two-year period. The children, up to the age of fourteen, were to be admitted outside the quota, and they were to be provided for by individuals or private agencies.[89]

The Wagner-Rogers Bill drew support from an extraordinarily broad cross section of American luminaries and organizations. Because they felt protected by this highly respected non-sectarian coalition, the Jewish organizations, in an uncommon show of unity, endorsed the proposed measure, yet kept a very low profile in public. And indeed, it was not long before opposition from patriotic and other right-wing groups, as well as from restrictionists within Congress, was voiced. The Non-Sectarian Committee for German Refugee Children, the coalition that organized public support for the measure, carefully selected the witnesses it summoned to testify on behalf of the bill. During four days in late April 1939 the hearings took place before a joint subcommittee of both houses on immigration.[90]

Despite the influential backing that the Wagner-Rogers Bill attracted, despite the carefully balanced strategy that was displayed during the hearings, and despite its modest demands, when the Senate finally reported the bill out of committee on June 30th, it was amended to death by including the children in the normal quota. Wagner opposed the amendment, which would have given the children first priority but would have abandoned those adults who were already on the list. Disappointed, he withdrew the bill. David Wyman has correctly located the reasons for this failure in the strong currents of nativism, anti-Semitism, and economic insecurity. As could have been expected, the response of the administration did not counter these trends; neither the State Department nor the president supported the bill.[91]

None of this could have caught the Jewish leadership by surprise; American Jews had encountered these low tides before. But in the state of existential turmoil they were in, both as Americans and as Jews, balancing the potential conflict between American and Jewish loyalty, which was always a difficult task, became all the more trying. It would, therefore, be a gross oversimplification to interpret the leadership's behavior as craven without taking due notice of what it reflected about American society. Indeed, the testimonies of the two Jews selected to appear at the Wagner-Rogers hearings reveal that in America any effort on behalf of a humanitarian measure required Jews to dissimulate their feelings and motives.

Sidney Hollander, president of the National Council of Jewish Federations, for example, did this by downplaying the Jewish factor. "Jews have been persecuted," he testified, "but they are not the only victims." "Concentration camps were established . . . for others before any were built for Jews." While this testimony was faithful to the facts, it certainly did not reflect the problem at hand. When asked about whether the measure would serve mainly Jewish children, he dodged the question by vowing "If it were, I doubt if I would so strongly urge passage of this bill." Clearly attuned to the absolute necessity of confirming his acceptance that nothing should be done for non-Americans which might disadvantage Americans, Hollander added: "If I thought for a moment that this would involve lessening of support for those [in need] in this country . . . I would hesitate to sponsor this bill."[92]

When Rabbi Stephen Wise, the second Jewish witness to appear before the sub-committee, took the stand, he hastened to assure committee members that "there is no intention whatsoever to depart from the immigration laws which at present obtain. I have heard no sane person propose any departure from the existing law now in force." While this opening caveat demonstrated remarkable consistency with Wise's testimony on the Dickstein measure in March 1933, there was, however, a striking variation, which, more than reflecting the deteriorating conditions of the Jews in Germany, revealed the depreciating position of the Jews in America. Wise continued:

> If there is any conflict between our duty to those children and our duty to our country, speaking for myself as a citizen, I should say, of course, that our country comes first; and if children cannot be helped, they cannot be helped, because we should not undertake to do anything that would be hurtful to the interests of our country.[93]

While none of the arguments underlying the defeat of the Wagner-Rogers Bill were uncommon or unknown, by rejecting them openly the Jewish spokesmen thought that they could make them ebb in popular consciousness. Indeed, judging by the testimonies of the two Jewish witnesses, it appeared that as Jews their self-assigned role was not to support the bill so much as to dispel the claim that it was intended to meet particular Jewish needs. What they failed to realize was that however much they professed their unqualified Americanism, in the popular imagination their Jewishness would not fade.

The leadership of the AJ Congress was ill at ease with its prudent public posture in the weeks prior to the congressional hearings, as it had been after the November pogrom in 1938. As then, there was a need to rationalize. While the *Congress Bulletin* did not address itself to the Wagner-Rogers proposal at all during this period, after the hearings on Capitol Hill it editorialized: "There was a great deal of necessary caution exercised on the part of responsible Jewish organizations." It went on to explain: "No reactionary group can accuse any liberal or Jewish organization of having shaped the decision of the Sub-Committee. . . .The names of those who testified are on record."[94]

The tragic saga of the *St. Louis* was another instance when American Jews could do little other than unburden their feelings of shame. The ship, with its "cargo of despair" of 936 refugees fleeing from Germany, was denied entry into America, after Cuba, their original destination, failed to accept them. "It did not even occur to Jews to appeal to the American government to find a way of saving the hapless passengers of the *St. Louis*," man of letters Jacob

Lestschinsky scolded his people, denouncing them for "showing increasing signs of becoming spiritually and morally reconciled to accept the ghetto and almost voluntarily to surrender the positions won by the Emancipation."[95]

This was powerful rhetoric, but nonetheless it was only rhetoric. For in fact the Jewish leadership was virtually paralyzed. Even Rabbi Wise, writing to his cousin just a day before the *St. Louis* docked in Havana, had to admit that "with the tragic Palestine situation* and the really rising tide of anti-Semitism everywhere, I do not know what to do!" Describing the events of the night before, he sounded terrified that "after Carnegie Hall was refused to the so-called Christian Front, made up of Coughlinites, they marched up and down 57th Street, shouting, 'Hang Rabbi Wise to a flagpole! Lynch Rabbi Wise!'—Thousands of them and the police didn't even interfere."[96] This was no exaggeration: the mood in New York and around the country was indeed terrifying.[97] But Wise also knew that succumbing to fear, however natural at times, was a luxury the powerless could ill afford. To his public Wise had to convey another message. Reflecting on the *St. Louis* affair he voiced an appeal to his followers through the pages of *Opinion:* "Let us not fear accusations of international intrigue from the Coughlinites et al. Our action must be determined not by fear of libel but by the courage of men and the heart of the Jews."[98] But again, this was a moral dictate, not a call for action.

Indeed, sympathy was virtually all that American Jews had to offer their despairing co-religionists. Hence, Frankfurter, for example, when forwarding to Billikopf a batch of the many letters he received from Jewish refugees asking for help, suggested "just a word of acknowledgment." Even that, he thought, would "make a difference and make them realize that we are not indifferent."[99] With regard to the many tragic appeals that came from the Jews of the Czech lands of Bohemia and Moravia, who on March 15th were brought under Nazi domination, Billikopf realized that "all we can possibly hope to do is to answer such appeals with letters of sympathy." He wrote to Frankfurter: "It is for this reason that I am constantly impressing upon the various organizations . . . that form letters should be used as a matter of last resort."[100]

Loyalty in the Shadow of War

Two days after the outbreak of war the ailing Cyrus Adler contemplated:

> While I think probably there ought to be a meeting of our Executive Committee, I confess that I do not see what program it could bring down at the present

---

*On May 17, 1939, Great Britain issued a white paper on Palestine virtually sealing off that sanctuary. Jewish immigration was to be limited to 75,000 over the next five years, after which no more Jews would be allowed to settle without the Arabs' approval.

time, if any. Our business is to protect Jews and Jewish rights wherever they are assaulted, and in time of war nobody has ever been able to do this.[101]

Some three weeks into the war, when the problems of relief and refugees became so staggering as to be "beyond calculation and even belief," Stephen Wise acknowledged that all that American Jewish leaders could do was to "give their full support to all that Britain and France mean and are attempting to achieve." This is what he conveyed to Dr. Maurice Perlzweig, then chairman of the British section of the World Jewish Congress, explaining why "it was no time to burden" the British prime minister. "The fate of the Jews," Wise reasoned, "is so utterly and entirely bound up with the fate of the Democracies that this is no time to bargain or make demands." Indeed, that time was long past, for as Wise so plainly admitted, "What would any statement now mean by the Democracies even if it could be gotten?"[102] When confronted with the horror of the impending catastrophe, with millions of Jews being swept under Nazi domination, the value of symbolic gestures depreciated to merely superfluous.

Indeed, the little that American Jewry could have done to influence public opinion and policy, or to effect the rescue of some of the European Jews, became less feasible after the German armies invaded Poland on September 1, 1939, and even more so after the United States entered the war in December 1941. For especially during times of international crisis Jewish leaders became concerned that the image of the "international Jew" as an element of internal subversion was liable to resurface and lead to an anti-Semitic backlash.

Viewed in such light, it is less surprising, perhaps, that when President Roosevelt, following his meeting with Brandeis, held extensive discussions with Harold Ickes on the use of Alaska as a refugee sanctuary, Jewish leaders reacted not to the essence of the proposal but out of fear of how it might reflect on the community. "It seems to me to be unwise to speak of Alaska as a place for Jews just because small numbers of Jews might settle there," Wise wrote to Frankfurter. "It makes a wrong and hurtful impression to have it appear that Jews are taking over some part of the country for settlement."[103] It seems that for American Jewry the most immediate and disquieting effect of the war in Europe was the imported "Jewish problem" that had been injected into the already fraught domestic scene. With anti-Semitism spreading and charges of warmongering and disloyalty mounting, retreat from the public sphere was envisioned as a sound means of protection.[104]

But backing such a tactic openly was also not simple, as an official of the St. Louis Jewish Community Council was to learn when he asked Rabbi Wise for advice. The local *St. Louis Globe-Democrat*, he complained, was "stress[ing] Jewish news too strongly," and he wondered if the editor should not be asked to "publish less news about the oppression of Jews." Wise, after justifying his delayed answer by being "overwhelmed with work . . . on behalf of the reelection of President Roosevelt," pronounced his judgment:

> If our status in America is so insecure that reading about these things will move the American people to treat American Jews as Jews are being treated throughout the Continent of Europe . . . then we have nothing left to protest and to safeguard. We ought to have a little more faith in America.[105]

Indeed, for those who had elevated Americanism to the status of a civil religion, expressing mistrust in America was perceived as no less than heretical. But what was prohibited in public was often expressed in private. Even Wise, who never lost faith in the greatness of America and the future for the Jews there, had to sadly admit after several fruitless trips to Washington during the darkest days of the war: "The truth is, in the midst of war, it is very difficult to make anyone see that we are most particularly hurt. These wounds are deeper and sorer than any other wounds inflicted."[106] But such disappointments were shared mostly between intimates.

In public, however, the Jewish establishment was not only careful to remain within the national consensus, it was also just as mindful of the need to voice its support for the national and presidential interests. Hence, domestic considerations were almost always paramount in deciding the Jews' response. Such was the case when Great Britain, America's undeclared ally, closed the doors to Palestine, the only possible asylum for the fleeing refugees from Europe prior to the outbreak of war. Wise asked for restraint even though America's Zionists were greatly angered. He was deeply convinced that "any demonstration now against Britain would merely furnish material to the Isolationists; in other words, give comfort to the enemies of F.D.R." Sharing this quandary with Justice Brandeis, he concluded, "This is the last thing in the world I want to do—the last thing in the world we have the right to do."[107] To his British colleague he explained it as follows:

> At present we are under the law of neutrality. Those of us who feel as deeply pro-British as I do, must be trebly careful because if too much be said in favor of the Democracies, the President will find it still more difficult to get from Congress the legislation which he desires and which he is going to get. Any too strong pro-British, pro-Democracies demonstration at this time could only hurt the President, so we must on every ground forebear.[108]

The American Jews' dependence on Roosevelt increased unremittingly with the advent of war. The underlying causes, however, were not as deeply rooted in events overseas as in the impact that these events had on the lives of American Jews. The Jews were "in a peculiarly difficult position," Wise explained to Alexander Easterman, another British associate in the WJC.

> We cannot forget the President's call to neutrality, which was as much a self-invocation as a command to his countrymen. We do not wish to give anyone . . . the right to charge us with war-mongering. Of course, they do it in any event. . . . Still . . . we Jews must not give the appearance of seeking to rush America into war. Hitler's blunders and crimes will effect that without any help or facilitation on our part.[109]

Although Wise, as well as others in the leadership, were perfectly aware that the charge of warmongering did not depend on how the Jews reacted, this hardly affected their behavior. As early as 1934, Rabbi William Braude of Rhode Island had warned Stephen Wise that "Europe is drifting toward war," and that the Jews' call for retaliation against Hitler would ally them with "the war party and the war makers in America."[110] Wise, although a pacifist of long standing who did not want his "country to go to war," realized after Munich that "the evil day has only been put off."[111] Indeed, on the very eve of the war he still held to the view that "war is hell," but he grew increasingly convinced that "peace through appeasement and surrender to Hitler would be deeper and fouler than hell."[112] Yet even when Wise became an interventionist, he took great care to emphasize that he was supporting war to defend democracy and not because Jews were being threatened.[113]

Reconciling what was viewed as a particular obligation of upholding the traditional maxim of Jewish solidarity with the no less sacred general obligation of supporting the nation's leader and its national interests presented a continuous challenge for American Jews. Morris Waldman, worried, perhaps, that the forthright and hasty Rabbi Wise might lose control, alerted him: "We should exercise the greatest caution in avoiding giving the impression that we Jews have special interests in the present situation. . . . Jews in Europe are not the only victims of the present turmoil."[114] As the war progressed, Jewish publications were also activated to dispel the dangerous allegation that "Jews are war-mongers." In a feature article in the *Contemporary Jewish Record*, Richard C. Rothschild avowed that "every American wants above all things to keep this country out of war," and went on to recommend that

> Rabbis and Jews in public life should express themselves in no uncertain terms along the lines of their beliefs, namely, that Americans must think of America first. The test of every proposition must be whether or not it makes for the security, happiness and well-being, not of a particular group, but of the American people as a whole, and, beyond that, of the world at large. American Jews are Americans, and if in the present crisis they *show* that they are *acting* as such, they will do much to deflect the impact of the war-monger propaganda which is being released against them.[115]

As the clouds of war descended over Europe and loomed ever nearer to their own backyard, as the United States joined the Allies on the battlefield and the combined forces of patriotism and nationalism came to define Americanism, most American Jews acted according to Rothschild's counsel. However, even if the particular circumstances had been different for American Jews, it is highly unlikely that they would have acted differently with regard to the evolving Jewish catastrophe in Europe. They had cast their lot with America, entrusting their own future and that of their beleaguered co-religionists to the American nation and its president.

9

"On Being an American"
(In Place of a) Conclusion

At some point history becomes like topography:
there is no *why* to it, only a *here* and a *there*.
—John Updike, *Memoirs of the Ford Administration*

The absolute devotion of Jews to their custodians—whether they were kings, kaisers, presidents, or states—goes back to the remote reaches of their historical experience. It was the benevolence of rulers that ensured the Jews' safety and to those rulers they declared their loyalty. Their allegiance was not diminished when they were granted political rights; instead, they extended it to the state institutions that sanctioned these rights. During times of crisis, this deep-seated sense of feebleness turned up in the subsoil of the Jewish mind, which tended to reaffirm the faith of Jews in the state and its leadership.

Things were not very different in the New World. American Jews, whose loyalty had always been doubted, misconstrued the meaning of patriotism; they accepted it as an end value. They treated loyalty to the nation as an article of faith; like religion, it was regarded as providing its own reward. Indeed, for Jews patriotism had a dual nature. In Weberian terms, it combined "a purely affectual" reaction of "an emotionally determined loyalty" with "a rational belief in the absolute validity of the order as an expression of ultimate values."[1] Although the democratic heritage assumes that loyal opposition should not be merely tolerated but valued and encouraged, America's political culture has imposed quite strict limits about where, when, and by whom dissent could be expressed.[2]

Priorities in the Face of Disaster

The campaign for his third term was the most difficult for Roosevelt and he needed every bit of help he could get. For loyal supporters like Wise there was every reason to be "deeply concerned about . . . the alienation of a certain group of voters from F.D.R."[3] For some, the economic measures of the New Deal had failed to end the Depression; in the eyes of others, Roosevelt was maneuvering the country toward war. As late as October 30, 1940, a Gallup poll showed Wendell Willkie running about even with the president nationally but ahead of him in New York and other key states.[4]

For Jewish supporters the president's shaky position during 1940 meant that they needed to be even more careful not to burden him with the situation of the Jews in Europe. But rather incredibly, Wise approached Ben Cohen to help him arrange a meeting with the president for Rabbi Maurice Perlzweig and Nahum Goldmann before the AJ Congress's annual conference:

> It would be an awfully nice thing if the Skipper were to ask some of us to one of his informal and brief luncheons. I do not want to press the matter, but I think that in the light of my devoted service through the years to the Skipper and his cause, it is not too much to ask some one [sic] of the courtesies or favors which I have suggested.[5]

It was indeed remarkable that in the midst of global chaos Wise thought of cashing in on his loyalty to FDR for a White House luncheon. Cohen's reply was fairly terse: "I don't feel that I should push myself into Jewish matters when the Skipper does not ask my advice."[6] Less than a month later Wise received a letter from Dr. Noah Barou, one of the key personalities in the British section of the WJC, in which he pleaded for the "strongest campaign possible to be instituted without delay against the Nazi bestialities in Poland." Options for action were shrinking, and Wise, feeling the need to do something, forwarded Barou's letter to Cohen. But this time he added, "I am not asking you to do anything about this, I merely want you to see how bitter and desperate they [the British Jews] feel."[7]

The little Wise could do was to sermonize to his co-religionists not to "over-evaluate a few anti-democratic, anti-American and therefore anti-Jewish voices."[8] But this soaring rhetoric rarely induced action. Although during 1940 dozens of special committees were formed to try to rescue selected groups of refugees in need of special considerations, the Jewish establishment continued to be guided overwhelmingly by domestic considerations. The Vaad ha-Hatzala (the Orthodox rescue committee), which was formed by the Union of Orthodox Rabbis in November 1939 with the aim of securing American visas for rabbis and yeshiva students and raising funds for their relocation expenses, provoked considerable controversy between Orthodox and non-Orthodox elements.[9] Opponents of the Vaad argued that the creation of a separate fund-raising campaign would further weaken Jewish relief efforts. When representatives of several key Jewish organizations met in August 1940 to discuss a plan to transfer the members of twenty yeshivoth who had fled from eastern Poland to Lithuania, Stephen Wise and other leaders thought that such a large number was inadvisable and that the absorption of just three to five yeshivoth would constitute an important contribution to Jewish culture on the part of American Jews. Wise further advised refraining from applying pressure on the administration to issue the necessary visas.[10] The Joint, which was urged to help in financing this rescue operation, was wary of its domestic impact, arguing that "[t]here were political and social and other implications in regard to the possibility of securing sufficient visas for the admission of any appreciable number of these people to the United States."[11]

"These people" were too Jewish, not only for the State and Justice Departments, but for many American Jews as well. Hitler's rise to power, and especially the war years, transformed the whole matrix of the relationships between Jews in America and Jews in (Eastern and Western) Europe in ways that were both dramatic and paradoxical. There can hardly be any doubt that among American Jews the conflagration in Europe resulted in a deeper sense of Jewish identification. But, irrefutably, it also intensified their Americanism. Indeed, the impact of the cumulative acculturation experience became increasingly more manifest during the war years.

It is tempting to point to "excessive assimilation" or "Americanization" as uniquely responsible factors in America for the limited Jewish response to the Holocaust. However, knowing as we do that much of the same distancing from the European catastrophe was manifested in the *Yishuv*'s response, it is just as plausible to argue that "excessive assimilation" or "Zionization" were responsible for the fact that "in Palestine daily life continued scarcely affected by the war."[12] Undoubtedly these elements played a major role in framing the response in both places, but hopes for the future far outweighed past memories and present ideologies. One second-generation American Jew spoke for many during those years when he said: "I might say that I do look with a certain amount of dread upon the present conflagration in Europe, but purely from a personal point of view. I wouldn't like to be involved. This life isn't a particularly sweet one, but it's the best I've known, and I'd like to know it a bit further."[13]

And to ensure a future—both in America and elsewhere—American Jews were not wrong in thinking that their best bet was Roosevelt. After all, it was against mostly Republican opposition that he led the United States into the war against Nazi Germany. True, the lack of an alternative, as well as Wise's particularly strong devotion to FDR, disabled the use of Jewish political support as a lever to press him harder for rescue efforts. But the truth of the matter was that the rescue of European Jews, as important as it was to Jewish leaders, never took precedence over all else. In a letter to Professor Otto Nathan, Rabbi Wise admitted as much when he reflected in September 1940:

> With regard to the political refugees, we are in the midst of the most difficult situation, an almost unmanageable quandary. On the one hand, the State Department makes all sorts of promises and takes all our lists and then we hear that the Consuls do nothing. A few people slip through, but we are afraid, this

> in strictest confidence, that the Consuls have private instructions from the De-
> partment to do nothing, which would be infamous beyond words. What I am
> afraid lies back of the whole thing is the fear of the Skipper's friends in the State
> Department that any large admission of radicals to the United States might be
> used effectively against him in the campaign. Cruel as I may seem, as I have
> said to you before, his re-election is much more important for everything that
> is worthwhile and that counts than the admission of a few people, however
> imminent be their peril.

With no apparent relation to the above, Wise ended this letter to Nathan
with the advice: "Sleep late; go to bed early; never think about the troubles of
others, and then you may survive, but you will be damned forever."[14] Clearly
Wise had not entirely tuned out the agony that was the price of his choice.
He was not "damned forever," for in his own mind he, at least, thought about
those troubles! But there was hardly anything he could do other than inform
those who he wished to believe could do more. Writing to Frankfurter in
March 1941 about the threat to Bulgarian Jewry, he emphasized "the pathos
of their confidence in the redemptive power of the Skipper." But he was careful to add, "I wish he might see this, but I know he cannot be burdened with
all this material."[15]

Indeed, over and above the news from abroad, there was enough on the
domestic American scene to keep the anxieties of Jews high. One such event
was the infamous speech of the American national hero Charles Lindbergh.
Addressing an America First Committee rally in September 1941, he named
the Jews as a major group "pressing America towards the war." Repeating the
usual anti-Jewish accusations before an audience of 8,000 zealous Americans, he counseled that instead of agitating for war "the Jewish groups in this
country should be opposing it in every possible way, for they will be among
the first to feel its consequences."[16] Although the speech was immediately
and harshly censured by the press, the churches, and many politicians, Jewish
organizations hastened to respond by trumpeting their Americanism.[17] In a
joint statement, the American Jewish Committee and the Jewish Labor Committee professed that Hitler was not a particular Jewish concern: "We will not
put even what he [Lindbergh] considers our 'interests' before those of our
country—since our interests and those of our country are one and indivis-
ible."[18] The AJ Congress's press release equaled the patriotic uplift of Lindbergh. It read: "Surely it is needless to state that we [Jews] are of and for
America as truly as any other group within the nation. . . . We have no view or
attitude in relation to foreign affairs that is not determined solely by American interests, the needs and interests of our own free country."[19] Although
Jewish officials had repeatedly tried to assure Americans that "no Jew on earth
has asked any nation to take up arms against Hitler," understandably perhaps,
their accommodating reactions were not always perceived as genuine.[20] The
ceaseless affirmations of Jewish loyalty to America were perhaps precisely
what reinforced the suspicions of some Americans.

TGFR—"Thank God for Roosevelt"

During the month of May 1942, daily reports reached the outside world from Hitler's man-made hell. On May 8th the torture and murder of "at least 100,000 Serbians and Jews" were reported; on the 11th the *Jewish Telegraphic Agency* published a speech by Nahum Goldmann in which he reported on the "slaughter of hundreds of thousands of Jews in German-occupied territories"; on the 13th an eyewitness described life in the Warsaw ghetto as "a veritable hell on earth."[21] Immersed in last-minute preparations for the war emergency conference sponsored by the AJ Congress, its leaders might have missed the significance of these reports.

When the conference opened in Chicago on May 16th, President Roosevelt sent greetings to its participants, commending "most highly" its "lofty aims . . . which are to help the United States win the war and win the peace and to develop a program designed to contribute toward the creation of a free world in line with the principles of the Atlantic Charter." Indeed, Roosevelt had every reason to be "very happy" with the Jews' "endeavor to advance these aims."[22] Although one resolution adopted by the conference called for "solidarity with all segments of the Jewish people," no demands were made on the administration other than to condemn "racial discrimination in the Army" and assail the subversive forces "which are seeking to separate group from group," both noble American principles.[23]

In May 1942 the Bund, the Jewish Socialist Party in Poland, smuggled out a report to England which opened with a stark statement: the Germans have "embarked on the physical extermination of the Jewish population on Polish Soil." The report, released in June, estimated that 700,000 Jews had already been killed.[24] The information evoked an emotional public response. The American Jewish Congress, together with B'nai B'rith and the Jewish Labor Committee, sponsored a mass rally at Madison Square Garden on July 21, 1942.[25] Ideological differences kept the American Jewish Committee from participating, and its new president Maurice Wertheim made do with a sympathetic message that he forwarded to the assembly.[26] President Roosevelt again sent greetings, which Rabbi Wise drafted for him. And again, he hailed the "determination of the Jewish people to make every sacrifice for victory over the Axis powers." Though American Jews were offered little more than sympathy, they were grateful for the promise that the "perpetrators of these crimes" would be held "to strict accountability in a day of reckoning which will surely come."[27]

With the situation in Europe growing progressively worse, Wise could genuinely rejoice "I am an American." Expressing his credo on the pages of *Opinion* in 1942, he wrote:

> I am doubly an American, because I am foreign-born. . . . Foreign-born Americans like myself do not take America for granted. We look upon American

citizenship as the most precious and sacred of boons. We understand what it is that we have left behind us—denial of the freedom of man, and we know what it is that has come to be our high destiny, to be a sharer in American freedom, to be a bearer of American responsibility, to be a devotee of the American Democracy, to use American freedom not for one's own advantage but for the service of the American Democracy.[28]

It was this unwavering belief, perhaps more than any other, that sustained Wise throughout the countless trials and tribulations that came his way during the worst times in the history of his people. As for his relationship with FDR, as in any unequal relationship it was very ambiguous and therefore inconsistent. There was no love at first sight, or ever. Circumstances turned Wise into a Roosevelt supporter, but it was his growing conviction that there was no one on the political horizon who could do better for America and the Jews that converted him into a loyal supporter. Wise's relationship with FDR was fraught with frustrations which he could not always ignore. But at the same time he was utterly convinced that no better alternative existed.

Among the few who still believed that action by Jewish organizations could make a difference with regard to rescue were some of the most recent to arrive in America. On July 27, 1942, Dr. Aryeh (Leon) Kubowitzki, the yet-to-be-acclimated Lithuanian-born and Belgium-educated lawyer who had moved to New York in late 1940 where he headed the WJC's executive committee, sent a memorandum to the organization's leaders briefing them on the situation of the Jews in Europe. Upon his initiative the administrative committee, which met on August 6th, decided to establish a special committee to consider a policy "aimed at stopping the mass slaughters and deportations of Jews." When some two weeks later Kubowitzki realized that "not a thing is being done," he dispatched an angry memorandum to the organization's top echelon, suggesting convening a conference of prominent non-Jews to whom one could "confess frankly our confusion and helplessness and ask for their advice and counsel." He further urged calling a press conference to protest the conspiracy of silence surrounding the massacres of Jews, canvassing leading political personalities to raise the issue in Congress in the way the Zionists sought to promote their cause, and publishing a special biweekly bulletin on the massacres and deportations so that those Jews and non-Jews who did not read Yiddish would become aware of the situation. He argued that "if it were known, public opinion would revolt." Kubowitzki believed that his assumption that knowledge was a prelude to action was reasonable. But he was learning fast. In a postscript to his memo, he referred to Roosevelt's statement on the atrocities which had just been released: "I am afraid it won't help us, there is not a word about the Jews, nor a word about the deportations."[29]

But clinging to his belief that if only the events were made known, action would follow, Kubowitzki reiterated in an August 26 memorandum his conviction that the "lack of reaction on the part of the Jewish public as well as of the American pubic opinion" was due to the shortage of published information in English. He suggested that the *Congress Weekly* should devote at least six pages of each issue to reports on the "slaughters and deportations of Jews." "The least we could do for our hard tried people," Kubowitzki pleaded, "is to tell what we know, tell the truth!" The editors were quick to reject his proposal, explaining that if so much space was allotted to news on the European Jews, the character of the publication would be changed and, perhaps, it would interest only a narrow section of the readership.[30] But perhaps there was also another reason.

Such was the case in some editorial decisions of the Jewish Publication Society. Fearing the "psychological effect" on American Jews of too much bad news from Europe, editor Solomon Grayzel wrote in early 1941: "I think the time has come when a responsible organization like ours must call a halt to terrorizing the Jewish population in this country—the last Jewish population which still retains its self-confidence." In line with this mindset Grayzel rejected two manuscripts, one a personal account of the concentration camps of Dachau and Buchenwald, and another a description of "The Massacre of the Jews in Vienna." Based on a similar argument—"in difficult times like those we are passing through, a book of Jewish humor might be considered escapist literature, and necessary"—the publication committee accepted S. Felix Mendelsohn's *Let Laughter Ring*. Based on the fact that this volume was the Society's biggest seller in 1941, the Jewish Publication Society must also be given credit for accurately reading the American Jewish mood.[31]

But for the leadership, at least, escapism became much harder when on Friday, August 28, 1942, just before the Sabbath, a telegram reached Rabbi Stephen Wise. The message had originated in Geneva on August 8th and was signed by Gerhard Riegner, the representative of the World Jewish Congress in Switzerland. Its text was as follows:

> Received alarming report stating that in Fuehrers headquarters a plan has been discussed and being under consideration according to which total of Jews in countries occupied controlled by Germany numbering three and half to four millions should after deportation and concentration in east be at one blow exterminated in order to resolve once for all Jewish question in Europe stop Action reported to be planned for autumn ways of execution still discussed stop It has been spoken of prussic acid stop Transmitting information with all necessary reservation as exactitude cannot be controlled by us beg to state that informer is reported to have close connections with highest German authorities and his reports to be generally reliable.[32]

The background to this message and its route to America and England have been extensively documented.[33] Suffice it to say here that Rabbi Wise did not receive the message from his own State Department, which thought it would be inadvisable in view of the "fantastic nature of the allegation, and the impossibility of our [the State Department's] being of any assistance if such action were taken, to transmit the information to Dr. Stephen Wise as suggested." Paul Culbertson, assistant chief of the European division, did not "like the idea of sending this to Wise but if the Rabbi hears later that we had the message and didn't let him in on it he might put up a kick."[34] He was unduly worried.

Riegner must have suspected that the information might be withheld from Wise, who was, after all, in the eyes of the bureaucrats, a private citizen. Hence, he asked that the message be also transmitted to the Allied governments as well as to Member of Parliament Sydney Silverman, who was also a member of the British section of the WJC.[35] The British Foreign Office held up the telegram for "just" seven days before it was passed on to Silverman, who on August 24th addressed it to Wise. This time, the War and State Departments cleared it, and it was delivered to Wise.[36]

Wise decided to appeal to Undersecretary of State Sumner Welles, unaware not only that he already had the information, but moreover that he had initialed the order to deny it to him. He wrote to Welles on September 2nd, some five days after the telegram reached him, although in his autobiography Wise recalled that he had contacted the undersecretary immediately. Welles spoke to Wise on September 3rd before he left for a week's vacation, and asked him to withhold the information from the press until the State Department had a chance to confirm it. He reluctantly agreed. It was only on November 24th, some ten weeks later, that Wise was released of his "oath" of secrecy and went to the press.[37]

On September 4th another cable arrived in New York, this time from Isaac Sternbuch, the Orthodox group's representative in Switzerland, informing the New York office of Agudat Israel that the Warsaw ghetto had recently been evacuated and 100,000 Jews bestially murdered. "Please do your best," the message pleaded, "to arouse such American intervention appealing to statesmen and public opinion. Inform [Stephen] Wise, [Abba Hillel] Silver, Lubavicer [Rabbi J. J. Schneerson], [Albert] Einstein, [philosopher Jacob] Klatzkin, [Nahum] Goldmann, Thomas Mann and others."[38]

Wise did not remain idle. Apart from contacting the already informed Welles, he urged Myron C. Taylor, the president's personal envoy to the Vatican, to appeal to the pope to intervene.[39] Wise also showed the two telegrams to Vice-President Henry Wallace and Assistant Secretary of State Dean Acheson. The same information was also shared with the very sympathetic Secretary of the Interior Harold Ickes.[40] As for President Roosevelt, he was not approached. Instead, Wise turned to his one-time regular conduit to the White House. Enclosing copies of the two telegrams, he wrote to Justice Frankfurter: "You may not be able to help any more, alas, than I can, but I want you to share the knowledge of this horror." For once Wise seemed starkly realistic. Hoping to recruit Frankfurter to deliver the "news" to FDR, Wise adopted a roundabout strategy. "I was tempted to call up Henry, Jr. [Morgenthau]," he wrote, "and ask him to put it before the Chief, just that he might know about it, even though, alas, he prove to be unable to avert the horror." But to assure Frankfurter that he recognized his unrivaled position vis-à-vis the president, Wise was quick to suggest: "Perhaps you will feel that in the face of this circumstantially confirming message from Berne," after the earlier message from Riegner, "the Chief ought to know about it." Indeed, it was not a simple message to pass on to the Chief; it could not be convincingly disguised that this catastrophe was first and foremost a Jewish tragedy. With many disappointments behind him, Wise did not expect too much of the president. "Perhaps he will not be able to avert the thing," he wrote to Frankfurter. But with little else on his side than faith, he added, "One somehow feels that the foremost and finest figure in the political world should not be without knowledge."[41] The president's Jews, not unexpectedly, were reluctant to approach him. And Wise, although growing increasingly anxious and impatient, had no other choice than to resort to another familiar tactic. "I don't know whether I am getting to be a Hofjude," he wrote to Frankfurter on September 16th, but dutifully performing the role of responsible leader and model American, he added, "I find that a good part of my work is to explain to my fellow Jews why our Government cannot do all the things asked or expected of them."[42] In the meantime, the leaders of American Jewry held fast to the belief, inspired in part by Welles and the Polish ambassador, that "for the present" the Jews of the Warsaw ghetto were not being killed but were being sent to work in munitions factories and to build fortifications.[43]

But information continued to stream in that told a different story. In mid-September Wise received another harrowing report, this time from Richard Lichtheim, the Geneva representative of the Jewish Agency for Palestine. The report mentioned Belzec by name; it also reported that the Jews from the Warsaw ghetto were being moved to a special camp and shot and that deportations from various European countries were taking place. All of it meant death.[44] Maurice Perlzweig, by then serving in the World Jewish Congress headquarters in New York as head of the department of international affairs, was "frankly shocked by the recklessness of the document." He sent out an angry memo:

> We ought to be more careful not to be led astray. Certainly it is a sheer waste of time, labor and money to circulate stuff like this, and it should be stopped without delay. We don't really need to convince ourselves that Hitler is capable of anything, and if we want to convince others, we must be sure that we have evidence of some value.[45]

Wise nonetheless delivered the new information to Welles on September 23rd. Most of the information contained in the report proved to be accurate, but there was little to do but cry out in grief.

On September 28th, exactly one month after the Riegner telegram had reached him, Rabbi Wise spoke at a rally at Madison Square Garden against the Nazi atrocities without violating the promise to secrecy he had made to Undersecretary of State Welles. The next day he wrote to a friend in London that "it was a great" demonstration. But Wise was facing the grim reality dauntlessly when he observed that "in time of war it is very difficult to get people excited, generally speaking, about atrocities. . . . It is difficult to move people with respect to special atrocities, even though they are special and, in the case of the atrocities practiced against us, unbelievable."[46]

Exactly a month later, on October 28, 1942, the WJC's Advisory Council on European Jewish Affairs met under the chairmanship of Dr. Nahum Goldmann. His statement made it clear that the 1933 paradigm prevailed:

> Our only weapon is public opinion. We plan to have the President or Cordell Hull receive a delegation of Jewish representatives. . . . A statement would then be issued, and a press conference held. Coming from such high authorities, the story would get front page publicity, and this is the best way to reach the public.

The participants in the meeting, most of whom did not represent the American Jewish establishment, did not spare their criticism of the recognized leadership, demanding action and castigating their docility. Zerach Wahrhaftig, a member of the Vaad ha-Hatzala, wondered, "How can we expect sympathy or help, when we are afraid to publicize our own disasters and think only of hiding them?" Another warned, "We must not make the mistake of being too diplomatic," and yet another participant insisted, "We must stop playing politics and rely on the strength and support of the people." Goldmann was rather blunt when he answered his anguished but naive critics: "If I were in your position, I would no doubt say the same as you have said," but was quick to try to set the record straight. "We face tremendous difficulties," he acknowledged, and went on to describe the attempts to gain the cooperation of the State Department in publicizing the plight of the Jews, and when that failed, the independently held press conferences that "had scarcely any effect at all." And as Goldmann had put it, the stark truth was that:

> Nothing can be done to check them [the Nazis]; we can only work for victory. The only thing that would really impress Hitler would be the shooting of 100,000 Nazis in America; Americans, however, could never do that. . . . The truth of the matter is, that even if we had done everything that was suggested here—and within twenty-four hours—it still would not have saved any Jewish lives. We are helpless; all we can hope to do is to establish a record which will help us after the war.[47]

In such circumstances faith was the only recourse. And as Goldmann made clear, the object of the Jews' faith was America and its President. Rabbi Wise swallowed his pride and overcame his qualms, and on December 2, 1942, some three months after the Riegner telegram had reached him, he wrote to the president to ask for a meeting with a Jewish delegation. The groundwork was laid by Myron Taylor, Sumner Welles, and David Niles.[48] Never since the gates to the White House had been opened to him in early 1936 had Wise hesitated for so long before trying to "break through" to FDR.

Wise opened his letter to the president under these extraordinary circumstances with the ordinary niceties: "I do not wish to add an atom to the awful burden which you are bearing with magic and, as I believe, heaven-inspired strength at this time." "But," he continued, "you do know that the most over-whelming disaster of Jewish history has befallen Jews." As if to prove that he had earned the right to approach the president, he informed him that he had succeeded in keeping the reports out of the press and kept in constant touch with the State Department. As was customary, Wise notified the president of the purpose of the requested meeting: to present a memorandum on the situ-ation of the Jews. He expressed the "hope" that the "Chief" would "speak a word which may bring solace and hope to millions of Jews who mourn, and be an expression of the conscience of the American people." Wise noted that on that very day, December 2nd, American Jews were observing a day of mourning and prayer, maybe intimating that a word from their protector would go a long way toward assuring their continued loyalty. "It would be gravely misunderstood," he concluded, "if, despite your overwhelming pre-occupation, you did not make it possible to receive our delegation. . . . I beg you will somehow arrange to do this."[49]

A somewhat reluctant president, who had suggested a meeting in the State Department instead, met with the Jewish delegation on December 8th.[50] The State Department–approved delegation carried two memoranda: one a sum-mary of the events, and the other a list of recommendations.[51] Two requests were listed: to warn the Nazis that they would be held to strict accountability for their crimes, and to form a commission to collect evidence of Nazi bar-barity.[52] While the president reassured his guests that the government was "very well acquainted with most of the facts,"[53] queries concerning the fate of the European Jews to which answers might have been sought were noticeably absent.

The half-hour meeting won Roosevelt's agreement to issue the war crimes warning; it did not produce a promise of establishing a fact-finding agency.[54] When the delegation asked for a statement that could be released immedi-ately, FDR authorized the re-issuance of a statement, without any change in wording, that he had released for the Madison Square Garden rally in July and which had not specifically emphasized Nazi crimes against Jews. The press release issued by the Jewish delegation exceeded the president's instruc-tions and quoted him as saying that he was shocked to learn that two million Jews had already perished.[55]

Wise was satisfied. It was his impression that all those present "were moved by the earnestness and vigor with which the President reacted to our pleas for his help." It was evident, Wise went on, that FDR and the State Depart-ment "comprehended the magnitude of the crime against our brother Jews throughout the lands occupied by Hitler, and that our Government is deter-mined to avert by all possible means the continuance of the wrong which has been and is being done to the Jewish People."[56] A day after the meeting with the president, Wise still felt elated. The "Chief" could not have been more "friendly and helpful." He was "cordiality itself," he wrote to David Niles: "Thank God for Roosevelt. We ought to distribute cards throughout the country bearing just four letters, TGFR, and as the Psalmist would have said, thank Him every day and every hour."[57]

"For the Record"

On March 24, 1943, the Polish ambassador forwarded a note that had arrived from the Jewish National Committee in Poland:

> The remnants of the Jewish communities in Poland exist in the conviction that during the most terrible days of our history you have not brought us help. Respond at least now in the last days of our life. This is our final appeal to you.[58]

A week later in his war diary, *Pages From Fire*, Mordecai Tenenbaum-Tamaroff told of a certain Aryeh (believed to be the poet and essayist Leibel Weinstein) who did not wish to pass on to him some of his poems and essays. Aryeh explained his reluctance thus: "I do not want some Stephen Wise or some other Jew to cry after I am gone with crocodile tears; I do not wish to provide him with material for lectures, for rhetoric." Tenenbaum-Tamaroff added, "These are the feelings of all of us—we lost faith not only in ourselves, but also in the vengeance of those who will come after us."[59]

The divide that separated those in need from those they thought had the means to rescue them could not be anything but intractable. But it was not only the victims who felt that not enough was being done. In America as well there were a few voices who called for a collective confession of guilt. One such call came at the American Jewish Conference in late summer 1943 from Rabbi Israel Goldstein:

> Let us forthrightly admit that we American Jews, as a community of five millions, have not been stirred deeply enough, have not exercised ourselves passionately enough, have not risked enough of our convenience and our social and civic relations, have not been ready enough to shake the bond of so-called amicability in order to lay our troubles upon the conscience of our Christian neighbors and fellow citizens.[60]

Yet this kind of catharsis so late in the day, however sincere, was still of little real consequence. If we prefer to attain an understanding rather than reach a judgment, then analyzing individual or group behavior on the basis of an idealized vision of human nature, where the exception is expected to be the rule, is of little avail. American Jews were thoroughly normal fallible human beings. With over half a million of them serving in the armed forces, their prime commitment was to victory. These sentiments were proclaimed by Rabbi Stephen Wise at the American Jewish Conference in August 1943. Upon its commencement he vowed:

> We are Americans, first, last, and at all times. Nothing else that we are, whether by faith or race or fate, qualifies our Americanism. . . . We and our fathers chose

to be, and now choose to abide[,] as Americans. . . . Our first and sternest task, in common with all other citizens of our beloved country . . . is to win the anti-Fascist war. Unless that war be won, all else is lost.[61]

Much was already lost. Three million of the Jews who were entrapped by the Nazi occupation had already vanished into Hitler's machinery of extermination. As for the rest, there was little American Jews could do but hope that some would survive to see V-E Day. As such, Rabbi Wise registered his "unchanged faith in the deep humanity of the foremost leader of free men in the world today, Franklin Delano Roosevelt," pledged the dedication of American Jews "to the triumph of our Nation's cause," and declared the nation's "deep and unchangeable confidence in the integrity and goodwill of its Commander-in-Chief."[62]

Probably few would contest the wisdom of American Jews in embracing their nation's interest. Rather more difficult to accept is their deep affection for the "chief" who had done so little to help them lessen the tragedy of their European counterparts. But that too can be grasped when we acknowledge that despite what they had endured in America, they were eternally grateful, especially during the difficult times of the 1930s, for the protection their adopted country gave them from a far worse fate. Although there was still abiding separateness behind the phenomenon of rapid acculturation, American democracy, as Felix Frankfurter noted in his May 1944 address "On Being an American," was "the political framework within which reason can strive most generously . . . on the widest scale—least hampered, that is, by the accidents of personal antecedents."[63] And for that American Jews loved their country as only people who have been subjected to politics of unreason could.

With a past so painful and a present so hopeless, it is not surprising that the agenda of the American Jewish Conference focused on the future. A lone voice of protest cried bitterly: "Unless we do our job in the Rescue Committee, there may be no Jews for whom a post-war scheme of things will be necessary."[64] But for most of world Jewry, as Nahum Goldmann put it, there was not much to do but lament that while "one-half of the generation is being slaughtered before our eyes . . . the other half has to sit down and cannot prevent this catastrophe."[65] Among the leadership it was widely held that for the present all that could be done was to establish a record for after the war. Goldmann, for example, although quite certain that negotiations with Germany were futile, held to the opinion that "Germany should have been approached for the record, so that we may not go down in history as not having done the necessary."[66] The *National Jewish Monthly* (which addressed the B'nai B'rith constituency) also pleaded to "continue to make our protest heard throughout the world, that history may record that the voice of justice and decency was not silent in 1943." But a word of caution, consistent with the American position, was added: "Let us not . . . divert our energies one whit from the immediate task at hand. . . . There is only one way to stop the Nazi massacres, and that is by crushing the Nazis in battle, wholly, completely, and irrevocably. . . . Everything for victory!" The *New Palestine*, echoing the views of American Zionists, held a similar view when it editorialized that the need for a "spiritual catharsis" was understandable, but the main task was "doggedly, grimly, resolutely, defiantly . . . [to] turn our full attention to the task of crushing the enemy."[67]

The reports about extermination made one thing clear: the time for rescue had passed. Whatever chances there had been had disappeared together with the Jews of Europe in the eastern wastelands. Among Zionists both in America and in Palestine this reality pushed to the foreground the need to work for a postwar Jewish state and, moreover, it provided a rationale for relegating the rescue issue to the background.[68] At a meeting of the American Zionist Emergency Council in May 1944, Abba Hillel Silver warned that Diaspora Jews could "undermine the Jewish state, because the urgency of the rescue issue could lead the world to accept a temporary solution." His advice was to "place increased emphasis on fundamental Zionist ideology." Emmanuel Neumann agreed and further explicated the logic behind this line of thinking:

> It is not a question of a conflict between stressing the refugee issue and stressing Zionist ideology. It is a matter of emphasis. The main issue is whether we place our stress on the present Jewish refugee problem or the eternal Jewish refugee problem. . . . The typical non-Jew thinks that the Jewish problem is the refugee problem perpetrated by Hitler. In reality, it is the recurrence of such tragedies that is peculiar to Jewish life and that has to be addressed.[69]

Whether useful or not, historical paradoxes often continue to linger as a theme of present pain. Indeed, a major problem in understanding history is dealing with its ironies while not letting go of its sardonic memories. Life in America presented the Jews with what has been called a tribal dilemma in the form of a conflict between individualism, which most Jews valued, and group identity, which they also cherished. In the resulting clash, tribal cohesion tended to lose out, despite the recognition that acceptance on an individual basis did not remove collective stigmatization, despite "all sentimental denials and institutional investments to the contrary."[70] Intense anti-Semitism continued to coexist comfortably with a high level of assimilation, as was true not only in New York but also in prewar Berlin, Vienna, Prague, and Budapest. For in fact it was during the 1930s and 1940s, in an era of gathering darkness, that American Jews experienced the rites of passage into American life. Precisely when feeling least welcomed in America they underwent the height of their Americanization process. And it was this enigmatically framed experience—their wish to gain acceptance at the height of rejection—which had a most significant bearing on shaping their defensive response to the Jewish catastrophe. Their Americanization experience played a more powerful role in determining American Jewry's response to the atrocities in Europe than the events themselves, and it is to their American context that American Jews resonated and responded most readily. Their need and desire to conform to their environment were more powerful than other factors and, once established, the patterns of behavior that resulted could not be breached until after the apocalypse.

One cannot but accede to the fact that the writing of history is subject to the vicissitudes of time. Only by narrowing the distance between voice and text can we come closer to the past's more authentic pitch. As John Updike observed, "At some point history becomes like topography: there is no *why* to it, only a *here* and a *there*." And ultimately it is the actors of history, both here and there, that should have the last word.

In July 1942, Richard Lichtheim, the representative of the Jewish Agency in Geneva, was asked for a report from Europe.[71] In a letter from Henry Montor, the president of the United Palestine Appeal, he was invited "to review the position of the Jews in Europe" in 1,500 words. In the article he sent on August 13th, he wrote: "This I cannot do because the Jews of Europe are today no more in a 'position' than the waters of a rapid rushing down into some canyon, or the dust of the desert lifted by a tornado and blown in all directions." He went on to concede, "I cannot even tell you how many Jews there are at present in this or that town, in this or that country, because at the very moment of writing thousands of them are fleeing hither and thither. . . . Trapped mice running in circles."

Although when Lichtheim sent his essay he was not privy to the information about a plan for the total extermination of Jews under Nazi domination that Gerhard Riegner had transmitted to the State Department five days earlier, it was not facts that he was lacking.[72] On the contrary, "I am bursting with facts," he went on to explain, "but I cannot tell them in an article of a few thousand words. I would have to write for years and years. . . . Nobody will ever tell the story—a story of five million personal tragedies[,] every one of which would fill a volume."

But, as he was well aware, the great divide that separated the "here" from the "there" was not born from want of facts, but from the inability to fathom the unthinkable human brutality, the lurid horror that accompanied millions to their end. Revealing penetrating insight and rare sensitivity, Lichtheim realized that grasping the death of millions can only be reached through grasping the death of one, that those who were fated to die by mass extermination could only be remembered one by one by one.

> Try to think the last thoughts of the three Jews who were paraded through the Polish town and hanged for having tried to obtain some food from non-Jews. Feel the feelings of the Jewish mother in Paris who threw her six children and then herself out of the window when the police came to take her away to a camp and then to Poland.

Recognizing the numbing effects of facts and figures, their ineptness in translating knowledge into understanding, Lichtheim tried to overcome the es-

trangement between the here and the there by downplaying the importance
of the facts and reaching out instead to the hearts.

> So now you know. Do you, I wonder. . . . Of course you do not want any emo-
> tional stuff, you want facts and figures.
>   But what are facts? There are always facts behind a fact, many of them, and it
> is these facts which you must know to grasp the atmosphere, to see the back-
> ground, to think the thoughts and feel the feeling of one man or woman or
> child connected with one single incident, which is just part of one little fact,
> fifty thousand of which form *the* fact which is a newspaper item of 5 lines.
>   You wanted facts and figures. Have I stated the facts? Some of them, but very
> few. Think of the facts behind the facts, of the rivers of tears and the streams of
> blood, the broken limbs and the naked bodies, the bleeding feet and the crying
> children, the stench of the filth, the biting cold and the gnawing hunger, the
> black despair in millions of hearts.

Lichtheim concluded his essay by reiterating again, "Have I stated the facts?
I have written 4,000 words and I have said nothing." All he could do was to
urge his readers, "Use your imagination. Please."
    But Lichtheim's account intended for "here" landed on a somewhat rough
terrain. In 1940 one young American Jew described its landscape as follows:

> The concept of the Jewish people throughout the world as a unit may not be
> strange to him [the American Jew] ideologically. . . . But personally he has
> already lost the feeling of unity with the larger whole. . . . Only the slimmest
> cultural and psychic ties bind him to Jews of Poland, Palestine, Germany, or
> Russia. . . . The immensity of the tragedy appalls him . . . but not sufficiently to
> make him a living part of the drama. Between him and the European scene
> there lie years . . . of life in America. These years, with all the cultural baggage
> that was accumulated in them, he does not share with Europe's Jews; and they
> stand between him and them.[73]

notes

Introduction

1. In addition to the following partial list of books, numerous articles and a good many dissertations have been written about various facets of America and the Holocaust. Among the most eminent books, in terms of scholarship or passionate argumentation, are: Arthur D. Morse, *While Six Million Died: A Chronicle of American Apathy* (New York, 1968); David S. Wyman, *Paper Walls: America and the Refugee Crisis, 1938–1941* (Amherst, 1968); Henry L. Feingold, *The Politics of Rescue* (New York, 1970); Saul S. Friedman, *No Haven for the Oppressed: United States Policy toward Jewish Refugees, 1938–1945* (Detroit, 1973); Martin Gilbert, *Auschwitz & the Allies: The Politics of Rescue* (New York, 1981); Yehuda Bauer, *American Jewry and the Holocaust: The American Jewish Joint Distribution Committee, 1939–1945* (Detroit, 1981); Moshe R. Gottlieb, *American Anti-Nazi Resistance, 1933–1941: An Historical Analysis* (New York, 1982); David S. Wyman, *The Abandonment of the Jews: America and the Holocaust, 1941–1945* (New York, 1985); Monty Noam Penkower, *The Jews Were Expendable: Free World Diplomacy and the Holocaust* (Urbana and Chicago, 1983); Haskel Lookstein, *Were We Our Brothers' Keepers? The Public Response of American Jews to the Holocaust, 1938–1944* (New York, 1985); M. J. Nurenberger, *The Sacred and the Doomed: The Jewish Establishment vs. the Six Million* (New York, 1985); Richard Breitman and Alan M. Kraut, *American Refugee Policy and European Jewry, 1933–1945* (Bloomington, 1987); David Kranzler, *Thy Brother's Blood: The Orthodox Jewish Response during the Holocaust* (New York, 1987); Rafael Medoff, *The Deafening Silence* (New York, 1987); Leon Weliczker Wells, *Who Speaks for the Vanquished? American Jewish Leaders and the Holocaust* (New York, 1987); Aaron Berman, *Nazism, the Jews and American Zionism, 1933–1948* (Detroit, 1990); David Morrison, *Heroes, Antiheroes and the Holocaust: American Jewry and Historical Choice* (Jerusalem and London, 1995); William D. Rubinstein, *The Myth of Rescue* (London and New York, 1997).

2. Henry L. Feingold, "Who Shall Bear Guilt for the Holocaust: The Human Dilemma," originally published in *AJH* 68 (March 1979): 261–82. Quoted here from the reprinted version in the 1980 edition of Feingold's *The Politics of Rescue*, 309.

3. Michael R. Marrus, *The Holocaust in History* (London, 1988), 156.

4. Jonathan Sarna, "American Jewish History," *Modern Judaism* 10, no. 3 (October 1990): 355–56.

5. This agenda is being rapidly realized. See, for example, Peter Novick, *The*

Holocaust in American Life (New York, 1999); and Jeffery Shandler, *While America Watches: Televising the Holocaust* (New York and Oxford, 1999).

6. Sarna, "American Jewish History," 355–56.

7. With regard to the American bystanders, the two noticeable exceptions are Breitman and Kraut, *American Refugee Policy*, and Berman, *Nazism, the Jews and American Zionism*. Both of these authors devote proportional attention to the prewar years.

8. Jonathan Frankel, "The Crisis as a Factor in Modern Jewish Politics, 1840 and 1881–1882," in Selwyn Ilan Troen and Benjamin Pinkus, eds., *Organizing Rescue: National Jewish Solidarity in the Modern Period* (London, 1992), 33.

9. Marc Bloch, *The Historian's Craft*, translated by Peter Putnam (Manchester, 1954), 29–35.

10. George L. Mosse, *The Culture of Western Europe: The Nineteenth and Twentieth Centuries* (Chicago, 1961), 2.

11. See Sarna, "American Jewish History," 355; Jacob Katz, "On Jewish Social History: Epochal and Supra-Epochal Historiography," *Jewish History* 7, no. 1 (Spring 1993).

12. Hannah Arendt, *Eichmann in Jerusalem: A Report on the Banality of Evil* (New York, 1965), 125.

13. Marrus, *The Holocaust in History*, 157.

14. Feingold, *The Politics of Rescue*, 309.

15. Such an expectation is evident in the following works: Friedman, *No Haven for the Oppressed*, esp. 139–54; Wyman, *The Abandonment of the Jews*, 321–29; Finger, ed., *American Jewry during the Holocaust*, Appendix 8; Wells, *Who Speaks for the Vanquished?*; and Lookstein, *Were We Our Brothers' Keepers?*

16. Edward T. Linenthal, *Preserving Memory: The Struggle to Create America's Holocaust Museum* (New York: Viking, 1995), 6–10.

17. See, for example, Feingold, *The Politics of Rescue*, 301; Kranzler, *Thy Brother's Blood*, 123, and Wyman, *Paper Walls*. It is interesting that Feingold noted the fact that even in the critical year of 1941 only 47 percent of the German-Austrian quota was filled, 296.

18. Henry L. Feingold, "PBS's Roosevelt: Deceit and Indifference or Politics and Powerlessness?" in *Bearing Witness: How America and Its Jews Responded to the Holocaust* (Syracuse, 1995), 187, where he nonetheless concludes that "in neither period [refugee or rescue phase] was there much cause for hope." An earlier and shorter version of this essay appeared in *Dimensions* 8, no. 2 (1994): 9–14.

19. This is true of the earlier Feingold, as well as of Wyman, Medoff, and Penkower. Breitman and Kraut in *American Refugee Policy*, 291n, are among the few who correctly argue that mass rescue during this period was "infeasible."

20. It is interesting to note that the historiography that attends to the response of the bystanders in Germany focuses on the prewar years.

21. Felix Frankfurter to James G. McDonald, May 8, 1933, Mack's Papers, A 405 84/B, CZA.

22. Feingold, *The Politics of Rescue*, 3, 296, 327; Wyman, *Paper Walls*, 221–22. The pressure for visas increased between 1938 and 1941 after the *Anschluss* and *Kristallnacht*, and indeed, it was only in the fiscal year 1939 that the quota was filled for the first time since the crisis began. By late 1941 the American quota became immaterial; Nazi restrictions on legal exit from the German-controlled territories rendered it meaningless.

23. Cited in Linenthal, *Preserving Memory*, 223.

24. Henry L. Feingold, "Who Shall Bear the Guilt for the Holocaust? The Human Dilemma," *AJH*, 68, no. 3 (March 1979): 274.

1. "Amerika du hast es besser"

1. On "American Civilization as a Model of Modern Civilization," see the extremely innovative article of this name by Yehoshua Arieli in his *History and Politics* (in Hebrew) (Tel Aviv, 1992), 278–99.

2. See "The Future Dimension in the American Experience," in ibid., 271.

3. Michel-Guillaume St. John de Crèvecoeur, *Letters from an American Farmer* (1912; reprint, London, 1945), 41–43.

4. Zygmunt Bauman, "Exit Visas and Entry Tickets: Paradoxes of Jewish Assimilation," *Telos* 77 (Fall 1988): 45, 50.

5. Eli Lederhendler, *Jewish Responses to Modernity: New Voices in America and Eastern Europe* (New York and London, 1994), 106.

6. See the excellent volume edited by Pierre Birnbaum and Ira Katznelson, *Paths of Emancipation: Jews, States, and Citizenship* (Princeton, 1995), 11, 161–62.

7. See Joshua Trachtenberg, *The Devil and the Jews: The Medieval Conception of the Jews and Its Relation to Modern Anti-Semitism* (1943; reprint, New Haven, 1993).

8. Oscar Handlin, "American Views of the Jew at the Opening of the Twentieth Century," in Abraham J. Karp, ed., *The Jewish Experience in America: At Home in America*, 5 vols. (Waltham and New York, 1969), 5:12–13.

9. The literature on assimilation is vast. It is interesting to note that in the literature I have examined the majority-minority relationship is generally overlooked. Charles A. Price, "The Study of Assimilation," in J. A. Jackson, ed., *Migration* (Cambridge, 1969), 181–239, provides a most valuable summary as well as a critique of the literature. Milton S. Gordon, *Assimilation in American Life* (New York, 1964) is still one of the leading books on the subject. George F. Simpson sees assimilation as complete when "persons of diverse ethnic and racial backgrounds come to interact, free of these constraints, in the life of the larger community." Interestingly, he does not include religion as a diversifying factor. Simpson, "Assimilation," *International Encyclopedia of the Social Sciences* (hereafter *IESS*), 17 vols. (New York, 1968–1978), 1:468. John Slawson, an officer of the AJC, prefers the alternative concept of "integration," stressing integration of minorities without complete loss of their identity. Slawson, *Integration and Identity: The Jew on the American Scene Today* (New York, 1960) and *The Realities of Jewish Integration* (New York, 1960). Ben Halpern, *The American Jew: A Zionist Analysis* (New York, 1956), gives a most insightful analysis of the limits of assimilation. Acculturation usually refers to cultural effect or change that occurs when two cultural systems meet, or when individuals from one culture enter another culture. This is often referred to as cultural assimilation, as opposed to accommodation, which refers to tolerance but not full acceptance of the other.

10. Calvin Goldscheider and Alan Zuckerman (eds.), *The Transformation of the Jews* (Chicago, 1984), 80, 157, 169–71.

11. See Peter Y. Medding, "Toward a General Theory of Jewish Political Interests and Behaviour," *The Jewish Journal of Sociology* 2 (1977): 118–19.

12. David Biale, *Power and Powerlessness in Jewish History* (New York, 1986), 177.

13. For a critique of liberal theory and an interesting attempt to resolve the conflict between universalism and particularism in Jewish group behavior, see Gordon Lafer, "Universalism and Particularism in Jewish Law: Making Sense of Political

Loyalties," in David Theo Goldberg and Michael Krausz, eds., *Jewish Identity* (Philadelphia, 1993).

14. Ira Katznelson, "Between Separation and Disappearance: Jews on the Margins of American Liberalism," in Birnbaum and Katznelson, *Paths of Emancipation*, 159.

15. See, for example, Oscar Handlin, *Adventures in Freedom: Three Hundred Years of Jewish Life in America* (Port Washington, N.Y., 1971) and Henry L. Feingold, *Zion in America: The Jewish Experience from Colonial Times to the Present* (New York, 1974). See also Michael Kammen, "The Problem of American Exceptionalism: A Reconsideration," *American Quarterly* 45, no. 1 (March 1993): 1–43.

16. See, for example, Roger M. Smith, "The 'American Creed' and American Identity: The Limits of Liberal Citizenship in the United States," *Western Political Quarterly* 41, no. 2 (1988): 225–51.

17. Goldscheider and Zuckerman, eds., *The Transformation of the Jews*, xi, 4.

18. Benjamin Ginsberg, *The Fatal Embrace: Jews and the State* (Chicago, 1993), 5.

19. Cited in Naomi W. Cohen, *Encounter with Emancipation: The German Jews in the United States, 1830–1914* (Philadelphia, 1984), 11. On the German-Jewish migration to America, see Leon A. Jick, *The Americanization of the Synagogue, 1820–1870* (Hanover, N.H., 1976), 28–43.

20. For the overview of the German Jewish period I draw heavily on Jacob Rader Marcus, *United States Jewry, 1776–1985*, vol. 2, *The Germanic Period* (Detroit: Wayne State University Press, 1991); Cohen, *Encounter with Emancipation*; H. G. Reissner, "The German-American Jews (1800–1850)," *LBIY* 10 (1969).

21. Frederick C. Luebke, *Bonds of Loyalty* (De Kalb, 1974), 41.

22. Katznelson, "Between Separation and Disappearance," 174–75.

23. Rudolf Glanz, *Studies in Judaica Americana* (New York, 1970), 223–25, 234–36, 238–43, 248.

24. Cited in Cohen, *Encounter with Emancipation*, 42.

25. Cited in ibid., 14.

26. *Charleston Courier*, March 20, 1841, quoted in Louise Mayo, *The Ambivalent Image: Nineteenth-Century America's Perception of the Jew* (Rutherford, N.J., 1988), 145.

27. *New York Commercial Advertiser*, Oct. 16, 1822, quoted in ibid., 144.

28. Jick, *The Americanization of the Synagogue*, 44–46.

29. The following discussion on the Damascus affair is based on Jonathan Frankel's comprehensive study, *The Damascus Affair: "Ritual Murder," Politics, and the Jews in 1840* (Cambridge, 1997), especially Chapter 8; Joseph L. Blau and Salo W. Baron, eds., *The Jews of the United States, 1790–1840: A Documentary History* (New York and Philadelphia, 1963), 3:924–52; Marcus, *United States Jewry 1776–1985*, 1:653–61; and Jick, *The Americanization of the Synagogue*, 63–67, 104–105.

30. "Persecution of the Jews at Damascus," Aug. 21, 1840, cited in Frankel, *The Damascus Affair*, 225.

31. "Report on the Philadelphia Meeting," in Blau and Baron, *The Jews of the United States*, 3:935–37. Also cited in Frankel, *The Damascus Affair*, 225.

32. Frankel, *The Damascus Affair*, 226.

33. Cyrus Adler and Aaron M. Margalith, *With Firmness in the Right: American Diplomatic Action Affecting Jews, 1840–1945* (New York, 1946), 4–5.

34. Blau and Baron, *The Jews of the United States*, 3:951–52.

35. Quoted in Dorothy B. Goebel, ed., *American Foreign Policy* (New York, 1961), 25.

36. Lawrence H. Fuchs, *The Political Behavior of American Jews* (Glencoe, Ill., 1956), 30; Nathaniel Weyl, *The Jew in American Politics* (New Rochelle, N.Y., 1968), 37.

37. Reprinted in Blau and Baron, *Jews of the United States*, 3:934–37.

38. Cohen, *Encounter with Emancipation*, 215.

39. These estimates are by David Sulzberger, "The Growth of Jewish Population in the United States," *PAJHS* 6 (1897): 14; and Bertram W. Korn, *American Jewry and the Civil War* (Philadelphia, 1951), 1.

40. Katznelson, "Between Separation and Disappearance," 181–82.

41. Michael N. Dobkowski, *The Tarnished Dream: The Basis of American Anti-Semitism* (Westport, Conn., 1979), Chapter 8; Rudolf Glanz, *The Jew in Old American Folklore* (New York, 1961), Chapter 5; Mayo, *The Ambivalent Image*.

42. Jick, *The Americanization of the Synagogue*, 19–27, 44–47.

43. Ibid., 147–48.

44. Katznelson, "Between Separation and Disappearance," 179–80.

45. John Higham, *Strangers in the Land: Patterns of American Nativism, 1860–1925*, 2nd ed. (New Brunswick, N.J., 1988), 4–9. On the Know-Nothing movement, see also W. Darrell Overdyke, *The Know-Nothing Party in the South* (Baton Rouge, 1950); and Harry J. Carman and Reinhard H. Luthin, "Some Aspects of the Know-Nothing Movement Reconsidered," *South Atlantic Quarterly* 39 (1940).

46. Oscar Handlin and Mary F. Handlin, "The Acquisition of Political and Social Rights by the Jews in the United States," *AJYB* 56 (1955): 58–60.

47. Sidney E. Ahlstrom, *A Religious History of the American People* (New Haven, 1972), 386–87.

48. Cohen, *Encounter with Emancipation*, 67.

49. Lee M. Friedman, *Early American Jews* (Cambridge, 1934), 108–109.

50. Adler and Margalith, *With Firmness in the Right*, 299.

51. Ibid., 300. For a detailed treatment of the Swiss treaty episode see Sol M. Stroock, "Switzerland and American Jews," in Abraham J. Karp, ed., *The Jewish Experience in America* (Waltham and New York, 1969), vol. 3, *The Emerging Community*; and Naomi W. Cohen, "American Jews and the Swiss Treaty," *Solomon Goldman Lectures 3* (Chicago, Spertus College, 1982), 83–100.

52. Cohen, *Encounter with Emancipation*, 106–107.

53. Quoted in ibid., 106 (emphasis in the original).

54. The note was completed and presented to the Swiss government in May 1858. See Adler and Margalith, *With Firmness in the Right*, 319–22.

55. On the Thanksgiving proclamation and the Sunday Laws, see Cohen, *Encounter with Emancipation*, 73–80. The issue was one of religious equality, which was endangered with the growing popularity of the concept of a Christian nation, a concept expressed, to cite but two examples, by the Governor of Rhode Island, who in his Thanksgiving prayer in 1852 favored the believers in Christ, and in 1841 by President Tyler who appealed to the "Christian people" when he set aside a day of mourning for his predecessor. Laws compelling the observance of Sunday as the day of rest had existed in the United States since colonial times. Between 1845 and 1855 the matter was raised again by Jews, this time in broader terms. Not only were these laws economically discriminatory, they also violated constitutional rights, above all the principle of equality under the law.

56. Halpern, *The American Jew*, 39.

57. Ibid., 40.

58. The complete study on the subject is Bertram W. Korn, *The American Reaction to the Mortara Case* (Cincinnati, 1957). See also Ismar Elbogen, *A Century of Jewish Life* (Philadelphia, 1966), 30–31; and Jick, *The Americanization of the Synagogue*, 135, 168–70.

59. Korn, *The American Reaction to the Mortara Case*, 51–52.

60. Fuchs, *The Political Behavior of American Jews*, 32.

61. Cohen, *Encounter with Emancipation*, 216–17; Morris U. Schappes, *A Documentary History of the Jews in the United States, 1654–1875* (New York, 1950), 674; Fuchs, *The Political Behavior of American Jews*, 31–33.

62. A letter to the Charleston *Courier,* Oct. 1, 1832, cited in Schappes, *A Documentary History*, 185–86.

63. Cited in Rudolf Glanz, *Jew and Irish: Historic Group Relations and Immigration* (New York, 1966), 55–56.

64. Cited in Leonard Dinnerstein, *Anti-Semitism in America* (New York, 1994), 30.

65. Allan Tarshish, "The Board of Delegates of American Israelites (1859–1878)," reprinted in Karp, ed., *The Jewish Experience in America*, 3.125–28.

66. Nathan Glazer, "The American Jew and the Attainment of Middle-Class Rank," in Marshall Sklare, ed. *The Jews: Social Patterns of an American Group* (New York, 1958), 18–19; John Higham, *Send These to Me* (New York, 1975), 144.

67. Quoted in Cohen, *Encounter with Emancipation*, 32.

68. Korn, *American Jewry and the Civil War,* especially 156–88.

69. For the background of the order and its implications see Steven V. Ash, "Civil War Exodus: The Jews and Grant's General Orders, No. 11," *Historian* 44 (Aug. 1982): 505–23. The order is reproduced in Rufus Learsi, *The Jews in America: A History* (Cleveland, 1954), 106 (emphasis added).

70. Schappes, *Documentary History*, 472, 474, 702–703.

71. Korn, *American Jewry and the Civil War,* 132–38, 277; Joakim Isaacs, "Candidate Grant and the Jews," *AJAJ* 17 (April 1965): 3–16.

72. Cohen, *Encounter with Emancipation*, 150–51.

73. Ibid., 152.

74. Korn, *American Jewry and the Civil War,* 144–46.

75. Cohen, *Encounter with Emancipation*, 129–30, 148.

76. Ibid., 24–26; Dinnerstein, *Anti-Semitism in America*, 36–37. See also the excellent article by Barry E. Supple, "A Business Elite: German-Jewish Financiers in Nineteenth-Century New York," *Business History Review* 31 (1957): 145–78.

77. Higham, *Strangers in the Land*, 26.

78. See Stephen Birmingham, *Our Crowd: The Great Jewish Families of New York* (New York, 1967), and Supple, "A Business Elite."

79. Ginsberg, *The Fatal Embrace*, 63–75.

80. On patrician anti-Semitism, see Barbara M. Solomon, *Ancestors and Immigrants: A Changing New England Tradition*, rev. ed. (Boston, 1989); and Michael Dobkowski, *The Tarnished Dream* (Westport, Conn., 1979). For different interpretations of Populist anti-Semitism, see Richard Hofstadter, *The Age of Reform: From Bryan to F. D. R.* (New York, 1955), 70–82; and Walter Nugent, *The Tolerant Populists* (Chicago, 1963).

81. Handlin and Handlin, "The Acquisition," 71.

82. Higham, *Strangers in the Land,* 27; on the Jew between pariah and parvenu, see Hannah Arendt, *The Origins of Totalitarianism*, new ed. (New York, 1979), 56–68; and

Arendt, "The Jew as a Pariah: A Hidden Tradition," in *JSS* 6, no. 2 (April 1944): 99–122.

83. Arendt, *Origins*, 54, 55.
84. See Handlin and Handlin, "The Acquisition," 70–80.
85. Katznelson, "Between Separation and Disappearance," 182–84.
86. Halpern, *The American Jew*, 17.

2. A Community Transformed

1. C. Bezalel Sherman, *The Jews within American Society* (Detroit, 1960), 122–23. In the period before 1881, the primary movement of Russian Jews was to the southern provinces of the Pale. But as early as the 1840s there was another, much smaller but steady, movement of Jews out of the country, primarily to America. See Stephen M. Berk, *Year of Crisis, Year of Hope: Russian Jewry and the Pogroms of 1881–1882* (Westport, Conn., 1985), 27, 28.

2. Marcus Ravage, *An American in the Making* (n.p., 1917), quoted in Irving Howe, *World of Our Fathers* (New York, 1976), 76.

3. Cited in Feingold, *Zion in America*, 118–19.

4. See Berk, *Year of Crisis, Year of Hope*, 55, 57; Howe, *World of Our Fathers*; Ronald Sanders, *Shores of Refuge: A Hundred Years of Jewish Emigration* (New York, 1988); and Abraham J. Karp, *Haven and Home: A History of the Jews in America* (New York, 1985).

5. According to Samuel I. Joseph, between 1880 and 1914 approximately 1,895,000 Jews came to the United States from Russia, Austria-Hungary, and Romania; the Russian Jews accounted for 71.6 percent of the total. *Jewish Immigration to the United States* (New York, 1914), 93. In *AJYB* 50 (1948–1949): 753, Sidney Liskofsky confirms these figures almost exactly. According to this source, by the end of the nineteenth century (when the government started to keep records of arriving "Hebrews"), half a million or more East European Jews had arrived in the United States; another million and a half had come before the outbreak of World War One; and still another 350,000 came before the national quotas were imposed in 1924. Between 1899 and 1914, more than 90,000 Jews a year entered the United States, and thirteen out of fourteen stayed on. The number of American Jews increased from about 0.6 percent of the population in 1880 to 3.5 percent in 1917.

6. See Goldscheider and Zuckerman, eds. *The Transformation of the Jews*, 160–64, and Feingold, *Zion in America*, 113–28.

7. Higham, *Strangers in the Land*, 38.

8. John Higham, "Social Discrimination against Jews in America, 1830–1930," *PAJHS* 47, no. 1 (Sept. 1957): 12.

9. Higham, *Strangers in the Land*, 38–39. For a contemporary view of a Christian clergyman reformer on the lives of immigrants, see Josiah Strong, *Our Country: Its Possible Future and Its Present Crisis* (New York, 1885). Also see Jacob A. Riis, *How the Other Half Lives: Studies among the Tenements of New York* (1990; reprint, New York, 1997).

10. Cited in Zosa Szajkowski, "The Attitude of American Jews to East European Jewish Immigration," *PAJHS* 40 (March 1951): 264–71.

11. Louis Finkelstein, ed., *The Jews* (New York, 1956), 1564.

12. Quoted in Esther L. Panitz, "The Polarity of American Jewish Attitudes toward Immigration (1870–1890)," in Karp, ed., *The Jewish Experience in America*, vol. 4, *The Era of Immigration*, 40–41.

13. Elias Tcherikower, "Jewish Immigrants to the United States, 1881–1900," *YAJSS* 6 (1951): 158.

14. Cited in Szajkowski, "The Attitude of American Jews to East European Jewish Immigration," 232.

15. Quoted in Sheldon M. Neuringer, "American Jewry and United States Immigration Policy, 1881–1953" (Ph.D. diss., University of Wisconsin, 1969), 7.

16. Cited in Sanders, *Shores of Refuge*, 35.

17. Quoted in Gilber Osofsky, "The HEAS of the United States, 1881–1883," in Karp, ed., *The Jewish Experience in America*, 4:83.

18. Baron de Hirsch was a Bavarian-born Jewish philanthropist who had settled in Paris. See Samuel J. Lee, *Moses of the New World: The Work of Baron de Hirsch* (New York, 1970).

19. Neuringer, "American Jewry and United States Immigration Policy," 17.

20. On the tense relations between the German and East European Jews, see Steven E. Aschheim, *Brothers and Strangers: The East European Jew in German and German Jewish Consciousness, 1800–1923* (Madison, 1982).

21. See Lederhendler, *Jewish Responses to Modernity*, Chapter 5; and Higham, *Strangers in the Land*, Chapter 4.

22. Cited in Ginsberg, *The Fatal Embrace*, 81.

23. Ernest Samuels, ed., *The Education of Henry Adams* (Boston, 1973), 238.

24. Ginsberg, *The Fatal Embrace*, 79–81.

25. Cited in Sanders, *Shores of Refuge*, 279.

26. Ginsberg, *The Fatal Embrace*, 82.

27. The categories of "old" and "new" are often used by historians of immigration to distinguish between those who arrived from Northern and Central Europe and those who came later from Southern and Eastern Europe. The "old" were considered more easily assimilable, while the "new" (mostly Jews) were regarded as unassimilable.

28. Cited in Handlin, "American Views of the Jew at the Opening of the Twentieth Century," 11–12.

29. Ibid., 4; Higham, *Strangers in the Land*, 92–94.

30. Higham, "Social Discrimination against Jews in America," 13.

31. Marcus Jastrow, *The Causes of the Revived Disaffection against the Jews* (New York, 1890), 9–10, quoted in Cohen, *Encounter with Emancipation*, 228.

32. It is interesting to note that "Israelites" was dropped from the new name. This can be seen as a sign of accommodation to the new nationalistic mood in America.

33. Union of American Hebrew Congregations (UAHC), *Proceedings* (Cincinnati, 1881), 1070.

34. Jehuda Reinharz, *Fatherland or Promised Land: The Dilemma of the German Jew, 1893–1914* (Ann Arbor, 1975), 13–29. An uncommon exception to this passivity occurred in December 1880, when Moritz Lazarus convened a meeting of Jewish notables in Berlin to discuss defensive measures. See ibid., 25.

35. See Naomi W. Cohen, "American Jewish Reactions to Anti-Semitism in Western Europe, 1875–1900," in *Proceedings of the American Academy for Jewish Research* 45 (1978): 29–37, 45–48, 62–63. The noninterference of American Jews coincided with United States policy, which preferred to deal with the German government on the situation of the Jews on an informal basis.

36. Esther L. Panitz, "In Defense of the Jewish Immigrants," *AJHQ* 55, no. 1 (Sept. 1965), 57.

37. Ibid.; Howe, *World of Our Fathers*, 32.

38. Richard G. Gottheil, *Zionism* (Philadelphia, 1914), 208. Gottheil, the son of the prominent Reform Rabbi Gustav Gottheil, served as president of the American Federation of Zionists from 1898 to 1904.

39. Among the most prominent were Jacob H. Schiff, Oscar S. Straus, Jesse Seligman, Louis Marshall, and Simon Wolf. See Cyrus Adler, *Jacob H. Schiff*, 2 vols. (Garden City, N.Y., 1929); Oscar S. Straus, *Under Four Administrations* (Boston, 1922); Naomi W. Cohen, *Dual Heritage: The Public Career of Oscar S. Straus* (Philadelphia, 1969); Morton Rosenstock, *Louis Marshall: Defender of Jewish Rights* (Detroit, 1965); and Charles Reznikoff, ed., *Louis Marshall: Champion of Liberty*, 2 vols. (Philadelphia, 1957).

40. Quoted in Neuringer, "American Jewry and United States Immigration Policy," 9–10.

41. On the image of the Russian Jews in America, see Mayo, *The Ambivalent Image*, Chapter 6.

42. Cohen, *Encounter with Emancipation*, 303.

43. Ibid., 232.

44. Ibid., 117.

45. Quoted in Solomon, *Ancestors and Immigrants*, 111. Madison Grant's popular book, *The Passing of the Great Race*, published in 1916, and *The Old World and the New*, by Edward Ross, one of the pioneers of American sociology, published in 1914, are probably the best examples of the campaign for racial purity.

46. Adler and Margalith, *With Firmness in the Right*, 216–17. Smith's report to Secretary of State James G. Blaine, dated Sept. 25, 1890, is also in FRUS (Washington, D.C.: U.S. Government Printing Office, 1890), 701.

47. Adler and Margalith, *With Firmness in the Right*, 218–19. Blaine to Smith, Feb. 18, 1891, FRUS (1891), 737.

48. This line of reasoning was further pursued during the campaign to abrogate the Russo-American Treaty of 1832. See below.

49. Cohen, *Encounter with Emancipation*, 233.

50. See Philip Ernest Schoenberg, "The American Reaction to the Kishinev Pogrom of 1903," *AJHQ* 42 (March 1974): 262–83.

51. Straus, *Under Four Administrations*, 166.

52. Cyrus Adler, *The Voice of America on Kishineff* (Philadelphia, 1904), 472. Also cited in Karp, *Haven and Home*, 220.

53. Cohen, *Dual Heritage*, 135.

54. *AJYB* 10 (1908–1909): 191–92.

55. Cohen, *Encounter with Emancipation*, 115–16.

56. Cited in Feingold, *Zion in America*, 126.

57. Meeting of Dec. 1905. See Naomi W. Cohen, *Not Free to Desist: The American Jewish Committee, 1906–1966* (Philadelphia, 1972), 8–9.

58. Minutes of the second meeting for organization (of AJC), May 19, 1906. Quoted in ibid., 15.

59. For the history of the AJC see Cohen, *Not Free to Desist*. In 1901 the National German-American Alliance was established. But it stood for the preservation of the German cultural heritage in addition to defense against nativist prejudice.

60. Cohen, *Not Free to Desist*, 17, 19–21. See also Biale, *Power and Powerlessness*, 48–51.

61. On the AJC's abrogation campaign see Cohen, *Not Free to Desist*, 54–80. The

documentary material on the 1832 treaty and the ensuing battle for its abrogation is in Adler and Margalith, *With Firmness in the Right*, 208–295; and Cohen, "The Abrogation of the Russo-American Treaty of 1832," *JSS* 25 (1963): 3–41. See also Max J. Kohler, "The Abrogation of the Treaty of 1832 between the United States and Russia and the International Protection in Religious Minorities," in Luigi Luzzatti, *God in Freedom* (New York, 1930).

62. Adler and Margalith, *With Firmness in the Right*, 176–211; Kohler, "The Abrogation of the Treaty of 1832," 706–712.

63. Cited in Adler and Margalith, *With Firmness in the Right*, 278. A similar circular was issued in 1901.

64. Cohen, *Not Free to Desist*, 58.

65. Adler, *Jacob H. Schiff*, 2:146.

66. Cohen, "Abrogation," 5.

67. Ibid., 4–5. See Louis Marshall's noted address on the passport question in Reznikoff, ed., *Louis Marshall* 1:62.

68. *AJYB* 13 (1911–1912): 28–29.

69. Cohen, "Abrogation," 9.

70. Cited in ibid.

71. Schiff is quoted in Cohen, *Encounter with Emancipation*, 235; and Cohen, "Abrogation," 10.

72. Cohen, *Not Free to Desist*, 62–63.

73. Quoted in Cohen, "Abrogation," 13 n47.

74. Reznikoff, ed., *Louis Marshall*, 1:105.

75. Cohen, "Abrogation," 11–14.

76. On the signal to go ahead, see Reznikoff, ed., *Louis Marshall* 1:57–59.

77. Ibid., 1:59–71. This address, delivered on January 19, 1911, also appeared as a Senate Document, No. 839 of the 61st Congress, 3rd session.

78. Cohen, "Abrogation" 16.

79. Ibid., 27–30.

80. Marshall to Wolf, June 3, 1911, cited in ibid., 31. Indeed, Simon Wolf of the B'nai B'rith and the Union of American Hebrew Congregations was an example of those who spoke with two voices: while officially in agreement with the Committee, he urged his co-religionists at the same time to ease the pressure for abrogation and allow President Taft more time to pursue his tactics. Further doubt was expressed during the argument that developed within the Jewish ranks between those who supported abrogation and those who mitigated their claims by agreeing to an arbitration settlement with Russia.

81. Ibid., 35–37.

82. Feingold, *Zion in America*, 242.

83. Nathan Glazer, *American Judaism*, 2nd rev. ed. (Chicago, 1989), 72.

84. Robert Rockaway, "Ethnic Conflict in an Urban Environment: The German and Russian Jews in Detroit, 1881–1914," *PAJHS* 60 (Dec. 1970): 135.

85. See Higham, *Strangers in the Land*, 21; Handlin and Handlin, "The Acquisition of Political and Social Rights," 70; Howe, *World of Our Fathers*, 411.

3. Hard Times in the *Goldene Medine*

1. See Glazer, "The American Jews and the Attainment of Middle-Class Rank," 141; Nathan Glazer, "Social Characteristics of American Jews," *AJYB* 56 (1955): 18–

19; Higham, *Send These to Me*, 144; Glanz, *Studies in Judaica Americana*, 176; John Higham, "Social Discrimination against Jews in America, 1830–1930," *PAJHS* 47, no. 1 (1957): 14. For the most realistic and vivid description of a Catskill resort's "parvenu type" see Abraham Cahan, *Rise of David Levinsky* (1917; reprint, New York, 1993).

2. Two outstanding works which discuss the effects of the East European immigration on German Jewry are Aschheim, *Brothers and Strangers*; and Jack Wertheimer, *Unwelcome Strangers: East European Jews in Imperial Germany* (New York, 1987). Shulamit Volkov's "The Dynamics of Dissimilation: Ostjuden and German Jews" is an interesting attempt to analyze the *Ostjudenfrage* as a factor in the process of dissimilation among Germany's Jews, in Jehuda Reinharz and Walter Schatzberg, eds., *The Jewish Response to German Culture: From Enlightenment to the Second World War* (Hanover, N.H., 1985), 195–211. A similar process took place among the German Jewish elite in America, although obviously set in a distinctive American setting and nurtured by entirely different anti-Jewish traditions.

3. Wise to J. H. Holmes, April 16, 1926, in Carl H. Voss, ed., *Stephen S. Wise, Servant of the People: Selected Letters* (Philadelphia, 1970), 138–39.

4. Ibid.

5. See in Lederhendler, *Jewish Responses To Modernity*, the very insightful chapter "America: A Vision in a Jewish Mirror," 104–139.

6. For a general survey of philanthropic activities, see Boris D. Bogen, *Jewish Philanthropy* (1917; reprint, New York, 1969). See also Arthur A. Goren, *New York Jews and the Quest for Community* (New York, 1970); and Herman D. Stein, "Jewish Social Work in the United States," in Nathan Glazer, Joseph L. Blau, Herman D. Stein, and Oscar and Mary F. Handlin, *The Characteristics of American Jews* (New York, 1965), 160–61, 179; Glazer, *American Judaism*, 87–91; Feingold, *Zion in America*, 148–57, 208–213.

7. Quoted in Moses Rischin, *The Promised City: New York's Jews 1870–1914* (1962; reprint, Cambridge, Mass., 1977), 100.

8. Kaufmann Kohler, "American Judaism," reprinted in Paul R. Mendes-Flohr, and Jehuda Reinharz, eds., *The Jew in the Modern World: A Documentary History* (New York, 1980), 372–73 (emphasis added).

9. Ibid.

10. The apologetic literature produced by and in the name of American Jews has not yet received the systematic treatment it deserves. This literature may provide an interesting perspective on the attitudes of the Jewish elite toward the animus it confronted during periods of national crisis. The attempt to prove the Jews' patriotism and Americanism took a variety of forms and solicited the patronage of non-Jews as well. The following are some selective examples: on the occasion of the 400th anniversary of Columbus's first voyage, Oscar Straus "arranged" for European historian Meyer Kayserling to write a history of the discovery of the New World and to prove the significant contributions of Jews to that venture. Straus himself published in 1885 *The Origin of the Republican Form of Government in the United States of America*, a treatise which intended to demonstrate the influence of the Hebrew commonwealth on the early colonists' commitment to republicanism. Madison C. Peters, a Baptist minister, published *Justice to the Jew* (London and New York, 1899), and *The Jew as a Patriot* (New York, 1902), with an introductory essay by Oscar S. Straus. Not all Jews accepted Peters's philo-Semitism; see, for example, the opinion of Rabbi Stephen S. Wise, in letter to Richard Gottheil, March 8, 1918, in Voss, ed., *Stephen S. Wise*,

82. In 1894–1895, Max J. Kohler published a series of articles on "Incidents Illustrative of American Jewish Patriotism," in the *American Hebrew*. Simon Wolf's *The American Jew as Patriot, Soldier and Citizen* (1895) was for the most part a compilation of names and ranks of Jews who had fought in the Civil War, dealing also with earlier conflicts. Samuel Walker McCall, the author of *Patriotism of the American Jew* (New York, 1924), was a former member of the House of Representatives from Massachusetts. The book begins by quoting the opening sentences of a speech he delivered on the abrogation of the Russo-American Treaty in December 1911: "My sympathies are with this brilliant race. . . . The laws of almost all nations have discriminated against it; and yet it has shown such marvelous vitality that it has made for itself a proud place." Nowhere is there a mention that in 1895 the same McCall had introduced the literacy bill in the House, refusing immigration to men and women over the age of fourteen who could not read or write in some language. He had urged the literacy test as a clear line of distinction between Anglo-Saxon and Southern European immigrants, especially those coming from Italy. See Higham, *Strangers in the Land*, 103.

11. Handlin and Handlin, "Acquisition of Political and Social Rights," 77.

12. Lederhendler, *Jewish Responses to Modernity*, 128.

13. Higham, *Strangers in the Land*, 195.

14. See ibid., 195–98, 278–79, for the response of German Americans to World War One. On Paul Warburg and the Federal Reserve, see Ron Chernow, *The Warburgs: The Twentieth-Century Odyssey of a Remarkable Jewish Family* (New York, 1993), 137–40.

15. See Joseph Rappaport, "Jewish Immigration and World War I: A Study of American Yiddish Press Reactions" (Ph.D. diss., Columbia University, 1951).

16. *The Jewish Comment* (Baltimore), quoted in ibid., 222.

17. See Cohen, *Not Free to Desist*, 87.

18. Marshall to Jacob Schiff, Oct. 2, 1914, in Reznikoff, ed., *Louis Marshall*, 1:5–6.

19. Marshall to Charles Schwager, Dec. 17, 1928, cited in ibid., 5.

20. The Zionists among them favored the Allies almost from the start, hoping for Turkey's defeat.

21. Learsi, *The Jews in America*, 241–42.

22. *Morgen Journal*, Sept. 9, 1914, cited in Bernard D. Weinryb, "Jewish Immigration and Accommodation to America," in Marshall Sklare, ed., *The Jews: Social Patterns of an American Group* (Glencoe, Illinois, 1958), 20. For detailed reactions of East European immigrants to the war, see Rappaport, "Jewish Immigration and World War I."

23. Wise to Maurice Leon, cited in Voss, ed., *Stephen S. Wise*, 61–62.

24. Ben Halpern, "The Americanization of Zionism," *AJH* 69, no. 1 (Sept. 1979): 27.

25. Yonathan Shapiro, *The Leadership of the American Zionist Organization, 1897–1930* (Urbana, 1971), 80; Melvin I. Urofsky, *American Zionism from Herzl to the Holocaust* (Garden City, 1975), 166. On the formation of the American Jewish Congress, see Morris Frommer, "The American Jewish Congress: A History, 1914–1950" (Ph.D. diss., Ohio State University, 1978), Chapter 1.

26. Marshall to S. Schechter, Feb. 19, 1915, in Reznikoff, *Louis Marshall*, 2:506.

27. Marshall to Reading, Sept. 22, 1915, in Reznikoff, ed., *Louis Marshall*, 2:511. See also Frommer, "The American Jewish Congress," 58–60.

28. *AH*, April 30, 1915.

29. Jacob Schiff to Brandeis, Feb. 29, 1916, quoted in Cohen, *Not Free to Desist*, 92–93.

30. The Pittsburgh Platform was a declaration of principles adopted by a group of Reform rabbis at Pittsburgh in 1885. The definition of "Jewishness" set forth in the Platform guided its community until 1935, when the Central Conference of American Rabbis (CCAR)—the organization of the Reform movement—became officially neutral on Zionism. It was not until 1937 that the Pittsburgh Platform was replaced with what is known as the Columbus Platform. Reflecting the changing realities in the Jewish world and no less in the American Reform movement, it asserted: "We affirm the obligation of all Jewry to aid in its [Palestine's] upbuilding as a Jewish Homeland by endeavoring to make it not only a haven of refuge for the oppressed but also a center of Jewish culture and spiritual life." See Thomas A. Kolsky, *Jews against Zionism: The American Council for Judaism, 1942–1948* (Philadelphia, 1990), 33–34; the Pittsburgh principles are quoted in full in Glazer's *American Judaism*, 187–88.

31. Schiff to Marshall, March 10, 1916, quoted in Jonathan Frankel, *Prophecy and Politics: Socialism, Nationalism, and the Russian Jews, 1862–1917* (Cambridge, 1981), 527.

32. Cited in Cohen, *Encounter with Emancipation*, 295. This pro- and anti-Zionist discourse took place in 1907 with regard to the future character of the Jewish Theological Seminary, of which Schiff was the chief financial backer. Schiff conducted an exchange of letters with Solomon Schechter, the president of the Seminary, who had "dared" to reveal his pro-Zionist sentiments. Unlike Schecter, who did not agree to make his letters public, Schiff did, proclaiming his Americanism for all to see. These letters are reproduced in Adler, *Jacob H. Schiff*, 2:164–69. On Schecter and the Seminary project, see also Glazer's *American Judaism*, 74–78.

33. Frankel, *Prophecy and Politics*, 509; Urofsky, *American Zionism from Herzl to the Holocaust*, 117–63; Naomi W. Cohen, *American Jews and the Zionist Idea* (n.p., 1975), especially Chapters 1 and 2; Samuel Halperin, *The Political World of American Zionism* (Detroit, 1961), especially Chapter 1; Shapiro, *Leadership of the American Zionist Organization, 1897–1930*.

34. On Brandeis the progressive and his role as the architect of Wilson's New Freedom, see Richard Hofstadter, *The American Political Tradition and the Men Who Made It* (New York, 1948), 259; Melvin Urofsky, *A Mind of One Piece: Brandeis and American Reform* (New York, 1971), Chapter 5; Melvin Urofsky and David Levy, eds., *Letters of Louis D. Brandeis: Progressive and Zionist* (Albany, 1973), 2:218–21. On Zionism's compatibility with Americanism, see Cohen, *American Jews and the Zionist Idea*, 16.

35. *The Jewish Advocate*, June 18, 1915. This address was delivered before the Eastern Council of Reform Rabbis in June 1915, as part of the campaign of the Jewish Congress movement. Cited also in Frommer, "The American Jewish Congress," 1:67.

36. Dr. Stephen S. Wise, "American Israel and Democracy." Issued by the Executive Organization Committee for the American Jewish Congress, New York City. AJ Congress Papers, Box 6, Executive Committee Minutes and Reports, 1916–1949, AJHS.

37. Actually, during the peace negotiations much effort was devoted to avoiding the ominous word "national." The Zionists also tried to avoid the term, speaking instead about "rights of democracies and nationalities." Wilson was a fervent advocate of granting "racial, religious, and linguistic rights to minorities"; he feared that "'national rights' would prove harmful inasmuch as minority groups thus marked as

separate corporate bodies would be rendered thereby 'liable to jealousy and attack.'"
See Oscar J. Janowsky, *The Jews and Minority Rights* (New York, 1933), 351.

38. *Maccabaean*, March 1917, cited in Cohen, *American Jews and the Zionist Idea*, 20.

39. *Maccabaean*, Sept. 1917, cited in ibid.

40. For an interesting interpretation of the difference in historical experience between the *Ostjuden* and the *deutsche-Juden* in regard to the relationship between religion and nationality, see Glazer, *American Judaism*, 63–66.

41. *Central Conference of American Rabbis Yearbook* 28 (1918): 133–34, 174–75 (emphasis added). See also Charles Israel Goldblatt, "The Impact of the Balfour Declaration in America," *AJHQ* 57 (June 1968): 460–84.

42. Kolsky, *Jews against Zionism*, 30–31; Stuart E. Knee, *The Concept of Zionist Dissent in the American Mind* (New York, 1979), 49–50, 96–97.

43. The AJC statement on the Balfour Declaration was formulated by Marshall and approved at a special membership meeting in April 1918. It is cited in full in Cohen, *Not Free to Desist*, 109–10.

44. Naomi W. Cohen, "Friends in Court: An American-Jewish Response to Antisemitism," in Jehuda Reinharz, ed., *Living with Antisemitism: Modern Jewish Responses* (Hanover, N.H., 1987), 314. For an example of Jewish Americanism see Louis Marshall, "The Loyalty of the American Jew," an address delivered on May 3, 1925, in Reznikoff, ed., *Louis Marshall*, 2:803–805.

45. Fuchs, *The Political Behavior of American Jews*, 57.

46. See Frommer, "American Jewish Congress," 104–105. The Zionists, with a few notable exceptions such as Magnes and Lipsky, had joined forces with the AJC leadership to oppose the factions who were against postponement. For the arguments of the different groups see Frankel, *Prophecy and Politics*, 537–39.

47. President Wilson is cited in a letter by Stephen Wise to Harry Cutler, June 30, 1917, in Voss, ed., *Stephen S. Wise*, 81–82. The fact that Wilson asked Wise to postpone the convening of the Congress is interestingly enough relegated to a postscript (in which Wilson noted that he "should have added [it] in the body of the letter"). Cutler was active in the National Jewish Welfare Board, the Zionist Organization of America, the American Jewish Committee, etc.

48. Wise to Brandeis, Sept. 8, 1917, SSW Papers, AJHS; see also Frommer, "The American Jewish Congress," 105.

49. Marshall to Magnes, June 1, 1917 in Reznikoff, ed., *Louis Marshall*, 2:971–73. Magnes was married to Marshall's sister-in-law, Beatrice Lowenstein.

50. Ibid., 972.

51. Leiser to Richards, April 4, 1917, quoted in Frommer, "The American Jewish Congress," 105–106, n91 (emphasis added).

52. See Biale, *Power and Powerlessness*, 106–110.

53. Higham, *Strangers in the Land*, 196; Clifton James Child, *The German-American in Politics, 1914–1917* (Madison, 1939), 4–7, 43–55.

54. Higham, *Strangers in the Land*, 196.

55. McCall, *The Patriotism of the American Jew*, 160.

56. Janowsky, *Jews and Minority Rights*, 180–82.

57. American Jewish Congress, *Report of the Proceedings of the American Jewish Congress* (Philadelphia, 1918), 44–48, cited in Frommer, "The American Jewish Congress," 114 (emphasis added).

58. Although the Zionists viewed the issue of Palestine as important, they did not

regard it as superseding the case of minority rights for the Jews of Eastern Europe. They were realistic enough to acknowledge that Palestine could not provide a solution to their problem. See Frommer, "The American Jewish Congress," 134–36. On the various American as well as other Jewish groups and opinions at the Paris Peace Conference, see ibid., 125–48.

59. Ibid., 150–55.

60. Cyrus Adler, *I Have Considered the Days* (Philadelphia, 1941), 310.

61. The private opinions of leaders of America Jewry about American officeholders were often based on whether they were "good for the Jews" or not. Rabbi Wise wrote "confidentially" to Nathan Straus on February 26, 1920, "I do not think we have suffered any great loss as far as Jewish affairs go through the passing [resignation] of [Secretary of State Robert] Lansing!" Wise tended to think that Jewish affairs that touched upon national interests could be influenced by personal relations, as shown by his comment in the same letter that Lansing's successor, Bainbridge Colby, "is a personal friend and I think we shall find he will be helpful." See Voss, ed., *Stephen S. Wise*, 98.

62. National Executive Committee Meeting, June 1, 1919, cited in Frommer, "The American Jewish Congress," 156.

63. The phrase "friends in court" is used by Naomi Cohen to denote two distinct approaches to Jewish conduct in America. The first is the activity of the community steward who has entrée into the circle or "court" of the power brokers and intercedes for his fellow Jews. The second is the use of the *amicus curiae* brief, an impersonal way of advancing Jewish interests through general litigation. See Cohen, "Friends in Court," 313–32.

64. When Wilson offered the Embassy of Constantinople to Morgenthau, the latter conveyed some resentment that was felt by Jews at having this particular post set aside for Jews, since Oscar Straus had been a three-time appointee to this post. See Fuchs, *The Political Behavior of American Jews*, 59.

65. Jewish Congressman Julius Kahn was chosen by the anti-Zionists to deliver the petition to the State Department and to President Wilson (on March 4, 1919), for whom he had managed a military appropriations bill in the House. See Frommer, "The American Jewish Congress," 131. Stephen Wise, although annoyed by the petition, drew comfort from the fact that "the really great Jewish figures are not among the signatories." And those, like Morgenthau, who were would come to regret it one day. For Wise's statement and the reaction of President Wilson to the petition, see Wise to Lena and Nathan Straus, March 6, 1919 in Voss, ed., *Stephen S. Wise*, 87. Morgenthau, it should be mentioned, was an enthusiastic supporter of Wilson. In 1916 his public appeal to Jews qua Jews to support Wilson, which violated Jewish political neutrality, was severely criticized. See Justine Wise Polier and James Waterman Wise, eds., *The Personal Letters of Stephen Wise* (Boston, 1956), 159–60.

66. Henry Morgenthau, *All in a Lifetime* (New York, 1923), 351, 383–84.

67. Oscar Janowsky, *Nationalities and National Minorities* (New York, 1945), 110–23.

68. Janowsky, *Jews and Minority Rights*, 356–57, 373–75; P. Azcarate, *The League of Nations and National Minorities* (Washington, 1945), 24–27.

69. Stephen Wise, together with ex-President William Howard Taft and Lawrence Lowell, president of Harvard University, became very active in the campaign for American participation in the League. See Polier and Wise, eds., *The Personal Letters of Stephen Wise*, 173, 175, 177; for Louis Marshall's views on the League's effec-

tiveness, see his letter to the editor of the *NYT,* Nov. 25, 1919, in Reznikoff, ed., *Louis Marshall,* 2:678–81, especially 680 and 681 (note) where Marshall confesses to a change of heart, having been at first skeptical about the League.

70. *The Jewish Advocate* (Boston), Jan. 23, 1919, cited in Frommer, "The American Jewish Congress," 165.

71. Mack in the Executive Committee Meeting, Oct. 26, 1924, Executive Committee Minutes, 1924 folder, AJ Congress Papers, Box 6, Executive Committee, 1916–1949, AJHS. On the use of legal procedures for attaining political ends, especially vis-à-vis a defeated nation, it is worthwhile recalling Otto Kirchheimer's monumental study, *Political Justice: The Use and Legal Procedure for Political Ends* (1961; reprint, Princeton, 1980).

72. Azcarate, *The League of Nations,* 255–62, 323–90.

73. The subject of American immigration policies has been widely researched. The immigration legislation during the 1920s will be discussed later in this chapter only in relation to the American Jewish response to the absorption of Jewish refugees. For general works as well as those referring specifically to the Jewish case, see M. T. Bennett, *American Immigration Policies* (Washington, 1963); W. S. Bernard, *American Immigration Policy: A Reappraisal* (1950; reprint, New York, 1969); Breitman and Kraut, *American Refugee Policy;* David Brody, "American Jewry: The Refugees and Immigration Restriction, 1932–1942," *PAJHS* 45 (June 1956): 219–47; Robert A. Divine, *American Immigration Policy, 1924–1952* (New Haven, 1957); H. Fields, "Closing Immigration throughout the World," *American Journal of International Law* 26 (1936); and Higham, *Strangers in the Land.*

74. Brandeis to Alfred Brandeis, April 10, 1921, cited in Alpheus T. Mason, *Brandeis: A Free Man's Life* (New York, 1946), 530. See also Hofstadter, *The Age of Reform,* 273–74.

75. Marshall to Lucien Wolf, Secretary, Joint Foreign Committee of the Jewish Board of Deputies and the Anglo-Jewish Association, Aug. 15, 1922, in Reznikoff, ed., *Louis Marshall,* 1:204.

76. Thomas F. Gossett, *Race: The History of an Idea in America* (New York, 1965), 405.

77. Calvin Coolidge, "Whose Country Is This?" *Good Housekeeping* 72 (Feb. 1921): 14, cited in Gossett, *Race: The History of an Idea in America,* 405. Ironically, in mourning the death of Coolidge, the *American Hebrew,* Jan. 13, 1933, wrote in its editorial that "his memory will be revered" by American Jews, among others, because of his denunciation, in Oct. 1925, of "Nordic nationalism" when he expressed the conviction that "no race or creed has a monopoly of patriotism in this country."

78. Oscar Handlin, *Boston's Immigrants* (Cambridge, Mass., 1959), 149.

79. Cited in John D. Hicks, *Republican Ascendancy, 1921–1933* (New York, Evanston, and London, 1960), 25.

80. See Higham, *Strangers in the Land,* Chapter 7, 158.

81. Cited in Cohen, *Not Free to Desist,* 48, 53.

82. *Temporary Suspension of Immigration,* Sixty-Sixth Congress, 3rd Session, House of Representatives, Report no. 1109, Dec. 6, 1920 and Appendix A. Cf. "Hearings: Emergency Immigration Legislation" (Senate Committee on Immigration), Sixty-Sixth Congress, 3rd Session, 10. Reprinted in Mendes-Flohr and Reinharz, *The Jew in the Modern World,* 405–407.

83. Higham, *Strangers in the Land,* 311.

84. Cited in Lederhendler, *Jewish Responses To Modernity,* 109.

85. Ibid., 318.

86. On the 1917 act, see Higham, *Strangers in the Land*, 202–204.

87. Marshall to Lucien Wolf, Secretary, Joint Foreign Committee of the Jewish Board of Deputies and the Anglo-Jewish Association, Aug. 15, 1922, in Reznikoff, ed., *Louis Marshall*, 1:201–202, 204 (emphasis in the original).

88. Cited in Cohen, *Not Free to Desist*, 138.

89. Ginsberg, *The Fatal Embrace*, 93–96.

90. Higham, "Social Discrimination against Jews in America," 28.

91. Leo Ribuffo, "Henry Ford and the International Jew," *AJH* 69 (June 1980): 446–47. On the origin and spread of the *Protocols*, see Norman Cohn, *Warrant for Genocide: The Myth of the World-Conspiracy and the Protocols of the Elders of Zion* (New York, 1969), Chapters 1–4.

92. John Higham, "American Anti-Semitism Historically Reconsidered," in Charles Herbert Stember, et al., *Jews in the Mind of America* (New York, 1966), 247–48. Ford is quoted from *The Dearborn Independent*, May 22, 1920, pp. 1–3, in ibid., 247. See also Albert Lee, *Henry Ford and the Jews* (New York, 1980); and Ribuffo, "Henry Ford and the International Jew." While Higham generally links anti-Semitism to social and economic causes, without precluding religious animus, his downplaying of the significance of the racial conception of the Jews has been recently questioned by Robert Singerman in "The Jew as Racial Alien: The Genetic Component of American Anti-Semitism," in David Gerber, ed., *Anti-Semitism in American History* (Urbana and Chicago, 1987), 103–28. For an excellent and informative essay on the newer interpretation of American anti-Semitism, see Gerber's article in that volume, "Anti-Semitism and Jewish-Gentile Relations in American Historiography and the American Past," 3–54.

93. Higham, *Strangers in the Land*, 286.

94. For the most comprehensive study of the Frank case, see Leonard Dinnerstein, *The Leo Frank Case* (New York, 1968). The founding of the Anti-Defamation League was prompted by the Leo Frank case. See Deborah Dash Moore, *B'nai Brith and the Challenge of Ethnic Leadership* (Albany, N.Y., 1981), 102–108.

95. Susan E. Tifft and Alex S. Jones, *The Trust: The Private and Powerful Family Behind the New York Times* (Boston, 1999), 92–93, 95, 96.

96. Marshall to Julius Levy, dated Oct. 13, 1920, in Reznikoff, ed., *Louis Marshall*, 1:335n.

97. Cited in Cohen, *Not Free to Desist*, 131. Schiff died in 1920.

98. Cited in ibid., 132.

99. In attendance were representatives of B'nai B'rith, the CCAR, the United Synagogue of America, and the AJ Congress. See Report of the American Jewish Committee (transcript), Nov. 14, 1920; Minutes of Executive Committee Meeting, Nov. 13, 1920, RG 1, Records of the AJC Executive Offices (EXO), YIVO.

100. Marshall to John Davey, Feb. 4, 1921, in Reznikoff, ed., *Louis Marshall*, 1:355. For a similar reaction to the danger of the Ku Klux Klan, see Stephen Wise's letter to J. R. Gilber, Oct. 22, 1924, in Voss, ed., *Stephen S. Wise*, 128.

101. Wise to Mack, Jan. 20, 1922, in Voss, ed., *Stephen S. Wise*, 107–108.

102. See Gerber, ed., *Anti-Semitism in American History*, 20–22 for his categories of anti-Semitism; for Higham's categories see "Ideological Anti-Semitism in the Gilded Age," in his *Send These to Me*, 120.

103. Wise to Bernard G. Richards, Aug. 3, 1922, in Voss, ed., *Stephen S. Wise*, 117.

104. *Menorah*, Aug. 1903, p. 95, cited in Cohen, *Encounter with Emancipation*, 302.

For a most interesting account of Jewish thinking of the time, see David E. Hirsch, *Rabbi Emil G. Hirsch* (Chicago, 1968).

105. Handlin and Handlin, "Acquisition of Political and Social Rights," 74; Higham, "Social Discrimination," 16–18; Higham, *Strangers in the Land*, 161; see also Glazer, "Social Characteristics of American Jews," 16. Reznikoff, ed., *Louis Marshall*, 1:244–500, provides an invaluable account of the scope of discrimination and bigotry in the United States during the 1920s. What is particularly interesting is that Marshall, "the champion of liberty," while active in combating this behavior, was adamant that it should not be made into a public issue, although he acknowledged (in 1915) that social discriminations against Jews "may be said to be anti-Semitic in their origin" (ibid., 245–46).

106. See Haywood Brown and George Britt, *Christians Only: A Study in Prejudice* (1931; reprint, New York, 1974). See also Max Vorspan and Lloyd P. Gartner, *History of the Jews of Los Angeles* (Philadelphia, 1970), 206; Lloyd P. Gartner, *History of the Jews of Cleveland* (Cleveland, 1978), 94–98; Albert I. Gordon, *Jews in Transition* (Minneapolis, 1949), 43–68; Deborah Dash Moore, *At Home in America: Second-Generation New York Jews* (New York, 1981), 36, 38; Glazer, "Social Characteristics of American Jews," 26.

107. Marcia Graham Synnott, "Anti-Semitism and American Universities: Did Quotas Follow the Jews?" in Gerber, ed., *Anti-Semitism in American History*, 238. This article provides most interesting statistics on numbers and percentages of Jewish students at selected colleges and universities as well as medical schools.

108. Gerber, "Anti-Semitism and Jewish-Gentile Relations in American Historiography and the American Past," in Gerber, ed., *Anti-Semitism in American History*, 26; see also Higham, "Social Discrimination against Jews in America," 21–23; Marcia Graham Synnott, *The Half-Opened Door: Discrimination and Admissions at Harvard, Yale and Princeton, 1900–1970* (Westport, 1979), xvii–xx, and passim; Dash Moore, *B'nai Brith and the Challenge of Ethnic Leadership*; Oliver B. Pollock, "Antisemitism, the Harvard Plan, and the Roots of Reverse Discrimination," *JSS* 45 (Spring 1983): 113–22; Solomon, *Ancestors and Immigrants*, 205–206.

109. See Beth S. Wenger, *New York Jews and the Great Depression: Uncertain Promise* (New Haven, 1996).

110. See Lloyd Gartner, "The Midpassage of American Jewry," in Jonathan Sarna, ed., *The American Jewish Experience* (New York, 1986), 230; Abraham G. Duker, "Socio-Psychological Trends in the American Jewish Community Since 1900," *YAJSS* 9 (1954): 167.

111. On the organization and early activities of the Young Men's Hebrew Association (YMHA), which served the German immigration, see Benjamin Rabinowitz, "The Young Men's Hebrew Association," *PAJHS* 37 (1947). For a comparison of the YMHA and the YMCA, see C. Howard Hopkins, *History of the Y.M.C.A. in North America* (New York, 1951), Chapter 9. Concerning works on agencies that assisted the East European immigrants, see Bogen, *Jewish Philanthropy*, Chapter 9. For the Educational Alliance of New York, the most Americanizing agency within the settlement house movement, see William Wirtz, *The First Fifty Years, a History of the National Council of Jewish Women* (New York, 1943). Rischin, *The Promised City*, provides a concise description of the conflict between the uptown and downtown Jews in the immigrant generation.

112. On the emergence of the synagogue centers, see Dash Moore, *At Home in America*, 123–47.

113. Ira Katznelson, "Between Separation and Disappearance: Jews on the Margins of American Liberalism," in Birnbaum and Katznelson, *Paths of Emancipation*, 205.

114. Mordecai M. Kaplan, *Judaism as a Civilization* (1934; reprint, Philadelphia, 1981), Chapter 5, 47–79; Glazer, *American Judaism*, 85–87.

115. Glazer, *American Judaism*, 47–49.

116. Erich Rosenthal, "Studies of Jewish Intermarriage in the United States," *AJYB* 64 (1963): 3–53. For a summary and an extensive bibliography on the subject see Moshe Davis, "Mixed Marriage in Western Jewry: Historical Background to the Jewish Response," *The Jewish Journal of Sociology* 10 (1968): 177–220. For use of the term see, for example, Volkov, "The Dynamics of Dissimilation," 195–211.

117. George L. Mosse, *German Jews beyond Judaism* (Bloomington and Cincinnati, 1985), 3. On the meaning of *Bildung* see David Sorkin, "Wilhelm von Humboldt: The Theory and Practice of Self-Formation (*Bildung*), 1791–1810," *Journal of the History of Ideas* (Jan. 1983): 5–73.

4. A Crisis of Faith

1. Fuchs, *The Political Behavior of American Jews*, 62–64.

2. Manfred Jonas, *The United States and Germany: A Diplomatic History* (Ithaca and London, 1984), 154.

3. For a detailed study of the general relationship between the United States and Germany, see Lloyd E. Ambrosius, "The United States and the Weimar Republic, 1918–1923: From the Armistice to the Ruhr Occupation" (Ph.D. diss., University of Illinois, 1967). For more narrowly focused studies, one may consult the following: Werner Link, *Die amerikanische Stabilisierungspolitik in Deutschland, 1921–1932* (Düsseldorf, 1970); Herbert Feis, *The Diplomacy of the Dollar, 1919–1932* (New York, 1966); Joan Hoff Wilson, *American Business and Foreign Policy, 1920–1933* (Lexington, 1971); William C. McNeil, *American Money and the Weimar Republic: Economics and Politics on the Eve of the Great Depression* (New York, 1986).

4. Memorandum attached to letter, Hoover to Harding, Jan. 2, 1922, quoted in Link, *Die amerikanische Stabilisierungspolitik in Deutschland*, 107. It is interesting to note that this analysis is pre-Keynesian, assuming the necessity of a balanced budget.

5. The speech was delivered on Dec. 29, 1922. Portions of the advanced text are in Phillips to Herrick, in *FRUS* (1922), 2:199–202.

6. Hughes to Wiedfeldt, July 25, 1923, *FRUS* (1923), 2:23.

7. Jonas, *The United States and Germany*, 174.

8. Robert Murphy, *Diplomat among Warriors* (London, 1964), 15–16. Murphy served in Munich from 1920 to 1925. He returned to Germany as political advisor to the American military government during the American occupation of Germany following World War Two and was perhaps one of the most powerful persons in Germany until 1949.

9. See Eberhard Kolb, *The Weimar Republic*, trans. P. S. Falla (London, 1988), 47–50.

10. Jehuda Reinharz, "The Zionist Response to Antisemitism in Germany," *LBIY* 30 (1985): 111; See also Hugo Bieber, "Anti-Semitism in the First Years of the German Republic," *YAJSS* 4 (1949): 123–45.

11. Confidential report to the members of the ZVFD, quoted in Reinharz, "The Zionist Response," 112.

12. *Jüdische Rundschau*, no. 96, Nov. 9, 1923, p. 557, cited here in the English

translation by Reinharz in ibid., p. 113, emphasis in the original; see also Peter Baldwin, "Zionist and Non-Zionist in the Last Years before the Nazi Regime," *LBIY* 27 (1982): 87–108.

13. Reinharz, *Fatherland or Promised Land*, 46–48.

14. *Jüdische Rundschau* 96 (Nov. 9, 1923), p. 557, cited here in the English translation by Reinharz in "The Zionist Response," 113.

15. See Werner T. Angress, "The German Army's 'Judenzählung' of 1916: Genesis—Consequences—Significance," *LBIY* 23 (1978): 117–35.

16. Cited in Jacob Boas, "The Jews of Germany: Self-Perception in the Nazi Era as Reflected in the German Jewish Press, 1933–1938" (Ph.D. diss., University of California–Riverside, 1977), 41 (emphasis in the original). This call was a joint proclamation issued by the C.V. and the Verband der deutschen Juden on Aug. 1, 1914.

17. Reichsbund jüdischer Frontsoldaten, ed., *Kriegsbriefe gefallener Jude* (Berlin, 1935), 20–21, 16.

18. Baldwin, "Zionist and Non-Zionist," 88–89; Jacob Boas, "Germany or Diaspora? German Jewry's Shifting Perceptions in the Nazi Era (1933–1938)," *LBIY* 27 (1982): 109.

19. Boas, "Germany or Diaspora?" 110.

20. Max Horkheimer, *Über die deutschen Juden* (Cologne, 1961), 7. An interesting example of those who sought another identity is author-historian Emil Ludwig. Born Emil Ludwig Cohen, his father suggested he drop the Cohen to have a better chance at a professional career. Presumably that was not enough; he also converted to Christianity. See Mosse, *German Jews beyond Judaism*, 26. Visiting the United States in September 1933, he confessed at an evening gathering organized by the American Jewish Congress that on the day that Foreign Minister Rathenau had been murdered he had realized that he, Rathenau, "was too much German and too little Jew." "From that day on," Ludwig continued, "I felt myself to be more Jew than German." But Ludwig did not go all the way—while demanding that the Jews "must be recognized as a national entity," and having been greatly impressed with the work being done in Palestine, he insisted that even if that country had been able to accommodate 16 million Jews, "it would not be advisable to send all our people there. Both they and the remainder of the world would lose too much thereby." But Ludwig was not only advocating the need to preserve the "universal" Jew, he seemed just as anxious to assure a future for the German Jews in Germany: "The Jews are good citizens of the nations to which they belong and, at the same time, super-national." Text of Address Delivered by Dr. Emil Ludwig, Sept. 28, 1933, SSW Papers, Box 82/3, AJHS. Ludwig understandably first approached the AJC and asked to organize a speaking tour under its auspices, hoping to arouse world opinion to the plight of German Jewry. Cyrus Adler, in a telegram to Felix Warburg, April 6, 1933, rejected the offer, claiming that "opinion in America, England and other countries sufficiently aroused. Present day Germany will resent being told contributions Jews to German Culture." In a letter to Warburg, on the same day, Adler went even further in explaining his rejection of Ludwig's proposal, claiming that "even here in America . . . the public will very soon tire of the Jewish question in Germany"; he was of the opinion that hearing more of the same would not keep the issue in the news. Letter to Felix Warburg, April 6, 1933, both in Warburg's Papers, Box 286/5, AJA.

21. Baldwin, "Zionist and Non-Zionist," 90.

22. Reinharz, "The Zionist Response to Antisemitism in Germany," 114–15. For the most detailed study of the German Jews' defense work against anti-Semitism, see Arnold Paucker, *Der jüdische Abwehrkampf* (Hamburg, 1969). During the Reichstag

elections in May 1924, the NSDAP together with the DVFP (Deutschvölkische Frei-heitspartei) captured 32 seats, that is, 6.6 percent of the vote. But following the Dawes Plan of August 1924 Germany entered a period of "stabilization" which translated at the polls during the Dec. 7, 1924 elections into only fourteen seats for the NSDAP. In the May 20, 1928 elections, when Germany was at its height of economic recovery, the NSDAP won only twelve seats. See Richard F. Hamilton, *Who Voted for Hitler?* (Princeton, 1982), 77–78.

23. AJC, Annual Report, 1922, cited also in Cohen, *Not Free to Desist*, 147.

24. Baldwin, "Zionist and Non-Zionist," 102.

25. Cohen, *Not Free to Desist*, 147; Chernow, *The Warburgs*, 228; see also Frommer, "American Jewish Congress," 293.

26. Quoted in Cohen, *Not Free to Desist*, 147.

27. Ibid.

28. Quoted in an AJ Congress Confidential Bulletin No. 2, of Nov. 30, 1923, SSW Papers, Box 82, AJHS.

29. Telegram to His Excellency the German Ambassador, Washington, Nov. 8, 1923, ibid.

30. Cited in Gordon, *Assimilation in American Life*, 101.

31. Arthur Herzberg, *The Jews in America* (New York, 1989), 248, 250.

32. Wise to Rebekah Kohut, March 28, 1925, in Voss, ed., *Stephen S. Wise*, 129–30.

33. Jonas, *The United States and Germany*, 176, 180; see also Kolb, *The Weimar Republic*, 58–61, 71.

34. Jonas, *The United States and Germany*, 185.

35. Schurman's speech (April 1928) is cited in Robert A. Gottwald, *Die deutsch-amerikanischen Beziehungen in der Ära Stresemann* (Berlin-Dahlem, 1965), 97. It was delivered on the occasion of accepting an honorary doctorate from the University of Heidelberg. See also Jonas, *The United States and Germany*, 189.

36. Ibid., 190; Kolb, *The Weimar Republic*, 103–105; David Abraham, *The Collapse of the Weimar Republic: Political Economy and Crisis*, 2nd ed. (New York and London, 1986), 141–42, 149–52.

37. Jonas, *The United States and Germany*, 191.

38. Kolb, *The Weimar Republic*, 64, 104–106.

39. Detlev J. K. Peukert, *The Weimar Republic: The Crisis of Classical Modernity*, trans. Richard Deveson (New York, 1992), 196.

40. In the Landtag election in Baden in October 1929, the Nazis obtained 7 percent of the votes; in Lübeck in November, 8.1 percent; and in Thuringia in December, 11.3 percent. In Thuringia, thanks to a stalemate between the bourgeois and the socialist parties and the former's agreement to enter into a coalition, the Nazis for the first time became members of a Land government. Similar gains were achieved by the NSDAP in the municipal elections in November 1929. See Kolb, *The Weimar Republic*, 104–105.

41. Sidney M. Bolkosky, *The Distorted Image: German-Jewish Perceptions of Germans and Germany, 1918–1935* (New York, 1975), 164–65.

42. Ibid., 165.

43. Kurt Löwenstein, "Die innerjüdische Reaktion auf die Krise der deutschen Demokratie," in Werner E. Mosse, ed., *Entscheidungsjahr 1932*, 2nd revised and enlarged edition (Tübingen, 1966), 403.

44. Cited in Bolkosky, *The Distorted Image*, 166.

45. Ibid.

46. Boas, "The Jews of Germany," 41.

47. Morris Waldman toured Europe during the summer of 1928; Stephen Wise spent the summer of 1926 on the Continent mostly to attend to Zionist affairs, but he was also attuned to the Jews' situation in Germany and Eastern Europe.

48. JTA folders, 1926–1927, AJCA. The bulk of Landau's report is missing, as attested also by Cohen in *Not Free to Desist*, 574.

49. Minutes of Executive Committee, Dec. 12, 1926, AJCA; also cited in Cohen, *Not Free to Desist*, 149.

50. Chronological Files: Feb. 1928, AJCA; and Cohen, *Not Free to Desist*, 149, 156.

51. Chernow, *The Warburgs*, 322.

52. Marshall to Waldman, July 10, 1929, Morris M. Waldman Papers, 1912–1963, MS Col. 23 (hereafter, Waldman's Papers), Box 1/28, AJA. The Centralverein asked for $175,000 annually. During Wiener's visit in the United States the request was denied. Early in 1930 the AJC turned over to the Centralverein a sum of $7,500, of which $2,000 was the final balance of the Emergency Trust Fund which had originally been created to aid the Jews of Eastern Europe. See Minutes of the AJC Executive Committee Meeting of Jan. 12, 1930, AJCA, as well as Cohen, *Not Free to Desist*, 157.

53. Waldman to Marshall, July 15, 1929, Waldman's Papers, Box 1/28, AJA. Excerpts from the letters exchanged between Waldman and Marshall appear also in Morris D. Waldman, *Nor By Power* (New York, 1953), 40–41.

54. Ibid., 39.

55. Marshall to Waldman, July 21, 1929, Waldman's Papers, Box 1/28, AJA.

56. Ibid.

57. Ibid.

58. Marshall to Waldman, July 10, 1929, Waldman's Papers, Box 1/28, AJA.

59. Marshall to Waldman, July 10 and 21, 1929; Waldman to Marshall, July 19, 1929, both in Waldman's Papers, Box 1/28, AJA.

60. Waldman to Marshall, July 15, 1929, Waldman's Papers, Box 1/28, AJA.

61. Ibid.

62. See, for example, Gottlieb, *American Anti-Nazi Resistance*, xxi; Shlomo Shafir, "The Impact of the Jewish Crisis on American-German Relations, 1933–1939" (Ph.D. diss., Georgetown University, 1971), Part 1, vi.

63. Waldman to Marshall, July 18, 1929, Waldman's Papers, Box 1/28, AJA.

64. Emma Felsenthal, *Bernhard Felsenthal* (New York, 1924), 19, quoted also in Eric E. Hirshler, ed., *Jews from Germany in the United States* (New York, 1955), 51. Felsenthal, a Bavarian-born schoolteacher, was the founder of the Jewish Reform Society in Chicago in 1858.

65. Wise to Einstein, May 9, 1933, in Voss, ed., *Stephen S. Wise*, 187.

66. Hirshler, ed., *Jews from Germany in the United States*, 42–45, 51; Glanz, *Studies in Judaica Americana*, 98–101, 203–255.

67. On the C.V.'s programmatic declaration, see Werner E. Mosse, "From 'Schutzjuden' to 'Deutsche Staatsbürger Jüdischen Glaubens': The Long and Bumpy Road of Jewish Emancipation in Germany," in Birnbaum and Katznelson, *Paths of Emancipation*, 92–93.

68. Leni Yahil, "Jewish Assimilation vis-à-vis German Nationalism in the Weimar Republic," in Bela Vago, ed., *Jewish Assimilation in Modern Times* (Boulder, Colo., 1981), 42.

69. Reinharz, "The Zionist Response to Antisemitism in Germany," 131–32.

70. Baldwin, "Zionist and Non-Zionist," 102–103.

71. *Jüdische Rundschau* 38, no. 19 (March 7, 1933): 92, cited in ibid., 104.

72. The Social Democratic Party (SPD) won 143 seats. However, the NSDAP increased its votes from 800,000 in the previous election to approximately 6.4 million, and its share of the poll from 2.6 percent to 18.2 percent, while the SPD lost about half a million votes and ten seats as compared with its record success in 1928. See Kolb, *The Weimar Republic*, 107, 113, 189.

73. George A. Gordon to Secretary of State Henry Stimson, Sept. 17, 1930; U.S. Department of State, *FRUS* (1930), 3:77–79.

74. Jonas, *The United States and Germany*, 195.

75. James W. Prothro, *The Dollar Decade: Business Ideas in the 1920s* (Baton Rouge, 1954) is an interesting analysis of the business mood during the 1920s. See also McNeil, *American Money and the Weimar Republic*.

76. General Motors owned the Opel Automobile Works, Ford of Detroit the Ford Motor A. G., to mention but two. Attracted by an average yield on German bonds of 7–8 percent, Americans purchased $1,239,000,000 worth of all German loan issues from 1924 to 1930. The cartel and contractual agreements between key American firms and German industries were merely strengthened with Hitler's rise to power and later developments. See Gabriel Kolko, "American Business and Germany, 1930–1941," *Western Political Quarterly* 15, no. 4 (Dec. 1962): 714–28.

77. Ibid., 714–15. In "American Business and the Approach of War, 1935–1941," *Journal of Economic History* 13, no. 1 (Winter 1953): 78, Roland N. Stromberg concludes that "In the drift toward unneutrality and then war, business played no independent role. . . . It was dragged along in the wake of circumstances." However, his analysis and conclusions are based almost exclusively on business publications. In Kolko's article one can discern clearly the lack of correlation between words and actions.

78. Corwin D. Edwards, *Economic and Political Aspects of International Cartels* (Washington, D.C., 1946), 43–44, cited in Kolko, "American Business and Germany, 1930–1941," 725.

79. Robert H. Ferrell, *American Diplomacy in the Great Depression: Hoover-Stimson Foreign Policy, 1929–1933* (1957; reprint, New York, 1970), 106–19.

80. William R. Castle, Undersecretary of State to Ray Atherton, July 19, 1931, *FRUS* (1931), 1:280; Ferrell, *American Diplomacy in the Great Depression*, Chapter 7.

81. Herbert Hoover, *Memoirs of Herbert Hoover: The Cabinet and the Presidency, 1920–1933*, vol. 2 (New York, 1951), 330. Even such a militarist as Secretary of State Stimson trusted that the "surest way" to increase the efficacy of the Kellogg-Briand Pact was "not by seeking to add extraneous sanctions of force, but by providing the machinery for enlightening and strengthening the present sanction of public opinion." See Stimson to Walter Lippmann, Jan. 7, 1930, cited in Ferrell, *American Diplomacy in the Great Depression*, 26.

82. Sol Bloom, *The Autobiography of Sol Bloom* (New York, 1948), 227.

83. Margaret K. Norden, "American Editorial Response to the Rise of Adolf Hitler: A Preliminary Consideration," *AJHQ* 59, no. 3 (March 1970): 290–91.

84. *NYT,* Feb. 12 and Sept. 27, 1930.

85. Hans J. Morgenthau, *Politics in the 20th Century*, 3 vols. (Chicago and London, 1962), vol. 2, *The Impasse of American Foreign Policy*, 196.

86. *NYT,* Oct. 20, 1930.

87. *AH,* Sept. 19, Oct. 24, and Oct. 3, 1930.

88. *American Jewish Congress Index*, Oct. 1930.

89. "Special Conference of the American Jewish Committee," Nov. 9, 1930, RG1, EXO 37/4, on situation in Germany (hereafter, "Special Conference," Nov. 9, 1930), AJCA, Historical Document Section. The verbatim transcript consists of 58 pages. This meeting was held as an executive session of the Committee's annual meeting. Since it was declared as an off-the-record, secret meeting, the speakers appear to have expressed themselves very openly. Hence, our understanding of this section of American Jewry can be much enhanced by what appears to be a most authentic response to the German situation.

90. "The Anti-Semitic Menace in Germany," Report to the AJC at a Special Executive Session of its Annual Meeting, delivered on Nov. 9, 1930 (hereafter, "Waldman's Report," Nov. 9, 1930), AJC Records, Record Group (RG) FAD-1, Germany, Anti-Semitism, YIVO. An abridged version of this report appears in Waldman, *Nor By Power,* 42–47. All quotes in this section are from the original version.

91. Waldman, *Nor By Power,* 47.

92. The 1943 report is cited in full in ibid., 464–68, quote on 466.

93. See, for example, Cohen, *Not Free to Desist,* 157–58.

94. "Special Conference," Nov. 9, 1930, p. 2.

95. Ibid., 1, 7, 20, 47.

96. *AJYB* 33 (1931): 77.

97. "Special Conference," Nov. 9, 1930, pp. 15–16.

98. See Chapters 2 and 3.

99. Jeremiah 29:5–7.

100. "Special Conference," Nov. 9, 1930, p. 1.

101. Ibid., 21, 47.

102. Sander L. Gilman, *Jewish Self-Hatred, Anti-Semitism and the Hidden Language of the Jews* (Baltimore, 1986), 2.

103. Cohen, *American Jews and the Zionist Idea,* 31. For a similar ideological opposition in America to Zionism in a later period, see Kolsky, *Jews against Zionism.*

104. Gilman, *Jewish Self-Hatred,* 2.

105. "Special Conference," Nov. 9, 1930, pp. 40, 22–23, 27, 13.

106. Ibid., 19, 18.

107. Selma Stern, *The Court Jew* (Philadelphia, 1950), 13.

108. "Special Conference," Nov. 9, 1930, pp. 9–10.

109. Ibid., 5–7, 10–12, 28–29, 43–44, 50–52. Boas, who published in 1911 the classic indictment of racial thinking, *The Mind of Primitive Man,* continued to lead the attack on ideas of racial superiority with regard to immigration restrictions. See also his *Race and Democratic Society* (New York, 1945), especially 87–92, 168–71, and "What is Race?" *The Nation* 120 (1925).

110. "Special Conference," Nov. 9, 1930, pp. 10–11, 13. Schulman referred to the National Socialist program, where the term "German" blood is used.

111. Ibid., 1.

112. Ibid., 24. The speaker is Rabbi David Philipson. Adler agreed, stating: "We recognize the fact that the German Government is opposed to this anti-Jewish movement. We recognize the fact that at the present time a majority of the people in Germany are opposed to this anti-Jewish movement" (53).

113. Ibid., 24.

114. Ibid., 49.

115. Arendt, *Origins,* xiii.

116. "Special Conference," Nov. 9, 1930, p. 50.

117. Ibid., 25.

118. Ibid., 2 (emphasis added).

119. Ibid., 58.

120. Cited in Stephen S. Wise, *As I See It* (New York, 1944), 22.

121. *NYT,* Oct. 20, 1930, p. 44.

122. *NYT,* March 9, 1931, p. 22.

123. Richards to Tenenbaum, April 14, 1931, folder 4, Bernard G. Richards Mss., Jewish Theological Seminary, cited in Frommer, "American Jewish Congress," 296.

124. Report of Meeting of Sub-Committee on Germany of the American Jewish Committee, Oct. 8, 1931, AJC Records, Foreign Countries File (FAD 1), Germany 1931–1933, YIVO.

125. "Antisemitism in Germany," Memorandum by Jacob Landau, 1931, AJC Records, Foreign Countries File (FAD 1), Germany 1931–1933, YIVO. In Germany Landau met with Dr. Julius Brodnitz, Dr. Alfred Wiener, Dr. Bruno Weil, and Ernst Wallach of the Centralverein; Dr. Mark Wischnitzer of the Hilfsverein; Rabbi Leo Baeck of B'nai B'rith; and Kurt Blumenfeld of the Zionist Federation.

126. Administrative Committee Meeting, Oct. 27, 1931, AJ Congress Papers, Box 2, Administrative Committee, 1923–1933, 1931 Folder, AJHS.

127. Wise to Mack, Dec. 30, 1931, in Voss, ed., *Stephen S. Wise,* 170–71.

128. "Memo of Conference of German Situation," Jan. 28, 1932, Cyrus Adler Files, AJCA, New York (hereafter Adler Files). Also cited in Frommer, "American Jewish Congress," 301. Minutes of Joint Meeting of American Jewish Congress and American Jewish Committee, Jan. 28, 1932, Adler Files.

129. Brodnitz, Hollander, Baeck to the AJC, May 6, 1932, Felix M. Warburg Papers, 1895–1937 (hereafter Warburg's Papers), Box 295, AJA.

130. See Maurice J. Karpf, "Jewish Community Organization in the United States," *AJYB* 39 (1937–1938): 62–126.

131. Felix Warburg to Adler, Feb. 18, 1932, Warburg's Papers, Box 295, AJA.

132. Adler to Felix Warburg, Feb. 19, 1932, Warburg's Papers, Box 295, AJA.

133. "Memo of Conference on German Situation," Jan. 28, 1932, cited in Frommer, "American Jewish Congress," 301–302.

134. Administrative Committee Meeting, March 1, 1932, AJ Congress Papers, Box 2, Administrative Committee, 1923–1933, AJHS.

135. Administrative Committee Meeting, March 15, 1932, AJ Congress Papers, Box 2, Administrative Committee, 1923–1933, AJHS. On March 10 the *New York World Telegram* published a story that Adler, as president of the AJC, had asked Borah to issue a statement protesting Hitler's program. The AJ Congress considered this independent step as a breach of its agreement with the Committee, namely that both bodies would not go public on the German problem. Schneidermann of the Committee called Wise the next day and informed him that Adler had not authorized the statement to the press.

136. Minutes of the executive committee, March 13, 1932, AJC Records, YIVO; Administrative Committee Minutes, March 29, 1932, AJ Congress Papers, Box 2, AJHS.

137. See Wise, *As I See It,* 26, 87.

5. Jewish Leaders versus the Voice of America, 1933

1. Paul L. Murphy, "Sources and Nature of Intolerance in the 1920s," in Milton Plesur, ed., *The 1920s: Problems and Paradoxes* (Boston, 1969), 170.

2. John Spargo, *The Jew and American Ideals* (New York, 1922), 7, cited in Leo P.

Ribuffo, *The Old Christian Right: The Protestant Far Right from the Great Depression to the Cold War* (Philadelphia, 1983), 9.

3. See Warren I. Susman, *Culture and Commitment, 1929–1945* (New York, 1973), and "The Thirties," in Stanley Coben and Lorman Ratner, eds., *The Development of an American Culture* (Englewood Cliffs, N.J., 1970), 179–218.

4. Nathan Wachtel, *Vision of the Vanquished: The Spanish Conquest of Peru through Indian Eyes, 1530–1570*, trans. Ben and Siân Reynolds (Hassocks, 1977), 208, cited in David G. Roskies, *Against the Apocalypse: Responses to Catastrophes in Modern Jewish Culture* (Cambridge, Mass., 1984), 11.

5. Rosenberg to McDonald, Nov. 16, 1935, Warburg's Papers, Box 324, AJA. Also cited in Barbara McDonald Stewart, *United States Government Policy on Refugees from Nazism, 1933–1940* (New York, 1982), 167.

6. See Jacob R. Marcus, "Zionism and the American Jew," *American Scholar* 2 (July 1933): 289–92. The membership of the Zionist Organization of America alone rose from 8,900 in 1933 to 43,000 in 1939.

7. Johan J. Smertenko, "Hitlerism Comes to America," *Harper's Magazine* 167 (Nov. 1933): 66–70; Ribuffo, *The Old Christian Right*; Seymour Martin Lipset and Earl Raab, *The Politics of Unreason: Right-Wing Extremism in America, 1790–1970* (New York, 1970), 157–67.

8. Wise, *As I See It*, 29.

9. Lipset and Raab went so far as to characterize the 1930s as "an eccentric decade of right-wing extremism in America." Lipset and Raab, *The Politics of Unreason*, 150.

10. Verbatim report of a "Conference on the German Situation called by the American Jewish Committee," May 24, 1933, Savoy-Plaza Hotel, New York City, RG1, EXO 37/6, 35 (hereafter, "Conference on the German Situation," May 24, 1933), AJCA, Historical Document Section; Mack to Stephen Wise, May 17, 1933, SSW Papers, Box 115, AJHS.

11. Milton M. Alexander, "Proceedings of the Regional Conference of the American Jewish Committee, Chicago, 10 June 1934," RG 1, EXO 37/7, 42–43 (hereafter, "Regional Conference," June 10, 1934), AJCA, Historical Document Section.

12. Waldman to Jacob Landau, director of the JTA, letter marked "Personal and Confidential," Nov. 2, 1935, Waldman's Papers, Box 1/22, AJA.

13. Raymond Gram Swing, *Forerunners of American Fascism* (New York, 1935), 168, cited in Ribuffo, *The Old Christian Right*, 20–21; on the Nazi movement in the United States see Sander A. Diamond, "The Years of Waiting: National Socialism in the United States, 1922–1933," *AJHQ* 59 (March 1970): 256–71; and *The Nazi Movement in the United States, 1924–1941* (Ithaca, New York, 1974); Leland V. Bell, *In Hitler's Shadow: The Anatomy of American Nazism* (Port Washington, New York, 1973).

14. Bell, *In Hitler's Shadow*, 23.

15. Lipset and Raab, *The Politics of Unreason*, 150.

16. Harry Simonhoff, *Under Strange Skies* (New York, 1953), 308.

17. Ibid.

18. Mack to Wise and Frankfurter, April 3, 1933, SSW Papers, Box 115, AJHS. Wise to Mack, Sept. 13, 1932, SSW Papers, Box 82/1, AJHS. Wise was in fact alerted to the potential power of pressure from the Jewish financial world in America by his close friend Holmes, whose letter he quoted in part to Mack.

19. Wise to Mack, April 10, 1933, SSW Papers, Box 115, AJHS. Sarnoff did agree to host a dinner party in honor of Dr. Hjalmar Schacht in May of 1933, in which a number of leading American Jews participated, including Wise, Proskauer, Irving

Lehman, and Roger Straus.

20. Ibid.

21. *New York World Telegram*, Feb. 5, 1935, cited in Jerold S. Auerbach, "Review Essay on *Proskauer: His Life and Times*," *AJH* 69 (Sept. 1979): 110.

22. Conversation of Dr. Stephen S. Wise with Bernard S. Deutsch re James G. McDonald, May 4, 1933, SSW Papers, Box 109, AJHS.

23. Report of Meeting with Ambassador Dodd, Sept. 19, 1933, Jacob Billikopf Papers, 1900–1951, File 18/3, AJA. The report is addressed to Mack, Frankfurter, Irving Lehman, Judge Cardozo, Judge Proskauer, Felix Warburg, Morris D. Waldman, and others.

24. Laura Puffer Morgan, Associate Secretary of the National Council for Prevention of War, to Stephen Wise, March 3, 1934, SSW Papers, Box 82/4, AJHS.

25. Robert C. Dexter, "Understanding Hitler's Germany," *Church and Society* 6 (Nov. 1933); E. G. Homringhausen, *Christian Century*, July 26, 1933.

26. "A Most Interesting Jewish View," letter to the editor by Richard T Levy, Jr.; "A Jew Answers a Jew," letter to the editor by Grant Lewi, both in the *Evening Post*, March 31 and April 3, 1933 respectively. SSW Papers, Box 82/1, AJHS.

27. "Conference on the German Situation," May 24, 1933, p. 28.

28. Ibid., 28, 31, 32–34.

29. Adler to Felix Warburg, April 9, 1933, Warburg's Papers, Box 301, AJA.

30. "Regional Conference," June 10, 1934, pp. 4–6.

31. Stephen Wise, *Challenging Years: The Autobiography of Stephen Wise* (London, 1951), 262.

32. Elizabeth Janeway, *Powers of the Weak* (New York, 1980), 166 (emphasis added). See, for example, Walter Laqueur, *The Terrible Secret: Suppression of the Truth about Hitler's "Final Solution"* (Boston, 1980); Walter Laqueur and Richard Breitman, *Breaking the Silence* (New York, 1986); Yehuda Bauer, "When Did They Know?" *Midstream* 4 (1968): 51–58; Henry Feingold, "Did American Jewry Do Enough during the Holocaust?" *B. G. Rudolph Lecture* (Syracuse University, Pamphlet Form, April 1984); and "The Government Response," in Henry Friedlander and Sybil Milton, eds., *The Holocaust: Ideology, Bureaucracy, and Genocide* (Millwood, New York, 1980), esp. 245–46.

33. Wise, *Challenging Years*, 236–37.

34. Joseph Tenenbaum, chairman of the executive committee of the American Jewish Congress, and Morris Rothenberg, president of the Zionist Organization of America, both at Madison Square Garden, March 27, 1933, cited in the *AH*, March 31, 1933.

35. See statement of protest issued by American social scientists and a similar interpretation presented in a statement of protest issued by American churchmen in affiliation with the National Conference of Jews and Christians, which reads: "We acknowledge the grievous provocations which have led to the German revolution . . . by the terms of the peace. Our nation shares part of the blame for this situation." Quoted in "Clergy and Social Scientists Protest," *AH*, May 12, 1933, p. 446; See also Dexter, "Understanding Hitler's Germany."

36. Wise, *As I See It*, 85.

37. See Deborah E. Lipstadt, *Beyond Belief: The American Press and the Coming of the Holocaust, 1933–1945* (New York, 1986), 14. For typical examples of reports which did not focus on anti-Jewish excesses see *New York Herald Tribune*, March 1 and 2, 1933, and *New York Times*, March 6, 1933—all on the front page.

38. *Los Angeles Times*, March 6, 1933, cited in Lipstadt, *Beyond Belief*, 16. For fur-

ther examples of skepticism, contradictory assessments within days, and utter confusion in press reports, see Lipstadt, 16–18. See also *The Jews in Nazi Germany: The Factual Record of their Persecution by the National Socialists*, published by the AJC (New York, 1933), 21, 24–27.

39. Lipstadt, *Beyond Belief*, 31–32.

40. Bernhard Kahn was the JDC's representative in Europe from the 1920s until he retired in 1938. See Bauer, *American Jewry and the Holocaust*, 23; *AH*, March 31, 1933, p. 331.

41. "Let Synagogue Leadership Bring United Jewish Appeal to American Government," *AH*, May 19, 1933. See also Jonah Wise's report on his trip to Germany in a letter to Mack, May 18, 1933, Mack's Papers, A405 83/A, CZA; "A Note on a Visit to Germany, 28 May to 3 June 1933," Warburg's Papers, Box 286/5, AJA.

42. Billikopf began his trip on Aug. 12, 1933. The report was sent to FDR by Herbert Lehman and is dated Sept. 1, 1933; another report on his meeting with Ambassador Dodd is dated Sept. 19. Both were widely distributed. In FDR's letter to Herbert H. Lehman (Sept. 27, 1933) the president indicated that he had forwarded it to Secretary of State Cordell Hull and to the Undersecretary William Phillips. Billikopf's Papers, File 18/3, AJA.

43. Goldman to Wise, Feb. 8, 1933, WJCC, A23/1, AJA. See also another anonymous letter dated March 14, 1933, by one who was apparently active on behalf of the American Jewish Congress, in Wise, *Challenging Years*, 241–44.

44. Cited in Carl Herman Voss, *Rabbi and Minister: The Friendship of Stephen S. Wise and John Haynes Holmes* (New York, 1964), 287, undated letter; also in a different letter to his daughter from Geneva, 1933, in Polier and Wise, eds., *The Personal Letters of Stephen Wise*, 223. See also Wise's letter to Brandeis, Sept. 19, 1933, in which he refers to a conversation they had on Feb. 6, 1933, in Voss, ed., *Stephen S. Wise*, 194.

45. Wise, *Challenging Years*, 256.

46. Quite a few letters can also be found in Mack's Papers in the CZA. Some typical letters are reproduced in *The Jews in Nazi Germany*, 28–35. Wise wrote to Mack on March 29, 1933, "I have had a stack of letters which I could show you that have come to the sisters and brothers and cousins and parents and children here in America, and the recipients have brought them to me." SSW Papers, Box 115, AJHS.

47. Letter from Paris, May 10, 1933, cited in *The Jews in Nazi Germany*, 32.

48. Rabbi Jonah Wise to Mack, May 18, 1933, Mack's Papers A405 83/A, CZA.

49. Letter dated March 23, 1933, SSW Papers, Box 82/1, AJHS.

50. Abraham Margaliot, "The Reaction of the Jewish Public in Germany to the Nuremberg Laws," in *Yad Vashem Studies* 12 (1977): 103–104; see also a report of March 16, 1936 that was sent to the Council for German Jewry in London, under the title "Jüdische Auswanderung aus Deutschland und deren Vorbereitung," S 25/9810, CZA, cited in Margaliot, 104.

51. See Billikopf to Felix Frankfurter, Sept. 11, 1933, Billikopf's Papers, File 8/2, AJA; see also Lipstadt, *Beyond Belief*, 32–35.

52. *Christian Science Monitor*, Aug. 1933; *Nation*, Oct. 18, 1933, cited in Lipstadt, *Beyond Belief*, 35, 33.

53. Related in a letter by Jacob Billikopf to Felix Frankfurter, Sept. 11, 1933, Billikopf's Papers, File 8/2, AJA.

54. Williams to the Chairman of the Jewish Congress, May 22, 1933, Mack's Papers, A405 83/A, CZA. Originally Williams was to go to Germany on behalf of the AJ Congress. But Stephen Wise and Bernard Deutsch, fearful of what he might report

and its reception in America, succeeded in canceling the assignment. See Mack to Wise, June 12, 1933 and Wise to Mack, June 16, 1933, both in Mack's Papers, A405 83/A, CZA.

55. Wise to Mack, April 8, 1933, SSW Papers, Box 115, AJHS.

56. Cyrus Adler to Ginzberg, April 7, 1933, reprinted in Ira Robinson, ed., *Cyrus Adler: Selected Letters*, 2 vols. (Philadelphia and New York, 1985), 258.

57. Mack to McDonald, May 12, 1933, SSW Papers, Box 115, AJHS.

58. Felix M. Warburg to Chaim Weizmann, May 9, 1933, Warburg's Papers, Box 294/8, AJA.

59. Editorial, "A Sorry Chapter," *Opinion*, July 1933, cited in Michael N. Dobkowski, ed., *The Politics of Indifference: A Documentary History of Holocaust Victims in America* (Washington, D.C., 1982), 325–26.

60. Statement issued by the Federation of German Citizens of the Jewish Faith following the March 5, 1933 elections, cited in Abner Phillipson, "German Elections Pass without Violence to Jews," *AH*, March 10, 1933.

61. Editorial, "The Proposed Anti-Hitler Protest," *AH*, March 17, 1933. For Hitler's complete speech see Max Domarus, ed., *Hitler: Speeches and Proclamations*, vol. 1, *The Years 1932 to 1934*, trans. Mary Fran Gilbert (Wauconda, Ill., 1990), 265–66.

62. Amos Funkenstein, "Passivity as the Characteristic of the Diaspora Jew," in Funkenstein, *Perceptions of Jewish History from the Antiquity to the Present* (in Hebrew) (Tel Aviv, 1991), 232–42.

63. *The Nation*, May 3, 1933, cited in *AH*, May 12, 1933. See also Ludwig Lewisohn's autobiography, *Up Stream: An American Chronicle* (New York, 1922), for an agonized description of the lives of Jewish immigrants.

64. "Rabbi Stephen Wise on Hitlerism's Attack on World Jewry and Challenge to Civilization," n.d., SSW Papers, Box 82/2, Germany, March-May 1933, AJHS; Wise, "A Century of Jewish Progress," in *As I See It*, 29.

65. Wise, *Challenging Years*, 235; Felix Warburg to Chaim Weizmann, April 6, 1933, Warburg's Papers, Box 294/8, AJA.

66. See letter dated March 31, 1933, cited in Wise, *Challenging Years*, 248–49; and one by Otto W. Brodnitz, March 15, 1933, SSW Papers, Box 82/1, AJHS. For other criticism, see, for example, the editorial, "Well Meant but Ill Advised," *AH*, Feb. 17, 1933; editorial, "The Proposed Anti-Hitler Protest," March 17, 1933; "Fighting Hitlerism with Toy Pistols!" May 5, 1933, p. 435; editorial, "A House Divided," May 26, 1933.

67. Wise to Mack, March 29, 1933 and May 5, 1933, SSW Papers, Box 115, AJHS.

68. *NYT*, March 28, 1933. Also cited in Gottlieb, *American Anti-Nazi Resistance*, 33–34.

69. Earl Raab, "The Deadly Innocences of American Jews," *Commentary* 50, no. 6 (Dec. 1970): 31.

70. In a survey entitled "Jewish Handicaps in the Employment Market," *Jewish Social Service Quarterly* 2 (March 1926): 174, Bruno Lasker concludes that the "dislike [of Jews in America] springs from too rapid an adaptation of the Jewish immigrant and his children to American life." Cited in Kaplan, *Judaism as a Civilization*, 73.

71. "The Jewish Problem," *The Christian Century*, Feb. 28, 1934, p. 280.

72. Joseph Ernest McAfee, "Jewish Solidarity in America," *The Christian Century*, Jan. 3, 1934.

73. For such a claim see Rabbi Cohon, "How Christian Missions Feel to a Jew," *The Christian Century*, Dec. 6, 1933.

74. McAfee, "Jewish Solidarity in America."

75. Ibid.

76. "The Jewish Problem."

77. T. S. Eliot, *After Strange Gods: A Prime Modern Heresy* (New York, 1934), 20, cited in Edward Alexander, *Irving Howe: Socialist, Critic, Jew* (Bloomington, 1998), 38.

78. Edward S. Martin, "The Nazis and the Jews," *Harper's Magazine* 167 (June 1933): 125–27.

79. Newton D. Baker to Everet R. Clinchy, director of National Conference of Christians and Jews, March 29, 1933, quoted in McDonald Stewart, *United States Government Policy on Refugees from Nazism,* 171–72.

80. Newton D. Baker to Rabbi Barnett Brickner, May 1, 1933, Mack's Papers, A405 83/A, CZA.

81. Wise to Frankfurter, May 15, 1933, Mack's Papers, A405 83/A, CZA.

82. Wise to Mack, March 9, 1933, SSW Papers, Box 115, AJHS; On the Nazi anti-Jewish propaganda in the 1930s conducted under the cover of anti-Communism, see Zosa Szajkowski, "A Note on the American-Jewish Struggle against Nazism and Communism in the 1930s," *AJHQ* 59 (March 1970): 272–89. On Jews and Communism in general, the best work is still Nathan Glazer, *The Social Basis of American Communism* (New York, 1961), especially Chapter 4, "Jews and Middle-Class Groups and the Party," 130–68. See also Irving Howe and Lewis Coser, *The American Communist Party* (1957; reprint, New York, 1974).

83. Cable from the Carl Schurz Memorial Foundation, Inc., March 25, 1933, Warburg's Papers, Box 286/5, AJA.

84. Wise to Mack, May 10, 1933, SSW Papers, Box 115, AJHS.

85. Morris Waldman to Executive Committee, Aug. 17, 1933, Warburg's Papers, Box 301, AJA; see also Szajkowski, "A Note on the American-Jewish Struggle," 282–89, for Waldman's appearance before the National Civic Federation (NCF), a leading conservative anti-Communist organization, on June 5th, 1934. The NCF was of the opinion that Germany's suppression of Communism should not be opposed. An unsigned NCF memorandum dated Oct. 10, 1933, stated that "If the world is to find Hitler a conservative force fighting against a revolutionary war, it may forgive him his anti-Jewish insanities and offer a prayer for his success" (272).

86. This is not a uniquely Orthodox concept. Rabbi Isaac Mayer Wise, the founder of the American Reform movement, was also in favor of eliminating from the Jewish ritual "whatever makes us ridiculous before the world." Jerold Auerbach, *Rabbis and Lawyers: The Journey from Torah to Constitution* (Bloomington, 1990), 78; Charles Silberman, *A Certain People: American Jews and Their Lives Today* (New York, 1985), 30, describes the "modern" version of this characteristic as the Jewish obsession "with being nice."

87. A. A. Brill, M.D., "The Psychology of the Jew," *AH*, Jan. 13, 1933, p. 170.

88. Elmer Davis, "On the Gentility of Gentiles," *Harper's Magazine* 167 (July 1933): 150–51.

89. Ibid., 153.

90. "Is the American Jew Safe or Unsafe?" Excerpts from an Address of Rabbi Stephen S. Wise before the Free Synagogue at Carnegie Hall, Dec. 2, 1934, SSW Papers, Box 82/2, AJHS.

91. Ibid.

92. Ibid.
93. Wise to Holmes, June 6, 1934, SSW Papers, Box 53, AJHS. Wise was the founder of the Free Synagogue.
94. Lewis Weinstein, *Masa: Odyssey of an American Jew* (Boston, 1989), 305–306.
95. "Rabbi Silver Replies to Mr. McAfee," *The Christian Century*, Feb. 28, 1934, pp. 293–94.
96. Ibid.
97. *AH*, Jan. 20, 1933. The growing respect for Polish Jews was undoubtedly related to the militant spirit with which they reacted to the plight of German Jews, especially in the European Minorities' Congress, before and after Hitler came to power. On this relatively obscure chapter in European Jewish history, see Moshe Landau, *The Disappointing Alliance: Jews and Germans in the European Minorities' Congress* (in Hebrew) (Tel Aviv, 1992), especially 146–59.
98. Quoted in the *AH*, Feb. 3, 1933; also cited in Wolfgang Benz (ed.), *Das Exil der kleinen Lente: Alltagserfahrung deutscher Juden in der Emigration* (Munich, 1991), 16.
99. "Rabbi Stephen Wise on Hitlerism's Attack on World Jewry and Challenge to Civilization," n.d., American Jewish Historical Society, SSW Papers, Box 82/2, Germany, March-May, 1933, AJHS.
100. On the ideology of normalization and its similarity to the reinterpretation of the doctrine of divine election in American Judaism, see Biale, *Power and Powerlessness in Jewish History*, 130–33, 193.
101. *NYT*, Sept. 27, 1930; Oct. 20, 1930.
102. Ibid., March 7, 1933.
103. "Editorial Analyses and Interpretations," *AH*, Feb. 3, 1933.
104. Ibid.
105. Cited in Hildebrand, *The Third Reich* (London, 1984), 3. The fact is that Hitler won a victory over his conservative ministers on the very day of his appointment and immediately before the new cabinet was sworn in by Hindenburg. Contrary to an agreement reached between the Nazis and the Nationalists during the coalition talks, after the new government was formed, Hitler demanded the right to dissolve the Reichstag that had been elected in November 1932 and to hold new elections. As Hugenberg rightly feared, these elections did not improve the position of the DNVP; see ibid., 3–4.
106. "Haman, Hitler and Beyond," *AH*, March 10, 1933, p. 289.
107. Editorial, "Festival of Redemption," *AH*, April 7, 1933.
108. See, for example, Nathan Straus, Jr., in *AH*, March 7, 1933, p. 372: "Hitler's men will come and go as other tyrants have . . . but the Jewish people goes on. . . . We are an eternal people."
109. "Haman, Hitler and Beyond," *AH*, March 10, 1933, p. 289.
110. "Wie Wählen wir am 5. März?" (How do we vote on March 5th?) in the Hamburg *Israelitisches Familienblatt*, March 2, 1933, quoted in Moshe Zimmermann, "'Die aussichtslose Republik'—Zukunftsperspektiven der deutschen Juden vor 1933," in *Menora, Jahrbuch für deutsch-jüdische Geschichte 1990* (Munich, 1990), 164.
111. "Haman, Hitler and Beyond," *AH*, March 10, 1933, p. 289.
112. Ibid.
113. "Fighting Hitlerism with Toy Pistols!" *AH*, May 5, 1933, p. 435.
114. Ibid.
115. "Conference on the German Situation," May 24, 1933, p. 36.

116. *New York World Telegram,* Feb. 5, 1935, cited in Auerbach, Review Essay on "Proskauer: His Life and Times," 110. For State Department pressure see the AJC Executive Committee Minutes of Dec. 30, 1934, AJCA, Historical Document Section; Cyrus Adler to the AJ Congress, Dec. 6, 1934, SSW Papers, Box 84, AJHS.

117. Cited in Auerbach, "Review Essay on *Proskauer: His Life and Times,*" 109.

118. These lines are from a Hebrew poem, *Hakitzah ami* (Awaken, my people), written in 1863 by Judah Leib Gordon, cited in Arendt, *Origins,* 65.

119. Press Release, American Jewish Congress, Jan. 30, 1933, SSW Papers, Box 82, AJHS.

120. *Opinion,* March 21, 1932; Wise to Mack, Feb. 9, 1933, SSW Papers, Box 115, AJHS.

121. Earlier, in February 1933, the American Jewish Congress had sponsored a meeting at Carnegie Hall on "Hitlerism and Its Meaning"; on March 23, Jewish War Veterans had paraded to City Hall, joined by the Veterans of Foreign Wars, the Disabled American War Veterans, and the American Legion. See Frommer, "The American Jewish Congress," 2:310, 315.

122. Wise's address at Madison Square Garden, March 27, 1933, "To the Conscience of the World," in Wise, *As I See It,* 85–86; also in the *AH,* March 31, 1933.

123. Special Meeting of the American Jewish Committee, April 9, 1933, RG 1, EXO 37/5, p. 70, AJCA, Historical Document Section.

124. Julian Mack to Jacob Billikopf, Jan. 15, 1935, Billikopf's Papers, File 18/3, AJA. Mack was responding to a letter about the Austrian Jews, received by Billikopf from George S. Messersmith, who at the time headed the United States Legation in Austria. See also Messersmith to Billikopf, Jan. 3, 1935, Billikopf's Papers, File 19/10, AJA. Mack, however, noted that the behavior of the conservative Jews was "the same problem that we are having everywhere" and made it clear that he was referring to the situation among American Jews.

125. Mack to Shotwell, March 29, 1933, SSW Papers, Box 115, AJHS.

126. Ibid.

127. *The New Republic* 74 (April 5, 1933); Dorothy Thompson and Benjamin Stolberg, "Hitler and the American Jews," *Scribner's* 19 (Sept. 1933): 136–40.

128. Wise to Mack, March 29, 1933, SSW Papers, Box 115, AJHS. Among the non-Jewish speakers were former New York State Governor Alfred E. Smith, United States Senator Robert F. Wagner, Bishop William T. Manning, Bishop Francis T. McConnell, New York City Mayor John P. O'Brien, and William Green, president of the American Federation of Labor.

129. Waldman to Cyrus Adler, Nov. 6, 1938, Waldman's Papers, Box 1/1, AJA.

130. Felix Warburg to James McDonald, March 16, 1933, Warburg's Papers, Box 299, AJA.

131. Mack to James McDonald, May 12, 1933; Mack to Wise, May 18, 1933, SSW Papers, Box 115, AJHS.

132. *AH,* March 31, 1933.

133. See Stephen Wise to John Haynes Holmes, Oct. 19, 1933, in Voss, ed., *Stephen S. Wise,* 196.

134. American Jewish Congress, *The Case of Civilization against Hitlerism* (New York, 1934), 3–4, 113–15.

135. Waldman to Landau, Nov. 26, 1935, Waldman's Papers, Box 1/22, AJA.

136. Meeting of Stroock and Waldman with Louis D. Brandeis in the company of Stephen Wise and Horace Kallen. See Cohen, *Not Free to Desist,* 165.

6. Co-optation of Protest

1. Fuchs, *The Political Behavior of American Jews*, 100–103.
2. This figure increased to 85 percent in the 1936 elections and to 90 percent in 1940 and 1944. See Stephen D. Isaacs, *Jews and American Politics* (Garden City, N.Y., 1974), 151–52. After the 1936 elections, when the New Deal moved farther to the left, the Jews' "love affair" with FDR—in sharp contrast with other hyphenated groups—grew more impassioned, as the 1940 election results demonstrate. One can safely deduce that the evolving catastrophe in Europe was not a factor in deciding the Jewish vote. See Feingold, *The Politics of Rescue*, 300. There were some exceptions to the support FDR enjoyed from Jews. Initially, Jewish Socialists remained outside the fold, and some Jewish tycoons like Hollywood mogul Ben Hecht, along with other critics in the business sector, came to abhor the New Deal. See Cohen, "Crisis and Reaction," 84–88; and Ben Hecht, *A Child of the Century* (New York, 1955), 534–35.
3. Myron I. Scholnick, *The New Deal and Anti-Semitism in America* (New York, 1990), 5.
4. Ibid., 14, 22–28; Isaacs, *Jews and American Politics*, 60–65.
5. Ginsberg, *The Fatal Embrace*, 104.
6. Arthur M. Schlesinger, Jr., *The Age of Roosevelt: The Politics of Upheaval* (Boston, 1960), 224.
7. Isaacs, *Jews and American Politics*, 61.
8. For this "rating" of Cohen by Joe Rauh, another young maverick who clerked for Cardozo and Frankfurter, see Isaacs, *Jews and American politics*, 61–62; see also Schlesinger, Jr., *The Politics of Upheaval*, 226–27, 230.
9. Arthur M. Schlesinger, Jr., *The Age of Roosevelt: The Crisis of the Old Order, 1919–1933* (Boston, 1957), 404, 421, and quote on 452. See also Bernard M. Baruch, *Baruch: The Public Years* (New York, 1960), 238, 241, 249–50; Carter Field, *Bernard Baruch: Park Bench Statement* (New York, 1944), 238–50, 276–79; W. L. White, *Bernard Baruch* (New York, 1950), 78.
10. See John Morton Blum, *From the Morgenthau Diaries: Years of Crisis, 1928–1938* (Boston, 1959), 11–15; Henry Morgenthau III, *Mostly Morgenthaus: A Family History* (New York, 1991).
11. Steven Fraser, *Labor Will Rule: Sidney Hillman and the Rise of American Labor* (New York, 1991).
12. Samuel I. Rosenman, *Working with Roosevelt* (New York, 1952), 71; see also Samuel B. Hand, *Counsel and Advise: A Political Biography of Samuel I. Rosenman* (New York, 1981); Cohen, *Not Free to Desist*, 170, 198, 253. In his memoirs Rosenman makes no mention of the Jewish problem in Europe. However, according to Abba Eben, he was instrumental in the Weizmann-Truman discussions concerning the recognition of Israel. Abba Eben, "Tragedy and Triumph," in Meyer M. Weisgal and Joel Carmichael, eds., *Chaim Weizmann: A Biography by Several Hands* (New York, 1963), 309–10. Rosenman was to become the editor of Roosevelt's public papers and addresses.
13. Although Rosenman did eventually contribute to the establishment of the War Refugee Board, he did so under some pressure and with great reluctance to approach Roosevelt directly. See Henry L. Feingold, "'Courage First and Intelligence Second': The American Jewish Secular Elite, Roosevelt and the Failure of Rescue," *AJHS* 72, no. 4 (June 1983): 424, 434.

14. *AH*, May 11, 1934, cited in Scholnick, *The New Deal and Anti-Semitism*, 29–30.

15. Citations are from Auerbach, *Rabbis and Lawyers*, 160. In 1939 FDR refused to nominate Frank as a federal judge because he had just named Felix Frankfurter to the Supreme Court (he was in fact appointed at a later time). See Joseph P. Lash, *Dealers and Dreamers: A New Look at the New Deal* (New York, 1988), 219, 387, 454.

16. Lash, *Dealers and Dreamers*, 173, 175, 338. As a postscript it may be added that Roosevelt saw no problem with appointing a Jewish undersecretary under Ickes at the Interior Ministry in the 1940s, Abe Fortas.

17. Leonard Dinnerstein, "Jews and the New Deal," *AJH* 72 (June 1983), 476. A later version of this article is included in Dinnerstein, *Uneasy at Home: Antisemitism and the American Jewish Experience* (New York, 1987).

18. See Jonathan Daniels, *White House Witness, 1942–1945* (New York, 1975), 266–67.

19. See *Roosevelt and Frankfurter: Their Correspondence, 1928–1945*, annotated by Max Freedman (Boston, 1967), 19.

20. Schlesinger, Jr., *The Politics of Upheaval*, 225.

21. Felix Frankfurter, *Felix Frankfurter Reminisces*, recorded in talks with Dr. Harlan B. Phillips (Garden City, N.Y., 1962), 288.

22. Frankfurter to Billikopf, Nov. 15, 1938, Billikopf's Papers, File 8/2, AJA. Arthur Hays Sulzberger, the editor of the *New York Times*, headed the Jewish opposition to Frankfurter's appointment. He thought that Cardozo's Jewishness was no reason why his successor should be one, no reason why the Jews should have a "lien" on this position as they had on the ambassadorship to Turkey. It was enough, he thought, that in the mind of the American public the New Deal legislation was the product of Frankfurter's "brains." Sulzberger apparently had his views communicated to the White House via Henry Morgenthau, Sr. See Billikopf to Frankfurter, Nov. 2, 1938; Billikopf to Sulzberger, Nov. 4, 1938; Ben Cohen to Billikopf, Jan. 25, 1939, all in Billikopf's Papers, Files 8/2, 4/20, AJA. See also *Roosevelt and Frankfurter*, 481–82.

23. Frankfurter to Billikopf, Nov. 15, 1938, Billikopf's Papers, File 8/2, AJA.

24. Beginning with his first job fresh out of Harvard Law School when he was advised to change his name, he continued to be denounced as a sinister figure who used his personal influence with the president to satisfy goals remote from the national interest. See Joseph P. Lash, *From the Diaries of Felix Frankfurter* (New York, 1975), 4; *Roosevelt and Frankfurter*, 19; and Robert A. Burt, *Two Jewish Justices: Outcasts in the Promised Land* (Berkeley, 1988), 37–62, 129.

25. *Roosevelt and Frankfurter*, 472. Frankfurter had very politely reprimanded Lady Astor for accusing Jews of controlling American advertising (474–75).

26. Ibid., 619 (emphasis in the original), letter dated Oct. 24, 1941.

27. Ibid., 619–20, letters dated Oct. 27 and 29, 1941, respectively.

28. See Philippa Strum, *Louis D. Brandeis: Justice for the People* (New York, 1984), 381, 384; and Burt, *Two Jewish Justices*, 8–36.

29. Rexford Tugwell, *The Art of Politics as Practiced by Three Great Americans* (New York, 1958), 247.

30. Auerbach, *Rabbis and Lawyers*, 133–35.

31. Brandeis was alerted by the recommendations of the Peel Commission that Palestine be divided into a Jewish and an Arab state, a solution that was totally unacceptable to the Zionists and that was later also rejected by the Woodhead Commission as unfeasible. American Zionists as well as Christian supporters began lobbying the president against cessation of immigration to Palestine and attempted to con-

vince him of Palestine's capacity to absorb European Jews escaping the Nazi menace. Brandeis met FDR in October 1938 with no result. He did not approach FDR again until October 1939, after his resignation from the Supreme Court, and this time with regard to the MacDonald white paper of May 1939 calling for severe restrictions on Jewish immigration and land purchases. Writing to Rabbi Wise on the day of the meeting with the President, Oct. 24, 1939, he found FDR "as *sympathetic as in the past;* and as interested in all I was able to tell him about the present in Palestine. There is reason to hope that he will *say* something about Palestine." See Strum, *Louis D. Brandeis,* 385 (emphasis added).

32. Allon Gal, *Brandeis of Boston* (Cambridge, 1980), 206.

33. Auerbach, *Rabbis and Lawyers,* 132–38, quote on 137.

34. Cited in ibid., 155, 156.

35. Melvin I. Urofsky, *A Voice That Spoke For Justice: The Life and Times of Stephen S. Wise* (Albany, N.Y., 1982), 268.

36. Michael E. Parrish, *Felix Frankfurter and His Times: The Reform Years* (New York, 1982), 129–49; Bruce A. Murphy, *The Brandeis/Frankfurter Connection: The Secret Political Activities of the Two Supreme Court Justices* (New York, 1982); Burt, *Two Jewish Justices.*

37. AJC, Minutes of the Executive Committee Meeting, Jan. 8, 1933, AJCA; see also Adler to Irving Lehman, Jan. 12, 1933, Adler's Chronological File, RG 1, EXO 14, AJCA.

38. Irving Lehman to Adler, Jan. 20, 1933, in Adler's Chronological File, RG 1, EXO 14, AJCA. The "conference" refers to a meeting with FDR.

39. Ibid.; Minutes of the AJC Executive Committee Feb. 12, 1933, AJCA.

40. Administrative Committee Meeting, Feb. 7, 1933, AJ Congress Papers, Box 2, AJHS; Wise to Mack, Feb. 9, 1933, SSW Papers, Box 115, AJHS.

41. Prittwitz to the German Foreign Ministry, Feb. 8, 1933, cited in Shafir, "The Impact of the Jewish Crisis on American-German Relations," pt. 1, 36.

42. Wise, *Challenging Years,* 237.

43. AJ Congress, Administrative Committee Minutes, Feb. 28, 1933, AJ Congress Papers, Box 2, AJHS.

44. AJ Congress, *Submitted to the Eleventh (Emergency) Session of the American Jewish Congress* (n.p., n.d.), 42–43, AJ Congress Papers, Box 2, AJHS.

45. Adler to Strauss, March 3, 1933, Department of State 862.4016/31, cited in Shafir, "The Impact of the Jewish Crisis on American-German Relations," pt. 1, 38.

46. Stimson to Sackett, March 3, 1933, *FRUS* 1933, 2:320; Sackett to Hull, March 11, 1933, *FRUS* 1933, 2:322; Wise to Mack, March 8, 1933, SSW Papers, Box 115, AJHS.

47. The excerpts from Roosevelt's inauguration speech are cited in James MacGregor Burns, *Roosevelt: The Lion and the Fox* (New York, 1956), 163–64.

48. Domarus, *Hitler Speeches and Proclamations,* vol. 1, *1932–1934,* 262.

49. Burns, *Roosevelt: The Lion and the Fox,* 166.

50. See Robert Dallek, *Franklin Roosevelt and American Foreign Policy, 1932–1945* (Oxford, 1979), 35–36.

51. Robert E. Herzstein, *Roosevelt & Hitler: Prelude to War* (New York, 1989), 78–79.

52. Herbert Lehman to Marguerite ("Missy") LeHand, March 11, 1933, FDR Papers, OF 198, cited in Shafir, "The Impact of the Jewish Crisis on American-German Relations," pt. 1, 222.

53. Wise to Mack, March 8, 1933, SSW Papers, Box 115, AJHS. For a detailed chronicle of the riots, see Kurt Jakob Ball-Kaduri, *Das Leben der Juden in Deutschland im Jahre 1933* (Frankfurt am Main, 1963).

54. Wise to Mack, March 8, 1933, SSW Papers, Box 115, AJHS. For the relationship and mutual admiration between Brandeis and Roosevelt, see Strum, *Louis D. Brandeis*, especially 381–87.

55. Wise to Mack, March 8 and 9, 1933, SSW Papers, Box 115, AJHS. In the correspondence the names of Louis D. Brandeis and Felix Frankfurter were abbreviated "LDB." and "FF."

56. *Administrative Report, July, 1932 to May, 1933*, 41, AJ Congress Papers, Box 2, AJHS.

57. *NYT*, March 20, 1933, cited in Gottlieb, *American Anti-Nazi Resistance*, 29.

58. *NYT*, March 21, 1933, cited in Gottlieb, *American Anti-Nazi Resistance*, 30.

59. Ibid.

60. Frommer, "The American Jewish Congress," 2:313.

61. Isaacs, *Jews and American Politics*, 24.

62. Raab, "The Deadly Innocences of American Jews," 38.

63. *NYT*, March 21, 1933, cited in Gottlieb, *American Anti-Nazi Resistance*, 31.

64. *NYT*, March 22, 1933; Stephen Wise, *Challenging Years*, 248–49; Gottlieb, *American Anti-Nazi Resistance*, 36–38, 45–47.

65. Phillips's statement March 21, 1933, cited in Shafir, "The Impact of the Jewish Crisis on American-German Relations," pt. 1, 53.

66. Memorandum of Hull's Press Conference, March 22, 1933, *FRUS*, 1933, 2:327–28 (emphasis added).

67. Wise to Brandeis, March 23, 1933, SSW Papers, Box 106, AJHS.

68. Howe had never forgiven Wise for embarrassing FDR in the Walker scandal the year before (see Chapter 7, 422–23). He was instrumental in keeping the rabbi out of the White House and in fact it was only after his death that Wise was invited to meet FDR there. Urofsky, *A Voice*, 256.

69. Wise to Brandeis, March 23, 1933, SSW Papers, Box 106, AJHS.

70. Wise to Gottheil, March 20, 1933, SSW Papers, Box 947, AJHS.

71. *NYT*, March 20, 1933.

72. Frommer, "American Jewish Congress," 2:315.

73. Wise to FDR, May 2, 1933, cited in Shafir, "The Impact of the Jewish Crisis on American-German Relations," pt. 1, 200.

74. Wise to Mack, April 15, 1933, SSW Papers, Box 115, AJHS.

75. Michael Parenti, *Power and the Powerless* (New York, 1978), 212.

76. Ibid., 212–13.

77. *Special Meeting of the American Jewish Committee, Sunday April 9, 1933, Savoy-Plaza Hotel, New York*, 2–3, EXO 37/5 (hereafter, Special Meeting), AJCA, Historical Document Section.

78. Adler and Margalith, eds., *With Firmness in the Right*, 365; Adler to Felix Warburg, March 24, 1933, Warburg's Papers, Box 286/5, AJA.

79. *Special Meeting*, 1–21; Adler and Margalith, eds., *With Firmness in the Right*, 365–66.

80. *Special Meeting*, 15.

81. Adler to Felix Warburg, March 24, 1933, Warburg's Papers, Box 286/5, AJA.

82. Ibid.

83. Cf. Parenti, *Power and the Powerless*, 212.

84. Hull's telegram of March 26, 1933, reprinted in Adler and Margalith, eds.,

With Firmness in the Right, 366. The telegram was addressed to Cohen of BB, Wise of the AJ Congress, and Adler of the AJC. Only Wise and Deutsch of the AJ Congress prepared a reply to Hull which was dispatched on the night of March 26th. After expressing their gratitude for the "sympathetic interest," the Congress leaders alluded to their real expectations by writing that "the enlightened opinion of America must watch with profoundest anxiety the development of events in Germany." See Gottlieb, *American Anti-Nazi Resistance,* 40–41.

85. Joseph Goebbels, *Vom Kaiserhof zur Reichskanzlei* (Munich, 1934), 288–89, quoted in Konrad Heiden, *Der Fuehrer: Hitler's Rise to Power* (1944; London, 1967), 456.

86. *I Will Bear Witness: The Diaries of Victor Klemperer, 1933–1941,* abridged and translated from the German edition by Martin Chalmers (London, 1998), 9.

87. Domarus, *Hitler Speeches and Proclamations,* 1:298–302.

88. David Bankier, "Hitler and the Policy-Making Process on the Jewish Question," *Holocaust and Genocide Studies* 3, no. 1 (1988): 4.

89. Saul Friedländer, *Nazi Germany and the Jews,* vol. 1, *The Years of Persecution, 1933–1939* (New York, 1997), 20; Memoranda of telephone conversation between the State Department and the U.S. Embassy in Berlin, March 31, 1933, *FRUS,* 1933, 2:342 ff.

90. On the meeting with Göring and its outcome, see Daniel Fraenkel, *On the Edge of the Abyss: Zionist Policy and the Plight to the German Jews, 1933–1938* (in Hebrew) (Jerusalem, 1994), 47–52.

91. Henry Friedlander and Sybil Milton, eds., *Archives of the Holocaust,* vol. 17, *American Jewish Committee New York,* ed. Frederick D. Bogin (New York, 1993), 4.

92. Confidential Report on the Zionist Situation in Germany," London, March 24, 1933, Z-4/10095, CZA, cited in Fraenkel, *On the Edge of the Abyss,* 49.

93. Ibid.

94. Wise to Ruth Mack Brunswick, April 6, 1933; Wise to Mack, March 29, 1933, both in SSW Papers, Box 115, AJHS.

95. Wise to Holmes, April 3, 1933, SSW Papers, Box 53/1, AJHS. While most references in the secondary literature are to a meeting on March 30, according to Wise's letter to Frankfurter he and Deutsch "practically lived at the State Department on Thursday and Friday," meaning March 30 and 31. See Wise to Frankfurter, April 3, 1933, SSW Papers, Box 109, AJHS. In the April 3, 1933 letter to Holmes, Wise again refers to March 31st (Friday), writing that "Phillips practically lived on the Berlin telephone on Friday." While no other confirmation is available, since the details of the discussions were never made public, it appears that the AJ Congress representatives were indeed welcomed for two days at the State Department. See Gottlieb, *American Anti-Nazi Resistance,* 41.

96. Wise to Frankfurter, April 3, 1933, SSW Papers, Box 109, AJHS. Wise noted that Senator William Borah, a progressive Republican from Idaho, had been replaced as chairman of the Foreign Relations Committee with Senator Key Pittman (Democrat from Nevada) "who does not know his job," and with Hull (the new Secretary of State) "who is not on the job."

97. Wise to Mack, April 2, 1933, SSW Papers, Box 115, AJHS.

98. Frankfurter to Wise, April 3, 1933, SSW Papers, Box 109, AJHS.

99. Wise to Holmes, April 3, 1933, SSW Papers, Box 53/1, AJHS; Wise to Frankfurter, April 3, 1933, SSW Papers, Box 109, AJHS; Wise to Mack, April 2, 1933, SSW Papers, Box 115, AJHS.

100. See *The Jews in Nazi Germany* (1935 edition), 35–37.

101. Wise to Frankfurter, April 3, 1933.

102. Wise to Mack, April 5, 1933, SSW Papers, Box 115, AJHS. On the same day Wise also wrote in a similar, if somewhat mitigated, vein to Justice Brandeis: "You will note that we have maintained silence during these last three days, in part at the request of the State Department. But we feel that today there is need for a clear statement." Wise to Brandeis, April 5, 1933, SSW Papers, Box 106, AJHS.

103. *Jewish Daily Bulletin*, April 7, 1933, also quoted in part in Gottlieb, *American Anti-Nazi Resistance*, 44.

104. Frankfurter's report is cited by Wise in letter to Mack, April 10, 1933, SSW Papers, Box 115, AJHS.

105. Ibid.

106. Dallek, *Franklin D. Roosevelt and American Foreign Policy*, 39–40, 51–54.

107. Wise to Mack, April 10, 1933, SSW Papers, Box 115, AJHS. Hitler, as we know, was not present at the talks, which opened in Washington on April 21st.

108. Ibid.

109. Adler to Irving Lehman, April 10, 1933, Adler's Chronological File, RG 1, EXO 14, AJCA.

110. Irving Lehman to Cyrus Adler, April 11, 1933, Adler's Chronological File, RG 1, EXO 14, AJCA. Reportedly, Lehman first approached Roosevelt on March 14th, asking the President to modify Herbert Hoover's 1930 order which barred anyone likely to become a public charge from qualifying to immigrate to the United States. But having seemingly read the "Chief's" mood, he was quick to adopt a more American stand. It is not clear if Lehman met with FDR or spoke with him over the telephone; see Breitman and Kraut, *American Refugee Policy*, 11–12, and 252 n2.

111. Frankfurter to Moley, April 24, 1933, cited in Breitman and Kraut, *American Refugee Policy*, 252 n3; see also 12–18.

112. Adler to Felix Warburg, April 6, 1933, Warburg's Papers, Box 286/5, AJA.

113. Wise to Mack, April 8, 1933, SSW Papers, Box 115, AJHS.

114. Wise to Rabbi George Alexander Kohut, April 26, 1933, in Voss, ed., *Stephen S. Wise*, 186.

115. See Cordell Hull, *The Memoirs of Cordell Hull* (New York, 1948), 1:599.

116. On April 13th and 16th, Samuel Untermyer—former vice-president of the AJ Congress, a well-known figure in the political circles of New York City and one of America's renowned attorneys—made his first public statements in support of an anti-Nazi boycott, an alarm signal for Wise and the more "responsible" leadership. See Gottlieb, *American Anti-Nazi Resistance*, 51–52; Wise to Mack, April 16, 1933, SSW Papers, Box 115, AJHS.

117. Wise to Frankfurter and Mack, April 15, 1933, SSW Papers, Box 115, AJHS; Adler to Hull, May 3, 1933, cited in Morse, *While Six Million Died*, 122–23; Martin Gilbert and Richard Gott, *The Appeasers* (Boston, 1963), 26–30; *AJYB* 35 (Philadelphia, 1933): 48–49; Gottlieb, *American Anti-Nazi Resistance*, 52.

118. There were no demands that the quotas be enlarged, but rather an attempt to allow review of consular refusals of visas. See *AJYB* 34 (1932–1933): 38; Brody, "American Jewry, the Refugees and Immigrations Restriction, 1932–1942," 220–21; Medoff, *The Deafening Silence*, Chapter 1.

119. Wise to Mack, March 29, 1933, SSW Papers, Box 115, AJHS.

120. Wise to Frankfurter, April 15, 1933, SSW Papers, Box 109, AJHS.

121. Wise to Mack, April 15, 1933, SSW Papers, Box 115, AJHS.

122. Lawrence Berenson to Mack, May 24, 1933, Mack's Papers, A405 83/A, CZA. Berenson added in handwriting "Wise needs you badly and I hope you will get back soon." Berenson's letter followed a long meeting with Wise on the same day, during which Wise showed him the letter he had written to Frankfurter on April 15, 1933.

123. Wise to Mack, April 15, 1933.

124. See Janeway, *Powers of the Weak*, 157–67.

125. Wise to Frankfurter, April 15, 1933.

126. Adler to Felix Warburg, April 25, 1933, Warburg's Papers, Box 286/5, AJA.

127. Adler to Leo Weil, May 3, 1933, cited in Breitman and Kraut, *American Refugee Policy*, 92.

128. *American Jewish Committee Executive Committee Minutes*, June 5, 1933, p. 174, AJCA, Historical Document Section.

129. Wise to Frankfurter, April 15, 1933 (emphasis added).

130. Ibid.

131. Wise to Mack, April 16, 1933, SSW Papers, Box 115, AJHS.

132. Wise to Frankfurter, April 16, 1933, SSW Papers, Box 109, AJHS (emphasis in original).

133. Wise to Mack, April 16, 1933.

134. Frankfurter to Perkins, April 14, 1933, SSW Papers, Box 109, AJHS; and Frankfurter to Moley, April 14, 1933, Moley Papers, Folder 106/I, Hoover Institute. The latter contains Frankfurter's handwritten comment that the drafts had been sent to FDR. See Breitman and Kraut, *American Refugee Policy*, 13, 253 n5.

135. See Wise to Frankfurter, April 16, 1933, SSW Papers, Box 109, AJHS; Frankfurter to FDR, April 16, 1933, National Archives, RG 59, Social Matters, Race Problems file, CDF 862.4016/586 GC, in Breitman and Kraut, *American Refugee Policy*, 92; Secretary Hull to Frankfurter, May 6, 1933, Mack's Papers, A405 83/A, CZA.

136. Secretary Hull to Frankfurter, May 6, 1933, Mack's Papers, A405 83/A, CZA.

137. Frankfurter to Proskauer, May 18, 1933, Mack's Papers, A405 83/A, CZA.

138. Frankfurter to Hull, May 23, 1933, Mack's Papers, A405 83/A, CZA.

139. Wise to Mack, May 4, 1933, SSW Papers, Box 115, AJHS. Indeed, Frankfurter avoided Hull and did not reply to his letter of May 6, 1933 until some two and a half weeks later. See Frankfurter to Hull May 23, 1933, Mack's Papers, A405 83/A, CZA.

140. Frankfurter to Frances Perkins, April 27, 1933, cited in Breitman and Kraut, *American Refugee Policy*, 93.

141. Frankfurter to Moley, April 24, 1933, SSW Papers, Box 82/12, AJHS. Another letter of the same date from Frankfurter to Moley is cited in note 111 above. The copy in my possession was sent to Wise marked in Frankfurter's handwriting: "SSW, Read & Destroy, FF."

142. Frankfurter to Proskauer, May 18, 1933, Mack's Papers A405 83/A, CZA (emphasis added); also cited in Breitman and Kraut, *American Refugee Policy*, 93. There are subtle indications that Frankfurter's frustrations in Washington drew him somewhat closer to Jewish affairs: in his above letter to Proskauer, he insisted that Stephen Wise be part of a delegation which would try to meet with the president. The fact that Frankfurter sent Mack a copy of his letter to Proskauer may indicate that he wished to touch base with the Jewish leadership. See Mack to Frankfurter, May 22, 1933, SSW Papers, Box 115, AJHS.

143. Frankfurter to Hull, May 23, 1933, Mack's Papers A405 83/A, CZA; see also

Frankfurter's letter to Secretary Perkins, to whom he also wrote: "For once in my life I wish that, for a brief period, I were not a Jew." Frankfurter to Perkins, April 27, 1933, cited in Shafir, "The Impact of the Jewish Crisis on American-German Relations," pt. 1, 144.

144. For a sociological representation of these ideas, see William A. Gamson, *Power and Discontent* (Homewood, Ill., 1968), 96.

145. See Saul S. Friedman, "The Power and/or Powerlessness of American Jews, 1939–1945," in Seymour Maxwell Finger, ed., *American Jewry during the Holocaust* (New York, 1984), 18–19.

146. Wise to Mack, April 28, 1933, SSW Papers, Box 115, AJHS (emphasis added).

147. Medoff, *The Deafening Silence*, 31.

7. The Demise of the Myth of Jewish Power

1. Biale, *Power and Powerlessness*, 205, 133, 206.

2. Martin, "The Nazis and the Jews," 126–27.

3. For the above discussion I am greatly indebted to Lafer, "Universalism and Particularism in Jewish Law: Making Sense of Political Loyalties," 177–211.

4. Rabbi Samuel Schulman (of Temple Emanu-El in New York), cited in "American Palestine Campaign Launched," *AH*, Jan. 20, 1933, p. 186.

5. Cited in *AH*, March 3, 1933, p. 281.

6. Henry Hurwitz in a signed opening statement of an issue devoted to the postwar reconstruction of Jewish life, *Menorah Journal* 21 (Jan.-March 1943).

7. Michael Parenti, *Power and the Powerless*, 3.

8. I draw here on Parenti, 4, 7–12 (emphasis in the original).

9. On the illusions of power among American Jews, see the insightful essay by Raab, "The Deadly Innocences of American Jews."

10. See Feingold, *The Politics of Rescue*, 300.

11. Brody, in "American Jewry, the Refugees and Immigration Restrictions, 1932–1942," 227. For a sample of case histories, forwarded to the State Department, of applicants who were refused visas and the reasons given, see Morse, *While Six Million Died*, 141–43. For an excellent study, soon to be published, on the work of U.S. consuls in Germany, see Bat-Ami Zucker, *In Search of Refuge: Jews and US Consuls in Nazi Germany, 1933–1941* (Essex, 2000). I wish to thank Professor Zucker for her generosity in sharing her work with me.

12. Brody, "American Jewry, the Refugees and Immigration Restrictions, 1932–1942," 219.

13. U.S. Department of State, "Press Release," Sept. 13, 1930 (emphasis in the original), cited in Zucker, "In Search of Refuge," 18. Immigration from Germany dropped from 241,700 in 1930 to 35,576 in 1932, of which 2,755 were Jews. See *AJYB* 47 (1945–1946): 653, and Zosa Szajkowski, "The Attitude of American Jews to Refugees from Germany in the 1930s," *AJHQ* 61, no. 2 (Dec. 1971).

14. Cited in Friedman, *No Haven for the Oppressed*, 22.

15. "Special Meeting of the American Jewish Committee," April 9, 1933, EXO 37/5, AJCA, Historical Document Section.

16. Chamberlain to McDonald, Aug. 25, 1934, cited in Szajkowski, "The Attitude of American Jews," 103–104.

17. *B'nai B'rith Magazine* 49 (March 1935): 135, cited in Brody, "American Jewry, the Refugees and Immigration Restrictions, 1932–1942," 223.

18. Brody, "American Jewry, the Refugees and Immigration Restrictions, 1932–1942," 238.

19. Since the Democrats had gained control of the House of Representatives following the 1930 elections, Dickstein, the new chairman of the Immigration Committee, had been successful in keeping bills for drastic cuts in the quotas from reaching the floor of the House. In 1931 a bill for a 90 percent reduction in all quotas passed the House and had a good chance of passing with a large majority in the Senate, but the legislative session ended before it came to a vote. See Divine, *American Immigration Policy, 1924–1952*, 79–86.

20. H. R. 67 was introduced by Rep. S. Dickstein on March 22, 1933, *Congressional Record*, 73rd Congress, 1st Session, 1933, vol. 77, pt. 1, 779. See also McDonald Stewart, *United States Government Policy on Refugees from Nazism*, 43.

21. Adler to S. Dickstein, March 28, 1933, reprinted in Michael N. Dobkowski, ed., *The Politics of Indifference*, 313–14 (emphasis in the original).

22. Kohler to Dickstein, March 31, 1933, reprinted in ibid., 315–16.

23. "Nazi Persecution Stressed by Wise," *NYT*, March 22, 1933, cited in Medoff, *The Deafening Silence*, 24.

24. "State Department Calls for Full Report on the German Situation from U.S. Embassy and Consulate Following Visit by Wise, Deutsch," *JTA Daily News Bulletin*, March 23, 1933, p. 1, cited in Medoff, 24.

25. "Review of Refusal of Visas by Consular Officials; Hearings Before the Committee on Immigration and Naturalization—House of Representatives, 73rd Congress, 1st Session; Hearing No. 73.1.2 (Revised and Completed), May 18, 23, 1933" (Washington D.C.: U.S. Government Printing Office, 1933), 2, 5, 6, cited in Medoff, *The Deafening Silence*, 25, 26–27; "Carr Fights Easing of Curbs on Aliens," *NYT*, March 30, 1933, p. 2.

26. Kohler to Dickstein, March 31, 1933, reprinted in Dobkowski, ed., *The Politics of Indifference*, 315–16.

27. Frankfurter to Billikopf, Sept. 12, 1933, Billikopf's Papers, Box 8/2, AJA.

28. Wise to Frankfurter, Nov. 29, 1935; Frankfurter to Wise, Nov. 30, 1935, both in SSW Papers, Box 109, AJHS.

29. Statement issued by the Department of State on April 28, 1933, reprinted in Adler and Margalith, *With Firmness in the Right*, 366.

30. Memorandum of Stephen S. Wise and Bernard S. Deutsch, Friday, April 28, 1933, Washington, Mack's Papers, A 405 84/A, CZA. The meeting of the AJ Congress representatives was arranged through the intervention of Senator Wagner and Bernard Baruch; Adler to Hull, May 3, 1933, Warburg's Papers, Box 286/5, AJA.

31. Wise to Frankfurter, May 23, 1933, SSW Papers, Box 109, AJHS.

32. Feingold, "'Courage First and Intelligence Second'," 427–28.

33. Adler to Hull, May 3, 1933, Warburg's Papers, Box 286/5, AJA. On Hull's economic views see Dallek, *Franklin D. Roosevelt and American Foreign Policy*, 33, 38.

34. Adler to Hull, May 3, 1933, Warburg's Papers, Box 286/5, AJA.

35. Confidential Address, "Extracts of Address by James G. McDonald, at Town Hall, 123 West 43 St., New York City, May 4, 1933, at 8:30 P.M." Mack's Papers, A 405 84/B, CZA.

36. Wise to Frankfurter, Brandeis, and Mack, May 4, 1933, SSW Papers, Box 109, AJHS; Wise to Mack, May 4, 1933, SSW Papers, Box 115, AJHS.

37. Wise to Mack, May 4, 1933, SSW Papers, Box 115, AJHS; see also Wise to Frankfurter, May 17, 1933, Mack's Papers A 405 83/A, CZA.

38. Wise to Frankfurter, Sept. 16, 1940, SSW Papers, Box 109, AJHS.

39. Frankfurter to Brandeis, May 9, 1933, SSW Papers, Box 109, AJHS; Brandeis to Wise (Confidential), May 11, 1933, Mack's Papers, A 405 84/B, CZA.

40. Mack to Wise, May 19, 1933, SSW Papers, Box 115, AJHS.

41. "Memorandum of conversation with Raymond Moley about the Jewish situation in Germany held from 8–10 A.M., Sunday, May 14, 1933," with a certain Weinstein, Mack's Papers, A 405 83/A, CZA; Mack to Wise, May 19, 1933, SSW Papers, Box 115, AJHS.

42. Frankfurter to Proskauer, May 18, 1933, Mack's Papers, A 405 83/A, CZA; Frankfurter to Wise, June 7, 1933, SSW Papers, Box 109, AJHS; Frankfurter to Wise, Feb. 27, 1936, SSW Papers, Box 109, AJHS.

43. Brandeis to Wise, May 11, 1933, Mack's Papers A 405 84/B, CZA.

44. See telegram from Schacht to Hitler, May 15, 1933 in *Documents on German Foreign Policy, 1918–1945*, Series C 1933–1937, vol. 1 (Washington, D.C., 1957), 423. Also report on the Schacht meeting from May 26, 1933 submitted in a Cabinet meeting, p. 487.

45. In the following correspondence we find extensive discussion about the preparations for the meeting, but no report on what transpired. Brandeis to Wise, May 11, 1933, Mack's Papers A 405 84/B, CZA; Wise to Mack, May 9 and 10, 1933, SSW Papers, Box 115, AJHS; Mack to Wise, May 19, 1933, SSW Papers, Box 11, AJHS. Avraham Margaliot was also unable to locate any records of the meeting from a Jewish source. See his *Between Rescue and Annihilation, Studies in the History of Germany Jewry 1932–1938* (in Hebrew) (Jerusalem, 1990), 159 n104.

46. Roosevelt to Irving Lehman, May 18, 1933, cited in Shafir, "The Impact of the Jewish Crisis on American-German Relations," pt. 1, 119. See also Dallek, *Franklin D. Roosevelt and American Foreign Policy*, 57–58.

47. Wise to Frankfurter, May 17, 1933, Mack's Papers, A 405 83/A, CZA.

48. Wise to Rabbi Louis Newman, July 19, 1932, SSW Papers, Box 117, AJHS.

49. Although neither Wise nor Holmes supported FDR in 1932, the split between them seemed to be mended after Roosevelt's election. They wrote the president-elect a warm congratulatory letter, to which FDR replied in an equally friendly and frank letter. Wise's "competitors" in the AJC and elsewhere highly exaggerated this split, arguing that Wise was not suitable to lead American Jewry. In a letter to Frankfurter, Mack informed him of the "miserable editorial" in the *Jewish Daily Bulletin* which urged Wise to stay away from the centers of power in Washington. "I only wish," he added to Frankfurter, "that you had stated specifically that Wise, despite the letters during the Walker investigation is not [added in handwriting, not clear whose] persona ingrata [*sic*] with F.D.R." Mack to Frankfurter, May 22, 1933, SSW Papers, Box 115, AJHS; Burns, *Roosevelt: The Lion and the Fox*, 140–41; Frommer, "The American Jewish Congress," 2:311; Voss, ed., *Stephen S. Wise*, 174–75; and Wise, *Challenging Years*, 217–18.

50. Wise to Frankfurter, Sept. 8, 1932, SSW Papers, Box 108, AJHS; Urofsky, *A Voice*, 254.

51. Wise to Mack, May 8, 1933, Mack's Papers, A 405, 84/B, CZA.

52. Memorandum of Stephen S. Wise and Bernard Deutsch, Friday, April 28, 1933, Washington, Mack's Papers, A 405 84/A, CZA; Wise to Mack, May 4, 1933, SSW Papers, Box 115, AJHS; Dr. Harry Friedenwald to Wise, May 16 1933, Mack's Papers, A 405 83/A, CZA.

53. Wise to Frankfurter, May 17, 1933, Mack's Papers, A 405, 83/A, CZA.

54. Wise to Frankfurter, March 2, 1936, SSW Papers, Box 109, AJHS; Frankfurter to Moley, April 24, 1933, ibid., Box 82/2; Wise to Frankfurter, July 5, 1933, ibid., Box 109.

55. Wise to Frankfurter, May 17, 1933, Mack's Papers, A 405 83/A, CZA.

56. "Mr. Wise's Report on his Activities in Europe," *Administrative Meeting of the American Jewish Congress*, Sept. 23, 1933, SSW Papers, Box 87, AJHS.

57. It was Senator Tydings who persuaded a group of Jews of this opinion, but it had previously been articulated by people like Adler and Wise. See Harry Friedenwald to Wise, May 16, 1933, Mack's Papers, A 405 83/A, CZA.

58. "Mr. Wise's Report on his Activities in Europe," *Administrative Meeting of the American Jewish Congress*, Sept. 23, 1933, SSW Papers, Box 87, AJHS. His other reasons for having opposed the boycott, to which the AJ Congress had lent its support on Aug. 20, 1933, were his beliefs that it should be a "world Jewish boycott," and that the government should support it.

59. Minutes of the Executive Committee Meeting, June 5, 1933, RG 1, Records of the AJC Executive Offices, Minutes Books, AJCA (emphasis added); for Adler's support of the president's public silence and his acceptance of Rosenman's analysis, see Adler to Rabbi Samuel Schulman, June 2, 1933, Adler's chronological file, RG 1, EXO 14, AJCA.

60. "Memorandum of conversation with Raymond Moley about the Jewish situation in Germany held from 8–10 A. M., Sunday, May 14, 1933," with a certain Weinstein, Mack's Papers, A 405 83/A, CZA.

61. "Mr. Wise's Report on his Activities in Europe," *Administrative Meeting of the American Jewish Congress*, Sept. 23, 1933, SSW Papers, Box 87, AJHS.

62. Ibid.

63. Proskauer to Rabbi Louis I. Newman, Oct. 2, 1933, Bernard G. Richards Papers, Jewish Theological Seminary, New York, cited in Auerbach, Review Essay on "Proskauer: His Life and Times," 109.

64. The "larger concerns" were the World Economic Conference which took place in London. Proskauer's address at the "Conference on the German Situation," May 24, 1933, p. 24, AJCA, Historical Documents Section.

65. See, for example, Wyman, *Paper Walls*, 14–23, and *The Abandonment of the Jews*, 9; see also the excellent study of Ribuffo, *The Old Christian Right*; Gerber, ed., *Anti-Semitism in American History*, 21–22; Lipset and Raab, *The Politics of Unreason*, Chapter 5; Dinnerstein, *Anti-Semitism in America*, Chapter 7.

66. Cited in Arnold M. Eisen, *The Chosen People in America: A Study of Jewish Religious Ideology* (Bloomington and Indianapolis, 1983), 30.

67. "Regional Conference," June 10, 1934, vol. 1, Sunday Morning Session, 4, AJCA, Historical Documents Section.

68. Proceedings of the Regional Conference of the American Jewish Committee, Standard Club, Chicago, Illinois, June 16, 1934, vol. 2, Sunday Afternoon Session, 53, 57, AJCA, Historical Documents Section.

69. Ibid., 57 (emphasis added).

70. Gottlieb, *American Anti-Nazi Resistance*, 60, 61, 63, 68–70; Waldman to Untermeyer, May 9, 1933, cited in Frommer, "The American Jewish Congress," 2:343–53.

71. Proskauer to Untermeyer, June 26, 1934, quoted in Gottlieb, *American Anti-Nazi Resistance*, 63.

72. Dinnerstein, *Anti-Semitism in America*, 109–111.

73. "(Strictly Confidential) Memorandum of Meeting of Sol M. Stroock, Morris

D. Waldman, Professor Horace M. Kallen and Stephen S. Wise with LDB [Brandeis]," May 15, 1934, Washington, D.C., SSW Papers, Box 106, AJHS.

74. Brandeis to Wise, Aug. 9, 1934, SSW Papers, Box 106, AJHS.

75. W. I. Thomas, in Robert K. Merton, *Social Theory and Social Structure* (New York, 1957), 421.

76. Julian Mack, "Memorandum of Washington Trip—October 30, 1933," Billikopf's Papers, Box 18/3, AJA. If the bond had been posted and accepted by the secretary of labor it would have prevented the consuls from barring applicants on the grounds that they were likely to become public charges. Under Secretary William Phillips, who initiated Mack's visit, had planned a slightly different order of business. The Departments of State and Labor were looking for a liaison between the Jewish organizations and themselves. Mack was considered an "agreeable" Jew and was asked to serve in this capacity, but he refused on grounds of his judicial work and poor health. For Assistant Secretary of State Wilbur J. Carr, Mack was a perfect choice to arbitrate between the Departments of State and Labor, for while he "disclosed quite frankly" his "strong liberal immigration views" he also emphasized his agreement that the Jews "could not under the law be given exceptional treatment." As Mack put it, Carr felt that "I would lean backward in favor of the State Department just because of my inclinations the other way around." Generally speaking, Carr was right.

77. Breitman and Kraut, *American Refugee Policy*, 21, 27.

78. Julian Mack, "Memorandum of Washington Trip—October 30, 1933."

79. Ibid.

80. Wyzanski to his parents, Oct. 30, 1933, in Breitman and Kraut, *American Refugee Policy*, 20.

81. The formal opinion was signed by Attorney General Homer Cummings, who referred to the "excellent memorandum" prepared by Wyzanski and authorized Perkins to proceed with the bonding procedures. Ibid., 21.

82. Wyzanski to parents, Jan. 12, 1934, in ibid., 22; Mack to Brandeis, Jan. 9, 1932, Mack's Papers, A 405 229, CZA.

83. Edwin Mims, Jr., "German Refugees and American Bureaucrats," *Today*, Jan. 20, 1934; Breitman and Kraut, *American Refugee Policy*, 23; on the repercussions of the article on the State Department, see Morse, *While Six Million Died*, 140–44.

84. Cyrus Adler to Abram C. Joseph, Nov. 22, 1933, Morris Waldman Files, RG 1, EXO-29, Germany Folder, YIVO.

85. Isidore D. Morison to Cyrus Adler (in agreement with Adler's opinion), Oct. 30, 1934, Warburg's Papers, Box 315, AJA.

86. Mack to Joseph Proskauer, Irving Lehman, Max Kohler, Stephen Wise, Bernard Deutsch, and others, June 6, 1934, Mack's Papers, A 405 229, CZA.

87. Irving Lehman to Mack, June 12, 1934, Mack's Papers, A 405 229, CZA.

88. Ibid.

89. Ibid.

90. Harold Fields, "Our Interest in Immigration Legislation," *Opinion*, June 1935, p. 12.

91. Wise to Frankfurter, May 23, 1933, with copies to Mack and Brandeis, SSW Papers, Box 109, AJHS.

92. Ibid.

93. "Memorandum of telephone conversation between SSW [Stephen S. Wise] and Congressman Sabath, Washington," June 1, 1933, Mack's Papers, A 405 84/B, CZA.

94. Wise to Frankfurter, June 1, 1933, SSW Papers, Box 109, AJHS.

95. For McFadden's speech see United States *Congressional Record,* 73rd Congress, 1st Session, 1933, LXXVII, 4538–40, quoted also in Scholnick, *The New Deal and Anti-Semitism,* 101–102.

96. Edward S. Shapiro, "The Approach of War: Congressional Isolationism and Anti-Semitism, 1939–1941," *AJH* 74, no. 1 (Sept. 1984): 47–49.

97. Stephen Wise and Bernard Deutsch memo, April 28, 1933, Mack's Papers, A 405 83/A, CZA.

98. "Fish Urges House to Call For Reich Jewry's Safety, Resolution Asks President to Use Good Offices," *NYT,* May 25, 1933.

99. Lawrence Berenson to Mack, May 25, 1933; Fish to Berenson, May 26, 1933; Wise to Mack, June 3, 1933; Wise to Proskauer, June 4, 1933, all in Mack's Papers, A 405 83/A, CZA.

100. Rosenman's instructions for Wise, as related to him by Dr. Louis I. Newman, are quoted in a letter by Wise to Mack, June 3, 1933, Mack's Papers, A 405 83/A, CZA.

101. Ibid.

102. In Voss, ed., *Stephen S. Wise,* 196.

103. Wise, June 13, 1933, quoted in Gottlieb, *American Anti-Nazi Resistance,* 77.

104. Waldman to Proskauer, Aug. 8, 1933, Waldman's Papers, 1/31, AJA.

105. Ibid.

106. "Confidential and Urgent, Memo to A. I. Spiro from Lillie Shultz," Nov. 6, 1933, SSW Papers, Box 93, AJHS.

107. Wise to Holmes, Sept. 18, 1933, Box 53/1, AJHS.

108. Wise to Benjamin Schloss, Nov. 8, 1933, cited in Urofsky, *A Voice,* 271.

109. Frankfurter to Jacob Billikopf, Oct. 16, 1933, Billikopf's Papers, Box 8/2, AJA.

110. Klemperer, *I Will Bear Witness,* 70–71 (emphasis in the original).

111. Felix Warburg to Mack, Sept. 27, 1934, Mack's Papers, A 405 83/B, CZA. These opinions were expressed in a conference that Warburg and other members of the AJC and the Joint had with Prof. Nathan of Princeton, Dr. Ernst Kahn of the Refugee Committee in London, and Dr. Kotsching, who represented James McDonald, the high commissioner on refugees.

112. Wise to Brandeis, July 14, 1934, SSW Papers, Box 106, AJHS; for Hitler's speech of July 14, 1934, before the Reichstag, see Domarus, *Hitler, Speeches and Proclamations,* 1:483–503.

113. Brandeis to Mack, July 17, 1934, Mack's Papers, A 405 83/B, CZA.

114. Waldman to Stroock, July 8, 1934 (from Paris), Waldman's Papers, Box 2/7, AJA.

115. Cable by Waldman to Stroock, July 5, 1934, Waldman's Papers, Box 2/7, AJA.

116. Waldman to Stroock, July 8, 1934 (from Paris), Waldman's Papers, Box 2/7, AJA.

117. Sobeloff to Max Kohler, Jan. 15, 1934, Mack's Papers, A 403 83/13, CZA. For the text of the resolution introduced by Senator Millard E. Tydings of Maryland, see Adler and Margalith, *With Firmness in the Right,* 369.

118. Unsigned (probably Kohler) to Simon E. Sobeloff, June 28, 1934, Mack's Papers, A 405 83/B, CZA. (The letter in my possession is a typed copy, and very likely the date ought to be Jan. 28, 1934.)

119. Adler to Rothenberg, June 25, 1934, Warburg's Papers, Box 315, AJA. Also cited in Zosa Szajkowski, "Relief for German Jewry: Problems of American Involvement," *AJHQ* 62, no. 2 (Dec. 1972): 142.

120. Waldman to Sol Stroock, July 8, 1934, Waldman's Papers, Box 2/7, AJA.

121. Report from Germany, Nov. 29, 1934, SSW Papers, Box 88, AJHS.

122. Wise to Holmes, Dec. 12, 1934, SSW Papers, Box 55/1, AJHS.

123. For a detailed description of the riots and the reactions of the American Jewish organizations, see Moshe Gottlieb, "The Berlin Riots and Their Repercussions in America," *AJHQ* 59 (March 1970): 302–328.

124. Cited in Adler and Margalith, eds., *With Firmness in the Right*, 367.

125. Memo of Joint Delegation to Phillips, July 26, 1935, cited in Shafir, "The Impact of the Jewish Crisis on American-German Relations," pt. 1, 485.

126. Cited in Gottlieb, "Berlin Riots of 1935," 317.

127. Phillips Diary, entry for July 26, 1935, cited in Shafir, "The Impact of the Jewish Crisis on American-German Relations," pt. 1, 485.

128. Cited in Gottlieb, "Berlin Riots of 1935," 318.

129. J. Wise to Waldman, Aug. 4, 1935, Waldman's Papers, 12/6, AJA.

130. Wise to Einstein, Sept. 23, 1933, in Voss, ed., *Stephen S. Wise*, 207.

131. Mack to James McDonald, May 12, 1933, SSW Papers, Box 115, AJHS.

132. Dallek, *Franklin D. Roosevelt and American Foreign Policy*, 95–96, 102–108.

133. McDonald to Warburg, Oct. 10 and 29, 1935, in Edgar B. Nixon, ed., *Franklin Delano Roosevelt and Foreign Affairs* (hereafter *FDR and Foreign Affairs*) (Cambridge, Mass., 1969), 3:51–52, 66; Mack to Carl Austrian, Sept. 19, 1935, Mack's Papers, A 407, 83/B, CZA.

134. Herbert Lehman to FDR, Nov. 1, 1935, quoted in *FDR and Foreign Affairs*, 3:60–62.

135. FDR to Lehman, Nov. 13, 1935; Lehman to FDR, Nov. 15, 1935; FDR to Lehman, Dec. 10, 1935, in ibid., 64–66.

136. Felix Warburg to McDonald, Nov. 20, 1935, quoted in McDonald Stewart, *United States Government Policy on Refugees from Nazism*, 142.

137. "Memorandum of statement on Nuremberg Laws, September 15, 1935," Oct. 22, 1935; "Analysis of the present situation," Dec. 3, 1935, Morris Waldman Files, RG 1, EXO-29, Germany Folder, YIVO. With respect to financial assistance, since 1935 it had been standard policy of the Joint not to send dollars to Germany, so as "not [to] be guilty of helping the Hitler regime." The exception was a relatively small sum of money that was given to the American Friends Service Committee (the Quakers), which was used for undercover aid to individuals in Germany. See Bauer, *American Jewry and the Holocaust*, 26.

138. Lazaron to Moore, July 2, 1935, cited in Shafir, "The Impact of the Jewish Crisis on American-German Relations," pt. 1, 510–11, where there is also information about the CCAR, as well as in Shafir, pt. 2, 870.

139. For the Zionist reaction to the Nuremberg Laws see Yoav Gelber, *New Homeland, Immigration and Absorption of Central European Jews 1933–1948* (in Hebrew) (Jerusalem, 1990), 92–111.

140. Laski to Waldman, Sept. 17, 1935, Waldman's Papers, 1/23, AJA.

141. Secretary of the Paris-based Comité des Délégations Juives (signature not clear) to Judge Mack, Oct. 18, 1935, Mack's Papers, A 405 83/B, CZA.

142. James Rosenberg to Waldman, June 26, 1935, Waldman's Papers, 1/33, AJA.

143. Waldman, *Nor By Power*, 56. McDonald's letter, dated Dec. 27, 1935, included 34 pages and an Annex that contained an analysis of the German measures against "non-Aryans" and their effects in creating refugees. The supplement was prepared by Melvin Fagen, who was on the AJC's staff as an expert on international law, and by Professor Oscar Janowsky, an authority on minority rights. It was reprinted in the

New York Times, Dec. 30, 1935, in the *Jewish Chronicle,* Jan. 3, 1936, and in the *Christian Century* in a supplement to the Jan. 15, 1936 issue.

144. "Memorandum of luncheon with James N. Rosenberg, James G. McDonald, Professor J. P. Chamberlain, Morris R. Cohen, Oscar I. Janowsky," drafted by Melvin Fagen, June 20, 1935, Waldman's Papers, 1/33, AJA. Fagen to Waldman, Nov. 29, 1935; Rosenberg to Felix Warburg, Dec. 4, 1935; both in Warburg's Papers, Box 331, AJA.

145. Waldman to Jacob Landau, Nov. 26, 1935, Waldman's Papers, Box 1/33, AJA.

146. Klemperer, *I Will Bear Witness,* 136–37.

8. FDR

1. Wise to Holmes, Feb. 3, 1936, SSW Papers, Box 189/32, AJHS.

2. Wise to Niles, Sept. 26, 1935, Box 68/5, AJHS.

3. Ibid.

4. Wise to Holmes, Feb. 5, 1936, Box 189/32, AJHS. One such intermediary was Maldwin Fertig, Roosevelt's former counsel. According to Wise, Frankfurter probably put in "a good word" for him as well.

5. Breitman and Kraut, *American Refugee Policy,* 99.

6. Wise to Holmes, Feb. 3, 1936, SSW Papers, Box 189/32, AJHS; Holmes to Wise, Feb. 11, 1936, Box 53/2, AJHS.

7. Wise to Brandeis, Jan. 12 1936, Box 106, AJHS.

8. Frankfurter to Wise, Jan. 30, 1936, Box 109, AJHS.

9. Ibid. On the relationship between Wise and FDR see also Wise, *Challenging Years,* 218; Urofsky, *A Voice,* 238–59.

10. Wise to Frankfurter, Jan. 28 1936, in Voss, ed., *Stephen S. Wise,* 210.

11. Wise to Frankfurter, March 2, 1936, SSW Papers, Box 109, AJHS.

12. Ibid.

13. Wise to Mack, April 10, 1936, Box 115; Wise to Frankfurter, April 10, 1936, Box 109. Both in AJHS. Moley to LeHand, April 4, 1936, in Nixon, ed., *FDR and Foreign Affairs,* vol. 3, 279–80.

14. Hull to Roosevelt, April 21, 1936, in Nixon, ed., *FDR and Foreign Affairs,* 282–83.

15. Scholnick, *The New Deal and Anti-Semitism,* 62–96, 105–116; Shafir, "The Impact of the Jewish Crisis on American-German Relations," pt. 2, 612–21. See also the series of letters: Wise to Frankfurter, Oct. 2, 1936; Frankfurter to Wise, Oct. 27, 1936; Wise to Frankfurter, Oct. 30, 1936, Wise Memorandum to Frankfurter and Mack, Dec. 15, 1936, all in SSW Papers, Box 109, AJHS.

16. Wise to Niles, Oct. 7, 1936, Box 118, AJHS.

17. Shafir, "The Impact of the Jewish Crisis on American-German Relations," pt. 2, 613–17.

18. Wise to Frankfurter, April 10, 1936, SSW Papers, Box 109, AJHS.

19. Wise's Statement to the Democratic National Committee, Sept. 24, 1936, cited in Shafir, "The Impact of the Jewish Crisis on American-German Relations," pt. 2, 609. On Wise's efforts to dismiss the allegations against a "Jewish vote" see Wise to Frankfurter, Oct. 26, 1936, SSW Papers, Box 109, AJHS.

20. Jonah Wise to Herbert H. Lehman, Oct. 27, 1937, cited in Szajkowski, "The Attitude of American Jews to Refugees from Germany in the 1930's," 103.

21. Michael J. Cohen, *Palestine and the Great Powers* (Princeton, 1982), 6. For the

events in Palestine during 1936 see Cohen, *Palestine: Retreat from the Mandate* (London and New York, 1978).

22. Frankfurter to Mack, May 20, 1936, SSW Papers, Box 109, AJHS.

23. Wise to FDR, May 18, 1936; FDR to Wise, June 8, 1936, both in Box 68, AJHS.

24. Wise to Brandeis, July 24, 1936, in Voss, ed., *Stephen S. Wise*, 212.

25. Wise to Holmes, September 1936 (no exact date), in Polier and Wise, eds., *The Personal Letters of Stephen Wise*, 233–34.

26. Wise to Harry Friedenwald, Oct. 12, 1936, and Wise to Emanuel Neumann, Oct. 13, 1936, both in Voss, ed., *Stephen S. Wise*, 216–17; Urofsky, *American Zionism from Herzl to the Holocaust*, 402–403.

27. Urofsky, *A Voice*, 284.

28. "Report of a Visit of Dr. Stephen S. Wise to President Franklin D. Roosevelt at Hyde Park, October 5, 1936 (Strictly Confidential)," sent to Brandeis, Frankfurter, and Mack, SSW Papers, Box 189/32, AJHS.

29. Wise to Frankfurter, Dec. 22, 1936, SSW Papers, Box 109, AJHS.

30. In the House of Representatives the Democrats won 331 seats out of 435, and in the Senate 76 out of 96.

31. Herbert Lehman to Roosevelt, June 15, 1936; Roosevelt to Herbert Lehman, in Nixon, ed., *FDR and Foreign Affairs*, 3:323–24, 341.

32. Cited in Morse, *While Six Million Died*, 195.

33. Ibid., 195–98; Breitman and Kraut, *American Refugee Policy*, 48–49.

34. Ibid., 50.

35. Cited in Medoff, *The Deafening Silence*, 33.

36. Wise erroneously cited Beck as demanding the emigration of three million Jews in a letter to FDR, Jan. 15, 1937, SSW Papers, Box 68/6, AJHS. At an international conference Beck had also referred to his country's "surplus" Jewish population and hoped for an annual emigration of between 80,000 and 100,000 Jews, who would leave their assets behind. See Michael R. Marrus, *The Unwanted: European Refugees in the Twentieth Century* (New York, 1985), 142.

37. Wise to FDR, Jan. 15, 1937, SSW Papers, Box 68/6, AJHS. Wise's suggested text read: "Every American citizen is the subject of his country's interest and concern. Nor will the American Democracy ever hold any faithful and law-abiding group within its borders to be superfluous." FDR to Wise, Jan. 23, 1937, SSW Papers, Box 68/6, AJHS. "Roosevelt's Second Inaugural Address," in Samuel Rosenman, ed., *The Public Papers and Addresses of Franklin D. Roosevelt*, 13 vols. (New York, 1938–1950), 6:1–6.

38. See Donald S. Strong, *Organized Anti-Semitism in America* (1941; reprint, Washington, D.C., 1979); Ribuffo, *The Old Christian Right*; Diamond, *The Nazi Movement in the United States, 1929–1941*; Mary Christine Athans, *The Coughlin-Fahey Connection* (New York, 1991); Donald Warren, *Radio Priest: Charles Coughlin, the Father of Hate Radio* (New York, 1996).

39. Eisen, *The Chosen People in America*, 33–36.

40. See Wyman, *Paper Walls*, 14–23.

41. Text of letter reprinted in "Jews In Action: Five Years of the Jewish People's Committee," 6, cited in Medoff, *The Deafening Silence*, 34.

42. Wise to Neumann, June 23, 1937, in Voss, ed., *Stephen S. Wise*, 220.

43. Wise to Frankfurter, April 12, 1937, SSW Papers, Box 109, AJHS.

44. Wise to Mack, Nov. 10, 1937, in Voss, ed., *Stephen S. Wise*, 222–23.

45. Quoted in a Memo from M. Boraisha to Wise, Jan. 3, 1938, SSW Papers, Box 90, AJHS.

46. See Morse, *While Six Million Died*, 200–201 for excerpts from the *New York Times* of March 16, 18, 20 and 23, 1938. For the diverse European reaction see Shlomo Z. Katz, "Public Opinion in Western Europe and the Evian Conference of July 1938," *Yad Vashem Studies* 9 (1973): 105–127. See also Friedländer, *Nazi Germany and the Jews*, 241–68.

47. Klemperer, *I Will Bear Witness*, 241.

48. Feingold, *Bearing Witness*, 75.

49. *FRUS*, 1938 (Washington, D.C., 1950), 1:740–41, March 23, 1938.

50. Cited in Anthony Read and David Fisher, *Kristallnacht: Unleashing the Holocaust* (New York, 1989), 231.

51. Frankfurter to FDR, March 26, 1938, cited in Shafir, "The Impact of the Jewish Crisis on American-German Relations," pt. 2, 705; Herbert Lehman to FDR, March 28, 1938, and FDR to Herbert Lehman, March 30, 1938, cited in Feingold, *The Politics of Rescue*, 24; Wise to FDR, March 28, 1938, SSW Papers, Box 68/6, AJHS; Wise to Mack, March 29, 1938, Box 115, AJHS.

52. Wise to Frankfurter, April 19, 1938; Frankfurter to Wise, March 28, 1938; Wise to Frankfurter, April 25, 1938. All in Box 109, AJHS.

53. Frankfurter to Wise, April 27, 1938, Box 109, AJHS. Two days earlier Frankfurter had written to Wise in similar vein: "As I see the great problem, it is to prevent F.D.R.'s generous will from being attenuated by men of prudence so-called, and even by men of not such good will." Frankfurter to Wise, April 25, 1938, Box 109, AJHS.

54. Wise to Frankfurter, March 30, 1938, Box 109, AJHS; Wise to Mack, March 29, 1938, Box 115, AJHS.

55. Wise to Frankfurter, March 30, 1938, Box 109, AJHS.

56. Schneiderman to Waldman, April 5, 1938, account of Executive Committee Meeting, Morris Waldman Files, RG 1, EXO-29, Immigration File 1938–1939, YIVO.

57. See also Medoff, *The Deafening Silence*, 42–43; and Wyman, *Paper Walls*, 68.

58. Waldman to Stroock, June 9, 1938, Morris Waldman Files, RG 1, EXO-29, Immigration File 1938–1939, YIVO.

59. Rosenman, ed., *The Public Papers and Addresses of Franklin D. Roosevelt*, 7:171; Wise, "No Human Dumping," *Opinion*, Aug. 1938, p. 4, cited in Medoff, *The Deafening Silence*, 45.

60. Peter Loewenberg, "The Kristallnacht as a Public Degradation Ritual," *LBIY* 32 (1987).

61. Quoted in Friedländer, *Nazi Germany and the Jews*, 273.

62. Lipstadt, *Beyond Belief*, 99. On the reaction of the international press, see Read and Fisher, *Kristallnacht*, 166–79. On the American Jewish reaction to the November pogrom see Lookstein, *Were We Our Brothers' Keepers?*, 35–80. See also Alfred Gottschalk, "The German Pogrom of November 1938 and the Reaction of American Jewry," *The Leo Baeck Memorial Lecture* (Leo Baeck Institute, New York, 1988); Sander A. Diamond, "The *Kristallnacht* and the Reaction in America," *YAJSS* 14 (1969): 196–208.

63. Wise to Mrs. Henry Pereira-Mendes, Nov. 12, 1938, SSW Papers, Box 96, AJHS; Wise to Brandeis, Nov. 11, 1938, SSW Papers, Box 106, AJHS.

64. Wise to Brandeis, Nov. 11, 1938, SSW Papers, Box 106, AJHS. Ben Cohen remembered things slightly differently: "I did counsel against your rushing down to Washington, but . . . I approved your suggestion that the Bishop of Washington might see the Skipper on the German situation." Cohen to Wise, Nov. 14, 1938, SSW Papers, Box 64, AJHS.

65. Wise to Niles, Nov. 14, 1938, SSW Papers, Box 118, AJHS.

66. Cited in Lookstein, *Were We Our Brothers' Keepers?*, 59.

67. Report dated Nov. 18, 1938, SSW Papers, Box 89, AJHS.

68. This account is based on Lookstein, *Were We Our Brothers' Keepers?*, 57–59, 71–73.

69. Wise to Frankfurter, Nov. 17, 1938, SSW Papers, Box 109, AJHS; Wise, *Challenging Years*, 264–65.

70. Wise to Ben Cohen, Nov. 17, 1938, SSW Papers, Box 64, AJHS.

71. Cited in Medoff, *The Deafening Silence*, 53.

72. Journal entry, Nov. 14, 1938, Jay Pierrepont Moffat, *The Moffat Papers, 1919–1943*, ed. Nancy H. Hooker (Cambridge, Mass., 1956), 221–22.

73. Memo of a conversation, Nov. 17, 1938, cited in Morse, *While Six Million Died*, 234.

74. "Report of a Meeting of SSW [Stephen Wise], Saturday Morning, Jan. 22, 1938," SSW Papers, Box 189/32, AJHS.

75. "Minutes of the Second Session of the President's Advisory Committee on Political Refugees, May 19, 1938," SSW Papers, Box 65, AJHS; "Confidential Memorandum [by Stephen Wise] on the Conference with the President and State Department, Wednesday Morning and Afternoon, April 13, 1938, Washington, D.C.," SSW Papers, Box 68/6, AJHS. In this memo, Wise referred to a joke that was going around Washington that FDR had named Baruch as one of the Jewish representatives on the President's Advisory Committee on Political Refugees "in order to punish him for his recent testimony before a Senate Committee on the New Deal, knowing . . . Baruch's preference for being regarded as a great American financier rather than as a leading Jew." Baruch to Hull, April 13, 1938, cited in Breitman and Kraut, *American Refugee Policy*, 102.

76. "Confidential Memorandum [by Stephen Wise]."

77. Cited in Lookstein, *Were We Our Brothers' Keepers?*, 68–69.

78. Rosenman to FDR, filed Dec. 12, 1938, President's Personal File, FDR Library, cited by Breitman and Kraut, *American Refugee Policy*, 230. Rosenman gave an almost verbatim reply when he was asked by Myron C. Taylor for his opinion on liberalizing the quota system; see Rosenman to Taylor, Nov. 23, 1938, quoted in Feingold, *The Politics of Rescue*, 42.

79. Breitman and Kraut, *American Refugee Policy*, 230.

80. Brandeis to Wise, Nov. 23, 1938, SSW Papers, Box 106, AJHS.

81. Harold L. Ickes, *The Secret Diary of Harold L. Ickes*, vol. 2, *The Inside Struggle 1936–1939* (New York: Simon and Schuster, 1954), 510, entry of Dec. 3, 1938.

82. For FDR's statement, issued on Nov. 15, 1938, prepared for him by Secretary Hull, and the changes made, see Lookstein, *Were We Our Brothers' Keepers?*, 41–42.

83. *Morning Journal*, Nov. 23, 1938, cited in ibid., 70.

84. Wise, *As I See It*, 107.

85. Waldman to Adler (Very Confidential), Nov. 6, 1938, Waldman's Papers, Box 1/1, AJA.

86. Editorial, *Congress Bulletin*, Dec. 16, 1938. Also cited in Lookstein, *Were We Our Brothers' Keepers?*, 50.

87. Waldman to Adler, Nov. 6, 1938, Waldman's Papers, Box 1/1, AJA.

88. Geist to Messersmith, Dec. 5, 1938, cited in Breitman and Kraut, *American Refugee Policy*, 67.

89. For a detailed description of the origin and reception of the Wagner-Rogers Bill, see Wyman, *Paper Walls*, 75–92.

90. Breitman and Kraut, *American Refugee Policy*, 107; Wyman, *Paper Walls*, 77–92.

91. Wyman, *Paper Walls*, 94–97.

92. "Admission of German Refugee Children, Joint Hearings Before a Subcommittee of the Committee on Immigration, United States Senate and a Subcommittee of the Committee on Immigration and Naturalization, House of Representatives; 76th Congress, 1st Session, on S. J. Res. 64 and H. J. Res. 168—Joint Resolutions to Authorize the Admission into the United States of a Limited Number of German Refugee Children, April 20, 21, 22, and 24, 1939" (Washington, D.C.: U.S. Government Printing Office, 1939), 95 (hereafter "Joint Hearings"), cited in Medoff, *The Deafening Silence*, 57.

93. Wise was questioned by one congressman about the idea of expanding the Wagner-Rogers proposal to include German Jewish children stranded in Poland, England, and Czechoslovakia, to which he responded: "Hard as it may be to answer your question . . . I feel that the country and the Congress should not be asked to do more than take care of a limited number of children. The bill provides for 10,000 each year for a period of two years. After all, we cannot take care of all of them. Germany has a population of five or six hundred thousand Jews." "Joint Hearings," 155, 158–59, cited in Medoff, *The Deafening Silence*, 57–58.

94. *Congress Bulletin*, May 12, 1939, p. 4. Also cited in Medoff, *The Deafening Silence*, 58.

95. "Where Do We Stand?" *Congress Bulletin*, June 16, 1939, p. 5. Rather ironically, the State Department did try, but unsuccessfully, to pressure the Cuban government to reverse its decision and later tried to persuade European governments to provide refuge for the passengers. See Irwin F. Gellman, "The *St. Louis* Tragedy," *AJHQ* 61 (Dec. 1971).

96. Wise to Rosemary Krensky, May 26, 1939, in Voss, ed., *Stephen S. Wise*, 233.

97. Lookstein, *Were We Our Brothers' Keepers?*, 91–92.

98. *Opinion*, July 1939, p. 3.

99. Frankfurter to Billikopf, Jan. 31, 1939, Billikopf's Papers, Box 8/4, AJA.

100. Billikopf to Frankfurter, March 15, 1939, Billikopf's Papers, Box 8/4, AJA.

101. Cited in Frederick A. Lazin, "The Response of the American Jewish Committee to the Crisis of German Jewry, 1933–1939," *AJH* 68, no. 3 (March 1979): 301.

102. Wise to Perlzweig, Sept. 21, 1939, SSW Papers, Box 91, AJHS.

103. Wise to Frankfurter, Oct. 17, 1939, SSW Papers, Box 109, AJHS. See also Harold L. Ickes, *The Secret Diary of Harold L. Ickes*, vol. 3, *The Lowering Clouds, 1939–1941*, 56–57; and Wyman, *Paper Walls*, 102. The Alaska settlement act, the King-Havenner Bill, was debated in Congress in early 1940, but opposition kept it from reaching the floor. The only Jewish group that backed the King bill was the very small faction of Poale Zion (Labor Zionists of America), who were willing to set aside their ideological preference for settlement in Palestine. See Medoff, *The Deafening Silence*, 68–69.

276 *Notes to pages 206–211*

104. In November 1933 Adler had already thought that "there is too much public discussion and we Jews are promoting too much of it and that it is not unlikely that our Christian fellow citizens will get tired of us." Cited in Breitman and Kraut, *American Refugee Policy*, 93.

105. Wise to M. J. Slonim, St. Louis Council, Oct. 29, 1940, SSW Papers, Box 82/6, AJHS.

106. Wise to Margaret Solomon, Aug. 6, 1942, and to Florence Luntz, Nov. 1, 1942, cited by Urofsky, *A Voice*, 327.

107. Wise to Brandeis, July 19, 1939, SSW Papers, Box 106, AJHS.

108. Wise to Perlzweig, Sept. 21, 1939, SSW Papers, Box 91, AJHS.

109. Wise to Easterman, Sept. 8, 1939, SSW Papers, Box 90, AJHS.

110. Rabbi William Braude to Wise, May 16, 1934, SSW Papers, Box 82/4, AJHS.

111. Wise to Holmes, Feb. 3, 1938; Holmes to Wise, Feb. 4, 7, and 18, 1938; Wise to Holmes, Sept. 30, 1938; all in SSW Papers, Box 53, AJHS.

112. Wise to Florence Luntz, Aug. 31, 1939, quoted in Urofsky, *A Voice*, 310.

113. Ibid., 311.

114. Waldman to Wise, Sept. 13, 1939, cited in Bauer, *American Jewry and the Holocaust*, 36.

115. Richard C. Rothschild, "Are American Jews Falling into the Nazi Trap?" *Contemporary Jewish Record* (Jan.-Feb. 1940): 9–17 (emphasis in the original).

9. "On Being an American"

1. Max Weber, *The Theory of Social and Economic Organization* (New York, 1947), 126–27.

2. Kammen, *Mystic Chords of Memory*, 5.

3. Wise to Frankfurter, Aug. 29, 1940, SSW Papers, Box 109, AJHS.

4. Breitman and Kraut, *American Refugee Policy*, 233. On FDR's 1940 campaign see also Burns, *Roosevelt, The Lion and the Fox*, 431–55; and Rosenman, *Working with Roosevelt*, 200–255.

5. Wise to Ben Cohen, Feb. 1, 1940, SSW Papers, Box 64, AJHS.

6. Cohen to Wise, Feb. 7, 1940, SSW Papers, Box 64, AJHS.

7. Barou to Wise, Feb. 26, 1940, and Wise to Cohen, March 12, 1940, SSW Papers, Box 64, AJHS.

8. Rabbi Stephen Wise, "In response to the greetings and the presentation of the Synagogue Building," March 17, 1940, SSW Papers, Box 82/5, AJHS.

9. Breitman and Kraut, *American Refugee Policy*, 108–111. See also Efraim Zuroff, "Rescue Priority and Fund Raising as Issues during the Holocaust: A Case Study of the Relations between the Vaad Ha-Hatzala and the Joint, 1939–1941," *AJH* 68, no. 3 (March 1979): 306–307. In the latter part of 1943, which is outside the framework of this study, Vaad ha-Hatzala changed its focus to the rescue of all Jews. See Kranzler, *Thy Brother's Blood*, 123–29.

10. Zuroff, "Rescue Priority," 312–13.

11. Moses Leavitt (secretary of the American Jewish Joint Distribution Committee) to Samuel Goldsmith, Jan. 27, 1941, cited in ibid., 312.

12. On the *Yishuv*'s response see Dina Porat, *The Blue and the Yellow Stars of David: The Zionist Leadership in Palestine and the Holocaust, 1939–1945* (1986; Eng. trans. Cambridge, Mass., 1990), 41–42, 54–55, 62–63; Tom Segev, *The Seventh Million: The Israelis and the Holocaust* (1991; Eng. trans. New York, 1993), 67–186.

13. Cited in David Steven Cohen, ed., *America, the Dream of My Life: Selections from the Federal Writers' Project's New Jersey Ethnic Survey* (New Brunswick and London, 1990), 211.

14. Wise to Professor Otto Nathan, Sept. 19, 1940, SSW Papers, Box 78/19, AJHS; see also Wise to Frankfurter, Nov. 27, SSW Papers, Box 109, AJHS.

15. Wise to Frankfurter, March 5, 1941, SSW Papers, Box 109, AJHS.

16. *JTA*, Sept. 15, 1941, p. 2.

17. Dinnerstein, *Anti-Semitism in America*, 129–30.

18. *JTA*, Sept. 19, 1941, p. 4.

19. "American Jewish Congress in Rosh Hashonah Message: Answer Charles A. Lindbergh," For Release Monday, Sept. 22, 1941, SSW Papers, Box 54, AJHS.

20. Wise to Holmes, n.d., 1941, in Polier and Wise, eds., *The Personal Letters of Stephen Wise*, 255.

21. All appeared in the *JTA*'s bulletins, May 8, 1942, p. 1; May 11, 1942, p. 3; May 13, 1942, p. 2.

22. Roosevelt to Wise, May 14, 1942, SSW Papers, Box 68/8, AJHS.

23. "Resolutions of the War Emergency Conference," cited in Medoff, *The Deafening Silence*, 77–78.

24. On the Bund report and its circulation see Bauer, "When Did They Know?," 52–57. See also Wyman, *The Abandonment of the Jews*, 40, 53; *JTA*, June 26, 1942, pp. 1–2.

25. On the organization of the rally and the central role played by the AJ Congress, see World Jewish Congress, *Unity in Dispersion: A History of the World Jewish Congress* (New York, 1948), 161. The event was followed by a nationwide day of fasting and prayer for Jews on Aug. 12, 1942.

26. Cohen, *Not Free to Desist*, 240.

27. Wise's handwritten draft (n.d.) and Roosevelt to Wise, July 17, 1942, both in SSW Papers, Box 68/8, AJHS.

28. "I Am An American," *Opinion* (July 1942): 5.

29. Memo by Leon A. Kubowitzki to Dr. Wise, Dr. Goldmann, Rabbi Miller, Dr. Perlzweig, Mr. Robinson, Dr. Tartakower, Mr. James W. Wise, Aug. 21, 1942, WJCC, C6/4, AJA.

30. Memo to Dr. Wise, Mr. Lipsky, Mr. Sherman, Mr. Boraisha, Mr. Caplan, cc: Dr. Goldmann, Rabbi Miller, Dr. Robinson, From: Dr. Kubowitzki, Aug. 26, 1942, WJCC, C6/4, AJA; Caplan and Boraisha to Dr. Kubowitzki, Aug. 28, 1942, 185-A, Box 4, AJA.

31. Quoted in Jonathan D. Sarna, *JPS: The Americanization of Jewish Culture, 1888–1988* (Philadelphia, 1989), 186–87.

32. Text of telegram in Raul Hilberg, *Perpetrators, Victims, Bystanders: The Jewish Catastrophe 1933–1945* (New York, 1992), 238–39. Morse, who discovered the telegram, cited one of its later formulations, edited to conform to English usage, in *While Six Million Died*, 8. See also the more recent descriptions by Breitman and Kraut, *American Refugee Policy*, 146–66; Lookstein, *Were We Our Brothers' Keepers?*, 107–145; and Hilberg, *Perpetrators, Victims, Bystanders*, 238–48.

33. See Raya Cohen, *The Story of Witnesses to Destruction: Jewish Emissaries in Switzerland, 1939–1942* (in Hebrew) (Tel Aviv: Am Oved, 1999).

34. Memo of Elbridge Durbrow of the European Division, Aug. 13, 1942, cited in Breitman and Kraut, *American Refugee Policy*, 149; Note by Paul Culbertson, assistant chief of the European Division, cited in Morse, *While Six Million Died*, 9.

35. Morse, *While Six Million Died*, 8–9.

36. Bernard Wasserstein, *Britain and the Jews of Europe* (New York and Oxford, 1979), 168–69, which also gives the reaction of the Foreign Office to the Riegner message. Gilbert, *Auschwitz and the Allies*, 59–60. Telegram from Silverman to Wise, Aug. 24, 1942, WJCC, Alphabetical Files—Switzerland, 184 A, Box 1, AJA. For clearance by State and War Departments, see Wyman, *Abandonment of the Jews*, 44.

37. Wise to Welles, Sept. 2, 1942, SSW Papers, Box 66, AJHS; see also Wise, *Challenging Years*, 275. Wise to Frankfurter, Sept. 4, 1942, Wise to Goldmann, Sept. 4, 1942, Wise to Frankfurter, Sept. 16, 1942, all in SSW Papers, Box 109, AJHS. According to Wyman, a notation on Wise's letter at the State Department indicates that Welles phoned Wise on Sept. 3rd. *Abandonment of the Jews*, 362 n10.

38. "Copy of Cablegram Sent to Dr. Jacob Rosenheim, of Agudas Israel, from Berne Switzerland, Sept. 4, 1942." Sent to him, decoded, from State Department in Washington. SSW Papers, Box 82/6, AJHS. See also Kranzler, *Thy Brother's Blood*, 91–2.

39. Wise to Fanny Mayer Korn, Sept. 9, 1942, in Voss, ed., *Stephen S. Wise*, 250. On the request for the Vatican's confirmation of the reports, see Wyman, *Abandonment of the Jews*, 49; and Breitman and Kraut, *American Refugee Policy*, 153–54.

40. Wise to Frankfurter, Sept. 16, 1942, SSW Papers, Box 109, AJHS; Wyman, *Abandonment of the Jews*, 47.

41. Wise to Frankfurter, Sept. 4, 1942, SSW Papers, Box 109, AJHS.

42. Wise to Frankfurter, Sept. 16, 1942, SSW Papers, Box 109, AJHS.

43. Ibid. and Wise to Goldmann, Sept. 4, 1942, SSW Papers, Box 109, AJHS.

44. Lichtheim to Lauterbach, Aug. 30, 1942, enclosing the report, in Henry Friedlander and Sybil Milton, eds., *Archives of the Holocaust*, vol. 4, ed. Francis Nicosia (New York, 1990), 61–63. For a detailed account of the report and its background, see Cohen, *The Story of Witnesses to Destruction*.

45. "Memo from Dr. M. L. Perlzweig," WJCC, Alphabetical Files—Switzerland, 184 A, Box 1, AJA.

46. Wise to Bakstansky, Sept. 29, 1942, SSW Papers, Box 104, AJHS.

47. Minutes of WJC Advisory Council on European Jewish Affairs, Oct. 28, 1942, WJCC, D 93/1, AJA. Other speakers included Rabbi Isaac Lewin of Agudat Israel, Vitalis Nachmias, Dr. Hugo Marx, Dr. Edward Kleinlerer, Rabbi Isaac Rubinstein, Prof. Robert Mosse, Dr. Kubowitzki.

48. Wise to FDR, Dec. 2, 1942, SSW Papers, Box 68/8, AJHS; Wise to Niles, Dec. 2, 1942, SSW Papers, Box 118, AJHS; Minutes of Meeting on European Affairs, Nov. 5, 1942, WJCC, D 92/2, AJA.

49. Wise to FDR, Dec. 2, 1942, SSW Papers, Box 68/8, AJHS.

50. On FDR's reluctance to meet the Jewish delegation, see Wyman, *Abandonment of the Jews*, 71; and Breitman and Kraut, *American Refugee Policy*, 243.

51. The delegation included Wise, Maurice Wertheim of the AJC, Henry Monsky of B'nai B'rith, Adolph Held of the Jewish Labor Committee, and Rabbi Israel Rosenberg of the Union of Orthodox Rabbis. The State Department vetoed a suggestion that representatives of the Synagogue Council, the American Federation of Polish Jews and the Orthodox Agudat Israel—all too militantly Jewish—join the delegation. See Wise to Tartakower, Dec. 15, 1942, WJCC, Alphabetical Files—Poland, 205 A, Box 3, AJA.

52. Memorandum with summation submitted to Roosevelt on Dec. 8, 1942, WJCC, Alphabetical Files—Poland, 205 A, Box 3, AJA.

53. Adolph Held, "Report on the Visit to the President" [Dec. 12, 1942], cited in Wyman, *Abandonment of the Jews*, 73.

54. Ibid., 72. The war crimes declaration was issued on Dec. 17, 1942 by the United States, Great Britain, and ten Allied governments in exile.

55. According to Held's account of the meeting, quoted by Penkower, *The Jews Were Expendable*, 85–86; "Jewish Delegation Press Release," Dec. 8, 1942, Morris Waldman Files, AJCA, RG 1, EXO-29, Germany/Nazism/American Jewish Congress, YIVO.

56. Wise to Tartakower, Dec. 15, 1942, WJCC, Alphabetical Files—Poland, 205 A, Box 3, AJA. Held of the Jewish Labor Committee wrote up a less enthusiastic report. See Wyman, *Abandonment of the Jews*, 72–73.

57. Wise to Niles, Dec. 9, 1942, SSW Papers, Box 118, AJHS.

58. Ciechanowski to Tartakower (with note attached), March 24, 1943, WJCC, Institute of Jewish Affairs—Jacob Robinson's Papers, 1936–1951, U 320, Box 4, AJA.

59. Mordecai Tenenbaum-Tamaroff, *Pages From Fire: Dappim Min Hadleka* (in Hebrew) (Yad Vashem, Beit Lohamei Hagetaot, HaKibbutz HaMehuchad, n.d.), 60, diary entry dated March 31, 1943 (my translation). Aryeh (Leibel Weinstein) was active in the Jewish underground and HaShomer HaTzair. None of his work survived.

60. Alexander S. Kohanski, ed., *The American Jewish Conference: Organization and Proceedings of the First Session, 29 August to 2 September 1943* (New York, 1944), 79.

61. Stephen S. Wise, "The American Jewish Conference," in *As I See It*, 67.

62. Wise, "The American Jewish Conference," in *As I See It*, 78.

63. "On Being An American," Address of Mr. Justice Felix Frankfurter on "I Am An American Day" in the District of Columbia, May 21, 1944, SSW Papers, Box 109, AJHS. Frankfurter had been awarded a Medal of Honor as a foreign-born American back in 1938. See Wise to Frankfurter, May 19, 1938, SSW Papers, Box 109, AJHS.

64. Dr. Maurice Perlzweig, who until 1942 was chairman of the British section of the WJC, was head of the department of international affairs of the WJC in New York in 1943. See Alexander S. Kohanski, ed., *The American Jewish Conference: Organization and Proceedings of the First Session, 29 August to 2 September 1943* (New York, 1944), 1–6. The American Jewish Conference's Committee on the Rescue of European Jewry, of which Perlzweig was a member, was established at the very last moment in response to domestic criticism that the leadership translated as a sign that "the delegates and the community wanted action in this field." Kohanski, ed., *The American Jewish Conference: Proceedings of the Second Session, 3–5 December 1944*, Pittsburgh, Pa. (New York, 1945), 217.

65. Nahum Goldmann, quoted in Berman, *Nazism, the Jews and American Zionism*, 98–99.

66. Minutes of WJC Advisory Council on European Jewish Affairs, May 10, 1943, WJCC, D 93/1, AJA.

67. Both quoted in Lookstein, *Were We Our Brothers' Keepers?*, 124–25.

68. See the monumental study by Tuvia Friling, *Arrow in the Dark: David Ben-Gurion, the Yishuv Leadership and Rescue Attempts during the Holocaust*, 2 vols. (in Hebrew) (Sede Boqer, 1998); Shabtai Teveth, *Ben-Gurion: The Burning Ground, 1886–1948* (Boston, 1987), 947–48; Segev, *The Seventh Million*, 102; Berman, *Nazism, the Jews and American Zionism*, 98–99.

69. Silver and Neumann in David S. Wyman, ed., *America and the Holocaust*, vol. 5: *American Jewish Disunity* (New York, 1990), 351–52. Both are paraphrases by Wyman of a document he was not permitted to reproduce.

70. Seymour Martin Lipset and Earl Raab, *Jews and the New American Scene* (Cambridge, Mass., 1995), 7.

71. "What Is Happening to the Jews of Europe," attached to a letter from Lichtheim to Montor, Aug. 13, 1942, L22/79, CZA.

72. See Raya Cohen, "Confronting the Reality of the Holocaust: Richard Lichtheim, 1939–1942," *Yad Vashem Studies* 23 (1993).

73. Shlomo Katz, "What Should We Write?" *Jewish Frontier* 7 (May 1940): 16.

bibliography

Note: Since I used the collections at the American Jewish Historical Society and at YIVO, they have been moved to the new Center for Jewish History in New York City.

Primary Sources

ARCHIVES

American Jewish Archives (AJA), Hebrew Union College, Cincinnati, Ohio
Jacob Billikopf Papers, 1900–1951
Morris M. Waldman Papers, 1912–1963
Felix M. Warburg Papers, 1895–1937
World Jewish Congress Collection, 1918–1982
   Series C: Institute of Jewish Affairs, 1925–1979
   Sub-series 1: Executive Files and Correspondence, 1926–1979
   a) Jacob Robinson Papers, 1936–1951

American Jewish Committee Archives (AJCA), Historical Documents Section, Blaustein Library, New York, N.Y.
Cyrus Adler, Chronological File
Jewish Telegraphic Agency
Minutes of Executive Committee
Selected Correspondence

American Jewish Historical Society (AJHS), Brandeis University, Waltham, Mass.
American Jewish Congress Papers
Stephen S. Wise Papers, 1893–1969

Central Zionist Archives (CZA), Jerusalem
Julian W. Mack Personal Papers (A405), 1893–1969
Political Department of the Jewish Agency (S25)

YIVO Institute for Jewish Research, New York, N.Y.
American Jewish Committee Records
Morris Waldman Files
NCRAC Files (National Community Relations Advisory Council)

DOCUMENTS, DIARIES, LETTERS AND SPEECHES

American Jewish Committee. *The Jews in Nazi Germany: The Factual Record of their Persecution by the National Socialists*. New York: American Jewish Committee, 1933; expanded edition, 1935.

Blau, Joseph L., and Salo W. Baron, eds. *The Jews of the United States, 1790–1840: A Documentary History*. 3 vols. New York: Columbia University Press, 1963.

Blum, John Morton. *From the Morgenthau Diaries: Years of Crisis, 1928–1938*. Boston: Houghton Mifflin, 1959.

Dearborn Independent. *The International Jew: The World's Foremost Problem*. Dearborn, Mich.: Dearborn Publishing Company, 1920. Vol. 1: *The International Jew;* Vol. 2: *Jewish Activities in the United States;* Vol. 3: *Jewish Influences in American Life;* Vol. 4: *Aspects of Jewish Power in the United States*.

Dobkowski, Michael N., ed. *The Politics of Indifference: A Documentary History of Holocaust Victims in America*. Washington, D.C.: University Press of America, 1982.

Documents on German Foreign Policy, 1918–1945. Series C 1933–1937, vol. 1. Washington, D.C.: 1957.

Domarus, Max, ed. *Hitler: Speeches and Proclamations*. Vol. 1: *The Years 1932 to 1934*. Trans. Mary Fran Gilbert. Wauconda, Ill.: Bolchazy-Carducci Publishers, 1990.

Freedman, Max, ed. *Roosevelt and Frankfurter: Their Correspondence 1928–1945*. Boston: Little, Brown, 1967.

Friedlander, Henry, and Sybil Milton, general eds. *Archives of the Holocaust*. 19 vols. New York: Garland Publishing, 1990–1993.

Ickes, Harold L. *The Secret Diary of Harold L. Ickes*. 3 vols. New York: Simon and Schuster, 1954.

Klemperer, Victor. *The Diaries of Victor Klemperer, 1942–1945*. London: Weidenfeld and Nicolson, 1999.

———. *I Will Bear Witness: The Diaries of Victor Klemperer, 1933–1941*. Abridged and translated from the German edition by Martin Chalmers. London: Weidenfeld & Nicolson, 1998.

Kohanski, Alexander S., ed. *The American Jewish Conference: Organization and Proceedings of the First Session, August 29 to September 2, 1943*. New York: American Jewish Conference, 1944.

———. *The American Jewish Conference: Proceedings of the Second Session, December 3–5, 1944, Pittsburgh, Pa.* New York: American Jewish Conference, 1945.

Lash, Joseph P. *From the Diaries of Felix Frankfurter*. New York: W. W. Norton, 1975.

Mendes-Flohr, Paul R., and Jehuda Reinharz, eds. *The Jew in the Modern World: A Documentary History*. New York: Oxford University Press, 1980.

Moffat, Jay Pierrepont. *The Moffat Papers, 1919–1943*. Ed. Nancy H. Hooker. Cambridge, Mass.: Harvard University Press, 1956.

Nixon, Edgar B., ed. *Franklin Delano Roosevelt and Foreign Affairs: Selected Papers from the Franklin D. Roosevelt Library at Hyde Park*. 3 vols. Cambridge, Mass.: Belknap Press of Harvard University Press, 1969.

Polier, Justine Wise, and James Waterman Wise, eds. *The Personal Letters of Stephen Wise*. Boston: Beacon Press, 1956.

Reichsbund jüdischer Frontsoldaten, ed. *Kriegsbriefe gefallener Jude*. Berlin, 1935.

Reznikoff, Charles, ed. *Louis Marshall: Champion of Liberty*. 2 vols. Philadelphia: JPS, 1957.

Robinson, Ira, ed. *Cyrus Adler: Selected Letters*. 2 vols. Philadelphia and New York: JPS and the Jewish Theological Seminary of America, 1985.

Rosenman, Samuel, ed. *The Public Papers and Addresses of Franklin D. Roosevelt.* 13 vols. New York: Random House, 1938–1950.

Schappes, Morris U. *A Documentary History of the Jews in the United States, 1654–1875.* New York: Citadel Press, 1950.

Union of American Hebrew Congregations (UAHC). *Proceedings 1881.*

Urofsky, Melvin, and David Levy, eds. *Letters of Louis D. Brandeis: Progressive and Zionist.* 5 vols. Albany: State University of New York Press, 1972–1978.

U.S. Congress. House Committee on Immigration and Naturalization. *Review of Refusal of Visas by Consular Officers.* 73rd Cong., 1st sess., 1933. Washington, D.C.: U.S. Government Printing Office, 1933.

U.S. Congress. *Admission of German Refugee Children. "Joint Hearings Before a Subcommittee of the Committee on Immigration, United States Senate and a Subcommittee of the Committee on Immigration and Naturalization, House of Representatives, on S.J. Res. 64 and H.J. Res. 168—Joint Resolutions to Authorize the Admission into the United States of a Limited Number of German Refugee Children."* 76th Cong., 1st sess., 1939. Washington, D.C.: U.S. Government Printing Office, 1939.

U.S. *Congressional Record.* Washington, D.C.: U.S. Government Printing Office.

U.S. Department of State. *Foreign Relations of the United States: Diplomatic Papers.* Vols. 1–3. Washington, D.C.: U.S. Government Printing Office, 1948–1950.

Voss, Carl H., ed. *Stephen S. Wise, Servant of the People: Selected Letters.* Philadelphia: JPS, 1970.

Wyman, David S., ed. *America and the Holocaust.* Vol. 5: *American Jewish Disunity.* New York: Garland Publishing, 1990.

Secondary Sources

BOOKS

Abraham, David. *The Collapse of the Weimar Republic: Political Economy and Crisis.* 2nd ed. New York and London: Holmes & Meier, 1986.

Adler, Cyrus. *I Have Considered the Days.* Philadelphia: JPS, 1941.

———. *Jacob H. Schiff.* 2 vols. Garden City, N.Y.: Doubleday, Doran, 1928.

Adler, Cyrus, ed. *The Voice of America on Kishineff.* Philadelphia: Jewish Publication Society of America, 1904.

Adler, Cyrus, and Aaron M. Margalith. *With Firmness in the Right: American Diplomatic Action Affecting Jews, 1840–1945.* New York: American Jewish Committee, 1946.

Ahlstrom, Sidney E. *A Religious History of the American People.* New Haven, Conn.: Yale University Press, 1972.

Alexander, Edward. *Irving Howe: Socialist, Critic, Jew.* Bloomington: Indiana University Press, 1998.

American Jewish Congress. *The Case of Civilization against Hitlerism.* New York: R. O. Ballou, 1934.

Arendt, Hannah. *The Origins of Totalitarianism.* New edition with added prefaces. San Diego: Harcourt Brace Jovanovich, 1979.

Arieli, Yehoshua. *History and Politics* (in Hebrew). Tel Aviv: Am Oved, 1992.

Aschheim, Steven E. *Brothers and Strangers: The East European Jew in German and German Jewish Consciousness, 1800–1923.* Madison: University of Wisconsin Press, 1982.

Athans, Mary Christine. *The Coughlin-Fahey Connection.* New York: Peter Lang, 1991.

Auerbach, Jerold. *Rabbis and Lawyers: The Journey from Torah to Constitution.* Bloomington: Indiana University Press, 1990.

Azcarate, Pablo. *The League of Nations and National Minorities.* Washington, D.C.: Carnegie Endowment for International Peace, 1945.

Ball-Kaduri, Kurt Jakob. *Das Leben der Juden in Deutschland im Jahre 1933.* Frankfurt am Main: Europaische Verlagsanstalt, 1963.

Baruch, Bernard M. *Baruch.* Vol. 2: *The Public Years.* New York: Holt, Rinehart & Winston, 1960.

Bauer, Yehuda. *American Jewry and the Holocaust: The American Jewish Joint Distribution Committee, 1939–1945.* Detroit: Wayne State University Press, 1981.

Bell, Leland V. *In Hitler's Shadow: The Anatomy of American Nazism.* Port Washington, N.Y.: Kensal Press, 1973.

Bennett, Marion T. *American Immigration Policies.* Washington, D.C.: Public Affairs Press, 1963.

Berk, Stephen M. *Year of Crisis, Year of Hope: Russian Jewry and the Pogroms of 1881–1882.* Westport, Conn.: Greenwood Press, 1985.

Berman, Aaron. *Nazism, the Jews, and American Zionism, 1933–1948.* Detroit: Wayne State University Press, 1990.

Bernard, W. S. *American Immigration Policy: A Reappraisal.* 1950. Reprint, Port Washington, N.Y.: Kennikat, 1969.

Biale, David. *Power and Powerlessness in Jewish History.* New York: Schocken Books, 1986.

Birmingham, Stephen. *Our Crowd: The Great Jewish Families of New York.* New York: Harper, 1967.

Birnbaum, Pierre, and Ira Katznelson. *Paths of Emancipation: Jews, States, and Citizenship.* Princeton, N.J.: Princeton University Press, 1995.

Bloch, Marc. *The Historian's Craft.* Trans. from the French by Peter Putnam. Manchester: Manchester University Press, 1954.

Bloom, Sol. *The Autobiography of Sol Bloom.* New York: G. P. Putnam's Sons, 1948.

Boas, Franz. *The Mind of Primitive Man.* New York: Macmillan, 1911.

———. *Race and Democratic Society.* New York: J. J. Augustin, 1945.

Bogen, Boris D. *Jewish Philanthropy.* 1917. Reprint, Montclair, N.J.: Patterson Smith, 1969.

Bolkosky, Sidney M. *The Distorted Image: German-Jewish Perceptions of Germans and Germany, 1918–1935.* New York: Elsevier Scientific Publishing Company, 1975.

Brandeis, Louis D. *The Jewish Problem: How to Solve It.* New York: Zionist Essay Publication Committee, 1915.

Breitman, Richard, and Alan M. Kraut. *American Refugee Policy and European Jewry, 1933–1945.* Bloomington: Indiana University Press, 1987.

Brown, Haywood, and George Britt. *Christians Only: A Study in Prejudice.* 1931. Reprint, New York: Da Capo Press, 1974.

Burns, James MacGregor. *Roosevelt: The Lion and the Fox.* New York: Harcourt, Brace and Company, 1956.

Burt, Robert A. *Two Jewish Justices: Outcasts in the Promised Land.* Berkeley: University of California Press, 1988.

Cahan, Abraham. *The Rise of David Levinsky.* 1917. Reprint with an introduction and notes by Jules Chametzky, New York: Penguin Books, 1993.

Chernow, Ron. *The Warburgs: The Twentieth-Century Odyssey of a Remarkable Jewish Family.* New York: Random House, 1993.

Child, Clifton James. *The German-American in Politics, 1914–1917.* Madison: University of Wisconsin Press, 1939.

Cohen, David Steven, ed. *America, the Dream of My Life.* New Brunswick, N.J.: Rutgers University Press, 1990.

Cohen, Michael J. *Palestine: Retreat from the Mandate.* London and New York: Holmes & Meier, 1978.

———. *Palestine and the Great Powers.* Princeton, N.J.: Princeton University Press, 1982.

Cohen, Naomi W. *American Jews and the Zionist Idea.* N.p.: Ktav Publishing House, 1975.

———. *Dual Heritage: The Public Career of Oscar S. Straus.* Philadelphia: JPS, 1969.

———. *Encounter with Emancipation: The German Jews in the United States, 1830–1914.* Philadelphia: JPS, 1984.

———. *Not Free to Desist: The American Jewish Committee, 1906–1966.* Philadelphia: JPS, 1972.

Cohn, Norman. *Warrant for Genocide: The Myth of the World-Conspiracy and the Protocols of the Elders of Zion.* New York: Harper & Row, 1967.

Cohen, Raya. *The Story of Witnesses to Destruction: Jewish Emissaries in Switzerland, 1939–1942* (in Hebrew). Tel Aviv: Am Oved, 1999.

Crèvecoeur, Michel-Guillaume St. John De. *Letters from an American Farmer.* New York: E. P. Dutton, 1957.

Curti, Merle. *The Roots of American Loyalty.* 1946. Reprint, New York: Atheneum, 1968.

Dallek, Robert. *Franklin Roosevelt and American Foreign Policy, 1932–1945.* Oxford: Oxford University Press, 1979.

Daniels, Jonathan. *White House Witness, 1942–1945.* Garden City, N.Y.: Doubleday, 1975.

Diamond, Sander A. *The Nazi Movement in the United States, 1924–1941.* Ithaca, N.Y.: Cornell University Press, 1974.

Dinnerstein, Leonard. *Anti-Semitism in America.* New York: Oxford University Press, 1994.

———. *The Leo Frank Case.* New York: Columbia University Press, 1968.

———. *Uneasy at Home: Antisemitism and the American Jewish Experience.* New York: Columbia University Press, 1987.

Divine, Robert A. *American Immigration Policy, 1924–1952.* New Haven, Conn.: Yale University Press, 1957.

Dobkowski, Michael N. *The Tarnished Dream: The Basis of American Anti-Semitism.* Westport, Conn.: Greenwood Press, 1979.

Eisen, Arnold M. *The Chosen People in America: A Study of Jewish Religious Ideology.* Bloomington: Indiana University Press, 1983.

Elbogen, Ismar. *A Century of Jewish Life.* Philadelphia: JPS, 1966.

Feingold, Henry L. *Bearing Witness: How America and Its Jews Responded to the Holocaust.* Syracuse, N.Y.: Syracuse University Press, 1995.

———. *The Politics of Rescue: The Roosevelt Administration and the Holocaust, 1938–1945.* New York: Walden Press, 1970.

———. *A Time for Searching: Entering the Mainstream, 1920–1945.* Baltimore: Johns Hopkins University Press, 1992.

———. *Zion in America: The Jewish Experience from Colonial Times to the Present.* New York: Twayne Publishers, 1974.

Feis, Herbert. *The Diplomacy of the Dollar, 1919–1932.* 1950. Reprint, New York: Norton, 1966.

Feldman, Egal. *Dual Destinies: The Jewish Encounter with Protestant America, 1920–1945.* Baltimore: Johns Hopkins University Press, 1992.

Felsenthal, Emma. *Bernhard Felsenthal, Teacher in Israel: Selections from His Writings, with Biographical Sketch and Bibliography.* New York: Oxford University Press, 1924.

Ferrell, Robert H. *American Diplomacy in the Great Depression: Hoover-Stimson Foreign Policy, 1929–1933.* 1957. New York: W. W. Norton, 1970.

Field, Carter. *Bernard Baruch: Park Bench Statement.* New York: McGraw-Hill, 1944.

Finger, Seymour Maxwell, ed. *American Jewry during the Holocaust.* New York: American Jewish Commission on the Holocaust, 1984.

Finkelstein, Louis, ed. *The Jews.* 1956. 4th ed. New York: Schocken Books, 1971.

Friling, Tuvia. *Arrow in the Dark: David Ben-Gurion, the Yishuv Leadership and Rescue Attempts during the Holocaust* (in Hebrew). 2 vols. Sede Boqer: Ben-Gurion University of the Negev Press, 1998.

Fraenkel, Daniel. *On the Edge of the Abyss: Zionist Policy and the Plight of the German Jews, 1933–1938* (in Hebrew). Jerusalem: Magnes Press, 1994.

Frankel, Jonathan. *The Damascus Affair: "Ritual Murder," Politics, and the Jews in 1840.* Cambridge: Cambridge University Press, 1997.

———. *Prophecy and Politics: Socialism, Nationalism, and the Russian Jews, 1862–1917.* Cambridge: Cambridge University Press, 1981.

Frankfurter, Felix. *Felix Frankfurter Reminisces.* Recorded in talks with Dr. Harlan B. Phillips. Garden City, N.Y.: Doubleday, 1962.

Fraser, Steven. *Labor Will Rule: Sidney Hillman and the Rise of American Labor.* New York: Free Press, 1991.

Friedländer, Saul. *Nazi Germany and the Jews.* Vol. 1: *The Years of Persecution, 1933–1939.* New York: HarperCollins, 1997.

Friedman, Lee M. *Early American Jews.* Cambridge, Mass.: Harvard University Press, 1934.

———. *Jewish Pioneers and Patriots.* New York: Macmillan, 1943.

Friedman, Saul S. *No Haven for the Oppressed: United States Policy toward Jewish Refugees, 1938–1945.* Detroit: Wayne State University Press, 1973.

Fuchs, Lawrence H. *The Political Behavior of American Jews.* Glencoe, Ill.: Free Press, 1956.

Gal, Allon. *Brandeis of Boston.* Cambridge, Mass.: Harvard University Press, 1980.

Gamson, William A. *Power and Discontent.* Homewood, Ill.: Dorsey Press, 1968.

Gartner, Lloyd P. *History of the Jews of Cleveland.* Cleveland: Western Reserve Historical Society and the Jewish Theological Seminary of America, 1978.

Gelber, Yoav. *New Homeland: Immigration and Absorption of Central European Jews 1933–1948* (in Hebrew). Jerusalem: Yad Yitshak Ben-Tsevi, 1990.

Gerber, David A., ed. *Anti-Semitism in American History.* Urbana: University of Illinois Press, 1987.

Gilbert, Martin. *Auschwitz and the Allies.* New York: Holt, Rinehart and Winston, 1981.

Gilbert, Martin, and Richard Gott. *The Appeasers.* Boston: Houghton Mifflin, 1963.

Gilman, Sander L. *Jewish Self-Hatred: Anti-Semitism and the Hidden Language of the Jews.* Baltimore: Johns Hopkins University Press, 1986.

Ginsberg, Benjamin. *The Fatal Embrace: Jews and the State.* Chicago: University of Chicago Press, 1993.

Glanz, Rudolf. *Jew and Irish: Historic Group Relations and Immigration*. New York: Waldon Press, 1966.

———. *The Jew in Old American Folklore*. New York: Waldon Press, 1961.

———. *Studies in Judaica Americana*. New York: Ktav Publishing House, 1970.

Glazer, Nathan. *American Judaism*. 2nd rev. ed. Chicago: University of Chicago Press, 1989.

———. *The Social Basis of American Communism*. New York: Harcourt, Brace, 1961.

Glazer, Nathan, Joseph L. Blau, Herman D. Stein, and Oscar and Mary F. Handlin. *The Characteristics of American Jews*. New York: Jewish Education Committee Press, 1965.

Goebel, Dorothy B., ed. *American Foreign Policy: A Documentary Survey, 1776–1960*. New York: Holt, Rinehart, and Winston, 1961.

Goldmann, Nahum. *The Autobiography of Nahum Goldmann: Sixty Years of Jewish Life*. New York: Holt, Rinehart and Winston, 1969.

Goldscheider, Calvin, and Alan Zuckerman, eds. *The Transformation of the Jews*. Chicago: University of Chicago Press, 1984.

Gordon, Albert I. *Jews in Transition*. Minneapolis: University of Minnesota Press, 1949.

Gordon, Milton S. *Assimilation in American Life*. New York: Oxford University Press, 1964.

Goren, Arthur A. *New York Jews and the Quest for Community*. New York: Columbia University Press, 1970.

Gossett, Thomas F. *Race; the History of an Idea in America*. New York: Schocken Books, 1965.

Gottheil, Richard G. *Zionism*. Philadelphia: Jewish Publication Society of America, 1914.

Gottlieb, Moshe R. *American Anti-Nazi Resistance, 1933–1941: An Historical Analysis*. New York: Ktav Publishing, 1982.

Gottwald, Robert A. *Die deutsch-amerikanischen Beziehungen in der Ära Stresemann*. Berlin-Dahlem: Colloquium Verlag, 1965.

Grant, Madison. *The Passing of the Great Race or The Racial Basis of European History*. New York: C. Scribner's Sons, 1916.

Hacker, Louis M., and Mark D. Hirsch. *Proskauer: His Life and Times*. University: University of Alabama Press, 1978.

Halperin, Samuel. *The Political World of American Zionism*. Detroit: Wayne State University Press, 1961.

Halpern, Ben. *The American Jew: A Zionist Analysis*. New York: Theodor Herzl Foundation, 1956.

Hamilton, Richard F. *Who Voted for Hitler?* Princeton, N.J.: Princeton University Press, 1982.

Hand, Samuel B. *Counsel and Advise: A Political Biography of Samuel I. Rosenman*. New York: Garland Publishing, 1979.

Handlin, Oscar. *Adventures in Freedom: Three Hundred Years of Jewish Life in America*. Port Washington, N.Y.: Kennikat Press, 1971.

———. *Boston's Immigrants, 1790–1865: A Study in Acculturation*. Cambridge, Mass.: Belknap Press of Harvard University Press, 1959.

Hecht, Ben. *A Child of the Century*. New York: Simon and Schuster, 1955.

Heiden, Konrad. *Der Fuehrer: Hitler's Rise to Power*. 1944. Reprint, London: H. Pordes, 1967.

Herzberg, Arthur. *The Jews in America*. New York: Simon and Schuster, 1989.

Herzstein, Robert E. *Roosevelt and Hitler: Prelude to War.* New York: Paragon House, 1989.

Hicks, John D. *Republican Ascendancy, 1921–1933.* New York: Harper Torchbooks, 1960.

Higham, John. *Send These to Me: Jews and Other Immigrants in Urban America.* Rev. ed. Baltimore: Johns Hopkins University Press, 1984.

———. *Strangers in the Land: Patterns of American Nativism, 1860–1925.* 2nd ed. New Brunswick, N.J.: Rutgers University Press, 1988.

Hilberg, Raul. *The Destruction of the European Jews.* New York: Harper Torchbooks, 1961.

———. *Perpetrators, Victims, Bystanders: The Jewish Catastrophe, 1933–1945.* New York: HarperCollins, 1992.

Hildebrand, Klaus. *The Third Reich.* Trans. P. S. Falla. London: George Allen & Unwin, 1984.

Hirsch, David E. *Rabbi Emil G. Hirsch: The Reform Advocate.* Chicago: Whitehall, 1968.

Hirshler, Eric E., ed. *Jews from Germany in the United States.* New York: Farrar, Straus and Cudahy, 1955.

Hofstadter, Richard. *The Age of Reform: From Bryan to F.D.R.* New York: Vintage Books, 1955.

———. *The American Political Tradition and the Men Who Made It.* New York: A. A. Knopf, 1948.

Hoover, Herbert. *Memoirs of Herbert Hoover: The Cabinet and the Presidency, 1920–1933.* Vol. 2. New York: Macmillan, 1951–1952.

Hopkins, Charles Howard. *History of the Y.M.C.A. in North America.* New York: Association Press, 1951.

Horkheimer, Max. *Über die deutschen Juden: Vortrag.* Cologne: M. DuMont Schauberg, 1961.

Howe, Irving. *World of Our Fathers: The Journey of the East European Jews to America and the Life They Found and Made.* New York: Schocken Books, 1976.

Howe, Irving, and Lewis Coser. *The American Communist Party.* 1957. Reprint, New York: Da Capo Press, 1974.

Hull, Cordell. *The Memoirs of Cordell Hull.* 2 vols. New York: Macmillan, 1948.

Isaacs, Stephen D. *Jews and American Politics.* Garden City, N.Y.: Doubleday, 1974.

Jackson, J. A., ed. *Migration.* London: Cambridge University Press, 1969.

Janeway, Elizabeth. *Powers of the Weak.* New York: A. A. Knopf, 1980.

Janowsky, Oscar J. *The Jews and Minority Rights.* New York: Columbia University Press, 1933.

———. *Nationalities and National Minorities.* New York: Macmillan, 1945.

Jick, Leon A. *The Americanization of the Synagogue, 1820–1870.* Hanover, N.H.: University Press of New England, 1976.

Jonas, Manfred. *The United States and Germany: A Diplomatic History.* Ithaca, N.Y.: Cornell University Press, 1984.

Joseph, Samuel I. *Jewish Immigration to the United States from 1881 to 1910.* New York: Columbia University Press, 1914.

Kallen, Horace. *Culture and Democracy in the United States.* New York: Bloch Publishing, 1924.

Kammen, Michael. *Mystic Chords of Memory: The Transformation of Tradition in American Culture.* New York: Knopf, 1991.

Kaplan, Marion A. *Between Dignity and Despair: Jewish Life in Nazi Germany.* New York: Oxford University Press, 1998.

Kaplan, Mordecai M. *Judaism as a Civilization: Toward a Reconstruction of American-Jewish Life.* 1934. Philadelphia: JPS, 1981.

Karp, Abraham J. *Haven and Home: A History of the Jews in America.* New York: Schocken Books, 1985.

Karp, Abraham J., ed. *The Jewish Experience in America: Selected Studies from the Publications of the American Jewish Historical Society.* 5 vols. Waltham, Mass.: American Jewish Historical Society, 1969.

Katz, Jacob. *Emancipation and Assimilation: Studies in Modern Jewish History.* Farnborough Hants: Gress International, 1972.

———. *From Prejudice to Destruction: Anti-Semitism, 1700–1933.* Cambridge, Mass.: Harvard University Press, 1980.

———. *Jewish Emancipation and Self-Emancipation.* Philadelphia: JPS, 1986.

———. *Out of the Ghetto: The Social Background of Jewish Emancipation, 1770–1970.* Cambridge, Mass.: Harvard University Press, 1973.

———. *Tradition and Crisis: Jewish Society at the End of the Middle Ages* (in Hebrew). Jerusalem: Mosad Bialik, 1963.

Kirchheimer, Otto. *Political Justice: The Use and Legal Procedure for Political Ends.* 1961. Reprint, Westport, Conn.: Greenwood Press, 1980.

Knee, Stuart E. *The Concept of Zionist Dissent in the American Mind.* New York: R. Speller, 1979.

Kolb, Eberhard. *The Weimar Republic.* Trans. P. S. Falla. London: Unwin Hyman, 1988.

Kolsky, Thomas A. *Jews against Zionism: The American Council for Judaism, 1942–1948.* Philadelphia: Temple University Press, 1990.

Korn, Bertram W. *American Jewry and the Civil War.* Philadelphia: JPS, 1951.

———. *The American Reaction to the Mortara Case: 1858–1859.* Cincinnati: American Jewish Archives, 1957.

Kranzler, David. *Thy Brother's Blood: The Orthodox Jewish Response during the Holocaust.* New York: Mesorah Publications, 1987.

Landau, Moshe. *The Disappointing Alliance: Jews and Germans in the European Minorities' Congress* (in Hebrew). Tel Aviv: University of Tel Aviv, 1992.

Laqueur, Walter. *The Terrible Secret: Suppression of the Truth about Hitler's "Final Solution."* Boston: Penguin Books, 1980.

Laqueur, Walter, and Richard Breitman. *Breaking the Silence.* New York: Simon and Schuster, 1986.

Lash, Joseph P. *Dealers and Dreamers: A New Look at the New Deal.* New York: Doubleday, 1988.

Lasswell, Harold D., and Abraham, Kaplan. *Power and Society.* New Haven, Conn.: Yale University Press, 1950.

Learsi, Rufus. *The Jews in America: A History.* Cleveland: World Publishing Company, 1954.

Lederhendler, Eli. *Jewish Responses to Modernity: New Voices in America and Eastern Europe.* New York: New York University Press, 1994.

Lee, Albert. *Henry Ford and the Jews.* New York: Stein and Day, 1980.

Lee, Samuel J. *Moses of the New World: The Work of Baron de Hirsch.* New York: T. Yoseloff, 1970.

Lewisohn, Ludwig. *Up Stream: An American Chronicle.* New York: Boni and Liveright, 1922.

Linenthal, Edward T. *Preserving Memory: The Struggle to Create America's Holocaust Museum.* New York: Viking, 1995.

Link, Werner. *Die amerikanische Stabilisierungspolitik in Deutschland, 1921–1932.* Düsseldorf: Droste Verlag, 1970.

Lipset, Seymour Martin. *Jews and the New American Scene.* Cambridge, Mass.: Harvard University Press, 1995.

Lipset, Seymour Martin, and Earl Raab. *The Politics of Unreason: Right-Wing Extremism in America, 1790–1970.* New York: Harper & Row, 1970.

Lipstadt, Deborah E. *Beyond Belief: The American Press and the Coming of the Holocaust, 1933–1945.* New York: Free Press, 1986.

Lookstein, Haskel. *Were We Our Brothers' Keepers? The Public Response of American Jews to the Holocaust, 1938–1944.* New York: Vintage, 1988.

Luebke, Frederick C. *Bonds of Loyalty.* De Kalb: Northern Illinois University Press, 1974.

Luzzatti, Luigi. *God in Freedom.* Trans. Alfonson Arbib-Costa. With American Supplementary Chapters, ed. Max J. Kohler. New York: Macmillan, 1930.

Marcus, Jacob Radar. *Early American Jewry.* 2 vols. Philadelphia: JPS, 1951, 1953.

———. *United States Jewry, 1776–1985.* Vol. 2: *The Germanic Period.* Detroit: Wayne State University Press, 1991.

Margaliot, Avraham. *Between Rescue and Annihilation: Studies in the History of Germany Jewry 1932–1938* (in Hebrew). Jerusalem: Yad Vashem, 1990.

Marrus, Michael R. *The Holocaust in History.* London: Weidenfeld & Nicolson, 1988.

———. *The Unwanted: European Refugees in the Twentieth Century.* New York: Oxford University Press, 1985.

Mason, Alpheus T. *Brandeis: A Free Man's Life.* New York: Viking Press, 1946.

Mayo, Louise. *The Ambivalent Image: Nineteenth-Century America's Perception of the Jew.* Rutherford, N.J.: Fairleigh Dickinson University Press, 1988.

McCall, Samuel Walker. *Patriotism of the American Jew.* New York: Plymouth Press, 1924.

McNeil, William C. *American Money and the Weimar Republic: Economics and Politics on the Eve of the Great Depression.* New York: Columbia University Press, 1986.

Medoff, Rafael. *The Deafening Silence.* New York: Shapolsky Publishers, 1987.

Merriam, Charles. *Political Power.* 1934. Reprint, New York: Collier Books, 1964.

Moore, Deborah Dash. *At Home in America: Second Generation New York Jews.* New York: Columbia University Press, 1981.

———. *B'nai Brith and the Challenge of Ethnic Leadership.* Albany: State University of New York Press, 1981.

Morgenthau, Hans J. *Politics in the 20th Century: The Impasse of American Foreign Policy.* Vol. 2. Chicago: University of Chicago Press, 1962.

Morgenthau, Henry. *All in a Lifetime.* Garden City, N.Y.: Doubleday, Page and Company, 1922.

Morgenthau, Henry, III. *Mostly Morgenthaus: A Family History.* New York: Ticknor & Fields, 1991.

Morrison, David. *Heroes, Antiheroes and the Holocaust: American Jewry and Historical Choice.* Jerusalem and London: Milah Press, 1995.

Morse, Arthur D. *While Six Million Died: A Chronicle of American Apathy.* New York: Random House, 1968.

Mosse, George L. *The Culture of Western Europe: The Nineteenth and Twentieth Centuries.* Chicago: Rand McNally, 1961.

———. *German Jews beyond Judaism.* Bloomington: Indiana University Press, 1985.

Murphy, Bruce A. *The Brandeis/Frankfurter Connection: The Secret Political Activities of the Two Supreme Court Justices.* Garden City, N.Y.: Anchor Books, 1982.

Murphy, Robert. *Diplomat among Warriors.* London: Collins, 1964.

Novick, Peter. *The Holocaust in American Life.* New York: Houghton Mifflin, 1999.

Nugent, Walter. *The Tolerant Populists.* Chicago: University of Chicago Press, 1963.

Nurenberger, M. J. *The Scared and the Doomed: The Jewish Establishment vs. the Six Million.* Oakville, N.Y.: Mosaic Press, 1985.

Overdyke, W. Darrell. *The Know-Nothing Party in the South.* Baton Rouge: Louisiana State University Press, 1950.

Parenti, Michael. *Power and the Powerless.* New York: St. Martin's Press, 1978.

Parrish, Michael E. *Felix Frankfurter and His Times: The Reform Years.* New York: Free Press, 1982.

Paucker, Arnold. *Der jüdische Abwehrkampf gegen Antisemitismus und Nationalsozialismus in den letzten Jahren der Weimarer Republik.* Hamburg: Leibniz-Verlag, 1969.

Penkower, Monty Noam. *The Jews Were Expendable: Free World Diplomacy and the Holocaust.* Urbana: University of Illinois Press, 1983.

Peters, Madison C. *The Jew as a Patriot.* New York: Baker and Taylor, 1902.

———. *Justice to the Jew.* London and New York: F. T. Neely, 1899.

Peukert, Detlev J. K. *The Weimar Republic: The Crisis of Classical Modernity.* Trans. Richard Deveson. New York: Hill and Wang, 1992.

Porat, Dina. *The Blue and the Yellow Stars of David: The Zionist Leadership in Palestine and the Holocaust, 1939–1945.* Cambridge, Mass.: Harvard University Press, 1990.

Prothro, James W. *The Dollar Decade: Business Ideas in the 1920s.* Baton Rouge: Louisiana State University Press, 1954.

Read, Anthony, and David Fisher. *Kristallnacht: Unleashing the Holocaust.* New York: Papermac, 1991.

Reinharz, Jehuda. *Fatherland or Promised Land: The Dilemma of the German Jew, 1893–1914.* Ann Arbor: University of Michigan Press, 1975.

Reinharz, Jehuda, ed. *Living with Antisemitism: Modern Jewish Responses.* Hanover, N.H.: University Press of New England, 1987.

Reinharz, Jehuda, and Walter Schatzberg, eds. *The Jewish Response to German Culture: From Enlightenment to the Second World War.* Hanover, N.H.: University Press of New England, 1985.

Ribalow, Harold U., ed. *Mid-Century: An Anthology of Jewish Life and Culture in Our Times.* New York: Beechhurst Press, 1955.

Ribuffo, Leo P. *The Old Christian Right: The Protestant Far Right from the Great Depression to the Cold War.* Philadelphia: Temple University Press, 1983.

Riis, Jacob A. *How the Other Half Lives: Studies among the Tenements of New York.* 1890. Reprint, New York: Penguin Books, 1997.

Rischin, Moses. *The Promised City: New York's Jews, 1870–1914.* 1962. Cambridge, Mass.: Harvard University Press, 1977.

Rosenman, Samuel I. *Working with Roosevelt.* New York: Harper, 1952.

Rosenstock, Morton. *Louis Marshall: Defender of Jewish Rights.* Detroit: Wayne State University Press, 1965.

Roskies, David G. *Against the Apocalypse: Responses to Catastrophes in Modern Jewish Culture.* Cambridge, Mass.: Harvard University Press, 1984.

Rubinstein, William D. *The Myth of Rescue: Why the Democracies Could Not Have Saved More Jews from the Nazis.* London: Routledge, 1997.

Samuels, Ernest, ed. *The Education of Henry Adams.* Boston: Houghton Mifflin, 1973.

Sanders, Ronald. *Shores of Refuge: A Hundred Years of Jewish Emigration.* New York: Schocken Books, 1988.

Sarna, Jonathan D. *JPS: The Americanization of Jewish Culture, 1888–1988.* Philadelphia: JPS, 1989.

Sarna, Jonathan D., ed. *The American Jewish Experience.* New York: Holmes and Meier, 1986.

Schlesinger, Arthur M., Jr. *The Age of Roosevelt: The Crisis of the Old Order, 1919–1933.* Boston: Houghton Mifflin, 1957.

———. *The Age of Roosevelt: The Politics of Upheaval.* Boston: Houghton Mifflin, 1960.

Scholnick, Myron I. *The New Deal and Anti-Semitism in America.* New York: Garland Publishing, 1990.

Schorsch, Ismar, *Jewish Reactions to German Anti-Semitism, 1870–1914.* New York: Columbia University Press and JPS, 1972.

Segev, Tom. *The Seventh Million: The Israelis and the Holocaust.* Trans. Haim Watzman. New York: Hill and Wang, 1993.

Shandler, Jeffrey. *While America Watches: Televising the Holocaust.* New York: Oxford University Press, 1999.

Shapiro, Yonathan. *The Leadership of the American Zionist Organization, 1897–1930.* Urbana: University of Illinois Press, 1971.

Sherman, C. Bezalel. *The Jews within American Society.* Detroit: Wayne State University Press, 1965.

Silberman, Charles. *A Certain People: American Jews and Their Lives Today.* New York: Summit Books, 1985.

Simonhoff, Harry. *Under Strange Skies.* New York: Philosophical Library, 1953.

Sklare, Marshall, ed. *The Jews: Social Patterns of an American Group.* New York: Free Press, 1958.

Slawson, John. *Integration and Identity: The Jew on the American Scene Today.* New York: American Jewish Committee, Institute of Human Relations, 1960.

———. *The Realities of Jewish Integration.* New York: American Jewish Committee, Institute of Human Relations, 1960.

Solomon, Barbara M. *Ancestors and Immigrants: A Changing New England Tradition.* Rev. ed. Boston: Northeastern University Press, 1989.

Spargo, John. *The Jew and American Ideals.* New York: Harper and Brothers, 1922.

Steinberg, Stephen. *The Ethnic Myth: Race, Class, and Ethnicity in America.* New York: Atheneum, 1981.

Stember, Charles Herbert, et al. *Jews in the Mind of America.* New York: Basic Books, 1966.

Stern, Selma. *The Court Jew.* Philadelphia: JPS, 1950.

Stewart, Barbara McDonald. *United States Government Policy on Refugees from Nazism, 1933–1940.* New York: Garland Publishing, 1982.

Straus, Oscar S. *The Origin of the Republican Form of Government in the United States of America.* New York: Putnam, 1885.

———. *Under Four Administrations.* Boston, New York: Houghton Mifflin, 1922.

Strong, Donald S. *Organized Anti-Semitism in America.* 1941. Reprint, Westport, Conn.: Greenwood Press, 1979.

Strong, Josiah. *Our Country: Its Possible Future and Its Present Crisis.* New York: Baker and Taylor, 1885.

Strum, Phillippa. *Louis D. Brandeis: Justice for the People.* New York: Schocken Books, 1984.

Susman, Warren I. *Culture and Commitment, 1929–1945.* New York: G. Braziller, 1973.

Synnott, Marcia Graham. *The Half-Opened Door: Discrimination and Admissions at Harvard, Yale and Princeton, 1900–1970.* Westport, Conn.: Greenwood Press, 1979.

Tenenbaum-Tamaroff, Mordecai. *Pages from Fire: Dappim Min Hadleka* (in Hebrew). Tel Aviv: Yad Vashem, Beit Lohamei Hagetaot, HaKibbutz HaMeuchad, 1947.

Teveth, Shabtai. *Ben-Gurion: The Burning Ground, 1886–1948.* Boston: Houghton Mifflin, 1987.

Tifft, Susan E., and Alex S. Jones. *The Trust: The Private and Powerful Family Behind the New York Times.* Boston: Little, Brown, and Company, 1999.

Trachtenberg, Alan. *The Incorporation of American Culture and Society in the Gilded Age.* New York: Hill and Wang, 1982.

Trachtenberg, Joshua. *The Devil and the Jews: The Medieval Conception of the Jews and Its Relation to Modern Anti-Semitism.* 1943. Reprint, Philadelphia: JPS, 1993.

Troen, Selwyn Ilan, and Benjamin Pinkus, eds. *Organizing Rescue: National Jewish Solidarity in the Modern Period.* London: Frank Cass, 1992.

Tugwell, Rexford. *The Art of Politics, as Practiced by Three Great Americans: Franklin Delano Roosevelt, Luis Munoz Marin, and Fiorello H. La Guardia.* 1958. Reprint, Westport, Conn.: Greenwood Press, 1977.

Urofsky, Melvin I. *American Zionism from Herzl to the Holocaust.* Garden City, N.Y.: Anchor Press/Doubleday, 1975.

———. *A Mind of One Piece: Brandeis and American Reform.* New York: Scribner Books, 1971.

———. *A Voice That Spoke for Justice: The Life and Times of Stephen S. Wise.* Albany: State University of New York Press, 1982.

Vago, Bela, ed. *Jewish Assimilation in Modern Times.* Boulder, Colo.: Westview Press, 1981.

Vorspan, Max, and Lloyd P. Gartner. *History of the Jews of Los Angeles.* Philadelphia: JPS, 1970.

Voss, Carl Herman. *Rabbi and Minister: The Friendship of Stephen S. Wise and John Haynes Holmes.* New York: Association Press, 1964.

Waldman, Morris D. *Nor by Power.* New York: International Universities Press, 1953.

Warren, Donald. *Radio Priest: Charles Coughlin, the Father of Hate Radio.* New York: Free Press, 1996.

Wasserstein, Bernard. *Britain and the Jews of Europe.* New York: Oxford University Press, 1979.

Weber, Max. *The Theory of Social and Economic Organization.* New York: Oxford University Press, 1947.

Weinstein, Lewis. *Masa: Odyssey of an American Jew.* Boston: Quinlan Press, 1989.

Wells, Leon Weliczker. *Who Speaks for the Vanquished? American Jewish Leaders and the Holocaust.* New York: Peter Lang, 1987.

Wenger, Beth S. *New York Jews and the Great Depression: Uncertain Promise.* New Haven, Conn.: Yale University Press, 1996.

Wertheimer, Jack. *Unwelcome Strangers: East European Jews in Imperial Germany.* New York: Oxford University Press, 1987.

Weyl, Nathaniel. *The Jew in American Politics.* New Rochelle, N.Y.: Arlington House, 1968.

White, William L. *Bernard Baruch.* New York: Harcourt, Brace, 1950.

Wilson, Joan Hoff. *American Business and Foreign Policy, 1920–1933.* Lexington: University Press of Kentucky, 1971.

Wirtz, William. *The First Fifty Years: A History of the National Council of Jewish Women.* New York: n.p., 1943.

Wise, Stephen S. *As I See It.* New York: Jewish Opinion Publishing Corporation, 1944.

———. *Challenging Years: The Autobiography of Stephen Wise.* London: East and West Library, 1951.

Wolf, Simon. *The American Jew as Patriot, Soldier and Citizen.* New York: Brentano's, 1895.

World Jewish Congress. *Unity in Dispersion: A History of the World Jewish Congress.* New York: World Jewish Congress, 1948.

Wyman, David S. *The Abandonment of the Jews: America and the Holocaust, 1941–1945.* New York: Pantheon Books, 1985.

———. *Paper Walls: America and the Refugee Crisis 1938–1941.* 1968. Reprint, New York: Pantheon Books, 1985.

Zucker, Bat-Ami. *In Search of Refuge: Jews and US Consuls in Nazi Germany, 1939–1941.* Essex: Vallentine, Mitchell (forthcoming 2000).

ARTICLES

Angress, Werner T. "The German Army's 'Judenzählung' of 1916: Genesis-Consequences-Significance." *LBIY* 23 (1978).

Arendt, Hannah. "The Jew as a Pariah: A Hidden Tradition." *JSS* 6, no. 2 (April 1944).

Ash, Steven V. "Civil War Exodus: The Jews and Grant's General Orders, No. 11." *Historian* 44 (August 1982).

Auerbach, Jerold S. "Review Essay on *Proskauer: His Life and Times.*" *AJH* 69 (September 1979).

Baldwin, Peter M. "Zionist and Non-Zionist Jews in the Last Years before the Nazi Regime." *LBIY* 27 (1982).

Bankier, David. "Hitler and the Policy-Making Process on the Jewish Question." *Holocaust and Genocide Studies* 3, no. 1 (1988).

Bauer, Yehuda. "When Did They Know?" *Midstream* 4 (1968).

Bauman, Zygmunt. "Exit Visas and Entry Tickets: Paradoxes of Jewish Assimilation." *Telos* 77 (Fall 1988).

Bieber, Hugo. "Anti-Semitism in the First Years of the German Republic," *YAJSS* 4 (1949).

Boas, Jacob. "Germany or Diaspora? German Jewry's Shifting Perceptions in the Nazi Era (1933–1938)." *LBIY* 27 (1982).

Brody, David. "American Jewry: The Refugees and Immigration Restriction (1932–1942)." *PAJHS* 45 (1955–1956).

Carman, Harry J., and Reinhard H. Luthin. "Some Aspects of the Know-Nothing Movement Reconsidered." *South Atlantic Quarterly* 39 (1940).

Cohen, Henry. "Crisis and Reaction." *AJAJ* 5, no. 2 (June 1953).

Cohen, Naomi W. "The Abrogation of the Russo-American Treaty of 1832." *JSS* 25 (1963).

———. "American Jewish Reactions to Anti-Semitism in Western Europe, 1875–1900." *Proceedings of the American Academy for Jewish Research* 45 (1978).

———. "American Jews and the Swiss Treaty," *Solomon Goldman Lectures* 3. Spertus College, Chicago, 1982.

———. "Anti-Semitism in the Gilded Age: The Jewish View." *JSS* 41 (Summer–Fall 1971).

———. "Friends in Court: An American-Jewish Response to Antisemitism." In *Living with Antisemitism: Modern Jewish Responses*, ed. Jehuda Reinharz. Hanover and London, 1987.

Cohen, Raya. "Confronting the Reality of the Holocaust: Richard Lichtheim, 1939–1942." *Yad Vashem Studies* 23 (1993).

Davis, Elmer. "On the Gentility of Gentiles." *Harper's Magazine* 167 (July 1933).

Davis, Moshe. "Mixed Marriage in Western Jewry: Historical Background to the Jewish Response." *Jewish Journal of Sociology* 10 (1968).

Dexter, Robert C. "Understanding Hitler's Germany." *Church and Society* 6 (November 1933).

Diamond, Sander A. "The *Kristallnacht* and the Reaction in America." *YAJSS* 14 (1969).

———. "The Years of Waiting: National Socialism in the United States, 1922–1933." *AJHQ* 59 (March 1970).

Dobkowski, Michael N. "American Anti-Semitism: A Reinterpretation." *America Quarterly* 29 (Summer 1977).

Duker, Abraham G. "Socio-Psychological Trends in the American Jewish Community since 1900." *YAJSS* 9 (1954).

Eben, Abba. "Tragedy and Triumph." In *Chaim Weizmann: A Biography by Several Hands*, ed. Meyer M. Weisgal and Joel Carmichael. New York: Atheneum, 1963.

Feingold, Henry L. "Anti-Semitism and the Anti-Semitic Imagination in America: A Case Study: the 1920s." In *A Midrash on American-Jewish History*, ed. Henry L. Feingold. Albany: State University of New York Press, 1982.

———. "'Courage First and Intelligence Second': The American Jewish Secular Elite, Roosevelt and the Failure of Rescue." *PAJHS* 72, no. 4 (June 1983).

———. "Did American Jewry Do Enough during the Holocaust?" B. G. Rudolph Lecture. Syracuse University, Pamphlet Form, April 1984.

———. "The Government Response." In *The Holocaust: Ideology, Bureaucracy, and Genocide*, ed. Henry Friedlander and Sybil Milton. Millwood, N.Y.: Kraus International Publications, 1980.

———. "Who Shall Bear the Guilt for the Holocaust: The Human Dilemma." *AJH* 68, no. 3 (March 1979).

Fields, Harold. "Closing Immigration throughout the World." *American Journal of International Law* 26 (1936).

Funkenstein, Amos. "Passivity as the Characteristic of the Diaspora Jew." In *Perceptions of Jewish History from Antiquity to the Present* (in Hebrew). Tel Aviv: Am Oved, 1991.

———. "The Political Theory of Jewish Emancipation from Mendelson to Herzl." *Jahrbuch des Instituts für Deutsche Geschichte* 9. Tel Aviv University, 1980.

Gellman, Irwin F. "The *St. Louis* Tragedy." *AJHQ* 61 (December 1971).

Gerber, David A. "Anti-Semitism and Jewish-Gentile Relations in American Historiography and the American Past." In *Anti-Semitism in American History*, ed. David A. Gerber. Urbana: University of Illinois Press, 1987.

Glazer, Nathan. "The American Jew and the Attainment of Middle-Class Rank." In *The Jews: Social Patterns of an American Group*, ed. Marshall Sklare. New York: Free Press, 1958.

———. "Social Characteristics of American Jews." *AJYB* 56 (1955).

Gleason, Philip. "American Identity and Americanization." In *Harvard Encyclopedia of American Ethnic Groups*, ed. Stephan Thernstrom. Cambridge: Belknap Press of Harvard University Press, 1980.

Goldblatt, Charles Israel. "The Impact of the Balfour Declaration in America." *AJHQ* 57 (June 1968).

Gottlieb, Moshe. "The Berlin Riots and Their Repercussions in America." *AJHQ* 59 (March 1970).

Gottschalk, Alfred. "The German Pogrom of November 1938 and the Reaction of American Jewry." The Leo Baeck Memorial Lecture. Leo Baeck Institute, New York, 1988.

Halpern, Ben. "The Americanization of Zionism." *AJH* 69, no. 1 (September 1979).

Handlin, Oscar. "American Views of the Jew at the Opening of the Twentieth Century." In *The Jewish Experience in America: Selected Studies from the Publications of the American Jewish Historical Society*, ed. Abraham J. Karp, Vol. 5. Waltham, Mass.: American Jewish Historical Society, 1969.

Handlin, Oscar, and Mary F. Handlin. "The Acquisition of Political and Social Rights by the Jews in the United States." *AJYB* 56 (1955).

Harrington, Mona. "Loyalties: Dual and Divided." In *Harvard Encyclopedia of American Ethnic Groups*, ed. Stephan Thernstrom. Cambridge, Mass.: Belknap Press of Harvard University, 1980.

Higham, John. "American Anti-Semitism Historically Reconsidered." In Charles Herbert Stember, et al., *Jews in the Mind of America*. New York: Basic Books, 1966.

———. "Ideological Anti-Semitism in the Gilded Age." In John Higham, *Send These to Me: Jews and Other Immigrants in Urban America*. New York: Atheneum, 1975.

———. "Social Discrimination against Jews in America, 1830–1930." *PAJHS* 47, no. 1 (September 1957).

Hymann, Herbert H. "Reference Groups," especially the section "Selection of Reference Groups." In *International Encyclopedia of the Social Sciences*, Vol. 13. New York: Macmillan, 1968.

Isaacs, Joakim. "Candidate Grant and the Jews." *AJAJ* 17 (April 1965).

Kammen, Michael. "The Problem of American Exceptionalism: A Reconsideration." *American Quarterly* 45, no. 1 (March 1993).

Karpf, Maurice J. "Jewish Community Organization in the United States." *AJYB* 39 (1937–38).

Katz, Jacob. "On Jewish Social History: Epochal and Supra-Epochal Historiography." *Jewish History* 7, no. 1 (Spring 1993).

Katz, Shlomo Z. "Public Opinion in Western Europe and the Evian Conference of July 1938." *Yad Vashem Studies* 9 (1973).

Kohler, Max J. "The Abrogation of the Treaty of 1832 between the United States and Russia and the International Protection in Religious Minorities." In *God in Freedom: Studies in the Relations between Church and State*, ed. Luigi Luzzatti. New York: Macmillan, 1930.

Kolko, Gabriel. "American Business and Germany, 1930–1941." *The Western Political Quarterly* 15, no. 4 (December 1962).

Kraut, Alan, and Richard Breitman. "Anti-Semitism in the State Department, 1933–44: Four Case Studies." In *Anti-Semitism in American History*, ed. David A. Gerber. Urbana: University of Illinois Press, 1987.

Lafer, Gordon. "Universalism and Particularism in Jewish Law: Making Sense of

Political Loyalties." In *Jewish Identity*, ed. David Theo Goldberg and Michael Krausz. Philadelphia: Temple University Press, 1993.

Lazin, Frederick A. "The Response of the American Jewish Committee to the Crisis of German Jewry, 1933–1939." *AJH* 68, no. 3 (March 1979).

Loewenberg, Peter. "The Kristallnacht as a Public Degradation Ritual." *LBIY* 32 (1987).

Löwenstein, Kurt. "Die innerjüdische Reaktion auf die Krise der deutschen Demokratie." In *Entscheidungsjahr 1932*, ed. Werner E. Mosse. 2nd ed., revised and enlarged. Tübingen: Mohr, 1966.

Marcus, Jacob R. "Zionism and the American Jew." *American Scholar* 2 (July 1933).

Margaliot, Abraham. "The Reaction of the Jewish Public in Germany to the Nuremberg Laws." *Yad Vashem Studies* 12 (1977).

Martin, Edward S. "The Nazis and the Jews." *Harper's Magazine* 167 (June 1933).

McAfee, Joseph Ernest. "Jewish Solidarity in America." *The Christian Century* 51 (3 January 1934).

Medding, Peter Y. "Toward a General Theory of Jewish Political Interests and Behaviour." *Jewish Journal of Sociology* 2 (1977).

Murphy, Paul L. "Sources and Nature of Intolerance in the 1920s." In *The 1920s: Problems and Paradoxes*, ed. Milton Plesur. Boston: Allyn and Bacon, 1969.

Norden, Margaret K. "American Editorial Response to the Rise of Adolf Hitler: A Preliminary Consideration." *AJHQ* 59, no. 3 (March 1970).

Osofsky, Gilber. "The HEAS of the United States, 1881–1883." In *The Jewish Experience in America: Selected Studies from the Publications of the American Jewish Historical Society*, ed. Abraham J. Karp. Vol. 4. Waltham, Mass.: American Jewish Historical Society, 1969.

Panitz, Esther L. "In Defense of the Jewish Immigrants." *AJHQ* 55, no. 1 (September 1965).

———. "The Polarity of American Jewish Attitudes toward Immigration (1870–1890)." In *The Jewish Experience in America: Selected Studies from the Publications of the American Jewish Historical Society*, ed. Abraham J. Karp. Vol. 4. Waltham, Mass.: American Jewish Historical Society, 1969.

Pollock, Oliver B. "Antisemitism, the Harvard Plan, and the Roots of Reverse Discrimination." *JSS* 45 (Spring 1983).

Raab, Earl. "The Deadly Innocences of American Jews." *Commentary* 50, no. 6 (December 1970).

Rabinowitz, Benjamin. "The Young Men's Hebrew Association." *PAJHS* 37 (1947).

Reinharz, Jehuda. "The Zionist Response to Antisemitism in Germany." *LBIY* 30 (1985).

Reissner, H.G. "The German-American Jews (1800–1850)." *LBIY* 10 (1969).

Ribuffo, Leo. "Henry Ford and the International Jew." *AJH* 69 (June 1980).

Rockaway, Robert. "Ethnic Conflict in an Urban Environment: The German and Russian Jews in Detroit, 1881–1914." *PAJHS* 60 (December 1970).

Rosenthal, Erich. "Studies of Jewish Intermarriage in the United States." *AJYB* 64 (1963).

Rothschild, Richard C. "Are American Jews Falling into the Nazi Trap?" *Contemporary Jewish Record* (January–February 1940).

Sarna, Jonathan. "America Is Different." *Midstream* 28 (February 1982).

———. "American Anti-Semitism." In *History and Hate: The Dimensions of Anti-Semitism*, ed. David A. Gerber. Philadelphia: JPS, 1986.

————. "American Jewish History." *Modern Judaism* 10, no. 3 (October 1990).

————. "Anti-Semitism and American History." *Commentary* 71, no. 3 (March 1981).

Schoenberg, Philip Ernest. "The American Reaction to the Kishinev Pogrom of 1903." *AJHQ* 42 (March 1974).

Selznick, Philip. "Coöptation: A Mechanism for Organizational Stability." In *Reader in Bureaucracy*, ed. Robert K. Merton, et al. Glencoe, Ill.: Free Press, 1952.

Shapiro, Edward S. "The Approach of War: Congressional Isolationism and Anti-Semitism, 1939–1941." *AJH* 74, no. 1 (September 1984).

Simpson, George F. "Assimilation." In *International Encyclopedia of the Social Sciences*, Vol. 1. New York: Macmillan, 1968.

Singerman, Robert. "The Jew as Racial Alien: The Genetic Component of American Anti-Semitism." In *Anti-Semitism in American History*, ed. David A. Gerber. Urbana: University of Illinois Press, 1987.

Smertenko, Johan J. "Have Jews a Divided Loyalty?" In *Mid-Century: An Anthology of Jewish Life and Culture in Our Times*, ed. Harold U. Ribalow. New York: Beechhurst Press, 1955.

————. "Hitlerism Comes to America." *Harper's Magazine* 167 (November 1933).

Smith, Roger M. "The 'American Creed' and American Identity: The Limits of Liberal Citizenship in the United States." *Western Political Quarterly* 41, no. 2 (1988).

Sorkin, David. "Wilhelm von Humboldt: The Theory and Practice of Self-Formation (*Bildung*), 1791–1810." *Journal of the History of Ideas*, January 1983.

Stein, Herman D. "Jewish Social Work in the United States." In Nathan Glazer, Joseph L. Blau, Herman D. Stein, and Oscar and Mary F. Handlin, *The Characteristics of American Jews*. New York: Jewish Education Committee Press, 1965.

Strauss, Herbert A. "Jewish Emigration from Germany: Nazi Policies and Jewish Responses (II)." *LBIY* 26 (1980).

Stromberg, Roland N. "American Business and the Approach of War, 1935–1941." *Journal of Economic History* 13, no. 1 (Winter 1953).

Stroock, Sol M. "Switzerland and American Jews." In *The Jewish Experience in America: Selected Studies from the Publications of the American Jewish Historical Society*, ed. Abraham J. Karp. Vol. 3. Waltham, Mass.: American Jewish Historical Society, 1968.

Sulzberger, David. "The Growth of Jewish Population in the United States." *PAJHS* 6 (1897).

Supple, Barry E. "A Business Elite: German-Jewish Financiers in Nineteenth-Century New York." *Business History Review* 31 (1957).

Susman, Warren I. "The Thirties." In *The Development of an American Culture*, ed. Stanley Coben and Lorman Ratner. Englewood Cliffs, N.J.: Prentice Hall, 1970.

Synnott, Marcia Graham. "Anti-Semitism and American Universities: Did Quotas Follow the Jews?" In *Anti-Semitism in American History*, ed. David A. Gerber. Urbana: University of Illinois Press, 1987.

Szajkowski, Zosa. "The Attitude of American Jews to East European Jewish Immigration." *PAJHS* 40 (March 1951).

————. "The Attitude of American Jews to Refugees from Germany in the 1930s." *AJHQ* 59, no. 2 (December 1971).

————. "A Note on the American-Jewish Struggle against Nazism and Communism in the 1930s." *AJHQ* 59, no. 3 (March 1970).

———. "Relief for German Jewry: Problems of American Involvement." *AJHQ* 62, no. 2 (December 1972).

Tarnish, Allan. "The Board of Delegates of American Israelites (1859–1878)." In *The Jewish Experience in America: Selected Studies from the Publications of the American Jewish Historical Society*, ed. Abraham J. Karp. Vol. 3. Waltham, Mass.: American Jewish Historical Society, 1968.

Tcherikower, Elias. "Jewish Immigrants to the United States, 1881–1900." *YAJSS* 6 (1951).

Thompson, Dorothy, and Benjamin Stolberg. "Hitler and the American Jews." *Scribner's* 19 (September 1933).

Volkov, Shulamit. "The Dynamics of Dissimilation: *Ostjuden* and German Jews." In *The Jewish Response to German Culture: From Enlightenment to the Second World War*, ed. Yehuda Reinharz and Walter Schatzberg. Hanover, N.H.: University Press of New England, 1985.

Weinryb, Bernard D. "Jewish Immigration and Accommodation to America." In *The Jews: Social Patterns of an American Group*, ed. Marshall Sklare. New York: Free Press, 1958.

Whitfield, Stephen. "The Presence of the Past: Recent Trends in American Jewish History." *AJH* 70 (December 1980).

Wiesel, Eli. "Telling the Tale." *Dimensions in American Judaism*, Spring 1968.

Wyman, David. "American Jews and the Holocaust." *New York Times Magazine*, May 8, 1982.

Yahil, Leni. "Jewish Assimilation vis-à-vis German Nationalism in the Weimar Republic." In *Jewish Assimilation in Modern Times*, ed. Bela Vago. Boulder, Colo.: Westview Press, 1981.

Zimmermann, Moshe. "'Die aussichtslose Republik'—Zukunftsperspektiven der deutschen Juden vor 1933." In *Menora. Jahrbuch für deutsch-jüdische Geschichte 1990*. Munich: Piper, 1990.

Zuroff, Efraim. "Rescue Priority and Fund Raising as Issues during the Holocaust: A Case Study of the Relations between the Vaad Ha-Hatzala and the Joint, 1939–1941." *AJH* 68, no. 3 (March 1979).

DISSERTATIONS

Ambrosius, Lloyd E. "The United States and the Weimar Republic, 1918–1923: From the Armistice to the Ruhr Occupation." Ph.D. diss., University of Illinois, 1967.

Boas, Jacob. "The Jews of Germany: Self-Perception in the Nazi Era as Reflected in the German Jewish Press, 1933–1938." Ph.D. diss., University of California, Riverside, 1977.

Frommer, Morris. "The American Jewish Congress: A History 1914–1950." Ph.D. diss., Ohio State University, 1978.

Hurwitz, Ariel. "American Jewry, the American Government and Society and the Destruction of European Jewry, 1942–1944" (in Hebrew). Ph.D. diss., Hebrew University, Jerusalem, 1990.

Neuringer, Sheldon M. "American Jewry and United States Immigration Policy, 1881–1953." Ph.D. diss., University of Wisconsin, 1969.

Rappaport, Joseph. "Jewish Immigration and World War I: A Study of American Yiddish Press Reactions." Ph.D. diss., Columbia University, 1951.

Schubert, Herzl. "Evian in Context: Refugees, Expulsions, Nationalism and Immigration Laws in the Inter-war Period" (in Hebrew). Master's thesis, Tel Aviv University, 1990.

Shafir, Shlomo. "The Impact of the Jewish Crisis on American-German Relations, 1933–1939." Ph.D. diss., Georgetown University, 1971.

NEWSPAPERS AND PERIODICALS

American Hebrew
American Jewish Congress Index
The Christian Century
Church and Society
Commentary
Congress Bulletin
Contemporary Jewish Record
Harper's Magazine
Jewish Daily Bulletin
Jewish Telegraphic Agency
The Nation
The New Republic
New York Times
Opinion

Gordon, Judah Leib, 256n118
Göring, Hermann, 145, 261n90
Gottheil, Gustav, 233n38
Gottheil, Richard, 36, 233n38
Grant, Madison, 233n45
Grant, Ulysses S., 23–24, 25, 26
Grayzel, Solomon, 215
Great Depression, 68, 86
Green, William, 256n128
Grossman, Louis, 57
group rights. *See* rights of individuals vs.
    rights of groups
Grynszpan, Herschel, 197–98
guilt, collective confession of, 220

Hakitzah ami (Gordon), 256n118
Halpern, Ben, 227n9
Haman, 95, 122
Harding, Warren G., 63, 67, 72, 243n4
Harper's Magazine, 116, 118
Harrison, Benjamin, 38–39
Hart, Abraham, 18
Hartman, Gustav, 96
Harvard University, discrimination in, 67
Haskalah, 59, 157
Hay, John, 39
Hebrew Immigration Aid Society (HIAS), 32
Hebrew Sheltering Society, 40
Hecht, Ben, 257n2
Herzl, Theodor, 36
Hexter, Maurice, 110
Higham, John, 24, 31, 67, 241n92
higher education, discrimination in, 67–68,
    242n107
Hillman, Sidney, 131
Hindenburg, Paul von, 78, 80, 97, 122–23,
    125
Hirsch, Baron de, 32–33, 232n18
Hirsch, Emil, 67, 241n104
historians, challenges for, 1–6, 91, 104, 109,
    159, 222–23
historical experiences of Jews, 36, 59, 95,
    118, 123, 255n108
Hitler, Adolf, 111, 113, 116–17, 137,
    247n76, 255n105; American Jews'
    misjudgment of, 121–24, 156, 178;
    anti-Semitism in Weimar Germany,
    80–83, 87–90, 95, 96–99, 249n135;
    boycott of German Jewish goods and
    services, 144–46; international
    economic talks in Washington, 148,
    262n107; putsch in 1923, 73
Hollander, Ludwig, 97
Hollander, Sidney, 203–204

Holmes, John Haynes, 50, 119, 146, 166,
    188, 250n18, 261n95, 266n49
Holocaust, historiography on, 2, 109
Hoover Executive Order of 1930, 161–64,
    262n110
Hoover, Herbert, 61, 86–87, 92, 97, 99, 136–
    37; as Secretary of Commerce, 63, 72,
    243n4
Horkheimer, Max, 75
host society, 13, 36, 92–93, 115
Hourwich, Isaac H., 55
House Committee on Immigration and
    Naturalization, 161
House Foreign Affairs Committee, 87
Howe, Louis McHenry, 141, 260n68
Huddle, Klahr, 192
Hugenberg, Alfred, 79, 122, 255n105
Hughes, Charles Evans, 72–73, 76–77,
    243n5
Hull, Cordell, 107, 140, 143–44, 149, 164–
    65, 191, 252n42, 260–61nn84,96,
    263n139
humanitarian diplomacy, American, 17–18,
    21–22, 77, 135, 140, 143
Hurwitz, Henry, 264n6

Ickes, Harold, 131, 201, 206, 216, 258n16
immigrants. *See* East European Jewish
    immigrants; German Jewish immi-
    grants; Russian Jewish immigrants
Immigration Act of 1917: bond issue, 170–
    71, 268nn76,81; LPC clause, 160, 164
immigration, restriction of, 30, 39, 45, 196,
    233n49, 248n109; American policies
    on, 160–65, 192–93, 197, 200–201,
    240n73; forces in favor of, 33, 38;
    particular, 235n10; quotas, 64–65, 94,
    265n19; quotas, German, 6, 150, 172,
    181, 226nn17,22, 262nn110,118,
    264n13; views of American Jews on, 36,
    161, 170–73, 194; World War One
    aftermath, 62, 63–65
Immigration Restriction League, 33
individual rights. *See* rights of individuals vs.
    rights of groups
industrialization, 25–26, 30–31, 33
"inside-outside" Jewish elite, 132–33, 154
intermarriage, 69, 243n116
"international Judaism," 18, 65–66, 93, 105,
    117, 174, 206
Isaacs, Stephen, 139
isolationism, American, 63, 72, 78, 160, 180,
    207
Italian-Ethiopian crisis, 180

GULIE NE'EMAN ARAD teaches American and European history at Ben-Gurion University of the Negev. She is the author of numerous articles and co-editor of the journal *History & Memory: Studies in Representation of the Past.*